THE NEHRU DEVELOPMENT MODEL

ADVANCE PRAISE FOR THE BOOK

'Panagariya has done the improbable. Once again, he has written a remarkable book on India that stands out in a field crowded with analyses and memoirs. In it, he tells the fascinating tale of India's early efforts under Pandit Jawaharlal Nehru to combat poverty through industrialization and growth, why they failed, and how the decisions made during those fateful decades continue to influence economic policies and outcomes till today'—Jagdish Bhagwati, University Professor, Columbia University

'Nehru's development model involved state planning and import licensing with the goal of fostering industrialization. Arvind Panagariya has written a fascinating study of its origins, effects and downfall. The book is a tremendous achievement, detailed but accessible to all readers, and interesting throughout. Young people in India who do not know this essential history should read this book to understand how good intentions, but bad economic policy, held India back for so many decades'—Douglas Irwin, John French Professor of Economics, Dartmouth College

THE NEHRU DEVELOPMENT MODEL

History and Its Lasting Impact

Arvind Panagariya

PENGUIN
VIKING
An imprint of Penguin Random House

PENGUIN VIKING

Penguin Viking is an imprint of the Penguin Random House group of companies whose addresses can be found at global.penguinrandomhouse.com

Published by Penguin Random House India Pvt. Ltd
4th Floor, Capital Tower 1, MG Road,
Gurugram 122 002, Haryana, India

Penguin Random House India

First published in Penguin Viking by Penguin Random House India 2024

10 9 8 7 6 5 4 3 2

ISBN 9780143466567

Typeset in Sabon Lt Std by MAP Systems, Bengaluru, India
Printed at Replika Press Pvt. Ltd, India

www.penguin.co.in

FSC www.fsc.org MIX Paper | Supporting responsible forestry FSC™ C016779

In memory of

Dr Ashok Panagariya

A neurologist par excellence, a Padma Shri awardee
and a brother like no other

Contents

Preface

This book is the result of two years of intense research and near-exclusive attention, apart from teaching duties and occasional diversions into writing articles that were too tempting to pass up. Though the process of researching and writing the book has been exciting and enjoyable, its beginnings were painful. After sending the final edits to the biography of my father, which came out in 2021, I began thinking about my next major project. This period coincided with the Delta wave of Covid-19. In late April 2021, my dear brother, Dr Ashok Panagariya, a distinguished neurologist who had first introduced the specialization to the state of Rajasthan and a Padma Shri awardee, fell victim to the virus. He was hospitalized in Jaipur and bravely battled the virus and multiple infections for nearly a month and a half. As the state's top neurologist since the early 1980s, he had literally given a second chance at life to many and a better living to many more. But, alas, when his turn came, nature did not offer him that same chance. On 11 June 2021, we lost him.

Merely two years apart in age, Ashok and I had grown up together and, therefore, had been as close as any two brothers can ever be. For all the difficult decisions in my life, I had habitually turned to him for advice. During the months of hospitalization and those that followed his passing, I became too distraught to concentrate on my work. All I could do was to seek diversion in biographies, Indian history immediately preceding and following Independence, and the speeches of India's first prime minister, Jawaharlal Nehru. I cannot now recall when this random reading turned into systematic research, then into what seemed like an interesting stand-alone article on Nehru's conversion from radical socialism to Fabian socialism, and finally, an idea for the book you now hold in your hand. It was as if, even as he passed into another world, my brother had given me a parting gift.

The greatest discovery for me when writing this book has been the amazing availability of archival material on the Internet. At the time my passive reading began turning into a book project, I had scarcely imagined that sitting in my New York apartment, I would be able to access nearly all the primary documents I would want to read and review to produce an authentic account of the Nehru-era economic history and thought. Websites of the Lok Sabha, Ministry of Culture, Internet Archive, planning commission and Gokhale Institute of Politics and Economics offer a wealth of documents from which it is possible to construct a detailed history of the evolution of a large part of the post-Independence economic history of India.

My only complaint is that as I entered the last six to eight months of work on the book, access to some of these websites, notably the planning commission and Gokhale Institute, closed down. Closure of the planning commission website proved particularly problematic since I was unable to find even such basic documents as the five-year plans, draft plans and mid-term appraisals on any other websites. The Ministry of Culture website also poses one important challenge: we can read the documents in its archives online but cannot download them. For researchers, having PDF copies is extremely convenient since it allows one to highlight the text that might be important for future reference. I mention these deficiencies not to be critical—as a beneficiary of the websites for the better part of the period of research on my book, that would be very ungrateful of me—but to flag the keepers of these websites for corrective action. With the document archives already there, the benefit-cost ratio of fixing the small problems is near infinity.

I was also fortunate in that Columbia University subscribes to the ProQuest Historical Newspapers archives for the *Times of India*, which are available on the website from January 1897 to the present. Being searchable, these archives proved to be extremely helpful in filling many gaps left by the document collections available on the websites. For example, the newspaper archives proved critical to the construction of the evolution of import and export policies on an annual basis, beginning with the Second World War. They were also helpful in tracking down contemporary thinking on the import and export policies in the media and among politicians and other commentators. On rare occasions when a particular report was not available on the Internet, newspaper reports helped fill the gap.

At the outset, I should warn the readers that while they will find parts of this book easy and exciting to read, they will also encounter parts that are tedious and dull. I deliberately chose not to cut corners to make either the readers' or my task easy. My hope is that a book like this will also serve as a reference on the economic history of the period covered.

I want to express my deep gratitude to Rana Hassan of the Asian Development Bank, and an anonymous referee, both of whom reviewed the manuscript. Rana provided several extremely helpful suggestions, leading to important revisions, especially at the beginning of the volume. The referee, in turn, suggested a line of inquiry that ended up forming the basis of the final chapter. My friends, Pravin Krishna of Johns Hopkins University, Rajeev Mantri of Navam Capital and Parth Shah of the Center for Civil Society read parts of the book when in progress and provided valuable feedback. Also helpful in answering certain questions was correspondence with Anand Swami of Williams College and David Lockwood of Flinders University. Sanjay Joshi, Ashutosh Jha and Vishnu Yadav of the Lal Bahadur Shastri National Academy of Administration provided critical assistance in locating the relatively sparse material on Sardar Patel's views on economic policy in independent India.

Last but not least, I can't thank Karthik Venkatesh and Ralph Rebello enough for the patience and care with which they have edited the volume, including the cover page, to give it the wonderful final shape that it has acquired. The volume is much improved from what I had originally submitted to Karthik.

A volume like this could not have been written without access to the numerous articles, books and documents referenced at its end. I wish to express my deep gratitude to all who authored these works. Books by Jagdish Bhagwati and Padma Desai, Sarvepalli Gopal, Baldev Raj Nayar, Jairam Ramesh and Vinay Sitapati have been particularly helpful. Numerous writings and speeches by Nehru were indispensable to shaping Part I of the book. For Part III, speeches by Lal Bahadur Shastri, Rajiv Gandhi and Narasimha Rao proved critical.

It is my hope that readers will come out better informed on the evolution of economic policy and economic thought in post-Independence India after reading the volume. I will also welcome more writing on these subjects, especially by economists who disagree with my analysis or conclusions. It is only through sharpening differences that we can separate the wheat from the chaff.

Columbia University Arvind Panagariya
New York, NY 10027
10 September 2023

1

Introduction

At Independence, Pandit Jawaharlal Nehru, India's first prime minister, embarked upon two foundational projects: one political and the other economic. His political project, consisting of the adoption of a democratic constitution with universal suffrage, so uncommon at the time, was a resounding success. It defied the early predictions that the tensions originating in caste- and language-based differences across regions would lead the country to either disintegrate or fall into the grip of authoritarian rule.[1] So robust turned out to be the institutions and democratic thought he nurtured that when his daughter, Prime Minister Indira Gandhi, decided to flirt with authoritarianism, the affair was short-lived. Within eighteen months, she self-corrected, returning the country to its chosen path of democracy. Today, seventy-seven years after Independence, India stands out not only as the world's largest democracy but also among its most stable and vibrant ones.

Unfortunately, however, this success was marred by an equally resounding failure of Nehru's economic project, built on the development of heavy industry, a rapidly expanding public sector and isolation from the world markets. Despite all the good intentions and its near-unanimous endorsement by all constituencies, the project not only failed to produce the growth necessary to rid India of, in Nehru's own famous words, 'appalling poverty' but also bequeathed an ethos that made a switch from it a real challenge during the decades following his departure.[2] Thanks to the entrenchment of socialist thought in the political, bureaucratic, intellectual and even business constituencies, more than seven decades after Independence, India continues to struggle to fully extricate itself from the Nehru-era economic policy framework.

Much has been written in recent times on the political history and political thought of the Nehru era and their long-term impact on Indian democracy. However, parallel analysis in the economic field has been almost entirely missing. This glaring gap in the literature is surprising in view of the fact that the big changes in modern India have been economic. Despite more than a hundred amendments to the Constitution, the essential foundations of Indian democracy have remained unshaken. In contrast, the economic policy framework has undergone a dramatic change. Though much work remains to be done, in the last three decades, India has turned from a primarily inward-looking and control-ridden economy into a primarily outward-oriented market economy.

Against this backdrop, the present volume is an attempt to systematically document the economic history of the Nehru era, contemporary economic thought and their impact on the post-Nehru political economy of policymaking. Though the pioneering 1970 study by Jagdish Bhagwati and Padma Desai provides an excellent description and analysis of the economic system as it existed in the late 1960s, many gaps remain.[3] How did this system evolve? What was the influence of Nehru's thinking on it? What impact, if any, did the thinking of other contemporary politicians and economists have? Above all, how did the economic history and thought of this era impact subsequent policymaking in India? These are the big questions that this volume attempts to answer, in addition to exploring numerous sub-themes that arise as a by-product.

The volume is divided into three parts. Part I is devoted to establishing that the economic model India adopted, beginning with the critical Second Five-Year Plan, is almost entirely due to Nehru. Though P.C. Mahalanobis prepared the Draft Plan-frame of the plan and the planning commission conducted extensive consultations with experts, including a panel of India's leading economists, foreign economists and statisticians, the final plan and policy framework had Nehru's stamp all over them. One economist, B.R. Shenoy, dissented, and two others, C.N. Vakil and P.R. Brahmananda of the Bombay School, offered alternative suggestions. However, none disagreed with the core features of the framework.

Part II describes in careful detail the policy regime, its implementation and the economic outcomes during the Nehru era. This part carries voluminous detail on the evolution as well as the content of the policy framework. It also describes in detail the implementation machinery of investment licensing, import licensing and the allocation of foreign exchange. Though Bhagwati and Desai have considered the policy regime and the administrative machinery earlier, I have filled the many gaps they leave, especially those relating to the evolution of the policies and the bureaucratic regime.

Finally, Part III develops the theme that by the time Nehru passed away, the socialist policy regime and thought had become sufficiently entrenched that a retreat from them in the foreseeable future was unlikely. It is as if India was on a deterministic path, with no prospects of a change of direction for a long time. Any change of direction required a leader who was convinced that a departure from the established path was called for. Moreover, in a democracy, the leader must persuade his followers of the desirability of the change. But given the inheritance of ideas across generations, it took time for such a leader to come along, even though it had been apparent that the path on which India had been travelling did not lead to the desired destination, at least not within the time originally envisaged. The first time that an opportunity arose, the leader was unable to persuade his fellow politicians to embrace the change. This was unlike an authoritarian country such as China, where, after the death of Mao, Deng Xiaoping could reorient the economy far more quickly and decisively.

To the extent possible, the account in this volume is based on original sources and documents to ensure authenticity. Only in the rare cases when I lacked access to the original sources did I choose to rely on the secondary ones. I have also chosen to let the sources speak for themselves through quoted text rather than paraphrase them. Finally, to fill many gaps in the available information, I have extensively searched the *Times of India* archives going back to the 1940s. The outcome of this search is reflected in the large number of references to the newspaper.

Economic Thought: Nehru and His Contemporaries

Two key ideas around which Nehru set out to build post-Independence India were democracy and socialism. As a seasoned politician, Nehru was a pragmatist, however, and demonstrated considerable flexibility of thought. He would listen to his opponents and modify his thinking if he could be convinced that a correction was warranted and it did not conflict with his core beliefs in democracy and socialism. He evolved over time and was keenly aware of it, so much so that in the preface to *The Discovery of India*, the last of his three books, he wrote that whenever he read something he had written sometime in the past, he felt as if it was written by someone else who was like him but different.

This evolution was on display in his thinking on socialism. It is commonly believed that he was already a convert to Fabian socialism in his youth while studying at the University of Cambridge in Cambridge and the Inner Temple in London. But this, my research demonstrates, is wholly incorrect. While he had exposure to socialism as a student, it was not until his second visit to Britain, topped by a visit to the Soviet Union on the way back in the late 1920s, that his ideas on socialism firmed up. By this time, he was already in his late thirties.

More interestingly, during this initial conversion, he had come to subscribe to a radical form of socialism, bordering on communism. His transition to the more moderate form, which is sometimes referred to as Fabian socialism, took place sometime between 1936 and 1946. This evolution of Nehru's thinking on socialism is the subject matter of Chapter 2 of the book.

Nehru's embrace of socialism was rooted in the belief that imperialism was the direct result of capitalism: capitalism gave rise to factories which, in pursuit of profits, sought cheap sources of raw materials and lucrative markets for the finished products. Colonies served both functions. Because international trade was the vehicle to gain access to raw materials in return for the finished products, this line of reasoning also led to the conclusion that it was to be avoided, with self-sufficiency being the goal. Nehru saw growth as the principal instrument to eradicate India's 'appalling poverty' and self-sufficiency as a way to avoid becoming a victim of imperialism. This latter objective led him to place the development of heavy industry on the front burner. Industrialization, the principal driver of growth, required factories that needed machines which, in turn, required steel. To be self-sufficient, India needed to make its own machines and steel.

The development of heavy industry fitted well within Nehru's philosophy of socialism. An important goal of socialism is to minimize inequality of income and wealth. Bringing the means of production progressively into the public sector provided an avenue to promote this goal. Because the private sector lacked the large volume of resources needed for investment in heavy industry, the public sector could take that responsibility. Being pragmatic, Nehru also realized that he needed the private sector to expand the output and national income rapidly. The logical consequence was the adoption of a mixed-economy model.

The remaining piece of Nehru's model of industrialization was the cottage and small industries, which were to be the primary source of employment for the masses. He recognized that he could not count on heavy industry to create adequate employment opportunities for India's large workforce. Therefore, he set aside light consumer goods for exclusive manufacture by the cottage and small industries. This also went well with the followers of Gandhi in the Congress, who were keen to ensure adequate protection for the cottage and small industries. Chapter 3 details the evolution of these ideas in Nehru's thinking.

Chapter 4 turns to a detailed examination of other contemporary, influential voices. The first and foremost among them is P.C. Mahalanobis, who translated Nehru's ideas into a formal model, which later came to be popularly known as the Mahalanobis Model. He also authored the Draft Plan-frame of the second plan, around which much of the discussion of this foundational plan took place. Nehru also appointed a panel of twenty-one leading economists of the country who contributed ideas through their own papers and a joint memorandum on the Draft Plan-frame by Mahalanobis. They included luminaries such as V.K.R.V. Rao, D.R. Gadgil, K.N. Raj, A.K. Das Gupta, C.N. Vakil, B.R. Shenoy and D.T. Lakdawala. With two exceptions, these economists not only gave the Draft Plan-frame a thumbs up but also recommended significantly tighter regulation of the private sector than Mahalanobis had advocated. The exceptions were Shenoy and Vakil. Shenoy submitted a dissent note in which he attacked the large deficit proposed to finance the ambitious plan. Vakil did not submit a dissent, but, through a paper with his colleague P.R. Brahmananda, advocated a greater focus on agriculture and limiting heavy industry to agricultural machinery. But none of these commentators questioned the key features of the plan, such as the centrality of heavy industry, a major role for the public sector, and the pursuit of self-sufficiency that were to result in the undoing of the economy in due course.

Among foreign experts, too, none expressed any reservations about the fundamentals of the planned approach, save

Milton Friedman. He offered a trenchant critique that proved prophetic. But unlike other foreign scholars whom the Government of India had invited, Friedman came on the initiative of the United States government. As a result, he had no chance of being heard. There is no evidence that there was any discussion of his short and succinct note in the government circles or the planning commission. In the voluminous literature that I have reviewed as a part of my research for this book, only P.T. Bauer, a fellow Mont Pelerin Society member of Friedman, refers to it in his 1961 critique of India's approach to development.[4]

Leading industrialists of India had been a part of the discussions in the Congress-appointed National Planning Committee during 1938–40 on the likely approach to industrialization upon winning independence. From available accounts, it may be concluded that there was a meeting of minds in these deliberations between Nehru and the industrialists. Accordingly, the main features of the Bombay Plan the industrialists produced in two parts in 1944 and 1945 were hardly distinguishable from the second plan. It acknowledged the need for heavy industry development, the role of the public sector in it, the concept of the mixed economy and the pursuit of self-sufficiency as an important objective.

In 1956, A.D. Shroff, an industrialist and banker, launched the Forum of Free Enterprise to give voice to the proponents of private enterprise and critics of Nehru's socialism. Those contributing to the forum's activities during its first five years included M.R. Masani, N.A. Palkhivala, Shenoy, Bauer, M.A. Master, K.C. Cooper and Shroff himself. But since Shroff had explicitly committed to limiting the forum's activities to informing and educating the public, it had no real impact on the government's policy choices.

Economic History: Policies and Their Implementation

How Nehru translated his vision into reality, what fruits it bore during his lifetime and why those fruits fell well short of his original goals are the subjects of Part II of the volume. To this end, Chapter 5 begins by describing the evolution and content of the industrial and labour policies. Under the British, industry was a State subject. The Government of India Act of 1935 provided for the enactment of laws making the development of certain industries a central subject, but no such law had been enacted until the end of the Second World War. The first such attempt was made in April 1945 when the central government released the Statement of Industrial Policy 1945. Anticipating that planning would require central control of certain industries, the statement identified twenty industries as good candidates for it. It provided for the development of heavy industry, direct ownership of certain basic industries by the government through investment and nationalization, and regulation and control of the private sector through licensing. The architect of this statement was Ardeshir Dalal, who had been one of the eight authors of part one of the Bombay Plan. Therefore, it is not surprising that the statement was wholly in the spirit of that plan, which was, in turn, heavily influenced by the discussions in the National Planning Committee of the Congress during 1938–40.

With the national leadership preoccupied with negotiations of independence with the British government, the 1945 statement did not translate into any laws that would lead to actual action. Soon after independence, the government enacted the Industrial Policy Resolution 1948 (IPR 1948), which, in addition to many provisions of the 1945 statement, provided for the creation of a National Planning Commission to formulate and execute programmes of development. But with conservatives providing the counterweight under the leadership of Sardar Vallabhbhai Patel, it differed from the 1945 statement and the National Planning Committee in one important respect: it explicitly ruled out nationalization of private undertakings, whether domestic or foreign owned, for ten years.

From IPR 1948 emanated the Industries (Development and Regulation) Act of 1951 (IDRA 1951), which laid down the legal framework for the licensing and regulation of private industry. It gave the government extensive powers over the private sector through strict licensing of all major sectors and powers to impose price and distribution controls over what it produced. In due course, regulations under this law were to become a serious burden on private entrepreneurs, a major drag on industrial growth and a source of corruption and bribery.

The Second Five-Year Plan considerably tightened the grip of the government over industry. It dramatically increased the share of industry in the total outlay relative to the first plan, which had devoted a significant proportion of the outlay to agriculture. The government now entered industrial activity on a significantly larger scale. To open the door wider to the public sector, Nehru also replaced IPR 1948 with the Industrial Policy Statement 1956 (IPR 1956), which expanded the scope of the public sector in the industry.

Nehru's socialism also found expression in the country's labour laws. Familiar with the history of the Industrial Revolution in Britain, he was keen on protecting the rights of industrial labour. Given that steel, textiles and other modern industries already had a significant presence under the British, some labour laws had already existed prior to independence. To these were added the Industrial Disputes Act of 1947, the Minimum Wage Act of 1948, the Employees State Insurance Act of 1948 and the Factories Act of 1948, even before the launch of the First Five-Year Plan. In the 1950s, they were followed by another six labour laws. These laws added a considerable burden on private industry, as Vakil and Brahmananda pointed out presciently as early as 1955 in one of the papers they submitted to the Panel of Economists.

The instruments to translate these policies into action were five-year plans with sector-specific production targets, public-sector production and implementation of industrial licensing. These are the subjects I address in Chapter 6. Even though the operational and bureaucratic procedures make for dry material—and I have had my share of pain writing it—I have chosen to present them in detail without cutting corners for two reasons. First, entrepreneurs in India born in and after the 1980s who feel haunted by the presence of the heavy hand of the government today might feel less sorry about themselves knowing the travails of their predecessors. Second, and more seriously, these details are necessary to fully understand the numerous sources of the inefficiency of what is popularly called the licence-permit raj.

The pursuit of self-sufficiency notwithstanding, heavy industry invariably required some combination of imported machinery, components, raw materials and spare parts. Therefore, industrial policy inevitably interacted with import policy. Accordingly, Chapters 7 and 8 discuss the evolution of import policy. Counting Chapter 9, which is devoted to export policy, trade policy occupies three chapters in the volume. In part, this disproportionate attention is the result of my passion for the subject, which led me to dig deeper into it. But it is also reflective of the important role that international trade policy plays in a country's development in the early stages.

Whereas the beginning of investment licensing can be traced to IDRA 1951, the history of import policy goes much farther back. To fully appreciate its conduct in the post-Independence era, it is necessary to begin with its pre-Independence history. Accordingly, I choose 1882 as the starting point since that year, the British adopted a free-trade policy in India. From 1882 to 1956, import policy in India remained liberal, with the brief exception of the Second World War era. Though the influential steel and textile industries sought and got some protection in the 1920s, and additional tariffs were levied subsequently, the overall incidence of protection remained low until the Second World War. Moreover, with rare exceptions, physical controls had their debut only after the beginning of the war. The war led Great Britain to introduce foreign-exchange control throughout the Empire. Import licensing in India was a natural by-product of this policy. The essentiality and domestic availability conditions, open general licensing, banned and restricted lists of imports, bureaucratic delays and corruption in issuing licences, which characterized import policy for decades in independent India, had their origins in the wartime import-policy regime.

It has gone entirely unnoticed in the literature that there remained a strong sentiment in favour of a liberal import policy for nearly a decade after the war. Not only newspapers and business groups but official reports and occasional ministers too called for liberalism in import policy during this decade. Although the wartime licensing machinery was left untouched, as long as the foreign exchange situation remained comfortable, import policy remained liberal. To his credit, Nehru rarely interfered with the day-to-day running of the import policy. Rather than use protection as the instrument of reaching self-sufficiency, his approach was to rejig the production basket gradually to the one desired by consumers. This liberal era is documented and analysed in Chapter 7.

With Chapter 8, we enter the darker era of import policy. During the Second World War, India had generated substantial surpluses in its trade account and, therefore, successfully accumulated a comfortable pool of foreign-exchange reserves. Since the reserves were held in pound sterling in London, they came to be known as sterling balances. By late 1956, the sterling balances depleted to a crisis level, forcing India to adopt foreign-exchange budgeting. Beginning in early 1957, the Department of Economic Affairs (DEA) in the Ministry of Finance instituted a system of six-monthly allocations of foreign exchange among different public-sector undertakings and government entities tasked with allocating their shares of foreign exchange among private-sector undertakings within their purview. An elaborate bureaucratic system of allocations that had to inevitably interact with both import-licensing and investment-licensing bureaucracies had to be devised. By the time Nehru died, consumer goods imports, except essential items such as food, had been completely banned, capital goods imports had to be largely financed by loans or investment by a foreign partner, and raw material, components and spare parts imports were subject to tight restrictions with foreign-exchange allocation required every six months.

These problems could have been alleviated if India had emerged as a successful exporter. But as Chapter 9 on export policy explains, conditions for success in this area did not exist. Deficit financing of the plans had resulted in high inflation, which, given the fixed exchange rate, made Indian products progressively less competitive vis-à-vis foreign products. At the critical moment in 1957 when the sterling balances ran out, devaluation of the rupee was an option, but there was no appetite for it. Nehru himself rejected it outright.

This general lack of competitiveness of Indian goods was reinforced by the fact that India's comparative advantage lay in light manufactures, but the government chose to relegate their production to village and cottage industries that lacked the necessary capital and skills to produce quality products at an efficient scale. They obviously made no headway in export markets. That left primary products such as tea and jute-based items as India's main exports. The export potential of these items was also undermined by export restrictions and export taxes imposed in the belief that with India having a large share of the world market, free exports would result in low prices. But over time, export-tax-induced high prices led buyers to look for substitute products and previously uncompetitive suppliers to become competitive. In the early 1950s, India had a vibrant textiles industry with a significant share of the export market. But this, too, was not allowed to flourish and grow lest it undermined the cottage and village industries.

Economic History: Outcomes and Analysis

Chapter 10 in Part II turns to the documentation of outcomes in areas such as growth, industrialization, poverty and education. The bottom line on this score is that despite some progress in industrialization, Nehru fell well short of achieving his goals.

The annual growth rate of 4.1 per cent represented a significant jump over the less than 1 per cent rate achieved during the first half of the twentieth century under the British. But with the population growing at 2.1 per cent, per-capita income grew just 2 per cent per year. This growth made almost no dent in poverty. Rural India, where the vast majority of the poor resided, saw little improvement in its fortunes due to the neglect of agriculture. In urban India, income increases benefited principally a few industrialists and organized labour. But much of the urban workforce suffering from poverty toiled in the informal cottage and small industries, which were denied all access to capital and hence saw no improvement in their fortunes.

Fundamentally, it was the decision to develop heavy industry upfront coupled with a fixed-exchange-rate regime rather than socialism or planning per se that necessitated the establishment of the vast bureaucratic regime characterized by investment licensing, autarkic import policy and price and distribution controls. Given the system of fixed nominal exchange rates with no appetite whatsoever to either periodically devalue the domestic currency or keep tight control of the money supply to hold down domestic prices, the licence-permit raj was unavoidable with or without elaborate planning and socialism. The only way to prevent the spillover of the scarce investment resources into the light industry was to either carry out the manufacturing activity in the public sector or regulate investment in the private sector through licensing or some combination of the two.

Arguably, the most detrimental effect of the heavy-industry-centred approach to industrialization was the exclusion of the vast majority of the population from the development process. Heavy industry absorbed the bulk of the meagre capital the country had in the early post-Independence era but only a tiny proportion of the workforce. This left nearly 95 per cent of the workforce in either agriculture or small, household and cottage industries. Because of this exclusionary feature, whatever limited industrialization and growth could be achieved as a result of the government's Herculean effort failed to contribute to either any movement of the workforce out of agriculture or to the eradication of poverty. The failure, in turn, led to the maligning of growth as the instrument of poverty reduction and paved the way for yet more radical, anti-growth and redistributive socialism under Nehru's daughter, Indira Gandhi.

The development of heavy industry required engineers and managers. Therefore, whatever little resources India could muster after meeting the needs of heavy industry investment and administration went to creating elite engineering and management institutions. The collateral damage was the neglect of school education. As Bauer put it in his 1961 book, the development expenditure on elementary education was about one-half the cost of each of the three steel plants in the public sector during the second plan. The near absence of capital in the cottage and small industries also meant that their employees learnt no new skills. Skill upgradation remained a distant dream for a long time.

The Lasting Impact

Nehru-era socialism left a lasting legacy effect on politicians, civil servants, policy analysts and even businessmen. This is the subject of the four chapters in Part III. Chapters 11 and 12 are devoted to the study of the legacy effect on political leadership during 1964–84 and 1985–23, respectively. Chapter 13 looks at the lasting effect of the Nehru era on the institutions and the business community, and Chapter 14 on economists and other policy analysts.

A necessary condition for a change of direction in policy is the willingness of the top leadership. In the Indian system of parliamentary democracy, this leader is the prime minister. In Chapter 11, I document that the influential leaders until 1984 were either the contemporaries of Nehru or had cut their teeth in politics during the time he ruled. They had, therefore, fully internalized socialism in their political thought. None of the prime ministers during the twenty years after the death of Nehru exhibited any appetite to fundamentally alter the direction of the economic policy. For several years after Nehru, socialism remained a sufficiently popular force that the more conservative opponents of Indira Gandhi lost the political battle against her. Though Indira Gandhi initiated some minor steps in the direction of deregulation during her last term from January 1980 to October 1984, upon her death, she left a policy regime with significantly tighter controls in all areas than in the time of Nehru.

Rajiv Gandhi, who came to office upon his mother's death in October 1984, was the first prime minister to have been untouched by socialism. For much of his life, he had no interest in politics. He spent the early years of his life studying in Britain and the 1970s as an Indian Airlines pilot. He entered politics at the urging of his mother upon the untimely death of his brother, Sanjay, in 1980. Sanjay had been the closest political associate of his mother, and with him gone, Indira Gandhi needed Rajiv Gandhi to help her.

Given this background, Rajiv Gandhi had experienced socialism not from the ruling but from the citizen end. As such, he realized that the system had not served ordinary citizens well and was keen to change it. Unfortunately, however, much of the remainder of the leadership within the Congress was still not ready to move away from the path Nehru had charted. It resisted Rajiv Gandhi, who, lacking political skills, was unable to move forward beyond a burst of some important liberalizing reforms in his first year. Only in the area of trade was he able to sustain modest reforms in the subsequent years.

The task of changing the direction of policy eventually fell on Narasimha Rao, who came to office in 1991 after Rajiv Gandhi himself was assassinated at a young age. The story of how and why a leader who was a contemporary and close associate of Indira Gandhi turned out to be the one to change the direction of policy is a fascinating one. In a nutshell, he was a leader apart from all his contemporaries. He was given to reading, writing and deep introspection but never revealed his mind publicly. He had observed and contributed to the liberalizing moves of both Indira Gandhi and Rajiv Gandhi. He had keenly watched Deng Xiaoping change the direction of policy in China. During his visits to the United States in the 1970s, he had been impressed by its achievements. He saw Nehru as someone who evolved as the world around him evolved. Therefore, he believed that changing direction did not mean abandoning Nehru but actually following him. Above all, unlike Rajiv Gandhi, he knew how to navigate the political system. At long last, he, therefore, successfully ushered in pathbreaking reforms in 1991.

Though the 1991 reforms reset the course of economic policy, the legacy of the Nehru era, buttressed by a yet deeper dive into socialism under Indira Gandhi, continues even if in a weakened form. This is partially reflected in the slow progress in the full transition to a market economy. The visible hand of the government can still be found everywhere, and the country continues to witness the instances of enactment of anti-reform policies, as exemplified by the Land Acquisition Act of 2013, the Right to Education Act of 2009, the retrospective taxation law and a return to protectionism.

The legacy effects of socialism through the bureaucracy, planning commission, laws and judiciary, and business community are considered in Chapter 13. When the reform involves stopping the bureaucracy from doing what it has been doing, implementation is easier. For example, when Rao ended industrial licensing, licensing applications stopped coming, and bureaucrats who were previously issuing licences no longer had that task to perform. In contrast, when a public-sector undertaking has to be privatized, which is one of the key outstanding reforms, the process is critically dependent on bureaucrats being heavily engaged. If they remain married to the socialist idea of a large public sector, privatization will inevitably face hurdles. It is in this sense that the Nehru-era legacy still continues to hold back the shift to a market economy.

The existence of the planning commission similarly proved a hurdle to change. Rajiv Gandhi had famously wanted to fundamentally alter the nature of the seventh plan by shifting the focus of development to urban India. His essential instinct was correct in that it is the growth of jobs in urban areas that drives migration out of agriculture into industry and services, raises the land per worker in agriculture and brings down poverty. But the planning commission establishment pushed back and kept the shift from taking place.

Socialist-era laws, too, have remained a challenge to the transition to a market economy. This is particularly true in the areas of labour. According to the Ministry of Labour and Employment, there currently exist forty central government labour laws. The balance of these laws is to protect the relatively few existing formal-sector workers. They discourage the creation of new formal-sector jobs, especially in the labour-intensive sectors where there exist more prospects for job creation for the masses. Though pro-market reforms began in 1991, until recently, no government has been willing to take the political risk of reforming these laws. In 2019 and 2020, the Modi government finally enacted four labour codes intended to replace more than two dozen existing labour laws. But with the socialism of yesterday still looming large in the Ministry of Labour and Employment, they have not been implemented even five years after the Parliament enacted them.

There has also been a history of the judiciary always passing judgments in favour of workers in industrial disputes, irrespective of the merit of the case. From the 1970s until recently, it was nearly impossible for employers to win a case in such disputes.[5] The lower courts still take this stand though the

Supreme Court has finally begun to consider the merits of the case in its rulings.[6]

The business community directly suffered the adverse consequences of the licence-permit raj. But in the early post-Independence years, when the economic system was being put in place, it had been supportive of the raj. It had expressed this support in the Bombay Plan, which had been authored by the who's who of the then business community. Until the early 1960s, its complaints were limited to the licensing procedures and not the system itself. But by 1966, with the negotiations with the World Bank underway, it was calling for the rollback of price and distribution controls and licensing. Nevertheless, so far as trade policy is concerned, it remained behind the curve. A sizeable section of the business community remained opposed to import liberalization even after the political leadership had begun to recognize the need for it and announced the 1991 reforms abolishing import licensing on products other than consumer goods. Today, the community broadly supports import-substitution policies, with even the export interests rarely coming forward in favour of liberal trade policies.

Finally, the legacy effect of the socialist era perhaps remains most visible in the area of teaching of and commentary on economic policy. After more than thirty years since the launch of economic reforms, it remains a challenge to find economists trained in India who are passionate advocates of pro-market reforms. Educators in colleges and universities, even in the leading universities, subscribe to the left ideology and end up imparting the same to their students. Some of these students become teachers for the next generation of students. The chain thus continues. With rare exceptions, economists who have supported and advocated reforms, whether from within the government or outside, have had substantial exposure to the Western or East Asian economies either as students or practitioners. These themes are fleshed out in considerable detail in Chapter 14.

Concluding Remarks

In this volume, I present the Nehru-era economic history and thought and draw their longer-term implications for shaping the thinking of the key stakeholders on the economic policy. I have made an effort to use minimal jargon without sacrificing rigour. I am acutely aware that the parts describing the procedures on investment licensing, import licensing and the allocation of foreign exchange are dreary, which many readers may choose to skip. But they are an essential part of the economic history, and the volume would not have been complete without their documentation.

My bottom-line conclusion from the research I undertook in the course of writing this book is that once the Nehru era was behind India, much of what followed was inevitable. Opportunities for change presented themselves on three occasions before the 1991 reforms, but no real change materialized on account of the dominance of the socialist ideology and the vested interests that the ideology had created. From 1967 to 1969, there was a struggle for the leadership of the Congress Party between Indira Gandhi and the conservative Syndicate. Gandhi won this battle by painting her opponents as friends of the business community. The second opportunity presented itself when in 1977 Morarji Desai became the prime minister following the end of the emergency rule of Gandhi. Desai had an opportunity to give a new direction to policy. However, despite his reputation as a conservative, his policies during his short-lived tenure were hardly distinguishable from those of Indira Gandhi. The third and final opportunity arose under Rajiv Gandhi in 1984. This was a truly genuine opportunity with Rajiv Gandhi entirely sincere and keen to change course. But even this opportunity passed due to a lack of support among his senior colleagues in the Congress.

One final question is whether it is possible to imagine a scenario in which economic policy could have taken a different course. I speculate on this issue in the final, concluding chapter, Chapter 15. My answer is that this was only possible if a leader other than Nehru had helmed the country during its immediate post-Independence years. For example, between them, if Nehru had been older and Patel younger, with the former departing the scene in December 1950 and the latter living till May 1964, we could have had a more market-oriented policy regime put in place in the 1950s. But short of such a scenario, it may be reasonably asserted that once Nehru had launched the second plan, he placed the economy on a deterministic path from which a retreat any time soon after his death was unlikely.

Part I

Economic Thought: Nehru and Others

2

Nehru: From Radical to Fabian Socialist

India won its independence from the British on 15 August 1947. Mahatma Gandhi, who had led the freedom movement, fell to an assassin's bullet less than six months later on 30 January 1948, leaving Pandit Jawaharlal Nehru as the top leader in the country. Sardar Vallabhbhai Patel, a close second, had the stature to be a challenger, but he passed away less than three years later on 15 December 1950. With no equal left, Nehru dominated the policy scene like no other leader during the following fourteen years until his death on 27 May 1964.

Whereas Gandhi devoted himself to winning political freedom and bringing about social change, Nehru also took a keen interest in India's economic problems. Indeed, he saw the economic salvation of the people of India as the ultimate goal of political freedom from the British. Having worked closely with peasants in the erstwhile United Provinces (modern-day Uttar Pradesh) in the first half of the 1920s, he had been acutely aware of the widespread poverty of rural India. Consequently, he had given much thought to the economic system India must adopt to overcome its poverty once it became independent.

The policy framework India eventually adopted, which has continued to serve as the foundation of the economy till today, was shaped principally by Nehru. To appreciate this framework fully, we must understand his economic philosophy. At a broad level, he was a socialist, and this creed greatly influenced the policy framework he adopted. But socialism itself comes in many hues. Therefore, what we require is an understanding of the particular brand of socialism that Nehru espoused. This, in turn, requires a look at the evolution of his thinking, a subject of considerable interest in its own right. Contrary to the common belief that he had become a convert to Fabian socialism while studying in Cambridge and London, his brand of socialism was his own. Moreover, he came to this brand through a more circuitous route several decades after he had completed his education in England.

Nehru returned from England to India with no ideological leanings towards socialism, Fabian or otherwise. Later, when he did embrace it, it was of a much more radical variety than the one he adopted in post-Independence India. This brand, bordering on communism, dominated his thinking till at least 1936. Sometime between 1937 and 1947, he transitioned into a more moderate form that came closest to Fabian socialism but is best viewed as his own, justifying the label 'Nehruvian socialism'. This brand became the basis of the economic-policy framework in India, beginning with the Second Five-Year Plan in 1956.

Not an Early Convert to Fabian Socialism

Nehru received his early education at home, first from a British tutor and then from an Irish-French theosophist. In 1905, at the age of sixteen, his father sent him to England, where he spent the first three years studying at Harrow (1905–7), an elite English school. Nehru then joined Trinity College at Cambridge (1907–10), followed by two years at the Inner Temple in London (1910–12). At Trinity, he did science tripos in chemistry, geology and botany, and at the Inner Temple, he appeared for the Bar examinations. When enrolled at the Inner Temple, he also spent time at the London School of Economics.

Nehru returned to India in 1912. He initially joined his father in practising law but did not find it satisfying. Though he had met Gandhi for the first time as early as 1916 at the twenty-ninth session of the Congress in Lucknow, he did not get seriously engaged with the freedom movement until 1919. After 1919, he actively participated in Gandhi's non-cooperation movement and worked closely with peasants in the United Provinces during the first half of the 1920s. There is little evidence of a trace of socialism in him during these years.

Nevertheless, there is a common impression that Nehru had already converted to Fabian socialism during his studies in England.[1] The likely source of this impression is a brief reference he makes to having been attracted to this form of socialism in his autobiography. He writes, 'My law studies did not take up much time and I got through the Bar examinations, one after the other, with neither glory nor ignominy. For the rest I simply drifted, doing some general reading, vaguely attracted to the Fabian and socialist ideas, and interested in the political movements of the day.'[2]

There are at least two reasons why this throwaway sentence on being 'vaguely attracted to the Fabian and socialist ideas' in the autobiography does not indicate his conversion to them. First, Sarvepalli Gopal, arguably the most authentic biographer of Nehru, gives an account of his years at Cambridge that casts considerable doubt on the possibility of him getting wedded to Fabian socialism when at Inner Temple. Gopal points out that during his first term at Cambridge, Nehru had attended a lecture by Bernard Shaw on 'Socialism and University Man' but went to it 'more to see the speaker than to hear him'.[3] More compellingly, he states,

> Fabianism, with its hopes of reforming capitalism and imperceptibly gliding to socialism, was at this time popular in Cambridge, but it seems to have attracted Jawaharlal little, and there is no reason to believe that he was a member of the Cambridge Fabian Society. Hugh Dalton, also at Cambridge at this time and prominent in the Fabian Society and the Union, knew Jawaharlal slightly but does not remember much else about him.[4]

Nehru had thus remained indifferent towards Fabian socialism at Cambridge, an institution where this ideology had been flourishing among his peers. Against this backdrop, it is improbable that his vague attraction to it would have translated into conversion to it at the Inner Temple.

According to Gopal, the figure that attracted Nehru more when studying in England was William Morris, a British textile designer, author and socialist activist. Morris founded the Socialist League in 1884. Its manifesto rejected the concept of socialism in one country and advocated proletarian internationalism and world revolution.[5] Gopal notes that Nehru had bought a full set of the collected works of Morris, which had begun coming out in 1910. He adds, 'There was clearly greater affinity with Morris than with Shaw. . . . The life of Morris was the story of the evolution of a revolutionary, the progress from aestheticism to the basic question of class power; and Jawaharlal may have been, in his own context, moving in the same direction.'[6]

The second and more compelling reason Nehru could not have become wedded to Fabian socialism yet is that there is little trace of it to be found in him for nearly one and a half decades following his return to India in 1912. Importantly, even when socialism became central to his thinking, it was not of the Fabian variety but instead, one preached by Morris. Upon his return to India, though Nehru took up law practice alongside his father, he remained uncertain regarding his profession for at least half a decade.[7] Only after he joined the freedom movement in 1919 did he feel he had discovered his life's mission. He then worked with peasants in the United Provinces, participated in the civil disobedience movement that Gandhi launched in 1922 and served three successive jail terms between 1921 and 1923.

Conversion to Radical Socialism

Against the backdrop of this engagement with the freedom movement alongside the masses, which included peasants and workers, the turning point in Nehru's conversion to socialism came during a visit to Europe and the Soviet Union from March 1926 to December 1927. The principal reason for the visit was the treatment of his wife, who had been ill. Though the visit failed to improve her condition, it proved transformational for him. A key event in this transformation was the International Congress Against Colonial Oppression and Imperialism, held in Brussels in February 1927. Nehru helped organize this conference and participated in it as the representative of the Indian National Congress. At the conference, he interacted intensively with leading communists and trade unionists from Europe and nationalists from Asia, Africa and Latin America. These interactions and the proceedings of the conference convinced him that imperialism, especially British imperialism, was an integral part of capitalism. Therefore, the only way to defeat it was to defeat capitalism and replace it with some form of international socialism. A visit to the Soviet Union that November reinforced this conviction. By December 1927, when he returned to India, he was a changed man. 'He who had sailed from India as a dedicated disciple of Gandhi returned a self-conscious revolutionary radical.'[8]

Nehru gave expression to this newfound radicalism in the speeches he delivered in different forums around the country soon after his return to India. The best example of it is his presidential address at the Punjab Provincial Conference on 11 April 1928. In it, he stated,

> Many of us who denounce British imperialism in India do not realize that . . . it is the necessary consequence of industrial development on capitalist line. For capitalism necessarily leads to exploitation of one man by another, one group by another, and one country by another. . . . The only alternative that is offered to us is some form of socialism, that is the state ownership of the means of production and distribution. We cannot escape the choice and . . . we cannot but cast our weight on the side of socialism.[9]

His speech in Calcutta the same year and Lahore the following year carried the same essential message.[10]

In 1931, an agrarian crisis resulting from repeated crop failures and excessive land rents in the United Provinces had led the Congress to seek a sharp cut in the rent collected by the landlords from tenants. Nehru was at the forefront of this intervention by the Congress. By this time, the British government had come to fear Nehru's radical socialism to such an extent that Malcolm Hailey, the governor of the United Provinces, wrote to Sir Findlater Stewart of the India Office in London, 'Jawaharlal and his school have of course a great influence locally, and there is no doubt that they have for a long time been bitten with the idea of making a kind of Soviet organization of peasant workers, which will first of all abolish the landlord and then possibly Sovietize Government.'[11]

Over time, Nehru's views on socialism acquired even sharper edges. In a series of articles published in the Indian press on 9, 10 and 11 October 1933, he opined that though capitalism had successfully solved the problem of production, it had failed to solve the allied problem of distribution. Moreover, the search for the sources of raw materials and markets for finished products had led the capitalist nations to imperialism and 'ever-increasing conflicts with the rising nationalism of colonial countries . . .'.[12] In this backdrop, he asked, 'Whither India?' and answered, 'Surely, to the great human goal of social and economic equality, to the ending of all exploitation of nation by nation and class by class, to national freedom within the framework of an international cooperative socialist world foundation.'[13]

Two months later, in a press release dated 18 December 1933, Nehru went a step further, stating that the only real choice any nation had was between fascism and communism, and he unequivocally chose the latter.[14] He elaborated on his ideas on the subject in his autobiography, written in jail in just nine months between June 1934 and February 1935.[15] Then, in 1936, he placed his case for radical socialism before the entire membership of the Congress in his presidential address.

At the forty-ninth session of the Congress during 12–14 April 1936 in Lucknow, Nehru devoted a significant part of his address to socialism. He said,

> I see no way of ending the poverty, the vast unemployment, the degradation, and the subjection of the Indian people except through socialism. That involves vast and revolutionary changes in our political and social structure, the ending of vested interests in land and industry, as well as the feudal and autocratic Indian States system. That means the ending of private property, except in a restricted sense, and the replacement of the present profit system by a higher ideal of cooperative service. . . . In short, it means a new civilization, radically different from the present capitalist order.[16]

Extolling the Soviet experience, Nehru said,

> Some glimpse we can have of this new civilization in the territories of the USSR [Union of Soviet Socialist Republics]. Much has happened there which has pained me greatly and with which I disagree, but I look upon that great and fascinating unfolding of a new order and a new civilization as the most promising feature of our dismal age. If the future is full of hope it is largely because of Soviet Russia and what it has done, and I am convinced that, if some world catastrophe does not intervene, this new civilization will spread to other lands and put an end to the wars and conflicts which capitalism feeds.[17]

He continued,

> Socialism is thus for me not merely an economic doctrine which I favour; it is a vital creed which I hold with all my head and heart. I work for Indian independence because the nationalist in me cannot tolerate alien domination; I work for it even more because for me it is the inevitable step to social and economic change. I should like the Congress to become a

> socialist organization and to join hands with the other forces in the world who are working for the new civilization.[18]

This address by Nehru, followed by statements by him along similar lines at different forums in the subsequent weeks, created much nervousness among Indian industrialists. They feared that if this thinking found traction in the Congress, it would leave little room for them to survive in post-Independence India. Therefore, industrialists opposed to the Congress launched a frontal attack on Nehru. At the same time, those actively partnering with it in the freedom movement worked behind the scenes with its conservative members and Gandhi to blunt the influence of Nehru's extreme ideas.[19] In the event, none of the resolutions the Congress Working Committee adopted at the end of the Lucknow session reflected Nehru's sentiments in favour of radical socialism. They diluted even his proposal to affiliate peasant and worker associations to the Congress.

Finding himself without support among senior leaders of the Congress, Nehru did not pursue his radical socialist ideas in the public space beyond 1936. Instead, as a loyal member of the organization, he got busy leading it in provincial elections slated for early 1937 under the Government of India Act of 1935. He proved exceptionally popular with the people during the campaign and helped Congress score election victories in seven out of eleven provinces. Provincial governments came into existence during the summer of 1937.[20] In the meantime, in December 1936, he was re-elected as the president of the Congress at the fiftieth session in Faizpur. He spent the bulk of 1937 defending provincial governments against their critics.

Critical Role of the Deliberations in the National Planning Committee

At the fifty-first session of the Congress, held in Haripur from 19 to 22 February 1938, Subhas Chandra Bose, another prominent figure in the Indian freedom movement, was elected the president. Like Nehru, he had been a committed socialist. The two also shared their enthusiasm for planning for industrialization once India became independent. For instance, in his presidential address at Haripur, Bose stated,

> I have no doubt in my mind that our chief national problems relating to the eradication of poverty, illiteracy and disease and to scientific production and distribution can be effectively tackled only along socialistic lines. The very first thing which our future national government will have to do, would be to set up a commission for drawing up a comprehensive plan of reconstruction.[21]

Striking a chord with Nehru and challenging the view of Gandhi on modern industry, he added,

> The planning commission will have to carefully consider and decide which of the home industries could be revived despite the competition of modern factories and in which sphere large scale production should be encouraged. However much we may dislike modern industrialism and condemn the evils which follow in its train, we cannot go back to the pre-industrial era, even if we desire to do so.[22]

Subsequently, on 2 October 1938, armed with a resolution of the Congress Working Committee, Bose convened a conference of the industries ministers of seven provinces with Congress governments to consider the problem of industrialization. This conference passed a resolution stating that 'the problems of poverty and unemployment, of national defense and of the economic regeneration in general cannot be solved without industrialization. As a step towards such industrialization, a comprehensive scheme of national planning should be formulated. This scheme should provide for the development of heavy key industries, medium scale industries and cottage industries . . .'[23]

To translate this resolution into action, Bose constituted the National Planning Committee with the charge to develop a comprehensive plan for implementation after Independence. He asked Nehru to chair this committee.[24] Nehru initially hesitated but accepted the responsibility because 'the work was after my own heart and I could not keep out of it'.[25] The committee had its first meeting on 18 December 1938 in Bombay, with Bose delivering the inaugural address.

The committee brought within its fold fourteen other eminent Indians from diverse fields. They included four industrialists, five scientists, three economists, a representative of industrial workers and a Gandhian.[26] Nehru also invited representatives of the then existing provincial governments and princely states interested in collaborating with the Congress. Nearly all provincial governments joined, including those headed by parties other than the Congress and several major princely states such as Hyderabad, Mysore, Baroda, Travancore and Bhopal.[27]

The original charge to the committee in the Industries Ministers' resolution was confined to evolving a strategy for industrialization. But as discussions progressed, the committee realized it could not ignore agriculture, the mainstay of people, or social services necessary to assist the poor. 'The more we thought of this planning business,' writes Nehru, 'the vaster it grew in its sweep and range till it seemed to embrace almost every activity.'[28]

The committee's work progressed well until September 1939, when the Second World War broke out. In November, the Congress governments in the provinces resigned, which removed the principal immediate clients of the committee from the scene. The committee, nevertheless, kept working. It nearly completed the subcommittees' reports and was writing the final overall report when, on 30 October 1940, Nehru was arrested and sentenced to a lengthy prison term. Because the Government of India refused to let Nehru complete the task from jail, the committee's work remained incomplete, with no final report issued.[29]

Predictably, the right wing of the Congress opposed the committee's work. It was wary of the consensus developing within the committee favouring State control of industry and agriculture. It also saw a potential challenge to the cottage industries and khadi in the committee's work. Gandhi supported this wing of the Congress and advised all his followers to keep away from the committee's work. He also vetoed Nehru's request for the publication of the subcommittee reports.[30]

A Shift to a More Moderate Socialism

Nehru spent the bulk of the next few years from his arrest on 5 December 1940 to 15 June 1945 in jail.[31] After coming out of jail, he got busy heading the Interim Government and the work of the Constituent Assembly. His speeches and writings from 1946 onward definitively indicate a significant shift in his position on socialism away from radicalism and towards moderation. He no longer harboured the ambition to set up a 'Socialist World Federation' that he had advocated in his Lucknow address. Even nationally, he now advocated only limited State ownership of the means of production, leaving considerable room for the private sector to operate. Indeed, in the Constituent Assembly debates and elsewhere, following independence, his task became one of defending private-sector enterprises, including those owned by foreigners, against calls for nationalization by radical socialists within the Congress and by the communists.

The report of the Economic Programme Committee, appointed by the All-India Congress Committee (AICC) under the chairmanship of Nehru on 17 November 1947, provides an early example of this shift. According to a summary of the report, which Nehru provided to the then Congress President Rajendra Prasad along with a letter dated 25 January 1948, the committee envisaged a monopoly of the public sector only over defence, key and public utility industries and undertakings that would serve more than one state. On the issue of nationalization, the summary stated, 'In respect of existing undertakings, the process of transfer from private to public ownership (on payment of equitable compensation) should commence after a reasonable period, so as to enable adequate arrangements to avoid dislocation of the economic life in the country or uneconomic acquisition of inflated assets.'[32] Thus, there was already a retreat from immediate nationalization and a recognition that acquiring assets at inflated prices would be a poor use of public resources.

Three weeks later, on 17 February 1948, Kazi Syed Karimuddin, a member of the Constituent Assembly, moved a resolution calling for the establishment of a 'socialist economy based on the principle of nationalization of key industries and co-operative and collective farming and socialization of the material resources of the country'.[33] In his response, Nehru pitched for a far more moderate approach arguing that it would be unwise to squander scarce government resources on acquiring what already existed instead of investing them in new ventures to create more wealth. To quote him,

> Now, it is well known, and we have often stressed this, that production is perhaps one of the most important things before us today: that is, adding to the wealth of the country. We cannot overlook other things. Nevertheless, production comes first, and I am prepared to say that everything that we do should be judged from the point of view of production first of all. If nationalization adds to production, we shall have nationalization at every step. If it does not, let us see how to bring it about in order not to impede production. That is the essential thing.[34]

Two months later, on 7 April 1948, Nehru spoke again on socialism as part of the debate on the Industrial Policy Resolution of 1948 (IPR 1948) in the Constituent Assembly. In this speech, he once again argued against indiscriminate nationalization to avoid sinking scarce resources in technologically obsolete ventures. He said,

> In fact, from the point of view of technological advance, it may well be a complete waste of money to acquire such obsolete machinery, factories and other installations. It is true that they are useful so long as new factories and new technological methods are not introduced, and if you have a vast quantity of money and resources, certainly acquire them and go ahead with other things. But if you have limited resources, then the main thing to do is not to think in terms of static technology, but to think in terms of changing technology, of the State acquiring the new processes, the new changes, and not the old, except when the old, obstruct, and hamper your planning and progress.[35]

In the same speech, Nehru later argued that India could not rely on pure capitalism either and needed to follow a 'mixed economy' approach. He reasoned,

> After all, in the world today, you know that various ideologies, economic and political, are in conflict. In the main, there are two: on one side the so-called capitalist ideology and on the other the so-called communist or Soviet ideology. . . . But it does not necessarily follow that you must have either this or that. There may be many intermediate ways. Now, you all know that capitalism . . . had a big problem before it—the problem of production. It has solved that problem in theory, and largely in practice in many parts of the world. Therefore, industrial capitalism has been, in spite of everything, a tremendous success. . . . Now, the other question arises . . .

> whether it can also solve the problem of distribution with equal success . . . If it cannot solve that problem, then some other way will have to be found. . . . In India, if we do not ultimately solve the basic problems of our country—the problems of food, clothing, housing, and so on it will not matter whether we call ourselves capitalists, socialists, communists or anything else. . . . Whatever the method may be, the method which delivers the goods . . . will justify itself and give hope. That method need not necessarily be an extreme method belonging to either of these two rival ideologies. It may be something in between.[36]

This statement was a definite climb down for Nehru from his earlier stance in the press release of 18 December 1933, in which he had declared that the only political systems available to us were fascism and communism and that he chose the latter.

IPR 1948, in whose defence Nehru delivered these remarks, was itself a far cry from Nehru's original radical socialism. It entirely ruled out the nationalization of private enterprises, including foreign-owned ones, for ten years. Criticism of the resolution by K.T. Shah, who had served as the general secretary of the National Planning Committee, confirms that it violated the spirit of the discussions in it. Shah expressed 'utter disappointment' with the resolution, saying, 'The National Planning Committee's list of industries which ought to be exclusively under State management has been most grievously curtailed. It is a matter of great regret that the head of our Government who was also the Chairman of our Planning Committee [meaning Nehru], should have subscribed to it.'[37]

Immediately following Independence, we observe a similar shift in Nehru's stance on agriculture. In his Lucknow address, he had extolled the Soviet model, which had resorted to forced collectivization of farming. However, his Economic Programme Committee of the AICC took a more conciliatory position, emphasizing the importance of production over other objectives. In the summary of the committee's report sent to Rajendra Prasad, Nehru noted,

> In agriculture the immediate aim should be to assure minimum levels of production of food, cloth and building materials in every Province and every prescribed area on the basis of a scheme of balanced cultivation. To increase efficiency in agricultural production the state should directly invest in non-recurring permanent land improvements, undertake and encourage experiment in cooperative farming and control the farmer in the interest of better farming.[38]

The summary went on to advocate the removal of all intermediaries between the farmer and the State and equitable distribution of land and then recommended something that would be anathema to today's socialists in India: replacement of land revenue by progressive agricultural income tax.

Nehru echoed a similar sentiment when speaking on agriculture in his speech at the Constituent Assembly on 17 February 1948. He noted, 'There has been talk about collective and cooperative farming. I should like to have collective and cooperative farming in this country.'[39] He added,

> Obviously, whatever decision we may make must have consent of a large number of people. We cannot force it down the throats of the vast majority of our peasants. We have to convert them. The best way to do that is to give them a living example in cooperatives, and show them how they will function: and then only can they be converted. India is a huge country. We may have various types of agricultural economy side by side and gradually the one that is best suited to the land will prevail.[40]

Explaining the Shift

How is this shift towards moderation in Nehru's views on socialism to be explained? Ideally, we would like to find evidence of transition in his own writings. Unfortunately, I have found no significant piece of writing or speech by him on socialism after 1936 and before Independence other than some incidental references to it in *The Discovery of India*. Therefore, the evidence I offer is in the nature of informed speculation.

Most likely, the seeds of the shift in Nehru's thinking got sown during his work in the National Planning Committee. Membership of this committee had included representatives from diverse fields, most notably industry. Four out of the fourteen members of the committee were from industry or had deep industry links.[41] They disapproved of wholesale nationalization and pushed against it in the committee discussions. Interactions with them may have begun to sensitize Nehru to the need to accommodate private capital. This possibility is hinted in *The Discovery of India*, the only major work Nehru produced during the 1940s before Independence. Describing how the discussions led the committee members to think along lines different from their original thinking, he writes,

> But I was agreeably surprised at the large measure of unanimity achieved by us in spite of the incongruous elements in our Committee. The big business element was the largest single group and its outlook on many matters, especially financial and commercial, was definitely conservative. Yet the urge for rapid progress, and the conviction that only thus could we solve our problems of poverty and unemployment, were so great that all of us were forced out of our grooves and compelled to think on new lines. . . . We knew our differences and yet we tried and often succeeded, after discussing every point of view, in arriving at an integrated conclusion which was accepted by all of us, or most of us.[42]

In the following paragraph, Nehru adds,

> Constituted as we were, not only in our Committee but in the larger field of India, we could not then plan for socialism as such. Yet it became clear to me that our plan, as it developed, was inevitably leading us towards establishing some of the

> fundamentals of the socialist structure. . . . And all this was to be attempted in the context of democratic freedom and with a large measure of cooperation of some at least of the groups who were normally opposed to the socialistic doctrine. That co-operation seemed to me worthwhile even if it involved toning down or weakening the plan in some respects.[43]

This account of the deliberations in the National Planning Committee brings out a far more accommodating and pragmatic Nehru concerning socialism than the one we witness in his earlier writings, especially his presidential address at the Lucknow Congress session. We may further hypothesize that once India won independence and Nehru confronted the task of building the nation's economy to deliver on his promise of ridding India of its appalling poverty, he realized that he could not implement his idealized version of socialism within the democratic polity which was integral to his post-Independence political architecture. By this time, industrialists were a powerful economic force. To move the economy forward, he needed their cooperation rather than to crush them. Furthermore, given the recognition of the citizen's right to property, for which unequivocal support existed among leaders such as Sardar Vallabhbhai Patel, wholesale nationalization would have required financial resources to compensate the owners of existing enterprises on a scale that the State did not have.

Remarks by N.G. Ranga of the Congress, a classical liberal who later became the president of the pro-market Swatantra Party at its founding in 1959, in response to the criticism of IPR 1948 by K.T. Shah, suggest that the clout Indian industrialists had acquired by this time indeed constrained Nehru in the framing of IPR 1948. The *Times of India* recorded this response a day after the passage of IPR 1948 thus,

> Prof. K.T. Shah's criticism of the policy of the Government, he [Ranga] said, was unjustified in as much as the present Government was a Nationalist one and not socialist and had

> received no mandate from the people to liquidate capitalism. It was a new Government placed in extraordinary circumstances and it had to come to some kind of terms with capitalists. What would happen if the capitalists went on a strike and refused to cooperate with the Government, he asked.[44]

Ranga was not engaging in empty rhetoric. Powerful private business interests in India had been pushing back against the expansion of the State in economic activity following Independence, just as they had done in the National Planning Committee. Moreover, even as popular a leader as Nehru was not in a position to ignore them. Michael Kidron describes the importance of this factor in his masterly narrative of political-economy forces at work in post-Independence India in these terms,

> Shaken by the social upheavals accompanying independence, afraid of the Government's populist leanings and of its tendency to formulate policy from general principles, Indian capital's major preoccupation in the first years was to *set the limits* of state economic activity. For its part, the Government was only too conscious of the need to ward off social chaos with increased production and employment. Since more than nine-tenths of total output and employment and more than seven-tenths of output in modern industry, were within the private sector, it was clear that private capital held most of the cards.[45]

Kidron goes on to suggest that the private sector had begun to set the terms of the debate even before the transfer of power from Britain to India had taken place. As evidence, he cites the following statement by G.D. Birla delivered at the annual session of the Federation of Indian Chambers of Commerce and Industry (FICCI) in March 1947, reflecting 'the utter exasperation with the state felt by him and his colleagues':[46]

> All that I ask at this stage is that they ought to declare their policy. If it is their desire that for the next few years they will rely on private enterprise they should say so; if on the other hand it is their desire to start industries of their own and manage them through their own agencies, they should declare it. All I can say is that the spirit of suspense is hindering production; and when I say this, I am not expressing any vague fears but only telling you what is today in every businessman's mind.

The account that follows in Kidron is highly suggestive of Nehru taking a conciliatory approach and meeting the private industry halfway. Once he had thus realized the limits to how far he could push socialism, as the nation's leader, he had no choice but to own that position. It was incumbent upon him to publicly defend the policy of his government. Therefore, even if his personal view remained sympathetic to a more radical form of socialism than that reflected in the policy, his speeches and public pronouncements had to conform to them.

Nehru's Personal Views Less Moderate than the Initial Policy

That Nehru's personal view may still have been less accommodating of private capital than his policy is evidenced by the fact that once Patel died and he was left with no equals to challenge him, he did push the socialist agenda further. While Patel lived, he was a formidable rival who held deeply conservative views, did not share Nehru's socialist philosophy and saw great merit in the role private industrialists could play in the country's development. Even if Nehru had wanted nationalization, he could not have won over Patel on it.

However, once Patel was gone, Nehru gradually consolidated his power to become the unchallenged leader of Congress and India. He then began pushing for greater State control over economic activity than that reflected in IPR 1948. In December 1954, he had the Parliament adopt a resolution to establish a socialist pattern of society in the country. Before that, in May 1953, nine existing airlines, including Air India, had been nationalized despite the assurance against nationalization for at least ten years. Then, in July 1955, the Imperial Bank of India was nationalized, with some state banks merged into it. Less than a year later, the Industrial Policy Resolution of 1956 (IPR 1956) replaced IPR 1948.

IPR 1956 dropped the guarantee against the nationalization of private enterprises. It also widened the space over which the public sector was to play an important role. In parallel, the Second Five-Year Plan set an ambitious target for public sector investment, a process continued in the Third Five-Year Plan. Finally, the more radical side of Nehru's socialism also saw expression in agriculture when he got Congress to adopt the Nagpur resolution in 1959. This resolution sought to implement, within three years, 'cooperative joint farming, the produce of land being shared partly in proportion to labour rendered and partly in proportion to land pooled'.[47] This project was reminiscent of the Soviet-style collectivization of agriculture and carried the risk of wholesale disruption in the countryside. Leaders such as C. Rajagopalachari and N.G. Ranga, who had emerged as champions of individual rights to property by this time, mounted a massive opposition. In the end, the resolution failed to advance beyond the Congress party apparatus.[48]

Compromise Not Alien to Nehru

A willingness to compromise and assume ownership of the position so evolved was neither alien to Nehru nor without precedence. Two earlier examples from his life illustrate the point. Soon after his return from Europe in December 1927, Nehru developed serious differences with Mahatma Gandhi on the ultimate goal of the freedom movement. Whereas Gandhi sought only Dominion Status at this point, Nehru wanted complete independence. At the Madras session of the Congress, where Gandhi was not present, he secured the passage of a resolution committing the Congress to complete independence. Gandhi immediately criticized the resolution as 'hastily conceived' and 'thoughtlessly passed' in his weekly newspaper *Young India*. He also told Nehru privately that he was proceeding too fast. Nehru first reacted sharply, telling Gandhi that their ideals were now very different, his (Gandhi's) leadership was hesitant and ineffective, and that he (Nehru) had considerable support. Gandhi confronted him head-on and offered to make their correspondence public. At that point, Nehru immediately recoiled and told Gandhi that their differences were only on a few points and need not spread to the many issues on which they agreed.[49]

The second instance relates to the Congress's Lucknow session, where Nehru delivered the presidential address advocating his radical socialist views. The resolutions Congress passed at the end of the session incorporated none of those views. Though he considered resigning his position in response, he did not do it for fear of precipitating matters. Later, in a letter dated 30 April 1936, Gandhi wrote to Agatha Harrison, 'But though he [Nehru] is extreme in his presentation, he is sober in his action . . . Whatever he does, he will do nobly. Though the gulf between us as to the outlook upon life has undoubtedly widened, we have never been so near each other in hearts as perhaps we are today.'[50]

Concluding Remarks

There is overwhelming evidence based on his writings and speeches that, at least until the late 1930s, Nehru subscribed to an extreme version of socialism that bordered on communism. However, as the prospects for independence began looking more and more realistic, the pragmatist in him came to supplant the idealist. He recognized that the extreme form of socialism he had once advocated required coercion of the citizenry, which was impossible within the democratic form of government he sought to establish in India. As a result, at independence, his original belief in complete ownership of the means of production and property by the government gave way to considerable accommodation of private entrepreneurship and property. Until the late 1930s, he had argued that nations' choices were limited to either capitalism or communism. However, by independence, he came to favour a path strictly between these two extremes, a path that later became known as a 'mixed economy.'

It bears noting that despite this turn to a more moderate form of socialism, Nehru's earlier radical ideas were not without consequences for his policy choices. For instance, the radical version of socialism had convinced him that imperialism resulted from the capitalist nations seeking to subjugate other nations to gain access to the sources of raw materials for their factories and markets for the vast volumes of finished goods they produced. That connection led him to take a highly sceptical view of international trade, lest it might leave newly independent nations exposed to the same imperialist forces. His decision to pursue economic self-sufficiency following India's independence had thus originated in his earlier, more radical variety of socialism.

Undoubtedly, the shift to the more moderate form of socialism by Nehru at independence saved the existing private industry from wholesale nationalization. Nevertheless, the damage even from this moderate form of socialism to India's economic fortunes was non-trivial, especially since it left the door ajar for future leaders to adopt a policy of more aggressive nationalization and State intervention. That possibility became a reality under his daughter, Indira Gandhi, who became prime minister in 1966. Political considerations led her to nationalize partially or wholly several sectors and enterprises and subject private-sector economic activity to much greater government control. The result was low growth for many more decades, which condemned India to continued high poverty levels for nearly half a century.

3

The Nehru Development Model

The economic policy framework India adopted after Independence carried the indelible mark of Nehru's thinking. Given that nearly all of the critical elements of this framework were due to him, it is wholly appropriate to characterize it as the Nehru Development Model. Past authors have generally not used this term because Nehru expounded his ideas informally, often in his speeches. Nevertheless, underlying these ideas was a core that meets the economist's definition of a formal model.[1]

Nehru had crystallized and firmed up nearly all of his economic ideas except those on agriculture by the time India became independent. For a pragmatic leader whose thinking was otherwise constantly evolving, it is remarkable how little these ideas changed in essentials during his seventeen-year-long unbroken tenure as prime minister.[2] In the 1960s, his opponents often attacked his strategy, but he remained firm in his belief that his chosen path was right and the only realistic one available to India. As it turned out, his development model survived for at least a quarter of a century after he died in 1964. Indeed, even after India had switched course and embraced pro-market reforms, his ideas continued influencing the thinking of many political leaders, bureaucrats and intellectuals, slowing the movement away from socialism.

Nehruvian socialism played a critical role in shaping the objectives, strategy and instruments that define what I have called the Nehru Development Model. To be sure, Nehru himself did not draw a sharp distinction across these three elements of the model. For instance, socialism, heavy industry and growth could appear as objectives, strategies or instruments in his speeches, depending on the context. Nevertheless, the distinction is both conceptually valid and helpful in understanding the logic of the economic edifice he created.

Objectives

In 1950, when Nehru appointed the Planning Commission, he chose to serve as its chairman himself. In this capacity, he was India's chief economic planner. However, he was also the country's prime minister. Therefore, it is not surprising that his goals included not merely economic but also political considerations. Though he and his fellow planners did not realize it, these goals were only partially consistent with each other. As a result, they were to result in serious adverse consequences, especially for economic efficiency and growth and hence poverty outcomes. These consequences became particularly damaging after his daughter, Prime Minister Indira Gandhi, pushed the policy towards a far more rapid expansion of public ownership of the means of production and tighter government control of private economic activity.[3]

The National Planning Committee and planners of post-Independence India had set for themselves two central objectives: removal of poverty and economic self-sufficiency. At the time, almost no one saw a conflict between these objectives, perhaps because the Soviet Union, whose example Nehru had been following, had seemingly pursued them successfully. However, in hindsight, the example was a red herring. The Soviet Union had paid a heavy price in human sacrifice to get to where it had gotten by the 1940s. As a democracy, India could not exact a similar price from its citizens.[4] Moreover, in the long run, the conflict between the two objectives caught up with even the authoritarian Soviet Union, leading to its disintegration by

1991. Massive economic inefficiencies, resulting from economic isolationism and State interventionism, played a critical role in the economic implosion that eventually led to the disintegration.

A third objective of the Nehru model was socialism. At a personal level, this objective was fundamental to Nehru's thinking in that poverty eradication and self-sufficiency were rooted in his socialist thought. While the National Planning Committee never adopted socialism as an explicit goal, it was very much present in the background throughout its discussions. 'Constituted as we were, not only in our Committee but in the larger field of India,' wrote Nehru, 'we could not then plan for socialism as such. Yet it became clear to me that our plan, as it developed, was inevitably leading us towards establishing some of the fundamentals of the socialist structure.'[5]

Removal of Poverty

Removal of poverty is an essential objective of policy in every welfare state, whether it is socialist or not. For a country committed to socialism, it is a given. Nehru had viewed even the freedom movement principally as an instrument of ridding India of its extreme poverty. In his influential article *Whither India*, written in 1933, he had stated, 'We cannot escape having to answer the question, now or later, for the freedom of which class or classes in India are we especially striving for [*sic*]? Do we place the masses, the peasants and workers, first, or some other small class at the head of our list?' Then, taking a dig at right-wing members of the Congress who refused to acknowledge the economic dimension of the freedom movement and insisted on casting it in purely political terms, he added, 'To say that we shall not answer that question now is itself an answer and taking of sides, for it means that we stand by the existing order, the *status quo*.' He further stated, 'The form of government is after all a means to an end; even freedom itself is a means, the end being human well-being, human growth, the ending of poverty and disease and suffering and the opportunity for everyone to live the "good life", physically and mentally.'[6] Further down the article, he asserted, 'The whole basis and urge of the national movement came from a desire for economic betterment, to throw off the burdens that crushed the masses and to end the exploitation of the Indian people.'[7]

Later, when the National Planning Committee began deliberations, it adopted poverty eradication as the central objective of planning. Nehru noted in *The Discovery of India*, 'Obviously we could not consider any problem, much less plan, without some definite aim and social objective. That aim was declared to be to ensure an adequate standard of living for the masses, in other words, to get rid of the appalling poverty of the people.'[8] In defining the objective precisely, the committee explicitly set a poverty line or what Nehru called an 'irreducible minimum' at Rs 15 to Rs 25 per month at pre-war prices. Noting that the estimated per capita income at the time was Rs 65 per month nationwide and just Rs 30 per month in rural areas, Nehru stated, 'These figures bring home the terrible poverty of the people and the destitute condition of the masses. There was lack of food, of clothing, of housing, and of every other essential requirement of human existence.'[9]

To its credit, when thinking about eradicating poverty, the committee did not merely consider income. Instead, its thinking extended to poverty's numerous manifestations, which we today describe as multidimensional poverty. In addition to the minimum income of Rs 15 to Rs 25 per month for all citizens, the committee set specific nutrition, clothing and shelter targets. For nutrition, it proposed a balanced diet with calorie intake between 2400 and 2800 units per adult worker per day; for clothing, it aimed to raise the availability of cloth from fifteen to thirty yards per capita per annum; and for shelter, it called for space of 100 square feet per person.[10]

Removal of poverty as the objective and growth and redistribution as joint instruments to achieve it remained integral to Nehru's thinking throughout his tenure as prime minister. Planners, in turn, incorporated this thinking into India's five-year plans. For instance, Chapter 1 of the First Five-Year Plan, which spanned fiscal years 1951–52 to 1955–56, states, 'The urge to economic and social change . . . comes from the fact of poverty and inequality of income . . . The elimination of poverty cannot, obviously, be achieved merely by redistributing existing wealth. Nor can a programme aiming only at raising production remove existing inequalities. The two have to be considered together . . .'[11] The plan discusses at length other social objectives, such as literacy; universal free education for children; raising life expectancy; reducing infant, child and maternal mortality; provision of tap water and sanitation; control of malaria and preventive healthcare of the rural population through health services for mothers and children. Subsequent five-year plans continued to echo these themes.

When the occasion demanded, Nehru returned to the theme of poverty and growth in his speeches in Parliament and elsewhere. One such occasion arose during the presentation of the Draft Outline of the Third Five-Year Plan in August 1960 in the Lok Sabha (House of the People). Challenging the sceptics who had argued that growth had bypassed the poor, he stated,

> The national income over the First and Second Plans has gone up by 42 per cent and the per capita income by 20 per cent. A legitimate query is made; where has this gone? To some extent, of course, you can see where it has gone. I address large gatherings in the villages and I can see that people are better fed, better clothed, they build brick houses and they are generally better.[12]

Self-Sufficiency

Self-sufficiency as an objective of policy commonly emerges from an extreme sense of nationalism or belief in protectionism as the means to promote domestic industry. However, in Nehru's thinking, it once again originated in socialism. He saw imperialism as the instrument capitalist nations used to gain access to the sources of raw materials and markets for finished products in their colonies.[13] In the specific context of India, Nehru wrote in *Whither India*,

> In this growth of capitalism, dominion over India was of vital importance to England. India's gold, in the early stages, helped in the further industrialization of England. And then India became a great producer of raw material to feed the factories of England and a huge market to consume the goods made in these factories.[14]

This reasoning led Nehru to equate any form of international trade with imperialism, against which he had waged the national freedom movement alongside Gandhi.

Once again, Nehru makes an explicit reference to this objective in *The Discovery of India* when reporting on the deliberations among the members of the National Planning Committee. He writes,

> The objective for the country as a whole was the attainment, as far as possible, of national self-sufficiency. International trade was certainly not excluded, but we were anxious to avoid being drawn into the whirlpool of economic imperialism. We wanted neither to be victims of an imperialist power nor to develop such tendencies ourselves.

He adds,

> The first charge on the country's produce should be to meet the domestic needs of food, raw materials, and manufactured goods. Surplus production would not be dumped abroad but used in exchange for such commodities as we might require. To base our national economy on export markets might lead to conflicts with other nations and to sudden upsets when those markets were closed to us.[15]

In principle, self-sufficiency can be achieved almost instantly by banning all international trade. This policy would deny the citizens access to all foreign products, forcing them to consume exclusively domestically produced products. However, Nehru did not consider this kind of protectionism in advocating self-sufficiency. Indeed, he rarely spoke or wrote about erecting trade barriers to achieve self-sufficiency. Instead, he wanted to plan the economy so that the production basket would adjust to the citizens' consumption needs, thereby eliminating the need for international trade in due course.

An excellent example of how Nehru viewed self-sufficiency is found in his address at the sixtieth session of the Congress at Avadi, delivered on 22 January 1955. In this address, he stated,

> The conception of planning today is . . . to measure the physical needs, that is to say, how much of food the people want, how much of clothes they want, how much of housing they want, how much of education they want, how much of health services they want, how much of work and employment they want, and so on. . . . Once we do that, we can set about increasing production and fulfilling these needs.[16]

He later added, 'What is really important is drawing up the physical needs of the people and then working to produce things which will fulfill such needs.'[17]

Given this conception, it is not surprising that we find hardly any discussion of a need for protectionist measures in the otherwise wide-ranging discussions of policy around the Second Five-Year Plan under the auspices of the Planning Commission. Though the government maintained the tariffs and import licensing inherited at Independence, it rarely chose to raise trade barriers as a part of the planning exercise during the 1950s. Only the adoption of foreign-exchange control in response to a balance-of-payments crisis in 1957 led to the tightening of import restrictions along the more traditional, protectionist lines.

Socialism

Participation in the International Congress Against Colonial Oppression and Imperialism held in Brussels in February 1927 had converted Nehru into a radical socialist. From then on, socialism became a central feature of his political and economic thinking. Some broad tenets of socialism, such as equitable distribution of material resources of the community and lack of concentration of wealth and means of production, were included in the Constitution. Later, as India embarked upon economic development and planning, the objective manifested itself in an assault on the most visible institutions of social inequity, such as the Zamindari system, princely privileges, and concentration of wealth as well as partial State ownership of the means of production.

Strategy

The critical question the National Planning Committee confronted in its deliberations was what path India must follow to rid its people of their massive poverty while also moving towards greater self-sufficiency. Despite socialism being the dominant ideology at the time, they recognized that the overall income of India was too low to solve this problem through redistribution alone. To quote Nehru again from *The Discovery of India*,

> To remove this lack and ensure an irreducible minimum standard for everybody the national income had to be greatly increased, and in addition to this increased production there had to be a more equitable distribution of wealth. We calculated that a really progressive standard of living would necessitate the increase of the national wealth by 500 or 600 per cent. That was, however, too big a jump for us, and we aimed at a 200 to 300 per cent increase within ten years.[18]

Nehru kept in sight the importance of growth for poverty alleviation as he began planning the economy after Independence. Though he proposed the resolution to establish a socialistic pattern of society in the Parliament and the Congress session at Avadi, he took extra pains to let radical socialists in the party know that there was little prospect of redistribution making a dent in India's poverty. In his address at the Avadi session, he forcefully stated:

> We cannot have a Welfare State in India with all the socialism or even communism in the world unless our national income goes up greatly. Socialism or communism might help you to divide your existing wealth, if you like, but in India, there is no existing wealth for you to divide; there is only poverty to divide. It is not a question of distributing the wealth of the few rich men here and there. That is not going to make any difference in our national income. We might adopt that course for the psychological good that might come out of it. But from the practical point of view, there is not much to divide in India because we are a poor country. We must produce wealth, and then divide it equitably.[19]

Nehru thus fully understood and appreciated the importance of growth for poverty alleviation. The question was, what was the right strategy to achieve growth? Illustratively, we can consider two extremes:

- Strategy 1, under which the country initially specializes in light manufactures such as clothing, footwear, furniture and other products of daily use that combine a large amount of its abundant factor of production, labour, with each unit of its scarce factor, capital. It exports a part of the output of these products in return for heavy industry products such as steel, machinery and transport equipment. Over time, capital becomes less scarce as incomes and investable resources grow, and the country can move into heavy industry. This approach explicitly relies on international trade and rules out self-sufficiency in the early stages of development. It has the potential to create decent jobs for the masses and deliver growth and poverty alleviation relatively fast, as the experience of Singapore, Taiwan and South Korea in the 1960s and 1970s demonstrates.

- Strategy 2, under which the country immediately embarks upon diversification into many products, including heavy industry products, and seeks faster convergence to self-sufficiency. This strategy relies on agriculture and cottage and small-scale enterprises dedicated to producing light industry products for job creation. It is the strategy India and China chose under two very different political systems. Complete self-sufficiency immediately turns out to be infeasible even under this strategy, however, since there are not enough investable resources available to establish production lines of all final products and their components and machines in the early stages of development.

One can also imagine an alternative strategy that falls between these extremes. Under this strategy, the country may engage in phased import substitution, protecting the assembly of final products in the first stage, production of components in the second stage and machinery in the third stage.

After Independence, Nehru and his planners opted for Strategy 2. Unfortunately, at the time, they failed to see the inherent conflict between self-sufficiency and poverty alleviation objectives. Systematic evidence from contrasting experiences of Singapore, Taiwan and South Korea, which followed Strategy 1, and India and China, which relied on Strategy 2, was still two decades away. Neither Nehru nor the economists and experts who advised him in framing the path-setting Second Five-Year

Plan foresaw that establishing heavy industry right away to achieve self-sufficiency would undermine growth on the one hand and exclude the vast majority of the population from the development process on the other. Both factors were to, in turn, undermine the poverty alleviation objective.[20] Instead, their unequivocal view was that heavy industry would lead to faster growth, and poverty reduction would go hand-in-hand with self-sufficiency.

Though the country did come to terms with its mistake and changed course in 1991, by then, it had lost four precious decades. Moreover, the history built over these decades continued to haunt its development efforts even after the change of course. For one thing, the base income remained low, given that the opportunity to grow rapidly had been missed in the early decades. Therefore, even an acceleration in growth to the 7 to 8 per cent range on a sustained basis could not deliver genuine prosperity for another few decades. Moreover, four decades of patronage of socialist ideas and policies came to hardwire Indian politicians, bureaucrats, intellectuals and even businesspeople in ways that made a swift march to a market economy politically challenging.

Against this background, consider the main elements of India's development strategy, beginning with the Second Five-Year Plan.

Heavy Industry

By far, the most critical elements in Nehru's strategy were heavy industry development and modern technology deployment. He spoke and wrote on their importance with passion and often. He considered them necessary for self-sufficiency, industrialization, growth, poverty alleviation and defence.

Heavy industry as the cornerstone of industrialization had already figured in the work of the National Planning Committee. Nehru touched on this theme in *The Discovery of India*, stating, 'I am all for tractors and big machinery, and I am convinced that the rapid industrialization of India is essential to relieve the pressure on land, to combat poverty and raise standards of living, for defense and a variety of other purposes.'[21] A few paragraphs later, he wrote,

> It can hardly be challenged that, in the context of the modern world, no country can be politically and economically independent, even within the framework of international inter-dependence, unless it is highly industrialized and has developed its power resources to the utmost. Nor can it achieve or maintain high standards of living and liquidate poverty without the aid of modern technology in almost every sphere of life.[22]

He even speculated that the absence of industrialization in a country would be an invitation to imperialist tendencies of industrialized nations: 'An industrially backward country will continually upset the world equilibrium and encourage the aggressive tendencies of more developed countries. Even if it retains its political independence, this will be nominal only, and economic control will tend to pass to others.'[23] He added, 'The economy based on the latest technical achievements of the day must necessarily be the dominating one. If technology demands the big machine, as it does today in a large measure, then the big machine with all its implications and consequences must be accepted.'[24]

Heavy Industry and Self-Sufficiency

These themes found expression on numerous occasions in Nehru's speeches after Independence. Emphasizing the importance of heavy industry for self-sufficiency, he stated in a speech delivered in Hindi in March 1953 at the FICCI,

> One thing is clear to me that if we do not develop heavy industry here then we either eliminate all modern things such as railways, airplanes and guns, as these things cannot be

> manufactured in small-scale industry, or else import them. But to import them from abroad is to be the slaves of foreign countries. Whenever these countries wished, they could stop sending these things, bringing our work to a halt; we would thus remain slaves.[25]

Two years later, on 2 October 1955, inaugurating a coach factory in Madras, he said, 'I shall venture to say that we cannot even maintain our freedom and independence as a nation without the big factory and all that it represents.'[26]

Heavy Industry, Industrialization and Growth

Nehru firmly believed that only heavy industry—and not light industry—could lead to industrialization and rapid growth. Addressing the Conference of the All-India Manufacturers' Organization in New Delhi on 14 April 1956, he stated,

> Previously people's idea of industrialization was one of increasing the output of consumer goods, with consequent employment. The idea now is, and I do not think it can be challenged, that if we really wish to industrialize, we must start from the heavy, basic, mother industries. There is no other way. We must start with the production of iron and steel on a large scale. We must start with the production of the machine which makes the machine. So long as you have not got these basic things, you are dependent on others and you can never really grow rapidly enough. Once you have got these basic things, you grow as rapidly as you like. It depends upon your own energy; you are not bound down by any external factor; you start a process of self-growth.[27]

Four years later, he had not changed his mind. Initiating the discussion on the Third Five-Year Plan in the Lok Sabha on 22 August 1960, he rejected the idea that establishing manufacturing of light industry products such as textiles could lead to industrialization.

> The beginning of industrialization really can now be seen in India. A number of textile mills in Ahmedabad or Bombay or Kanpur is not industrialization; it is merely playing with it. I do not object to textile mills; we need them; but our idea of industrialization will be limited, cribbed, cabined and confined by thinking of these ordinary textile mills and calling it industrialization. Industrialization produces machines, it produces steel, it produces power. They are the base. Once you have that base, it is easy to build.[28]

Heavy Industry and Defence

In Nehru's mind, heavy industry development was also intimately linked to defence. He referred to this link in many speeches, taking it up systematically in a speech he delivered in the Lok Sabha on 21 March 1956 during a debate on demands of the defence ministry. Responding to a house member who wanted India to concentrate on defence instead of five-year plans, Nehru said,

> That is a grave statement to make. But the Five-Year Plan is the defence plan of the country. What else is it? Because defence does not consist in people going about marching up and down the road with guns and other weapons. Defence consists today in a country being industrially prepared for producing the goods and equipment of defence.[29]

Nehru went on to explain how the capacity of a country to arm itself depended on its industrial development, especially of heavy industry. To quote him again,

> The real strength of a country develops by industrial growth, which implies the capacity to make weapons of war for the army, the navy or the air force. You cannot develop an isolated industry without a general background of industrial development. You cannot have a factory producing tanks in

> the absence of other industrial development in the country. A factory producing aircraft can be erected only if there is a large supply of technically trained people. Therefore, our immediate object should be, both from the point of view of economic development and that of defence, to build up industry, heavy industry in particular.[30]

Nehru also argued that a country could not rely on imports for its defence. He contended that one could import a machine or an aircraft; however, what if it broke down and one needed spare parts for repair? 'If somebody from whom you bought refuses to supply a part of it, it becomes useless, so that in spite of your independence you become dependent on others, and very greatly so.'[31] Defence, self-sufficiency and heavy industry development were thus intimately linked in his thinking.

Small Industry

Nehru had included a substantial section in *The Discovery of India* on the big versus small industry.[32] But he devoted this section principally to making his case for the big industry and arguing that Congress and Gandhi were never opposed to it. As far as the village, cottage, household and small industry (small industry for short) was concerned, he simply acknowledged that it would always be there without making a clear, positive case for it. The key sentence in this section says, 'It must be remembered that, however rapid might be the development of heavy industry in India, a vast field will remain open to small and cottage industries.'[33]

As discussions for five-year plans got underway, however, the relative indifference towards the small industry gave way to its emergence as one of the central elements in the strategy. In these discussions, the small industry, devoted to producing consumer goods and other light manufactures, became the second key component of Nehru's development strategy. Both political and economic considerations played a part in this shift. Politically, led by Gandhi, a section of the Congress had always seen his pursuit of heavy industry as an existential threat to small industry. Therefore, having already won the battle for a central place for heavy industry, it was good politics to make small industry an integral part of his development plan. Economically, Nehru needed small industry as a source of employment for the masses and consumer goods of daily use. Besides, bringing small industry centrally into the development strategy went well with his thinking that planning was all about achieving a balance.[34]

Speaking on the First Five-Year Plan in the Lok Sabha on 15 December 1952, Nehru noted the centrality of the small industry to ensure adequate employment opportunities. To quote him,

> It is obvious that India must be industrialized as rapidly as possible. And industrialization includes, of course, all kinds of industry—major, middling, small, village and cottage. However rapid our industrialization may be, it cannot possibly absorb more than a small part of the population of this country in the next ten, twenty or even thirty years. Hundreds of millions will remain who have to be employed chiefly in agriculture. These people must, in addition, be given employment in smaller industries like cottage industries and so on.[35]

He later added that the development of heavy industry would not solve the employment problem for the millions in the country. 'We have to develop the village and cottage industry in a big way, at the same time making sure that in trying to develop industry, big and small, we do not forget the human factor.'[36]

Later, after heavy industry, with its focus on producer goods such as steel and machinery, became the fulcrum of the Second Five-Year Plan, Nehru went on to acknowledge in his speeches the importance of small industry in providing balance in the economy as also its role as the supplier of consumer goods. Speaking at the All-India Congress Committee on 4 January 1957, he noted,

> We believe generally that the industrial progress of India will depend and must depend on the growth of heavy industry. There will be no industrial progress unless machines are made here, unless iron and steel are manufactured here. At the same time, we have always to remember that unless we balance heavy industry with the growth of village industry, we shall produce an unbalanced structure which may crack up and fall to pieces. Therefore, the importance of village industry, household industry, cottage industry and small industry is very great. It is great from the employment point of view, of course; but it is also great from the point of view of balanced production. It is great from the point of view of producing consumer goods.[37]

Those championing its cause feared that the small industry would fail to withstand competition from the large, heavy industry sector. To lay these fears to rest, Nehru and his planners decided that the latter would not be permitted to enter products produced by the former. The formal heavy industry sector and informal small industry sectors thus came to be divided into non-competing sectors specializing in different sets of products.

Agriculture

Nehru had been exposed to the plight of peasants in the United Provinces as early as the first half of the 1920s. He was painfully aware that while bigger zamindars prospered at their expense, the peasants lived in abject poverty. Despite this recognition, until the beginning of the plans, he was yet to pay systematic attention to the role of agriculture in development. The only crucial farmer-related issue that occupied him in his pre-Independence writings concerned the zamindari system.

In his autobiography, he wrote critically of it in several places and called for its abolition. He felt so strongly about it that he even criticized Gandhi scathingly for his relaxed attitude towards and accommodation of the zamindars and zamindari system.[38]

Later, in *The Discovery of India*, Nehru devoted several pages to discussing heavy industry but made only a passing reference to agriculture. Referring to the discussions in the National Planning Committee, he acknowledges that 'no planning could possibly ignore agriculture, which was the main stay of the people' but said nothing about what role agriculture should play in the nation's economic development.[39] After Independence but before the launch of the First Five-Year Plan, he discussed food shortages and its distribution policy on numerous occasions but not agriculture per se.

In all probability, the importance of agriculture in the development process entered Nehru's consciousness only when formulating and implementing the First Five-Year Plan. When delivering his major speech on this plan in the Lok Sabha on 15 December 1952, he made the first clear and substantial statement on the importance of this sector in economic development. After pointing out that the plan had allocated a significantly larger proportion of the expenditure to agriculture and irrigation than industry, he stated,

> 'We certainly attach importance to industry; but in the present context, we attach far greater importance to agriculture and food and matters pertaining to agriculture. If our agricultural foundation is not strong then the industry we seek to build will not have a strong basis either. . . . If our agriculture becomes strongly entrenched, as we hope it will, then it will be relatively easy for us to progress more rapidly on the industrial front, whereas if we concentrate only on industrial development and leave agriculture in a weak condition we shall ultimately be weakening industry. That is why primary attention has been given to agriculture and food and that I think, is essential in a country like India at the present moment.'[40]

After this speech, calls for a balance between agriculture and industry and references to the need to develop agriculture to eliminate the imports of food grains, even export them, became more frequent in his speeches. For instance, in a speech in the Lok Sabha on 21 December 1954, he referred to 'the terrific food shortage in this country' and reminded the house that the First Five-Year Plan had prioritized solving precisely this problem. 'We did that because we felt that unless we had a strong food basis, our industrial efforts might well be bogged down.'[41]

Then, initiating the debate on the Second Five-Year Plan in the Lok Sabha on 23 March 1956, he returned to these themes.

> In all this, agricultural production has a very special importance. First of all, there can be no really stable industrial economy in this country without a stable agricultural basis. We paid considerable attention to agricultural production in the First Five-Year Plan, and we made greater progress than we had expected. But we have to do a great deal more. We intend to have another forty per cent increase, and that is a great deal. We can do that, when we remember that our agricultural production is nearly the lowest in the world.[42]

These themes continued to find a place in the discussions on the Third Five-Year Plan. Introducing the draft outline of the plan in the Lok Sabha on 22 August 1960, Nehru said,

> We shall find that this industrial progress cannot be made without agricultural advance and progress. The fact is that the two cannot be separated. They are intimately connected because agricultural progress is not possible without industry, without tools, without the new methods and techniques. . . . Everyone knows that unless we are self-sufficient in agriculture we cannot have the wherewithal to advance in industries. If we have to import food, then we are doomed so far as progress is concerned.[43]

Instruments

The discussion of policy instruments for implementing the development strategy in this chapter is brief. We shall return to their detailed discussion in the later chapters. For the present purposes, we may divide the instruments into seven categories.

The Plan

The overall instrument Nehru relied on to translate his strategy into reality was planning. The planning commission prepared a detailed plan for each five years, with 1951–52 being the first year of the first plan. As Nehru noted when presenting the first five-year plan in the Lok Sabha on 15 December 1952, it integrated 'the agricultural, industrial, social, economic and other aspects of the country into a single framework of thinking'.[44] It also provided detailed physical targets for individual sectors, often at the product level, to be achieved over five years. The planners set the targets ostensibly to alleviate poverty and promote self-sufficiency. The working assumption was that absent government intervention, private entrepreneurs would seek to maximize their profits and choose a production basket different from what was required to achieve the social objectives.

Production by the Public Sector

The government decided to take it upon itself to produce one set of products as per plan targets. It did so in keeping with the spirit of socialism. The thinking was that progressively greater control of the means of production by the State would contribute to greater equality. In contrast to private-sector profits, which would increase the concentration of wealth in a few hands, public-sector profits would turn into public revenues and be used to promote public good. Over time, as more and more means of production moved into the public sector, the concentration of wealth would decline and contribute to the poverty-reduction objective.

At least initially, the government policy was to enter only basic, heavy industry sectors, such as steel and other metals, machines, railways and armaments. It divided public-sector industries into two categories. In the first category, the products were reserved exclusively for public-sector manufacturing. In the second category, the private sector could enter, but the public sector dominated the industries. As a matter of principle, the government kept the door open to itself in any industry it wanted to enter.

Licensing of Private-Sector Production

The government regulated private-sector production to achieve two objectives. First, it needed to keep large manufacturers from entering the manufacture of products that the small industry produced. Second, it needed to ensure that the scarce private capital chose the product and scale of production as per priorities laid down in the five-year plans. Investment licensing was the instrument used to achieve both objectives.

To achieve the first objective, the Nehru government fixed a relatively low threshold level of investment in plant and machinery above which an entrepreneur was to obtain a production licence from a government agency. It then adopted a policy of denying licences for manufacturing any product produced by the small industry. Beginning in 1967, the Indira Gandhi government formalized this policy through the so-called Small-Scale Industries (SSI) reservation policy. Under the policy, it drew up a list of light-industry products made off-limits to medium or large enterprises. To achieve the second objective, the government was open to issuing a licence for large-scale production of items not produced by the small industry. The licence specified the product and production capacity in line with the priorities in the plan.

Import Licensing and Tariffs

The British government had introduced import licensing during the Second World War. After Independence, India left this system untouched. Two important categories of licences under the system were those issued to 'Established Importers' and 'Actual Users'. A licence in the former category allowed the importer to freely sell imported products, usually consumer goods, to other buyers in the domestic market. On the other hand, Actual User licences were issued to producers and were for machinery and raw material. Importers were not allowed to sell these products to other buyers. Until about 1957–58, Established Importers accounted for almost one-third of the import licences in value terms. This share dropped to one-tenth by the early 1960s.[45]

Responding to the demands of Indian industrialists, the British government had also introduced some modest tariffs on imports in the 1920s. The Indian government retained these tariffs after Independence. However, they remained low throughout the Nehru era. Tariffs rose dramatically in the 1980s when the government decided to mop up quota rents (the gap between the domestic and border price, which existed due to quantitative limits on imports) to add to its revenue kitty.

Price and Distribution Controls

The self-sufficiency objective required diversification into as many product lines as possible within a short period. The five-year plans considered this fact and set the production targets accordingly. Investment licences in products not manufactured by the small industry were not issued freely. Instead, they followed plan priorities. The authorized capacity of many products fell short of domestic demand. As long as the foreign exchange was plentiful, imports could fill the gap. However, after the sterling balances ran out in 1957–58, the government adopted strict foreign-exchange control.[46] That, in turn, translated into strict quantitative limits on the imports of most products, with imports of consumer goods almost entirely prohibited. The resulting supply shortages created the prospects of high prices and, therefore, high profits for domestic manufacturers lucky enough to have been granted investment licences.

Given the sensitivity to private wealth accumulation in the prevailing socialist ethos, these profits led the government to impose price ceilings on many products. The ceilings, in turn, created a gap between demand and available supply, necessitating a mechanism to allocate the available supply among buyers seeking access to it. Distribution controls followed whereby a product buyer had to obtain a permit from a designated government agency before buying the product.

Institutions of Technical Education

Nehru knew that establishing basic and heavy industries would require technical expertise. Therefore, he made provision for creating many engineering and other technical education institutions in the five-year plans. Indian Institutes of Technology, Indian Institutes of Management, Indian Statistical Institutes and other engineering institutions, polytechnics and management institutions began to come up in India in the 1950s and 1960s. Institutions devoted to atomic energy and space research also emerged during these decades. In the early decades following the Second World War, India was well ahead of other developing countries in this area.

Land Reform, Community Development and Cooperative Farming

Nehru firmly believed that the zamindari system was exploitative of Indian farmers. Therefore, one of the first steps he took to safeguard the farmers' interests after becoming prime minister was its abolition. He accomplished this objective in approximately a decade.

To distribute farmland more equitably, Nehru also encouraged state governments to enact laws placing ceilings on land ownership, acquiring land above the ceiling from large landowners and distributing it among the landless. In addition, he urged states to end tenancy and vest ownership rights in the existing tenants. But these reforms, at best, met with partial success. Locally powerful large landowners successfully gamed the system to get around the ceilings. Most states did outlaw tenancy but failed to transfer ownership rights to tenants. The result was that the cure proved worse than the disease: tenancy went underground, with tenants left without any protection against the excesses of landowners.[47]

Early in his tenure, Nehru also promoted community development projects. These projects consisted of three phases: National Extension Service, Intensive Community Development and Post-Intensive Development. The first two phases were to last three years, and then the third phase launched. Each community development project covered 300 villages divided into three development blocks of 100 villages. Each block was, in turn, divided into twenty groups, with each group containing five villages. A Gram Sevak (village-level worker) served each group. The project sought holistic development in eight specified areas: agriculture, communication, education, health, training, social welfare, employment and housing. The idea was to bring about development from below with government officials guiding from above. The programme was launched on 2 October 1952 and spread rapidly over the First and Second Five-Year Plans.[48] During the second plan period, it came to cover all of India with 5200 blocks in all.[49]

During the early to mid-1950s, Nehru spoke glowingly of the projects, describing them on one occasion as 'bright, vital and dynamic sparks all over India from which radiate rays of energy, hope and enthusiasm'.[50] On another occasion, he extolled them as 'the great revolution' that was 'changing the face of India'.[51] However, the programme was unsuccessful because the commonality of interests among fellow villagers did not exist or necessary grassroots initiative was lacking. The assumption that government officials would put their heart and soul into the programme and impartially and honestly use the resources to navigate it for the benefit of all also proved incorrect.

The trigger for a change, of course, came from a bad harvest in 1957–58, which led to a sharp rise in food grain imports. This event coincided with the running out of the sterling balances and an acute need for restraining imports, including food grain imports. The result was a change in the government policy towards a greater focus on increasing the domestic output of food grains. It decided to drop 'nonessential' activities under community development projects and concentrate on activities directly related to boosting food grain output.[52]

As a part of this shift in policy, recognizing the small size of land holdings in India and drawing on the experience of China, Nehru turned to the introduction of cooperative and joint farming. His thinking, undoubtedly grounded in socialist philosophy, was that pooling of small holdings would help create larger holdings, allowing the exploitation of scale economies and the deployment of modern technology. At its session in Nagpur in 1959, Congress formally adopted a resolution stating, 'The future agrarian pattern should be that of cooperative joint farming, the produce of land being shared partly in proportion to labor rendered and partly in proportion to land pooled.'[53] Opposition leaders such as C. Rajagopalachari and N.G. Ranga vehemently opposed the move, characterizing it as a precursor to Chinese-style collectivization. In the event, the government limited its efforts to promoting cooperative farming on a voluntary basis. However, cooperative farming never seriously took off. Though agricultural output did improve in 1958–59 and subsequently during the Nehru era, the Green Revolution, which eventually made India genuinely self-sufficient in agriculture, took almost another decade to fructify.

Concluding Remarks

The conventional explanations for the poor performance of the Indian economy during the Nehru-Gandhi era have focused on licence-permit-autarky raj and the heavy involvement of the public sector in manufacturing activity. But deep down, the Achilles heel of the economy during this era was the decision by Nehru to make heavy industry the centrepiece of his strategy. This strategy represented the inversion of all development models, including the one based on the conventional import-substitution-industrialization. Even the ISI model does not recommend heavy industry as the starting point of industrialization.

The future can be altered but not divorced from the past. Though India has made a break from the Nehru Development Model, its journey away from it has been slow because of both the inherited industry structure and its intellectual legacy. Entrepreneurs like to invest in sectors in which they have succeeded in the past. Unfortunately, those with a record of success in producing light manufactures on a large scale are missing. Intellectuals are even slower to change, and, as educators, they continue to groom future generations in the old socialist ideas. The result is a political leadership and bureaucracy unwilling to embrace markets speedily. These twin factors have translated into a slow emergence of large-scale manufacturers operating in the global marketplace. Past failures have thus tilted the balance against the Nehru Development Model, but the market model is yet to score a decisive victory over it.

4

Other Contemporary Influential Voices

In retrospect, the development strategy Nehru adopted had serious flaws. Before we turn to a systematic dissection of these flaws, a pertinent question is whether there is a plausible scenario under which India could have opted for an alternative strategy. The answer to this question is unequivocally negative. Most of those who mattered at the time—politicians, leading Indian economists, eminent foreign advisers and business leaders—supported Nehru's strategy wholeheartedly. None among the small minority who disagreed objected to the centrality of heavy industries and the objective of self-sufficiency.[1] Besides, their objections, primarily centred on excessive deficit financing, lack of centrality of agriculture and insufficient economic space devoted to the private sector, had little resonance with the political leadership of the day and, as such, went unheeded.

Although some aspects of Nehru's development strategy began to be implemented during the first plan period spanning 1951–52 to 1955–56, it did not take centre stage in public discourse until the government initiated the formulation of the Second Five-Year Plan in the Fall of 1954.[2] The key document around which these discussions took place was the Draft Plan-frame, formally titled 'Draft Recommendations for the Formulation of the Second Five-Year Plan (1956-1961)'. Authored by Prasanta Chandra Mahalanobis, 'a physicist by training and a statistician by practice' (Bhagwati and Desai 1970, 236), the Draft Plan-frame served as the foundation document of the final Second Five-Year Plan. Having known and interacted with him since 1940, Mahalanobis understood Nehru's thinking on planning and industrialization well. Therefore, it is no surprise that his plan-frame incorporated all of the key elements of the Nehru Development Model.

At about the same time that the government tasked Mahalanobis with preparing the Draft Plan-frame, it had appointed a Panel of Economists with twenty leading Indian economists as members and Finance Minister C.D. Deshmukh as chairman. While Mahalanobis prepared the Draft Plan-frame, the panel members and economists from selected government bodies set out to prepare approximately forty background papers. Once the Draft Plan-frame became available, the panel members discussed it at length in the light of their own papers. Based on these discussions, they issued a consensus memorandum giving the plan frame a green light. One member of the panel, Professor B.R. Shenoy of the University of Gujarat, formally dissented from the consensus view. Another, Professor C.N. Vakil of the Bombay School of Economics, did not formally dissent but advocated a strategy centred on agriculture and agricultural machinery in one of the papers he and his co-authors submitted to the panel.

Several foreign statisticians and economists visited India during the winter of 1954–55. They were predominantly left-leaning and often admirers of the Soviet model. They naturally endorsed the development model underlying the Draft Plan-frame. A rare one, Milton Friedman, who advocated a market-oriented strategy, found no takers. At the time, there was little receptivity to a market-based approach to development in circles that mattered.

India's business leaders had been active participants in the discussions of the National Planning Committee during 1938–40. In all likelihood, those discussions led them to fully internalize Nehru's economic policy thinking. The Bombay Plan, which they had prepared in 1944 and 1945, broadly coincided with the approach taken in the Draft Plan-frame and, eventually, the full final Second Five-Year Plan.

Among politicians, B.C. Roy, chief minister of West Bengal, attacked the Draft Plan-frame for its overly ambitious size and limited employment potential. Later, after the Draft Plan was formally published and K.C. Neogy, a member of the Planning Commission, dissented, Roy and the chief ministers of Uttar Pradesh and Mysore (now Karnataka) threw their weight in his support. In the final stages, when the Draft Plan and the complete Second Five-Year Plan came up for discussion in the Parliament, some members criticized them for deficit financing while others argued favouring the Gandhian approach centred on village and cottage industries. But none among the critics challenged the central role assigned to heavy industries.

Mahalanobis and the Draft Plan-frame

Though a physicist by training, Mahalanobis had developed a keen interest in statistics and its applications while serving on the faculty of the Department of Physics at Presidency College, Kolkata.[3] In the 1920s, he formed an informal group of scholars to discuss statistical methods and their applications to practical problems. In 1932, some of these scholars founded the Indian Statistical Institute (ISI). The following year, they launched *Sankhya,* a journal in the field of statistics that quickly acquired an international reputation.

Mahalanobis hailed from the well-known Tagore family of Bengal and had met Nehru several times when the latter came to Kolkata to see Nobel Laureate Rabindranath Tagore. One evening in early 1940, when discussions on planning within the National Planning Committee were ongoing, Mahalanobis visited Nehru at his Allahabad home. After dinner, the two gentlemen had a long chat till 2 a.m. on the role of statistics in planning.[4]

Upon becoming the prime minister of independent India, in February 1949, Nehru appointed Mahalanobis as the

Honorary Statistical Adviser to his Cabinet. Later, as the time for formulating the Second Five-Year Plan came close, he forged a close working relationship among the Finance Ministry, the Planning Commission and the ISI. Under his instructions and with the help of a group of economists and statisticians drawn from these three entities, Mahalanobis prepared the Draft Plan-frame, the foundation document of the Second Five-Year Plan. In mid-1955, he submitted the document for discussion in the National Development Council (NDC), consisting of the Council of Ministers, Planning Commission members and states' chief ministers.

Underlying Model and Features of the Plan Frame

Mahalanobis discusses the analytic ideas underlying the Draft Plan-frame and an associated working paper in a long article published in *Sankhya* in 1955.[5] These ideas closely mirrored those of Nehru, with only occasional differences in shades rather than substance. Turning first to industry, he sought five features of its development pattern.

First, like Nehru, he saw heavy industries as the cornerstone of the entire development strategy. But unlike him, he emphasized machinery production more than steel and power. In the 1955 article, Mahalanobis wrote:

> The Plan-frame has stressed the need of establishing and expanding the basic industries to manufacture heavy machinery with all possible speed. This would enable India to install new plants for the production of steel, cement, and other investment goods with the help of machinery manufactured in India out of domestic resources; and to produce in increasing quantities machinery required for mineral prospecting and mining, hydro-electric projects, electrical appliances, railways and other forms of transport, and for the production of consumer goods generally.[6]

The conceptual foundations of this conclusion lay in what subsequently came to be known as the 'Mahalanobis Model' among economists. Published in 1953 in *Sankhya*, this model was a close cousin of a model developed earlier by Russian mathematician and economist Grigory Alexandrovich Feldman who had worked with the Soviet planning agency Gosplan from 1923 to 1931.[7] Taking a closed-economy context, the Mahalanobis model envisages a two-sector economy that can produce a consumer good and an investment good. Each additional unit of the investment good generates a larger value when deployed in the consumption good than when employed in the investment good. The output of the investment good in any given year determines the extent of additions to production capacities in the two goods in the following year.

The planner's problem is determining the allocation of the investment good each year between consumption and investment goods.

> As is to be expected . . . in the initial stage of development, the larger the percentage investment on consumer goods industries, the larger will be the income generated. But there is a critical range of time and as soon as this is passed, the larger the investment in investment goods industries the larger will be the income generated. Hence, it would be desirable to invest relatively more on the consumer goods industries provided we are interested in the immediate future. If, on the other hand, we are interested in the more distant future, relatively larger investment on investment goods industries would give distinctly better results.[8]

The model thus favours larger investment in the investment goods (machinery) sector if the objective is to maximize income in the long run.

In the Draft Plan-frame, Mahalanobis used a four-sector extension of his two-sector model with the investment goods such as machinery and steel, factory-produced consumer goods such as automobiles and scooters, small- and household-industry-produced consumer goods such as clothing and agricultural commodities and services representing the four sectors.[9] Because production efficiency, captured by the output-to-capital and output-to-labour ratios, was fixed by assumption and labour supply was plentiful, growth depended only on the overall investment and its allocation among the four sectors.

Mahalanobis argued that rapid industrial development required that investment be increased appreciably. 'We have suggested that it should be increased from about 7 per cent to about 10 or 11 per cent [of GDP] by the end of the Second Five-Year Plan or should be about 9 per cent on an average during the plan-period.'[10] He also suggested allocating 30 to 50 per cent of the net new investments to the investment good sector 'to attain a fairly rapid increase of income over, say, thirty years . . .'[11] The recommendation for the establishment of a machinery industry found explicit mention in the Draft Plan-frame: 'It has been proposed in the Plan-frame that a heavy machine building industry should be established in India so that as soon as possible India is able to fabricate machinery for the production of steel (or cement or other capital goods) to the value of say Rs. 40 or Rs. 50 crore per year.'[12]

The second feature of industrial development sought by Mahalanobis was economic self-sufficiency. Once again, he fully subscribed to Nehru's conviction that India had to be self-sufficient. Accordingly, he unhesitatingly assumed a closed-economy context in the two- and four-sector models. For him, placing machinery production at the top of the priority list was a means to rapid growth in the long run as well as bringing self-sufficiency at the earliest. Articulating this view, he wrote,

> India's present dependence on imports of capital goods is a fundamental structural weakness which must be corrected as quickly as possible. It would be obviously more economical from the national point of view to produce in India as much heavy machinery as possible because this would ensure a supply of capital goods which would make India increasingly independent of imports and would strengthen India's position

> in the world market. In my opinion, the development of the heavy machine building industry is so important that, if necessary, targets of even steel, coal, or transport should be reduced to give higher priority to heavy machines because this would facilitate a much quicker rate of industrialization after four or five years.[13]

The arguments that 'It would be obviously more economical from the national point of view to produce in India as much heavy machinery as possible' or that it would 'strengthen India's position in the world market' were, of course, wholly false. Given the enormous scarcity of capital and abundance of labour, the cost of machinery production in India was vastly higher than what it would have paid for its imports in terms of labour-intensive products in exchange. And keeping out of the world markets rather than engaging with them did not strengthen India's position in the world markets in any meaningful manner. This fact became progressively clearer when the country had to adopt strict foreign-exchange control within three years and progressively tighten import licensing. But with the consensus on the desirability of self-sufficiency, no one questioned the logical error in the argument.

As a third feature of industrialization, Mahalanobis fully shared Nehru's enthusiasm for assigning the public sector the key role in the development of heavy industries:

> The heavy machinery industry should be in the public sector. For rapid industrialization of an under-developed country, it would be desirable to keep the cost of capital goods as low as possible. The further removed the type of capital goods under consideration is from the production of final consumer goods the greater is the need of keeping the price low. Heavy machinery which would manufacture machinery to produce investment goods is the furthest removed from the consumption end. It is essential, therefore, that Government

> should have complete control over the heavy machinery industry so as to be able to fix prices to suit national needs.[14]

Whereas Nehru had advocated placing heavy industries in the public sector because the private sector lacked resources to invest on the scale necessitated by technology in these industries, Mahalanobis offered the novel argument that this was required to fix machinery prices at low levels. He did not explain, however, why it was necessary to fix the price of machinery below cost or why price controls could not be applied if machines were produced in the private sector. After all, the government did apply price controls on products such as automobiles and scooters, which were produced in the private sector. Once again, with few influential voices doubting the necessity of the public sector or its ability to achieve efficiency in production, the flaw in the argument went unnoticed.

Fourth, like Nehru, Mahalanobis saw small-scale and household industries as the key to creating employment opportunities for the masses. His view was that these enterprises would be expected to use minimum capital in the early phase of development but expressed the hope that, eventually, they would gain access to capital to attain higher efficiency. He wrote,

> It is, therefore, necessary to plan for a transition phase in which preference would be given to capital-light and labour-intensive small-scale and household industries to create as much employment as possible in the immediate future and, at the same time, to release capital resources for the heavy industries. However, as the economy expands, and employment increases, the need of giving preference to labour-intensive but low-efficiency production would decrease. As the supply of power, machinery and other capital goods increases, a gradual and steady change-over would be made to more efficient forms of production by the increasing use of machinery driven by power.[15]

A final feature of the industrial pattern sought by Mahalanobis was the wide dispersal of production activity by geography, enterprise size, and management and ownership. He advocated 'locating units of production in such a way that different regions of India can share equitably in the programme of production'.[16] While due consideration ought to be given to transport costs, 'planning should be deliberately aimed at achieving a broad parity in the level of production and of living in the different regions of India and preventing the formation of depressed areas'.[17]

As regards enterprise size, Mahalanobis classified industries into two distinct groups: those such as steel, cement, railway rolling stock, fertilizer, automobiles and heavy machinery in which technology mandated large-scale production and those such as clothing, footwear and furniture in which production could be carried out in small units. For the former, he recommended large factories that would be located 'in well-planned new industrial towns with adequate housing, schools, medical clinics, hospitals, and facilities for sports and cultural activities . . .'[18] For the latter, he recommended giving preference to the smallest units, which would be dispersed over villages and small towns.

On the subject of management and ownership, in the short run, Mahalanobis's view was aligned with that of Nehru: basic heavy industry products, especially machinery production, in the public sector and other products, including agriculture in the private sector consisting of cottage and small enterprises and larger corporate units. But in the longer run, he expressed a somewhat different view arguing, 'The future policy, in my opinion, should be to establish and bring all large units of production under direct Government control; to develop enterprises of a medium size on a co-operative basis; and leave small units of production to household enterprises.'[19] In making this recommendation, Mahalanobis went well beyond Nehru in seeking a shift away from the private sector and towards the public and cooperative sectors. Unlike Nehru, who was fully comfortable with the private sector managing large units, he wanted to bring all large units under the public or cooperative sector.

In designing the Draft Plan-frame, Mahalanobis sought a balance between basic heavy industries producing investment goods and consumer goods. Although the long-term growth objective was best served by maximizing investment in basic heavy industries, two factors constrained such investment. First, beyond a limit, the sacrifice of consumption was socially unacceptable. This fact placed a ceiling on the proportion of the total output that could be devoted to investment in any given year. Second, within the assumed closed-economy context, a balance was essential between income increases and consumption goods' availability if inflation was to be kept in check. Investment in basic industries was expected to generate income but not the supply of consumer goods. Therefore, unless small and household industries saw large increases in the output of consumer goods via increased employment or higher productivity, income generated in the basic industries risked generating high inflation.

Broad Outline of the Draft Plan-frame

The Draft Plan-frame had all the elements of what later became the final Second Five-Year Plan. The Plan-frame contained six chapters in all. Topics covered in the six chapters in chronological order were: aims and objectives; physical production targets for the major agricultural and industrial products; allocation of investment across sectors; quantitative estimates of employment by sectors; sources of financial and foreign exchange resources; and issues of organization and administration. A brief appendix to the second chapter provided a check on the internal consistency of available inputs and outputs.

The Draft Plan-frame set the target of 5 per cent annual growth in the national income and provided for the creation of a total of 11 million jobs over five years. Over the plan period, it pegged the total expenditures of the central government at 14 per cent of the national income. Of this, 7 per cent was to be plan expenditure and 7 per cent outside the plan. Out of the 7 per cent plan expenditure, 5.6 per cent was allocated to public sector investment. This overall plan size was widely regarded as ambitious at the time.

The Draft Plan-frame estimated the private sector investment over the plan period to be 3.6 per cent of the national income making the total investment (inclusive of the public sector investment) 9.2 per cent. The draft plan allocated 50 per cent of this total investment to industry, 24 per cent to construction, 17.1 per cent to agriculture and irrigation, and 8.1 per cent to warehousing and storage. Within the industry, 8.9 per cent of the total investment was to go to electricity, 16.1 per cent to transport and communication, and the remaining 25 per cent to heavy industries.

As regards resources to finance the proposed government expenditures, the Draft Plan-frame estimated tax and other revenues at 8.5 per cent of the national income, loans from the public at 1.6 per cent, railway surplus and foreign aid at 1 per cent, other taxes and profits from state enterprises at 1.3 to 1.6 per cent and money creation at 1.6 to 2 per cent. Money creation was to thus account for 11.4 to 13.6 per cent of the total expenditures. This was seen as potentially highly inflationary.

Memorandum by the Panel of Economists

A key step in advancing the Draft Plan-frame of Mahalanobis towards the final Second Five-Year Plan was its endorsement by the Panel of Economists. The Planning Commission had appointed the latter around the same time (January 1955) that the Standing Committee of the National Development Council tasked Mahalanobis with preparing the Draft Plan-frame. Finance Minister C.D. Deshmukh was the chairman, and twenty other economists were members. Thirteen member-economists were drawn from academic institutions in diverse states and union territories. The remaining seven came from the Planning Commission, the Reserve Bank of India and the Ministry of Food and Agriculture.[20] While the Draft Plan-frame was still in preparation, the panel members were asked to write background papers on several topics related to the second plan.[21]

The Draft Plan-frame was completed in mid-March 1955 and sent to the Panel of Economists for comments. Professor D.R. Gadgil of Gokhale School of Economics and Politics in Poona and the panel's vice chairman led the discussions among the member-economists. The panel completed its discussions on 10 April 1955 and summarized its comments in an approximately 9000-word memorandum entitled 'The Second Five Year Plan: Basic considerations relating to the Plan-frame'.[22] Forwarding the memorandum to Deshmukh, Gadgil wrote in his cover letter that it represented 'the broad consensus of opinion reached at our meetings'.[23] However, he added that one member, B.R. Shenoy, disagreed with this consensus view and would submit a separate dissent note.

Though the economists provided cautionary notes on some aspects of the Draft Plan-frame and made numerous recommendations in the memorandum, they gave it their unequivocal endorsement. This support, in turn, helped smooth out the path of the plan frame as it travelled through the National Development Council, the central ministries, state governments, the All India Congress Committee and, finally, the Parliament. Recognizing the endorsement's value, Mahalanobis later wrote, 'The strong support of the Panel of Economists at this stage was of decisive importance.'[24]

From our viewpoint, the value of the contents of the memorandum lies not in the role it played in shaping the second plan, which was peripheral at best and nil at worst, but in the valuable insights into contemporary Indian economic thought on development and planning that it provides. It shows that the vast majority of influential academic economists of the day had no faith whatsoever in the allocative power of prices and markets and firmly believed that the government had to control or, at the least, direct and regulate every aspect of economic activity. It is as if they were out to outdo the socialists at socialism and planners at planning.

The panel organized the memorandum around three broad headings: the size of the plan, its structure and content, and the policy and institutional implications of the proposed plan frame. It noted at the outset, 'These questions were considered by the Panel in the light of a large number of papers—about forty—received from its members and, also in the light of the papers prepared by the economists and statisticians in the Government of India and the Reserve Bank and at the Indian Statistical Institute.'[25] A review of individual papers confirms that they served as the sources of nearly all the ideas in the memorandum. However, two members, Shenoy and Vakil, differed from the consensus view of the panel. The former had serious disagreements, which became the basis of his dissent note. The latter, along with his associates from the Bombay School of Economics, contributed several papers that contained ideas at variance with those in the memorandum. But he did not submit a formal dissent.

The first part of the memorandum endorsed the goal of a 25 per cent increase in the national income and associated plan size. It argued, however, that the plan size required upping the game on taxation, stating,

> Our present tax structure is not such as to ensure even a proportionate increase in tax receipts as the national income goes up. What is needed, however, is more than this—an increase in the proportion of the national income that becomes available to the public sector. The measures recommended by the Taxation Enquiry Commission [of 1953–54] for a widening and deepening of the tax structure have, therefore, to be implemented expeditiously, and tax administration has

> to be strengthened to enable it to cope with the additional work and effectively to minimize evasion.[26]

The panel recommended a sharp increase in income and wealth taxation, including estate tax. It also called for a revision in the price policy of public enterprises to generate larger profits that could then be mobilized to finance developmental expenditures. It noted, however, that these efforts would still fall short of delivering necessary revenues and suggested a widening of the tax base by extending the sales tax to items of mass consumption.

The panel pointed out that the income increases were likely to be concentrated in workers' wages in construction, public works, irrigation projects and agriculture. But these wages remained out of the tax net. It reasoned,

> When so large a measure of effort is necessary to increase the *proportion* of tax revenues to the national income, which has remained so obstinately static, one cannot escape the logic of the fact that the mass of consumption is by the mass of the people. Unless this bears a somewhat higher burden of taxation, no perceptible change in the stubborn ratio of public revenues to the national income can be achieved.[27]

Therefore, it pitched for the acceptance of the recommendation by the Taxation Enquiry Commission for a constitutional amendment to remove the exemption from the sales tax of articles 'essential to the life of the community'.

On the question of deficit financing in the form of money creation, contrary to its dissenting member Shenoy, the panel took a relatively soft line: 'In an economy in which planned development is being undertaken, a part of the expenditure in planned development is being currently or within a short time reflected in increase in current production. There is, therefore, an increment in total production against which it is possible to increase money supply within the community.'[28] Going a step further, it added that 'with a constantly increasing level of the national income, an addition to money supply may not only not have inflationary consequences, but may be required to prevent a decline in prices which may lead to distress and distortions in the economy.'[29] The only qualification the panel noted was that money creation should be avoided when the economy is already facing inflationary pressures.

> It appears to us that at the present there is no general inflationary pressure in the economy. We do not, therefore, see any danger in undertaking deficit financing in a limited measure at the beginning of the second five-year plan period. For a year or two, deficit financing at a rate of Rs. 200 crores or so is safe—and even necessary.[30]

In the second part of the memorandum, the panel took up the question of investment structure across sectors. As in the first part, it gave the green light to the proposals expressing its general 'agreement with the investment pattern'.[31] Its more detailed discussion of the proposed investment allocations to heavy industries; power, transport and communication; construction; and warehousing and storage raised no notable concerns. It underlined the importance of agriculture but acknowledged the merit of greater emphasis on industry because, beyond a point, agricultural development depended on non-agricultural activities, especially industrial ones, which acted both as buyers of agricultural goods and suppliers of industrial consumer goods.

The panel devoted the remainder of the second part of the memorandum to a discussion of possible solutions to the problems of unemployment and underemployment. It made three specific recommendations, all extremely demanding on a government still in its infancy. First, it recommended the organization of a National Labour Force with those with little or no income as its members. It proposed that the government draw upon this labour force in implementing specific tasks of the general development programme. Second, it recommended converting several small towns around the country into industrial townships with planned provisions for small and light industries to create self-employment opportunities. Finally, the memorandum recommended that no significant investments be made during the second plan towards increasing the installed capacity in factory-produced consumption goods. To maximize employment creation, it instead pitched for leaving the expansion of the consumption goods sector entirely to small-scale and cottage industries called 'hand industries' in contemporary nomenclature.

Before concluding the second part, the panel raised the concern that due to their technical inferiority, these hand industries would not be able to compete with factory industries. Therefore, it recommended the creation of 'a common Production Programme that will provide a secure market for the products of these industries and at the same time provide for gradual improvement of techniques and skills among their workers'.[32] Regarding how this was to be accomplished, the panel's tentative suggestion was that 'there will have to be organized on a regional and a national scale cooperative and other forms of organization for the supply of raw materials and finance and for the marketing of finished products of the workers engaged in hand industries'.[33] The proposal was thus for the protection of hand industries not from foreign competition, which was taken for granted, but from the more efficient domestic factory sector. The panel did not understand or appreciate that the price mechanism is capable of accommodating enterprises with different production costs of identical products and products of different quality. Therefore, its solution was some form of government intervention in the supply of raw materials and finance to equalize the production costs of like products between hand industries and factories.

In the third part of the memorandum, the panel took it upon itself to offer many more suggestions relating to the extension of the public sector and regulation of the private sector. Implementing these suggestions required yet greater government control over the economy and its resources. Moreover, the suggestions assumed the ability to direct and manage the economy on the part of a young government, which even the most mature and capable governments normally lack.

At a philosophical level, the panel first noted that progress towards a socialistic pattern of society required that an increase in the scale of economic activity be principally brought about through cooperation, horizontal and vertical, among otherwise decentralized small units. It added that resort to centralized large-scale operation should be taken only when advantages of modern technology necessitated it. It called upon the government to assist and participate in forming cooperative units and to counter the effects of the exercise of monopoly power by large units.

The panel then pointed out areas where the government could consider expanding the public sector as the second plan progressed. Specifically, it pointed to the coal sector and electricity generation and distribution as potential candidates for nationalization. It observed that the main limitation to yet greater extension of the public sector was the ability of the government to cope with the administrative burden such extension would bring. 'If, however, during the course of the Plan period, circumstances become either more favourable from the administrative point of view or if it is found that opportunities for monopolistic or quasi-monopolistic exploitation are increasing in the private sector, there should be no objection to a further extension of the public sector.'[34]

Next, the panel discussed regulatory policies vis-à-vis the private sector. Here it first considered the extension of licensing. Taking hand industries first, it argued that confining all increases in consumption goods to them 'will make it necessary to extend the operation of licensing legislation to include even processing activities'. It added, 'The best way of dealing with the situation would be for all State Governments to bring within licensing and regulatory legislation such establishments carrying out the processing and preparation of primary products and the production of consumer goods as are not covered by the existing Regulation of Industries Act.'[35] In other words, state governments should set up their own licensing regimes to cover activities that the central government legislation had left out.

Elaborating on the regulation of supplies and prices of products, the panel advised,

> As the spheres common to machine and hand industry will cover a large number of consumption goods in general use, the prices and supplies of goods over this large sphere will have to be constantly under State observation and regulation. In a number of important producers' goods, such as cement and steel, the existing allocation controls will continue, and price controls could be imposed, if necessary.[36]

Regarding the prices of agricultural goods, it noted that their stability was of special importance and called upon the government to expeditiously implement the recommendations of the Rural Credit Survey Committee on the warehousing, processing and marketing of agricultural produce.

> We recommend that the warehousing system should be used by the State for purchase and sales of buffer stocks of agricultural commodities not only for the purpose of dealing with any sharp falls in agricultural prices such as we are witnessing today but also with the objective of preventing any sharp seasonal fall or rise in prices. Need for action in this regard may arise either in all commodities all over the country or only in an individual important commodity in particular regions.[37]

Ironically, having recommended these administratively and organizationally complex interventions, the panel went on to lament the government's lack of management and organizational capabilities. It pointed out that organizational backwardness could be experienced in every sphere, stating:

> It is felt in the administrative structure, its efficiency and its capacity to carry out additional responsibilities; it is experienced in local governmental authorities; it is seen in the lack of established and effective pattern for conduct of economic activity in the public sector. These difficulties are patent today in attempted development along established lines. They are felt all the more keenly when orientation of the economy, on the now agreed lines of decentralized self-employment or co-operative activity is attempted. The manifold advantages of such an organization can be reaped only when the large work it involves by way of distribution of supplies and collection of product, of storage and finance, of technical guidance and administrative supervision is efficiently organized and carried out. The creation of such organization is an immense national task without whose accomplishment the proper development of agriculture and rural industry in particular will be well-nigh impossible.[38]

The panel concluded the memorandum with a discussion of the policies it considered essential for progress towards the socialistic pattern of society. It first considered land reform, recommending four specific measures: consolidation of land holdings, a ceiling on land holdings, a floor on land holdings and cooperative farming. It followed up the recommendation of the ceiling on land with a ceiling on urban incomes: 'The acceptance of the idea of a ceiling on land must lead, in our opinion, logically to the acceptance of the parallel concept of a ceiling on all personal incomes for the urban and industrial sectors.'[39] To this end, it pitched for a speedy implementation of steeper estate duties and the introduction of a capital gains tax.

At the lower end of the income distribution, the panel recommended 'standardization of wages and fuller implementation of the Minimum Wages legislation in the country'.[40] It stopped short of recommending a general social security scheme to lessen income insecurity. Still, it noted, 'We would, however, recommend exploration of the possibilities of the State offering life insurance schemes wide-spread throughout the country. In the absence of measures of social security as such, we must look to the fullest extension of social service expenditure for doing something in this behalf.'[41] However, the panel did not point out where the resources for such expenditures were to come from, especially given the limitations on tax revenues and deficit financing that it had noted in the first part of the memorandum.

Dissent from within the Panel

As I have already noted, two members of the panel, Shenoy and Vakil, expressed views that differed from those contained in the memorandum of the Panel of Economists. Though their views did not impact the course of the policy, it is important to consider them in detail from the history of thought viewpoint.

The Dissent by Shenoy

In January 1931, when Friedrich Hayek, the great critic of socialism and advocate of individual freedoms and markets, delivered his famous lectures on monetary economics at the London School of Economics (LSE), Shenoy was pursuing his graduate studies there.[42] Though Shenoy found it difficult to follow Hayek, who spoke in English with a heavy Viennese accent, the lectures, having created a stir at LSE, attracted him to study Austrian economics. That exploration turned him into a lifelong follower of Hayek and Ludwig von Mises and a firm believer in the economics of markets.[43] Against this background, it is not surprising that he found himself fundamentally in disagreement with a Plan-frame that rested on Soviet-style socialist economics.[44]

Shenoy divided his dissent note into three parts: the size of the plan, money creation as the means to raise resources, and policy and institutional implications of the plan.[45] In the first part, he forcefully questioned the size of the plan given the limited availability of resources:

> To force a pace of development in excess of the capacity of the available real resources must necessarily involve uncontrolled inflation. In a democratic community where the masses of the people live close to the margin of subsistence, uncontrolled inflation may prove to be explosive and might undermine the existing order of society. . . . Probably the greatest enemy of the Kuomintang in China was the printing press.[46]

Shenoy correctly observed that setting aside foreign aid, total investment in the economy would have to equal total savings. The plan had pegged total investment at 9.2 per cent of the national income during the five years, whereas the savings rate at the time was only 7 per cent. In light of this experience and given the government's own objective of a reduction in income inequality, which would work towards lowering savings, it was unsafe to assume that the savings rate would rise beyond 8 per cent of the national income by the end of the second plan. He concluded, 'The size of the Plan Frame has been unduly inflated as result, on the one hand, of an overoptimistic growth in the national income, which it aims at, and, on the other, of an unduly high average rate of saving as applied to this assumed growth in income.'[47]

Turning to money creation as an instrument of mobilizing resources in the second part of the dissent note, Shenoy drew a sharp distinction between industrial and developing (called 'underdeveloped' at the time) economies. He noted that unemployment of resources in industrial economies referred to a simultaneous existence of excess capacity and less than full employment among workers. Under such circumstances, financing government expenditures through money creation could raise output without a time lag through fuller use of all resources. Such money creation would not generate inflation.

In contrast, the only factor abundantly available and underemployed in developing economies was unskilled labour. Other factors of production, such as machinery, materials and skilled personnel with engineering and managerial skills, were in short supply. True, unutilized capacity existed in some sectors in India then, but its economic significance was limited. It would not justify the massive money supply expansion proposed in the plan frame. In a paper submitted separately to the panel, he outlined more fully why money creation would end up being inflationary when unskilled labour was the only unemployed or underemployed factor of production.[48]

He hypothesized a situation in which some underemployed workers are transferred from agriculture to construct dams, roads or other investments with expenses financed by newly created money. By assumption, the output and money income in agriculture would remain unchanged. Therefore, the total money income in the economy would rise by the wages paid to the transferred workers.

> There was always a time lag between investment (whether in the construction of wells, roads, or factories), its completion, and the resulting increase in output. Much economic disturbance may occur during the interval. The currently available supply of consumer goods being unchanged, the rise in money incomes would cause a rise in the prices of consumer goods. The time interval was the crux of the problem and the rise in consumer prices, the starting point of the trouble.[49]

This 'interim' inflation would not liquidate itself in the future when the output does rise. 'As a financial counterpart to the increased output there will simultaneously accrue a corresponding increase in the income of those who directly or indirectly participated in it.'[50]

In the last part of the dissent, Shenoy objected to many of the recommendations of the Panel of Economists in their memorandum. He questioned the wisdom of legislative and administrative actions to increase the savings rate to finance a bigger and bolder plan because they would 'risk undue infringement of the liberty of the individual'.[51] He opposed the panel's proposal to extend the sales tax to articles essential to the community's life because there existed 'hardly room for a further reduction in the standard of living of the lower income groups in India'.[52] He disapproved of the creation of the National Labour Force, further extension of nationalization and continuation of controls and physical allocations proposed by the panel. 'Controls and allocations are an essential characteristic of communist planning. They do not very well fit in under planning in a free enterprise market economy.'[53]

Lastly, Shenoy made an impassioned case against support prices for agricultural produce. His arguments made over sixty-five years ago, continue to resonate even today. He stated,

> Price support of agricultural produce in India is a risky venture and we should be forewarned of the inherent dangers of it. About 50 per cent of Indian national income is drawn from agriculture. A policy of price support is, in essence, a subsidy by the rest of the community to the producers of the price-supported commodity. In countries where agriculture is a minor sector of the national economy, the incidence of the subsidy may be spread out thinly on the larger sector of the economy and the proceeds may provide substantial relief to farmers. The reverse would be the case in India.[54]

Though the share of agriculture in the national income has declined today to less than 15 per cent, the extension of the minimum support price being sought by farmers is beyond the financial means of the country.[55]

Surprisingly, despite his somewhat sweeping critique in the third part of the dissent, Shenoy raised few specific concerns on the basic strategy of the Draft Plan-frame. For instance, he expressed disapproval of controls and physical allocations but did not question the reliance of the proposed Plan-frame on disproportionately large investments in heavy industries. After all, given that markets would not have directed investment into these most capital-intensive industries, physical allocations were a natural outcome of the heavy industries strategy. Similarly, a free-market economist could be expected to lean explicitly and forcefully against self-sufficiency and make a case for openness to international trade. But he made no such case. It was only closer to the mid-1960s that he began touching on some of these themes.

The Bombay School: Vakil and Brahmananda

Facilitated by Vakil, economists from the Bombay School of Economics submitted as many as six out of thirty-three papers by the Panel of Economists.[56] Three of these papers expressed clear and important differences with the Draft Plan-frame and are relevant to our present discussion.

In 'Investment Pattern in the Second Five Year Plan', Vakil and Brahmananda argued a strategy centred on investment in agriculture, especially food and heavy industries that would be ancillary to agriculture.[57] As examples of the latter, they cited equipment necessary for irrigation and power plants, earth-moving equipment, equipment for fertilizer plants and intermediate inputs such as steel and cement. The reasoning, rooted in their wage-goods model, was that increased food production would give rise to an increased marketable surplus.[58] Since food was the principal commodity consumed by industrial workers, they would become the demanders of the surplus. With the revenues so received, farmers would then be able to buy agricultural machinery produced by the industrial workers. In this manner, industrial workers would become the source of demand for food and supply of agricultural machinery and farmers of demand for agricultural machinery and supply of food. A virtuous cycle of the increased marketable surplus of food leading to increased production of agricultural machinery and increased production of agricultural machinery leading to an increased marketable surplus of food would thus be created.

To the question of whether there was a need to invest in the production of machinery and equipment employed in consumer goods industries during the second plan, Vakil and Brahmananda answered that the demand for such machinery and equipment depended on the growth in the demand for consumer goods, which in turn depended on the growth in marketable surplus in agriculture. 'Thus, it is ultimately the growing agricultural base which enables indirectly the development of heavy industries.'[59] Vakil and Brahmananda recommended that proper studies be conducted on whether enough marketable surplus existed to generate plentiful demand for consumer goods before rushing into machinery and equipment used by them.

The authors also leaned against the recommendation in the Plan-frame to promote only heavy industries in the factory sector to the neglect of consumer goods industries. The rationale behind the recommendation was that future expansion of production capacity in consumer goods should be left to hand industries with the view to maximizing employment opportunities and sparing investable resources for heavy industries. Vakil and Brahmananda argued, 'By definition, heavy industries do not provide large employment. If, however, we can get cheap imports of equipment, and consumer goods industries within the country can be developed at a faster rate, the volume of employment can be continuously stepped up. There will be great scope for both large-scale and small-scale units.'[60] They also saw the possibility of the consumer goods industries serving as an important source of export revenues, arguing that 'a substantial stepping up of the expansion of consumer goods industries built up for export markets is an urgent need of the hour. Nothing should be done in the Plan period which negatives the cumulative progress in these industries over a period of four or five decades.'[61] They added that the plan should 'concentrate on expanding industries which have built up export markets and at the same time explore the potentialities of those industries which can build up export markets anew'.[62]

Finally, in an appendix to the paper, the authors made an important observation regarding large- and small-scale *industries* versus large- and small-scale *units* within an industry. The Plan-frame had classified industries into those predominantly suitable for large-scale production and those suitable for small-scale production. Vakil and Brahmananda correctly objected to such division because 'we cannot be definite about the changes in technology and what form they are going to take'. They added that more efficient production methods required considerable initial investment in equipment, technical skills and organization. By definition, small-scale units cannot incur such investments and therefore employ technologies that lead to higher per-unit production costs.

The last two points in the paper—relating to the relevance of export markets and large-scale production in any given industry—had far-reaching implications for the right approach to development. Taken together, they pointed to an export-oriented strategy with specialization in consumer goods industries with efficient firms, regardless of scale, permitted to enter or exit freely. Given the large size of the world markets, this would have allowed the export industries to create good jobs for the unskilled in vast volumes. But given the closed-economy context that Vakil and Brahmananda had chosen to make their own case for greater emphasis on agriculture and investment in agricultural machinery and equipment, they failed to make this connection. Instead, they stopped at pointing to export prospects of factory production of consumer goods industries as a source of much-needed foreign exchange and at using the sources of differences in per-unit production costs in large- and small-scale units to suggest strategies for improving the latter's efficiency.

Vakil and Brahmananda submitted a second paper to the panel entitled 'Institutional Implications of a Bolder Plan', in which they discussed a miscellaneous set of issues, including procurement of larger marketable surplus, utilization of idle or under-utilized labour, employment policy and labour welfare measures.[63] In the current-day context, their discussion of the last of these topics requires some elaboration. In discussing it, the authors anticipated at a rather early stage the problems associated with labour welfare measures in India that were to get bigger over time and go uncorrected for many decades.

The authors referred to several measures introduced, especially after Independence, to strengthen workers' bargaining power vis-à-vis employers'. These measures included welfare commitments whose burden fell on the firm, barriers to the retrenchment of workers and methods of dispute settlement that led to polarization between labour and capital. The authors noted, 'These tendencies have cumulatively placed an additional premium on the employment of capital-intensive methods. . . . There is some truth in the statement that the labour welfare policy of the Government is indeliberately [sic] causing difficulties to labour itself.'[64] The authors underlined the need for evolving a policy 'which would, within limits, permit considerable wage differentials between regions and between groups of workers'.[65] This warning was truly prescient though it went wholly unheeded, and, with labour laws becoming progressively more inflexible, production structure and technology became more and more capital- and skilled-labour-intensive over time. There was near total stagnation in creating formal-sector jobs for the unskilled for decades.

The third and last Bombay School paper taking a sharply contrary view to that of the Draft Plan-frame was by Professor B.V. Krishnamurthi on the role of the public sector. At a time when hardly anyone questioned the entry of the public sector into heavy industries and the expansion of its share in investment over time, Krishnamurthi unequivocally called for confining it to social overhead capital formation, admitting the possibility of only rare exceptions, such as fertilizer production. He noted,

> To start with, there can be little disagreement with regard to the Statement that the State should take upon itself the vital task of Social Overhead Capital Formation.
>
> For instance, the development of railways and highways, irrigation, hydroelectric power generation and distribution, and so on. These are socially urgent capital items that should be given the highest priority. . . . But outside this important group of projects, there is a vast area of producer goods and consumer goods industries that are well within the competence of the private sector and where the existing record of performance of private enterprise is quite creditable. To cite a few instances, Steel, Cement, Cotton Textiles, and Engineering Industries. It is difficult to understand why the State should enter these spheres of production where-in any desired programme of improvement and expansion could be safely entrusted to the private sector.[66]

As evidence, the author pointed to the superior performance of the organized private sector over the public sector during the first three years of the First Five-Year Plan. Citing data, he argued that the public sector had not only missed its targets by wide margins in many sectors but had also been slow to meet its spending goals. In contrast, the private industry had been highly successful in meeting its targets in such industries as cotton textiles, cement, and iron and steel.

Krishnamurthi concluded,

> Therefore, instead of an indiscriminate expansion of the public sector, what is called for is concentration of effort in raising the tempo of progress in the projects already on hand.

> Even after a satisfactory completion of these projects, the public sector could and should widen itself by undertaking similar additional projects, for instance, more railways and highways, more public schools and hospitals, and so on.[67]

He recommended the entry of the public sector in manufacturing only under rare circumstances: 'Even with regard to the other producer goods industries, if the private enterprise is not readily forthcoming or if the aggregate requirements are so enormous that there is room for both, there is a clear case for the State to step in. Fertilizers are an instance in point.'[68] Like all others, including his Bombay School colleagues, Krishnamurthi relied on a strictly closed economy context when making this concession. Else, the import of fertilizers offered an alternative to inefficient production by the public sector.

Foreign Experts

Several distinguished foreign economists and statisticians visited the Operational Research Unit, established in December 1953 within the Indian Statistical Institute, to advise Mahalanobis and his team on formulating the draft plan. Mahalanobis himself specifically mentions the names of Ragnar Frisch of Norway, Oskar Lange of Poland, Charles Bettelheim of France, Richard Goodwin of the University of Cambridge, and D.D. Degtyar of the Soviet Gosplan and his team of economists and statisticians. Because these experts were either entirely committed to planning or were statisticians who focused principally on data and consistency of models, they supported the work of the host institution. In turn, Mahalanobis acknowledged their contribution in unqualified positive terms stating, 'We profited much from our discussions with these distinguished experts. They helped us to think clearly; . . . The greatest benefit was that through contacts with such eminent experts from many different countries we gained confidence in our way of thinking.'[69]

The critical commentary came from Milton Friedman, who, rather than being invited by Mahalanobis, had been sent by the Eisenhower administration in response to a request for assistance by the Indian government. As Friedman himself noted more than four decades later, 'The administration recognized an opportunity to counter the influence of the left-wing advice by sending two strong proponents of free markets. Neil Jacoby was one of the two. I was the other one.'[70]

Upon arrival, Friedman was assigned to advise the then finance minister. By his own account, he spent a very intense one month in India and wrote a memorandum summarizing his advice. The memorandum was given to Finance Minister C.D. Deshmukh and officials in the International Cooperation Administration, the predecessor of the present-day U.S. Agency for International Development. Given the prevailing ethos of the time, it received no attention from Indian policymakers and economists.

Unsurprisingly, in the memorandum, Friedman anticipated nearly all major pitfalls of India's approach in the second plan.[71] Unlike any other observer at the time, he criticized its emphasis on the development of two extremes: heavy industry and handicrafts.

> This policy threatens an inefficient use of capital at the one extreme by combining it with too little labour and an inefficient use of labour at the other extreme by combining it with too little capital. The presumption for an economy like India's is that the best use of capital is in general somewhere in between, that heavy industry can best develop and be built upon a widely diversified and much expanded light industry.[72]

Friedman also foresaw the pitfalls of the public sector entering manufacturing activity. Referring to the post-war experience of Europe, he noted that country after country had moved towards expanding the public sector, and the results had been uniformly disappointing in every single case.

> This point may be especially important for India. The areas for which only Government can take responsibility are here so large, so vital, and require such large investments that they alone would be a heavy burden on the limited administrative personnel of high caliber. It seems the better part of wisdom therefore to avoid any activities that can be left to others.

Friedman was also critical of giving direction to private investment through licensing. 'It is impossible to predict in advance the lines of investment that will turn out to be the most productive, as the failure of so many private enterprises amply demonstrate. There is therefore great need for a system that is flexible and can change easily.' He anticipated that detailed direction would waste scarce energies of public servants in producing and enforcing regulations and of private individuals in trying to evade them. He further stated that policies such as excise tax on factory-made shoes and factory-made textiles and discrimination in favour of the cottage industry added to the inefficiency in the use of human resources. 'Granting them [cottage industry] special favour in the form of especially advantageous loans, guaranteed markets, refusal of licences to competitors, enforcing or even permitting private price-fixing and market-sharing agreements simply encourages inefficiency and wastes scarce resources.'

Finally, Friedman advised against protection and foreign-exchange control. Referring to the successful Canadian experience, he recommended adopting a flexible exchange rate to balance the demand for and supply of foreign exchange. Once this was done, the need for an elaborate system of import controls would also disappear. His critique of the system as it existed then is worth quoting at some length. He wrote,[73]

> The existing structure of exchange-controls and their associated system of import and export licenses and of discrimination between sources of purchases, seem to this writer a major obstacle to the growth and progress of the

> Indian economy. They involve waste and inefficiency in the use of foreign exchange. They introduce delay, uncertainty, and arbitrariness into domestic business activities. They impose on officials in charge of exchange control a task that is bound to be discharged most imperfectly, however able and devoted the officials may be. The criteria the officials use—and must use—tend to perpetuate the status quo ante, and therefore constitute an obstacle to dynamic change and adaptation in an area that traditionally has been one of the most dynamic sectors in the economy and the source of much of the impetus to change. Exchange controls necessarily involve the indiscriminate distribution of implicit subsidies to those granted import licenses, and they lend themselves to abuse as a means of granting administrative protection from foreign competition to inefficient or monopolistic domestic producers.

In this one paragraph, Friedman anticipated the essence of the more detailed and evidence-based critique of the import-control cum foreign-exchange allocation regime that Jagdish Bhagwati and Padma Desai would provide independently fifteen years later in what would be the first major work on the pitfalls of the controlled regime and the need for a shift to a more open and market-oriented economy.[74] Based on his analysis, Friedman concluded that India would be wise to abolish exchange control and import licensing. He then explained how a Canadian-style flexible exchange rates system could be adopted to solve the problem of increased demand for foreign exchange that would accompany the end of import licensing and foreign-exchange control.

Industrialists: The Bombay Plan

In most countries, industrialists represent the constituency for a pro-market policy regime in which they are free to pursue profits. But this was not the case in 1950s India. Through the

Bombay Plan, published in 1944 and 1945 in two parts, they endorsed the development strategy they expected Congress to pursue after Independence.

Leading industrialists, most prominently G.D. Birla, had been partners of Mahatma Gandhi and the Congress in the freedom movement against the British since 1920. There are at least two explanations for why they may have forged this partnership. One, as patriotic Indians, they saw the British rule through the same lens as Mahatma Gandhi and the Congress. And two, as historian David Lockwood has suggested, they may have expected their own business interests to be served better under a national rather than the British government. British policies inevitably gave primacy to British economic interests and, therefore, pursued policies not always conducive to the economic interests of Indian industrialists. In contrast, a national government would place Indian economic interests at the centre of its policies and, therefore, better serve the interests of Indian industrialists.[75]

The close association with Congress allowed Indian industrialists to participate in and influence its internal discussions on the economic strategy to be pursued once India became free. As already noted in the previous chapter, when the Congress constituted the National Planning Committee under Nehru to prepare the blueprint of post-Independence industrialization strategy in 1938, it had appointed four out of its fourteen members from the business community: Purshotamdas Thakurdas, A.D. Shroff, Walchand Hirachand and Ambalal Sarabhai. As committee members, these industrialists got the opportunity to sensitize Nehru to the needs and concerns of Indian industry and influence his thinking on the role of the private sector in India's future industrialization. Simultaneously, they acquired a better understanding of the economic vision Nehru had for an independent India and themselves became sensitized to the political constraints within which they would have to operate.

In October 1940, Nehru was arrested, and the National Planning Committee's work ended abruptly. The Congress itself did not actively return to planning until the Interim Government of 1946 appointed the Advisory Planning Board. But in the intervening years, the industrialists went to work and produced their own road map for post-Independence India's economic development. The full document consisted of two parts initially published sequentially in January 1944 and January 1945. Later, in April 1945, Penguin Books brought out the two parts together under the title *Memorandum Outlining a Plan of Economic Development for India*.[76] It became known as the Bombay Plan and gained the acceptance of Indian industry more broadly, including a formal endorsement by FICCI.

Apart from small differences in emphases, the Bombay Plan endorsed nearly all elements of what I have called the Nehru Development Model. Since the Draft Plan-frame of Mahalanobis itself was heavily influenced by the latter, the industrialists had de facto anticipated and endorsed it in advance. In all likelihood, they had understood Nehru's mind during discussions in the National Planning Committee and calibrated their position within the context of the constraints those discussions implied.

The Bombay Plan devoted Part I to outlining a fifteen-year production plan, divided into three five-year plans aimed at tripling the total income and doubling per-capita income. In conformity with the discussions in the National Planning Committee, it identified the elimination of poverty as its principal objective stating that '[I]increased production will be meaningless unless it is directed towards the eradication of poverty'.[77] Explaining the reason for placing the production plan on the front burner, it noted, '[I]n a country of comparatively low production such as India, no system of distribution, however meticulously framed, will help to raise the standard of living unless production is vastly increased.'[78]

With the additional goal of achieving self-sufficiency, the Bombay Plan also adopted the strategy of placing heavy industries at the centre of its production plan. Early in Part I, it noted,[79]

> It is an important part of our proposals regarding industrial development that in the initial stages attention should be directed primarily to the creation of industries for the production of power and capital goods. Nothing has more seriously hindered the development of India's industrial resources during the war than the absence of these basic industries and we consider it essential that this lack should be remedied in as short a time as possible. Apart from its importance as a means of quickening the pace of industrial development in India, it will have the effect of ultimately reducing our dependence on foreign countries for the plant and machinery required by us and, consequently, of reducing our requirements of external finance.

Later, in laying out the stages of development, the plan reiterated the need to develop the basic industries upfront to achieve self-sufficiency. To quote another memorable passage,[80]

> In carrying out the stages of development, we shall have to pay special attention to basic industries, such as the manufacture of machinery, chemicals, etc. On these industries will depend the development not only of all other industries but of the whole economic life of the country. Till these industries are developed, we shall naturally be at the mercy of foreign countries. To shorten this period of dependence it is necessary to give priority to basic industries over other industries and thus to speed up development.

Side-by-side with the development of heavy industries, the plan recommended that 'provision should be made at the same time for the manufacture within the country of the most essential classes of consumption goods, as otherwise a great deal of unnecessary hardship may be caused during the planning period'.[81] It suggested that 'in the production of these essential consumption goods, the fullest possible use should be made of small-scale and cottage industries. This will, besides providing employment, reduce the need for purchasing expensive plant and machinery.'[82]

In its discussion of agriculture, the plan saw the small size of agricultural holdings as the biggest problem to be solved. It noted that the average holding was no more than three acres scattered over the village in tiny fragments and viewed consolidation of holdings and increase in their size as one of the main reforms required. 'To bring it about,' noted the plan, 'co-operative farming appears to present less difficulties than any other method that may be suggested. It increases the size of the holding for purposes of cultivation without depriving the cultivators of their right to the ownership of their existing holdings.'[83] The Bombay Plan thus endorsed Nehru's idea of cooperative farming as well.

It may be hypothesized that the authors of the Bombay Plan were especially sensitive to the possibility of being accused of trying to secure profit opportunities for themselves through the plan to the detriment of the welfare of the masses. Therefore, they devoted the entire Part II of the plan to measures necessary for equitable income and wealth distribution. In this part, they began by noting that it could not be assumed that increased production would automatically solve the problem of poverty. 'In fact, increased production will be meaningless unless it is directed towards the eradication of poverty. Logically, an improvement in the general standard of living, therefore, involves both increased production and equitable distribution . . .'[84]

The authors set two explicit goals for policies aimed at achieving equity: '(i) to secure to everybody a minimum income essential for a reasonable standard of living and (ii) to prevent gross inequalities in the incomes of different classes and individuals.'[85] They then made extensive recommendations concerning taxation of wealth and income, employment opportunities, a minimum wage and living standard for all, equitable regional distribution of industries, free provision of education and health, redistribution of land and remunerative prices to farmers for their produce.

Finally, the plan acknowledged the need for all-round State intervention in the economy. 'It is inevitable that in executing a comprehensive plan of economic development, especially in a country where the beginnings of such development have yet to be laid, the State should exercise in the interests of the community a considerable measure of intervention and control.'[86] Concerning the form of intervention, the plan explicitly noted the need for going beyond the conventional functions of the State, such as coordination of economic activity, currency management, public finance, legislative activity and safeguarding the interests of economically weaker sections of society. It recommended,[87]

> We have, however, to deal here with another and a more specific set of functions that are being advocated by important sections of enlightened opinion both in this country and outside. These functions centre around (i) ownership, (ii) control, and (iii) management of economic enterprises. A widening of the economic functions of the State in these directions is advocated on the ground that unrestricted private enterprise under the capitalistic system of production has not served the interests of consumers and of the community generally as satisfactorily as it should have.

Among the three functions, the plan saw the exercise of control over economic activity to be the most important. 'Mobilization of all the available means of production and their direction towards socially desirable ends is essential for achieving the maximum amount of social welfare.'[88] The plan went on to acknowledge the need for government control in nearly all economic activity, explicitly mentioning production, distribution, consumption, investment, foreign trade, foreign exchange, wages and working conditions. Regarding ownership, it recommended the entry of the public sector whenever public interest justified it. It explicitly endorsed the entry of the public sector in post and telegraph, defence and industries entirely new to the country or specific regions.

In sum, the view of the industry, as outlined in the Bombay Plan, was already aligned with the Indian government's future planning and industrialization strategy. When discussions on the Draft Plan-frame, completed in mid-March 1955, began, the business community did criticize some specific aspects of it but uniformly endorsed its central features, namely, the emphasis on the development of heavy industry and the pursuit of self-sufficiency. For instance, a paper issued by FICCI questioned the role assigned to the public sector in production activity, arguing that the provision of power, education, health and sound institutional and policy framework constituted a wide enough agenda to occupy the government.[89] Similarly, large-scale textile manufacturers such as Lala Shri Ram, Shantilal Mangaldas and G.D. Birla questioned the low target for cloth production in the mill sector.[90] But these criticisms did not add up to a challenge to the fundamental features of the Draft Plan-frame. On the contrary, when the planning commission published the draft second plan on 10 February 1956, criticism of FICCI became much muted. Its spokesman welcomed the document for its emphasis on industrialization while expressing reservations on the 'rigid demarcation' between public and private sectors. 'If rapid industrialization is the goal,' he said, 'there should be no such rigid demarcation. But the whole sector should be treated as one national sector, and both should be allowed to develop.'[91] The spokesman had thus moved away from the original position of FICCI, which had called for the confinement of the public sector to power, education, health and a sound institutional and policy framework.

Later, when the government issued the Industrial Policy Resolution of 1956, which was to serve as the foundation of the second and subsequent plans, the business community offered, at best, muted adverse reactions. Commentary by A.D. Shroff in the context of the Industrial Policy Resolution of 1956 provides a glimpse of the readiness with which industrialists accepted government policies during this era:[92]

> The Industrial Policy statement of this year has certainly created further apprehensions not only in the minds of business men [sic] but of the investing public in general. The tragedy of the situation is this - that with a few exceptions, Indian business men [sic] and Indian public in general have not shown any due appreciation of the implications of this policy. Even a man like Sir John Strachey, who visited India some months ago, in his report has pointed out, although he is a man who has a definite Leftist bias, he was really surprised that when the Industrial Policy Statement was issued some Indian business men [sic] definitely welcomed it, while, most of them in general showed apathy or indifference about it.

The Bombay Plan had considerably weakened the hand of even the few politicians who were critical of Nehruvian policies and made a case for greater space for the private sector. As late as 1963, when the Swatantra Party members of Parliament challenged the basis of the government's economic strategy, Nehru could counter them by drawing their attention to the nod given by industrialists in the Bombay Plan.[93]

Forum of Free Enterprise

Our discussion of contemporary influential voices will be incomplete without a brief reference to the Forum of Free Enterprise founded by industrialist and banker A.D. Shroff to give voice to the proponents of private enterprises and critics of Nehru's socialism as it impacted business activity. Those who contributed to the forum's activities during its first five years included M.R. Masani, N.A. Palkhivala, B.R. Shenoy, P.T. Bauer, M.A. Master, K.C. Cooper and, most prominently and frequently, Shroff himself.

Unfortunately, while the contributions of these and other luminaries to the forum's activities are important from a history of thought viewpoint, there is little evidence that they had any perceptible influence on policy. This lack of influence is not surprising since the exercise of influence required political activism, and Shroff was committed to limiting the forum's role to educating the public. He explicitly laid down the policy of the forum in these terms: 'We are not a political organization. Our main, if not the only, objective is of an educative character.'[94] While the contributors to the forum wrote on subjects such as the importance and capabilities of the private sector, complexities of the tax system, wisdom of state trading, cooperative farming and inflationary aspects of budget proposals, they rarely attacked the overall policy framework underlying the second plan.

From the perspective of broad economic strategy, the thrust of the most influential contributors within this group was on the defence of the private sector without questioning the wisdom of the presence of the public sector. Contributions by Masani and Shroff best illustrate this point. In a 1961 article, Masani expressed his bewilderment at the sceptical view of the private enterprise of most of his colleagues in the Parliament, stating, 'I sat through a week of discussions in Parliament on the Companies Amendment Bill. One of the impressions I gathered was that the Government on one side and a fair section of members on the other looked upon a joint-stock company as some kind of necessary evil to be tolerated for the time being. It was not, as it is in most countries of the world, in America, Germany, Sweden, Japan or England, a very desirable form of organization . . .'[95] He said that in a country like India, few questioned the need for state enterprises in certain fields. What was unsettling, however, was that 'increasingly, in one field after another, not only that the State enters but the State puts out of business anyone else who happens to be there and asserts a monopoly or a near-monopoly in that particular sphere'.[96]

Earlier, in a 1956 article, Shroff had written similarly in reaction to the assertion by T.T. Krishnamachari, Minister of Commerce and Industry, that the private enterprise was showing neither initiative nor enterprise. To underline the dynamism of the private sector, he reminded him of the industrial development under the British when the latter had been wholly hostile to native entrepreneurs. He noted that even from 1951 to 1956, 'the overwhelming proportion of the increased production was contributed by Private Enterprise because the few State Enterprises which came into operation were mainly confined to the Sindri Fertilizer Factory, the Chittaranjan Locomotives, the Indian Telephone Factory at Bangalore, etc.'[97] Shroff also called out the adverse impact of the rising tide of regulations on private-sector economic activity.

> Even if you think of starting an industry on your own, unless you satisfy certain norms which have been established by the Planning Commission, you are not likely to get permission to go into that industry. There are also certain administrative procedures . . . where so much of red tape was involved that a number of industrial proposals which were put up in Madras and Bangalore had to be abandoned since the promoters got simply tired of travelling from Bangalore and Madras to New Delhi and back.[98]

In sum, the critiques of the contributors to the Forum of Free Enterprise were largely defensive. They took the form of pushback against the drive by government policies to undermine private enterprise without fundamentally questioning the policy framework itself. Even their intellectual arguments did not go far enough to question the central features of the development model, namely priority to heavy industries and pursuit of self-sufficiency. And, given the reluctance of the forum to go beyond playing the educational role, there was little prospect that it could change the course of the economy as set by Nehru.

Concluding Remarks

All evidence shows that when India adopted the Nehru Development Model, nearly all voices that mattered supported it. At least during the crucial discussions on the Mahalanobis Draft Plan-frame, even the isolated dissenting voices of Indian economists such as Shenoy, Vakil and Brahmananda did not question the fundamental features of the model. Shenoy expended much of his energy on pointing out the risks of deficit financing.[99] Vakil and Brahmananda pitched for greater emphasis on agriculture but endorsed developing heavy industry as long as it was ancillary to agriculture. Overall, it is difficult to disagree with the bottom line offered by Nayar: 'Over the years before independence, the heavy industry strategy had thus acquired a sacred quality in political and economic thinking in India, the very notion of planning had become identified with the heavy industry strategy. And one basic reason for this eminence for heavy industry was equation between industrialization and independence that was dominant in national thinking.'[100]

The only clear and comprehensive critique of the Nehru Model in 1955 came from Milton Friedman. In a memorandum containing less than 5000 words, he pointed a finger at nearly every single flaw in the model. But, alas, at the time, the ideas of Friedman were yet to gain wide acceptance even within the United States. As such, the prospects of their acceptance in the India of the time, so heavily dominated by Nehru and his followers, were nil.

Part II

The Economic History: Implementation and Outcomes

5

Industrial and Labour Policies

In a market economy, the actions of individual economic agents seeking profits determine the structure and time path of the industry. The government's job is to provide a secure environment where economic agents can freely transact. In contrast, Nehru and his planners sought a structure and time path of the industry quite different from the one profit-seeking and freely-transacting economic agents would have produced. They wanted the heavy industries to grow upfront and in a regionally balanced manner. At the same time, they wanted cottage, village and small-scale industries to flourish to provide employment opportunities and supply consumer goods nationwide. This industry structure and its time path required different implementation tools, including sector-wise planning, an overall policy framework and administrative machinery that would guide investment across enterprises and regions per pre-determined production targets in chosen geographical locations.

This was not an easy problem to solve. Whereas the market decentralizes investment, production, pricing and distribution decisions based on the actions of individual economic agents, the Nehru Development Model chose to centralize them in the hands of a small elite. At each stage, there was ample scope for slippage. That scope grew over time as the economy grew and became more complex. The task was made further difficult by the fact that the objectives of economic agents at the grassroots level, whether in the public or private sector, often conflicted with those of planners and decision-makers at the top.

The economic outcomes resulted from the overall policy framework, sector-wise production targets set by the planners and the plan's administration by a massive bureaucracy within the general policy framework. This was a vast multi-component exercise, and its study requires multiple chapters. In the present chapter, I begin by considering industrial and labour policies. Implementing these policies and import, export and foreign investment policies will constitute the subjects of the following chapters.

Industrial Policy

The Nehru-era industrial-policy framework was governed by the Industrial Policy Resolution of 1948 (IPR 1948), Industrial Policy Resolution of 1956 (IPR 1956) and Industries (Development and Regulation) Act of 1951 (IDRA 1956). Before considering these documents, however, it is useful to discuss another pre-Independence-era document titled 'Statement of Industrial Policy of 1945' (SIP 1945). While only the first three of the above documents have a direct bearing on the policy framework adopted by India, SIP 1945 is of interest for two reasons. First, despite being issued by the then colonial government, it bears a remarkably close resemblance to IPR 1948 and IPR 1956. And second, it has escaped the attention of the vast majority of writers of the economic history of this period, including Bhagwati and Desai, who are otherwise quite comprehensive.[1]

Statement of Industrial Policy of 1945

Until the First World War, the British government had followed a laissez-faire policy on the assumption that industrial progress was best achieved by unregulated private enterprise. Following the First World War, there was some shift in thinking, and tariff protection was granted to sectors such as textiles, and iron and steel. Nevertheless, the central government lost direct interest in industrial development after industry became a State subject under the Government of India Act of 1919.

The Government of India Act of 1935 empowered the central government to pass laws making the development of certain industries a central government subject, but no central government law had been passed as of April 1945 when the Statement of Industrial Policy was issued. As a result, the development of industries remained entirely the responsibility of state governments. According to the statement, a key reason for the government's decision to change this policy was the progress in planning, which had made the central control of certain industries attractive from the viewpoint of coordinated development. Accordingly, the statement lists twenty sectors it considers good candidates for central government control. The list includes nearly all major industries, such as iron and steel, prime movers, automobiles, tractors, trucks, aircraft, all kinds of heavy machinery, machine tools, chemicals, fertilizers, pharmaceuticals, textiles, rubber manufacture, cement, sugar, coal, electric power and radio engineering.

The statement sets out three objectives for the future industrial policy of the central government: maximizing the creation of wealth through the fullest use of available resources and its equitable distribution, building up the country's defence industry and achieving a high and stable level of employment. It reasons, 'If India is to make rapid headway and if the standard of living of the masses is to be effectively raised, a vigorous and sustained effort is necessary in which the State no less than private industry must take part.'[2]

The statement attaches special importance to the development of heavy industries noting,

> Government have decided to take steps to encourage and promote the rapid industrialization of the country to the

> fullest extent possible. They attach particular importance to the development of those industries which constitute the foundation of modern industrial life, such as the iron and steel industry, the heavy engineering industry, the machine tool industry, the heavy chemical industry, and so on.[3]

Turning to the direct role to be played by the government in ownership and management of industrial enterprises, the statement notes,

> Apart from ordnance factories, public utilities and railways, basic industries of national importance may be nationalized provided adequate private capital is not forthcoming and it is regarded as essential, in the national interests, to promote such industries. For the purpose of Government policy, basic industries can be defined as including aircraft, automobiles and tractors, chemicals and dyes, iron and steel, prime movers, transport vehicles, electrical machinery, machine tools, electro-chemical and non-ferrous metal industries.

The statement also proposes to nationalize industries such as salt manufacturing, which constituted a major source of tax revenue. But it leaves all other sectors to private enterprise under varying degrees of control, with stricter controls applying to industries of semi-monopolistic nature and those reliant on scarce natural resources.

A key instrument of control and regulation the statement proposes to introduce is the power to license industrial undertakings. It offers two rationales for it. First, left unregulated, industry would tend to concentrate geographically in ways contrary to the national interest. It reasons,[4]

> It seems unsound from the strategic point of view that so large a proportion of industry should be concentrated in a few cities which might well be vulnerable to attack. On the social side it

> is clear that concentration creates housing problems of a most acute type. Perhaps, an even more important consideration is that concentration deprives other areas of the country of the beneficent effects of diversified economy. Lastly, it is not clear that concentration is necessarily economically sound. The markets for textiles, for instance, are situated all over India, and cotton, the main raw material, is also grown in various parts of India. From the point of view of the consumer, it would obviously be right to cut out unnecessary transportation costs and to locate manufacture where both the raw material and the market are situated.

The second rationale for licensing the statement provides is to combat and control the tendency of capitalists to pursue quick returns. It argues that such tendency 'will lead to lopsided development—a scramble for some industries, with the danger of overproduction and excessive competition and inadequate attention to other industries which are equally necessary in the national interest'.[5] As a solution, it suggests fixing targets for the industries subject to such tendency, allocating them on a regional basis and enforcing them via licensing. Specifically,[6]

> Government propose that they should take power to license the starting of new factories and the expansion of existing factories, for, without this power, planned industrial development will be quite impossible. At the same time in order to avoid unnecessary delays, it is proposed to set a monetary limit to the plants or projects requiring license so that very small plants, moderate extension of existing plants or replacements which do not add to the output should not be subject to licensing.

The statement also proposes a set of measures to assist industries when the objectives of the policy demand so. These include loans to and equity investment in certain enterprises, guaranteed minimum dividend on capital for a fixed number of years, financial support to research organizations set up by industry associations, preference in government procurement, tax incentives, assistance in procurement of certain capital goods from abroad and expert advice. Finally, it proposes additional controls aimed at achieving a balance among agriculture, industry and services, securing fair wages for industrial workers, preventing excessive profits on private capital, ensuring the quality of industrial products and avoiding unhealthy concentration of assets in the hands of a few individuals or of a special community.

The proposals in this statement are broadly in the spirit of the discussions held under the auspices of the National Planning Committee of the Congress and the Bombay Plan. In conformity with them, it gives priority to heavy industries; proposes direct State ownership and management whenever these industries are seen as essential and adequate private investment in them is not forthcoming; envisages licensing of private production activity above a threshold level of investment; and recognizes the need for setting up product-wise targets for industrial production.

Coming from the colonial government, this resemblance between the statement and the positions of the Congress and Indian industrialists may seem surprising. It is unlikely that the government directly consulted Nehru before issuing the policy since he was still in jail. But the coincidence is explained once we recognize that beginning with the Government of India Act of 1935, there had been a slow Indianization of economic policy within the colonial government. In the present case, the statement had been authored in its entirety by Ardeshir Dalal, who had also been one of the eight authors of part one of the Bombay Plan. Soon after the latter's publication, the then Viceroy and Governor General of India Archibald Percival Wavell had appointed Dalal to the Viceroy's Executive Council as member in charge of the Planning and Development Department. In this capacity, the latter became the author of the Statement of Industrial Policy of 1945.[7]

Industrial Policy Resolution 1948

IPR 1948 provided the first framework for industrial policy after Independence. The essential ground for it had been prepared by the report of the Economic Programme Committee that the AICC had appointed at its November 1947 session under the chairmanship of Nehru. Other members of the committee were all influential senior members of the Congress.[8] The report of the committee, submitted to the Congress President in February 1948, provided detailed recommendations on agriculture, village and cottage industries, large-scale industries, the role of private and public sectors in the development of large-scale industries, investment licensing, nationalization of existing large-scale enterprises and industrial relations. Though IPR 1948 differed in its details from the recommendations of the committee, the latter had a visible influence on it. This was inevitable because of the seniority of the committee members within the Congress.

The Planning Commission and the Central Objective of the Resolution

At the outset, the resolution proposed establishing a National Planning Commission to formulate and execute development programmes. It went on to emphasize the critical role of wealth creation in the fight against poverty, stating, 'Any improvement in the economic conditions of the country postulates an increase in national wealth; a mere redistribution of existing wealth would make no essential difference to the people and would merely mean the distribution of poverty.'[9] Therefore, a continuous 'increase in production by all means' alongside equitable distribution was the key to the policy's success.

By placing wealth creation at its centre, the resolution sought to give greater space to the private sector than the past resolutions and discussions within the Congress had envisaged, and socialists within the party and communists had supported. It noted,

> The problem of state participation in Industry and the conditions in which private enterprise should be allowed to operate must be judged in this context. There can be no doubt that the state must play a progressively active role in the development of industries, but ability to achieve the main objectives should determine the immediate extent of state responsibility and the limits to private enterprise.

It argued that for some time to come, the State's scarce resources would be better used by expanding its activities in areas it was already operating and starting new production units in other fields rather than acquiring existing units in the private sector.

The Direct Role of the State in Industrial Production

In this background, the resolution made three provisions to define the direct role of the State (defined to include central and state governments and other public agencies such as municipal corporations) in the running of industrial enterprises. First, it confined its monopoly to just three sectors: the manufacture of arms and ammunition, the production and control of atomic energy, and the ownership and management of railway transport. Second, the resolution gave the State the exclusive right to establish new enterprises in coal; iron and steel; aircraft; shipbuilding; telephone, telegraph and wireless; apparatus except radio receiving sets and mineral oils. But even in these sectors, it left the door open to the government seeking the cooperation of the private sector in the national interest. Finally, while asserting the State's right to acquire any existing industrial unit in the public interest, as a matter of policy, the resolution ruled out such acquisition for ten years. This immunity from nationalization applied to foreign-owned enterprises as well. In exceptional cases, if the State did exercise its right to nationalize a private unit, the resolution promised fair and equitable compensation.

Private Corporate Sector

Except for power generation and distribution, which had just been brought under full control of the government, the resolution left the remainder of the industrial field open to the private sector. This did not mean that the State would play no role in these sectors. The State reserved the right to enter any sector it saw fit, as it had indeed done regarding fertilizers, essential drugs and synthetic oil from coal. Moreover, the State was also to regulate these sectors.

In particular, the resolution provided for the planning and regulation of certain basic industries of national importance, requiring substantial investment or a high degree of technical skills. Although it explicitly mentioned eighteen sectors such as salt, automobile, prime movers, electrical and heavy machinery, chemicals, fertilizers, pharmaceuticals, non-ferrous metals, cotton and woollen textiles, cement, sugar, newsprint, air and sea transport, and defence-related industries in this category, it cautioned that the list was not exhaustive.

The Cottage and Small-Scale Industry

The final section of the industry to get a mention in the resolution was that comprising cottage and small-scale enterprises. It noted, 'These industries are particularly suited for the better utilization of local resources and for the achievement of local self-sufficiency in respect of certain types of essential consumer goods like food, cloth and agricultural implements.[10]' The resolution called for adequate provision of raw materials, cheap power and technical advice for these enterprises and safeguarding the latter against competition by their large-scale counterparts. It also proposed the creation of 'small-size industrial co-operatives throughout the country' to fill the vacuum likely to result from inadequate access to capital goods for the large-scale industry.

The Role of the Provincial Governments and Other Public Agencies

The resolution covered four other subjects: the role of provincial governments and other public agencies in industrialization; the division of the fruits of production between labour and capital; the treatment of foreign capital; and tariff and tax policy. Regarding the first of these subjects, when assigning the responsibility of starting new units in industries such as coal, iron and steel, aircraft manufacturing and shipbuilding exclusively to the State, it explicitly defined the State as including the central and provincial governments and other public agencies like municipal authorities. Likewise, when discussing the industries that the State intended to regulate and control, it stated,

> The Government of India, while retaining the ultimate direction over this field of industry, will consult the Governments of the Provinces and States at all stages and fully associate them in the formulation and execution of plans. Besides these Governments, representatives of Industry and Labor will also be associated with the Central Government in the Industrial Advisory Council and other bodies which they propose to establish, as recommended by the Industries Conference.[11]

Division of the Fruits of Production between Labour and Capital

The resolution stated that the maximum increase in production could not be achieved without 'the fullest co-operation between labor and management and the maintenance of stable and friendly relations between them.' It went on to note the government's acceptance of the resolution by the Industries Conference recommending the sharing of net profits between labour and capital after provision has been made 'for payment of fair wages to labor, a fair return on capital employed in the industry and reasonable reserves for the maintenance and expansion of the undertaking.'[12] It provided the broad outline of an institutional structure aimed at fixing wages and determining the distribution of profits between labour and capital in ways that would minimize industrial disputes.

Treatment of Foreign Capital

Through its general immunity from nationalization to all private enterprises for ten years, the resolution laid to rest the immediate fears of existing foreign companies for their possible government takeover. The resolution anticipated opposition from domestic business interests and general hostility towards new foreign capital. Therefore, it chose to walk a thin line. While agreeing with the Industries Conference that foreign capital had a role to play in the country's rapid industrialization, it went on to state that the conditions of its participation 'should be carefully regulated in the national interest'. It promised to bring suitable legislation governing the approval of foreign investment proposals and the management of foreign enterprises. It envisaged that with rare exceptions, the major interest in ownership and effective control would be in Indian hands. As it turned out, however, such legislation was never enacted. Moreover, a statement in the Parliament by Nehru exactly a year later, which ended up substituting for the promised legislation, enunciated a significantly more liberal policy towards foreign capital.

Assistance to Private Enterprises and Tariff and Tax Policy

Finally, the resolution provided that, while taking full responsibility for industries exclusively reserved for it, the government would also extend assistance to private and cooperative enterprises, especially 'by removing transport difficulties and by facilitating the import of essential raw materials to the maximum possible extent. The tariff policy of government will be designed to prevent unfair foreign competition and to promote the utilization of India's resources without imposing unjustifiable burdens on the consumer.'[13] The resolution also promised to adjust the taxation to encourage savings and productive investment and prevent undue concentration of wealth in the hands of a few.

Industrial Policy Resolution of 1956

Although the First Five-Year Plan was formally launched in 1951–52, it was not placed before the Parliament in its final form until December 1952. Many industrial projects were already underway by this time, while many others had been identified. Therefore, industrialization during the first plan was largely governed by IPR 1948 and its implementing legislation IDRA 1951 (discussed below). When preparations began to launch the second plan, several developments led the government to issue a new industrial policy.

As the 1950s unfolded, with Sardar Patel having passed away in December 1950, Nehru emerged as the unquestioned leader of India. To be sure, advocates of private industry remained within Congress, but none of them could claim to be Nehru's equal. This development gave the latter a freer hand in moving his socialist agenda forward. In December 1954, he got the Parliament to adopt a resolution to establish a socialistic pattern of society in the country. In 1955, the Congress also adopted a similar resolution. The discussions around the Draft Plan-frame of the second plan, prepared by Mahalanobis, helped mobilize the support of the public as well as the political and intellectual class for a development strategy reliant on heavy industries, a progressively larger share of the public sector in investment, and greater control and regulation of the private sector by the State.

Against this background, the Industrial Policy Resolution of 1956 (IPR 1956) was promulgated to give an extra edge to Nehru's socialist agenda.[14] Though exhibiting continuity with its predecessor, this resolution differed from it in terms of widening the space for the public sector and placing greater emphasis on developing the private sector on cooperative lines. Recalling the acceptance by the Parliament of 'the socialistic pattern of society as the objective of social and economic policy', the resolution stated,

> In order to realize this objective, it is essential to accelerate the rate of economic growth and to speed up industrialization and, in particular, to develop heavy industries and machine making industries, to expand the public sector, and to build up a large and growing cooperative sector. . . . Accordingly, the State will progressively assume a predominant and direct responsibility for setting up new industrial undertakings and for developing transport facilities. It will also undertake State trading on an increasing scale. At the same time, as an agency for planned national development, in the context of country's expanding economy, the private sector will have the opportunity to develop and expand. The principle of cooperation should be applied whenever possible and a steadily increasing proportion of the activities of the private sector developed along cooperative lines.

The resolution then went on to spell out the details of the policy.

The Public Sector

In contrast to IPR 1948, IPR 1956 assigned the State direct responsibility for the future development of industries over a significantly wider area. According to it, achieving the socialistic pattern of society and planned rapid development 'required all industries of basic and strategic importance, or in the nature of public utility services should be in the public sector'.[15] Other industries that were essential and required investment on a scale that only the State could provide had also to be in the public sector. The list of these industries, provided in Schedule A of the resolution, included as many as seventeen broad sectors.

Among Schedule A industries, railways and air transport, arms and ammunition, and atomic energy were to be complete State monopolies. From being left in private hands by IPR 1948, air transport thus now jumped into the State monopoly list. To the list of industries in which only the State was to start new units, identified in IPR 1948, Schedule A added many forms of heavy plant and machinery manufacture; mining of minerals such as iron ore, manganese ore, gypsum, sulfur and diamond; and mining and processing of copper, lead, zinc, tin and molybdenum.

The resolution identified a second set of industries, listed in Schedule B, which were to be 'progressively state-owned and in which the State will, therefore, generally take the initiative in establishing new undertakings, but in which private enterprise will also be expected to supplement the efforts of the State.' Schedule B included twelve industries, such as all other major minerals not included in Schedule A, machine tools, all inputs required in chemical industries, antibiotics and other essential drugs, fertilizers, synthetic rubber, chemical pulp, and road and sea transport. Private entry into these sectors was not forbidden, but it would likely face higher barriers than industries not included in Schedules A and B.

Private Corporate Sector

The remaining industries were left to the private sector though entry into them was not entirely free. 'Industrial undertakings in the private sector have necessarily to fit into the framework of the social and economic policy of the State and will be subject to control and regulation in terms of the Industries (Development and Regulation) Act and other relevant legislation.' Nevertheless, to its credit, the resolution recognized the need for flexibility within this framework, stipulating,

> The Government of India, however, recognize that it would, in general, be desirable to allow such undertakings to develop

> with as much freedom as possible, consistent with the targets and objectives of the national plan. When there exist in the same industry both privately and publicly owned units, it would continue to be the policy of the State to give fair and nondiscriminatory treatment to both of them.[16]

Three further observations may be made concerning provisions relating to the public and private corporate sectors in the resolution. First, it recognized that the boundary between the public and private sectors would not be seen as absolute and unbreachable. If national interest so dictated, the private sector could be allowed in Schedule A industries. Likewise, the public sector retained the right to operate in sectors outside of Schedules A and B. Second, as in the past, the State would continue providing financial assistance to private enterprises, especially when organized along cooperative lines. When such assistance was large, it was expected to predominantly take the form of equity capital. Finally, unlike IPR 1948, the resolution made no explicit promise against the nationalization of private industrial units.

Cottage and Village and Small-Scale Industries

The resolution provided for the continuation of the government's 'policy of supporting cottage and village and small-scale industries by restricting the volume of production in the large scale sector, by differential taxation, or by direct subsidies'.[17] It noted, however, that the policy would aim at ensuring that this sector acquired sufficient vitality to be self-supporting. For this, it emphasized the need for constant upgrading of production techniques, extension of rural electrification and organization of industrial cooperatives.

Other Provisions

Other issues briefly addressed in the resolution included regional balance by bringing power, water supply and transport facilities in areas lacking industrialization; creation of technical and managerial personnel; improvement in living and working conditions of workers; maintenance of industrial peace and harmonious industrial relations; and speedy and decentralized decision-making in public-sector enterprises. It also explicitly noted that with IDRA 1951 having covered the division of responsibility between the centre and states, and the statement by the prime minister in the Parliament on 6 April 1949 having enunciated the policy on foreign capital, there was no further need to deal with these subjects.

Industries (Development and Regulation) Act of 1951

IDRA 1951 was the key legislation that implemented IPR 1948. Because IPR 1956 differed from IPR 1948 mainly in its greater emphasis on the public sector and expanded the scope of regulatory control over private sector activity, it required no new legislation. The shift into the public sector could be brought about through an increase in its share in investment in the five-year plans, and the expansion of regulatory control could be achieved by enlarging the industries to which IDRA 1951 was applied.

At the outset, the legislation summarizes itself pithily as 'An Act to provide for the development and regulation of certain industries'. Adhering to the spirit of IPR 1948, its framers had worded this sentence carefully to convey that the legislation was intended to cover only a subset of sectors. When introducing the bill in the Constituent Assembly in April 1949, the then Minister of Industry and Supply Shyama Prasad Mukherjee underlined this point once again, stating that the aim of the bill was 'to select certain industries which we consider to be all-India importance and to provide a machinery for the purpose of securing their regulation and development.'[18] The legislation expressed this intent by listing the industries covered by it in its First Schedule. But once the discussions for the Second Five-Year Plan got underway, thinking within the government changed.

Planners now wanted a much wider sway over the industry, as reflected in IPR 1956. Consistent with this resolution, the government expanded the First Schedule, adding more products and expanding its scope in other ways.[19]

On the development front, IDRA 1951 empowered the central government to appoint a development council for any industry or group of industries listed in the First Schedule. The council was to consist of persons representing the interests of owners of industrial undertakings, employees and consumers, and those with domain knowledge of the industry concerned. The council's functions were described in the Second Schedule of the legislation. They included such important matters as recommending production targets and coordinating production programmes, suggesting norms to improve efficiency and product quality, and recommending measures for fuller use of the installed capacity. Though the Development Councils were notified for several industries, they seldom functioned effectively.[20]

On the regulatory front, IDRA 1951 had three major provisions that later came to define the so-called licence-permit raj. The first and by far the most consequential one related to licensing of products. According to it:

1. All existing industrial undertakings in the scheduled industries were required to register in a manner prescribed by the central government;
2. All new industrial undertakings with investment in fixed assets (building, land, and plant and machinery) above a stipulated threshold in the scheduled industries were required to obtain a licence specifying the product, location, the minimum standards in respect of size and any other conditions prescribed by the central government;
3. No new article was to be produced by an undertaking without obtaining a licence or modification of an existing licence; and

4. No substantial expansion or change of location of an industrial undertaking was to be undertaken except under a licence issued by the central government. The legislation defined substantial expansion as an expansion of production capacity that 'amounted virtually to a new industrial undertaking' and explicitly excluded from the regulation 'such expansion as is normal to the undertaking'.

As we will see in greater detail in the next chapter, though the legislation applied only to undertakings employing fifty workers if using power and hundred workers if not using power in industries listed in the First Schedule, its scope grew much wider after the balance-of-payments crisis forced the government to adopt strict foreign-exchange control in 1957. Regardless of their size and industrial classification, undertakings found they could no longer access foreign exchange for machinery and raw material imports unless registered under IDRA 1951.

Over time, some of the flexibilities built into the legislation also got lost. For example, to avoid the creation of overly small units exhibiting high per-unit production costs, the legislation had provided for the specification of a minimum size of the undertaking. But following the emergence of the shortage of foreign exchange, licensing authorities adopted the practice of specifying the maximum capacity in the licence.[21] Similarly, the restriction on substantial capacity expansion, which intended to exclude 'such expansion as is normal to the undertaking', came to be interpreted as any expansion above 10 per cent of licensed capacity.[22]

While the first subject of regulation in IDRA 1951 was investment by private industrial undertakings, the second covered the pricing and distribution of their output. It empowered the central government to take any or all of the following actions on any article 'relatable to any scheduled industry' through a notification:

1. Fix the price at which the notified article may be bought or sold;
2. Regulate 'by licenses, permits or otherwise the distribution, transport, disposal, acquisition, possession, use or consumption of any such article';
3. Prohibit the withholding from sale of any such article that is ordinarily kept for sale;
4. Require any person manufacturing, producing or holding in stock any such article to sell the article partially or wholly;
5. Regulate or prohibit any class of commercial or financial transactions relating to the article;
6. Require sellers and traders of the article to mark it with the sale price and exhibit the available quantity in a visible place; and
7. Collect information and statistics for the purpose of regulation.

These were wide-ranging powers that could be applied not just to products listed in the First Schedule but also to any article related to them. These powers complemented those already available under the Essential Supplies (Temporary Powers) Act of 1946. Though this act expired in January 1955 under the Constitution's provisions, the Parliament enacted another similar act known as the Essential Commodities Act of 1955 (ECA 1955). Like its predecessor, this new act covered a subset of industrial products and many agricultural commodities. Industrial products included items such as coal, parts and accessories of automobiles, cotton and woollen textiles, drugs, fertilizers, iron and steel, paper including newsprint and petroleum and petroleum products. While the regulatory powers over price and distribution control under IDRA 1951 and ECA 1955 were similar, only a subset of commodities was common to them. For instance, the former did not cover agricultural commodities, while the latter did. A bigger difference was that while only the central government was empowered to take action under IDRA 1951, state governments could also act under ECA 1955 on subjects over which the Constitution gave them jurisdiction.

The third and final set of regulatory powers under IDRA 1951 relates to the central government's investigation and direct management or control of industrial undertakings. Investigation powers extended to causes of a substantial fall in output, marked deterioration in product quality, unjustified increase in price and management of the undertaking in a manner detrimental to the scheduled industry or public interest. If an investigation suggested a need for action, the government was empowered to regulate the quantity, quality, price and distribution of the product of the undertaking.

If an undertaking failed to comply with directives issued after an investigation or the investigation found that it was being managed in a manner highly detrimental to the scheduled industry or public interest, the central government could authorize any person or body of persons to take over its management for up to five years. This person or body of persons was required to take necessary steps to efficiently manage the business of the undertaking. These steps were to be taken per the provisions in the order notifying the undertaking's takeover.

Labour Policy

Strong protections for industrial labour had been a part of the Congress agenda, at least since the Karachi resolution of 1931. It had called for 'suitable legislation and in other ways, a living wage, healthy conditions of work, limited hours of labour, suitable machinery for the settlement of disputes between employers and workmen, and protection against the economic consequences of old age, sickness and unemployment'.[23] This sentiment carried over to the discussions in the National Planning Committee. Sensitized by those discussions, the

Bombay Plan, too, had devoted considerable space to the equitable distribution of the fruits of industrial activity between capital and labour. IPR 1948 and IPR 1956 emphasized the need for improved living and working conditions for workers.

A small but significant industrial labour force had come to exist because of railway building, textiles and jute manufacturing, steel mills and coal mining in India in the first half of the twentieth century. This had led to the enactment of several labour laws well before Independence. Most prominently, they included the Employees Compensation Act of 1923, the Indian Trade Unions Act of 1926, the Trade Disputes Act of 1929 and the Wage Payments Act of 1936. Against this backdrop, it is unsurprising that additional labour laws began to be enacted even before the Interim Government was formed in September 1946.

The Industrial Employment (Standing Orders) Act was enacted in April 1946, and the Industrial Disputes Act in April 1947. The latter replaced the Trade Disputes Act of 1929, which had proved inadequate for settling disputes between employees and the employer. Other important labour laws enacted almost concurrently with IPR 1948 and well before the launch of the development programme included the Minimum Wage Act of 1948, the Employees State Insurance Act of 1948 and the Factories Act of 1948. Six more labour laws were enacted in the 1950s, and another two in the first half of the 1960s. Industrial policy was thus complemented by a panoply of labour laws.

The detrimental impact of these laws on India's economy has been widely discussed in the context of post-1991 economic reforms.[24] Therefore, rather than consider these laws in detail, I may note that they ended up providing a high level of protection to the lucky few who could get jobs in larger industrial enterprises but became a barrier to the plentiful creation of such jobs. Over time, amendments to existing laws, as well as the enactment of new such laws, strengthened the rights of workers vis-à-vis employers, further encouraging a shift into capital- and skilled-labour-intensive industries and technologies at the expense of the mass of the workforce that either remained stuck in agriculture or ended up in low-paying jobs in informal-sector industry or services.

India has been unique in placing the social revolution ahead of the economic revolution through its high protection of industrial labour. Given that many among the Indian elite had been educated in Great Britain and nearly all of them were aware of the history of exploitation of industrial labour during the early phase of industrialization in Western countries, there was near unanimity among them on the merits of these laws. As a result, voices against adopting these labour laws were rare.

The earliest voice of caution I have been able to trace came in 1955 from Vakil and Brahmananda in one of the papers they submitted to the Panel of Economists during the discussions on the Draft Plan-frame of the second plan. As discussed in the previous chapter, they pointed out that the labour welfare policy of the Government had cumulatively placed an additional premium on the employment of capital-intensive technologies and disadvantaged labour itself. Subsequently, writing in 1962, American economist and a great friend of India, the late John P. Lewis, who also happened to be among my mentors at Princeton University, drew attention to 'the cost pressures and inhibitions to production expansion that comparatively strong unionization and strong labour-welfare legislation may create in so underdeveloped an economy as India's'.[25] He went on to add:

> I choose this emphasis not out of any reactionary bias against the rights or welfare of industrial labour. However, it does appear that in India—as one by-product of the lead that political development has gained over economic development—institutions for the benefit and protection of workers have achieved an advanced stage of development at a much earlier stage of industrialization than has been usual

> in other industrial processes. From a humanitarian point of view, this is all to the good. But it tempts organized labour, encouraged by its parliamentary and other political affiliates, to press for higher levels of, and higher rates of improvement in, compensation that the level of, and gains in, productivity in novice industries may justify.[26]

Unfortunately, voices such as these were not only rare but, coming from Bombay and the United States, they belonged to 'outsiders' as far as policymaking in Delhi was concerned. They found little traction with Indian policymakers. As a result, the march towards employment-unfriendly labour laws continued.

Concluding Remarks

In this chapter, I have considered India's industrial and labour policies that guided India's development during the Nehru era and beyond. A key difference between policies in the two areas was that, whereas the industrial policy was designed as the bulwark of India's planned industrialization in the forthcoming decades, the labour policy was a response to industrialization already underway. Substantial factory-based modern industry and industrial labour as a class had already emerged in India during the first half of the twentieth century. A need for the protection of the rights of these workers was felt even before Independence. Hence, many labour laws got put in place before Independence or soon after.

In contrast to labour policies, industrial policy evolved, considering future industrialization. Though its foundations had already been laid down by the Congress-led National Planning Committee during 1938–40, it underwent some evolution. In particular, the presence of Sardar Patel and other moderates ensured that the 1948 Industrial Policy Resolution provided for larger space for domestic and foreign private capital. But by the time the Second Five-Year Plan was launched, Nehru had emerged as a national leader with no equals. This dominance of his leadership found expression in the 1956 Industrial Policy Resolution, which expanded the areas of public-sector monopoly, investment and regulation as they related to industry. Such wide control over industrial activity was incompatible with achieving economic efficiency in the allocation of investment across different sectors and the selection of enterprises investing within each sector. In setting detailed production targets, planners had to take recourse to ad hoc decision-making. In the same vein, licensing authorities made no pretence to choosing among various applicants based on social rates of return. Instead, they considered applications as they came, with decisions based on the technical soundness of projects without regard to economic efficiency or a comparison of alternative projects. These are some of the issues we turn to in the next chapter.

6

Implementation: Target-Setting and Industrial Licensing

The government translated its objectives and policies into action through detailed planning, and setting product-level capacity and output targets. These targets were, in turn, converted into investments at the level of the enterprise in the public and private sectors. Both of these steps required a large bureaucracy whose different arms had to coordinate with one another. How this was done has been documented by government and parliamentary committees reporting in 1964 and subsequently.[1] Drawing upon the reports by these committees, Bhagwati and Desai have provided a comprehensive snapshot of the system as it existed in the mid to late 1960s.

Given the existence of these accounts, it may seem unnecessary to revisit the system in detail here. But two factors lead me to choose the opposite course. First, the committee reports are tedious to read, with the relevant details scattered across hundreds of pages. The account in Bhagwati and Desai solves this problem to some degree, but its limitations are that it only offers a snapshot of the system from the 1960s and sometimes leaves out useful details. Therefore, a more detailed account that captures the regime's evolution over time is called for. Second, detailed knowledge of the licensing regime helps us better understand the implications of the Nehru-era policies for efficiency and growth in the short and long run.

The Planning Commission and Target Setting

Established on 15 March 1950 by a resolution of the Government of India, the Planning Commission was delegated the responsibility to draw up a plan for every five years beginning with 1951–52. Though the Prime Minister served as the institution's chairman, the deputy chairman in the rank of a cabinet minister served as its de facto head.[2] Up to about half a dozen eminent individuals were appointed as members in the rank of minister of state and junior only to the deputy chairman. The commission staff was of a technical and administrative nature and was assisted by outside experts, including leading foreign scholars, especially during the Nehru era. The apex body of the commission was the National Development Council (NDC), headed by the Prime Minister. It included the deputy chairman, members of the Planning Commission, cabinet ministers and state chief ministers. The NDC played an important role in guiding and reviewing the work of the commission's staff. With state chief ministers as members, it also served as an effective sounding board for assessing the political feasibility of potentially controversial issues, such as raising financial resources through taxation, the degree of regulation and control over industry and criteria for the disbursement of transfers to states through the commission.

Apart from presenting a broad discussion of strategy, policy and programmes, each of the three plans implemented during the Nehru era had to grapple with three inter-related questions: what would be the overall size of the investment during the five years; how will this investment be allocated across different sectors; and what would be the specific production targets for the major products. On the first question, opinions differed between those who wanted rapid growth and therefore sought a 'bold' plan with a large size of investment and those who feared inflationary financing and therefore pitched for a small size of investment. On the second question, the planners had to agree on the allocation of investment between agriculture on the one hand and industry and services on the other. Once these broad allocations had been agreed upon, the Planning Commission also had to provide finer allocations of investment among subsectors within each broad sector and set physical targets for individual products, which would serve as the guide to the launch of public-sector undertakings and issuance of licences to private-sector enterprises.

Though the initial draft of the first plan had been presented to the Parliament in July 1951, its final version did not reach the latter until 15 December 1952.[3] Therefore, despite the expression 'five-year plan' in the title, the document was effectively only a three-year plan. When presenting the plan to the Parliament, Nehru was acutely aware of this fact. To use his own words, 'Although we still call this a Five-Year Plan, two years of it are already over. Now, it is really a plan for the next three years.'[4]

The draft first plan had been largely a collection of development projects that had already been underway and those that had not yet been launched.[5] The final version retained these projects, added a few more and polished the presentation further. The draft plan had pegged the total expenditure at the modest level of Rs 14.93 billion, which rose to Rs 20.69 billion in the final version. While Nehru lauded the plan as 'the first of its kind—certainly the first of its kind in India' in his speech to the Parliament, he recognized that it was principally a preparatory step towards the more ambitious second plan.[6] 'I have no doubt that when the time comes for a second Five-Year Plan, we shall be in a far better position and on firmer ground, because we will have gone through the process of thinking and planning and benefited from its consequences.'[7]

While the plan spelled out the allocation of the total plan outlay (investment plus current expenditure) across sectors, it contained only a small number of product-wise targets, and even those were largely projections derived from existing or expected additional capacities. Unlike its two successor plans, the first plan placed much greater emphasis on agriculture than on industry. It allocated as much as 44.6 per cent of the total plan expenditure to agriculture, community development, irrigation and power. In comparison, the allocation to industry was set at 8 per cent and to transport and communication at 24 per cent. Despite much talk around industrialization, emphasis on industry did not emerge as the central feature of this plan.

As a result of the relatively small expenditure allocation to industry, the role of the public sector in industrialization remained muted during the plan. Indeed, adhering to the spirit of IPR 1948, the plan document noted,

> The distinction between the public and the private sector relates to the mode of operation rather than to the ultimate objective. . . . The scope and need for development are so great that it is best for the public sector to develop those industries in which private enterprise is unable or unwilling to put up the resources required and run the risks involved, leaving the rest of the field free for private enterprise.[8]

Later, the document magnified this sentiment stating,

> While the emphasis of industrial expansion in the public sector during this five-year period is on initiating and promoting investment in certain basic lines and on completing the projects in hand, the initiative and responsibility for securing the necessary expansion over the bulk of the field of industry rest with private enterprise.'[9]

Though Nehru took full ownership of the plan when presenting it in the Parliament, he did not play the same hands-on role in its preparation as in the second plan. In all likelihood, a team of technocrats was largely responsible for crafting and drafting this document.

We have seen in earlier chapters that the planning process became significantly more elaborate, beginning with the second plan, which, in turn, became the foundation of policy, administrative machinery and economic structure to emerge in the following decades. We have also seen that as far as plan size is concerned, despite objections, most notably by B.R. Shenoy, those who sided with the 'bold' plan, as proposed in the Mahalanobis Draft Plan-frame, carried the day. In the final plan document, total public- and private-sector investments were pegged at Rs 38 billion and Rs 24 billion, respectively. The recommendations in the Mahalanobis Draft Plan-frame were not very different at Rs 34 billion and Rs 22 billion, respectively.

From the viewpoint of implementation, once an agreement had been reached on the plan size, the two remaining important tasks at the planning stage were allocating investment across different sectors and sub-sectors of the economy and fixing product-wise targets. Taking the former first, recall that Mahalanobis had employed a four-sector model to derive sectoral investment allocations. These allocations, in turn, served as the basis of the six-sector allocations he recommended in the Draft Plan-frame.[10]

A pertinent question at this point is whether Mahalanobis had chosen these allocations to achieve the best possible outcome for income and employment within his four-sector model. The answer to this question turns out to be in the negative. Economist Ryutaro Komiya demonstrated in a 1959 article that alternative allocations yielding higher levels of income and employment than those yielded by the allocations recommended by Mahalanobis existed within his own model.[11] Furthermore, even assuming that the Mahalanobis allocations were ideal in some limited sense, they were not adopted without modification in the final plan. The two allocations were markedly different to the extent that such a comparison can be made despite differences in classifications of sectors in the Draft Plan-frame and those in the final plan.[12]

The upshot of this discussion is that the final investment allocations, even at the broad sectoral level, were, at best, based on unspecified criteria and, at worst, no criteria. The story got murkier still when it came to more detailed planning involving allocating investment in each broad sector to its numerous sub-sectors and setting product-wise targets. For the former, the final plan provided allocations only at the level of the *total* plan outlay consisting of public-sector investment and current plan expenditure. The plan did not provide sub-sector-level public- or private-sector investment allocations. Regarding product-wise targets, it provided a long list of products with corresponding physical targets for installed capacity and actual production but without any rationale for the specific choices made. For instance, the plan did not explain how the specific products within heavy industry were chosen from numerous such products. It also did not explain the relationship between the targets for production and the installed capacity of a product.

Apart from a few improvements on the margin, the third plan exhibited the same broad characteristics as the second. Improvements included greater attention to the time-phasing of investment and the balance between input demands implied by different production targets and the availability of those inputs through domestic or foreign sources. Beyond these improvements, the ad hoc nature of allocation of total outlays in broad sectors to sub-sectors and product-wise production and capacity targets remained.

For example, it should have been clear from the beginning that given limited resources, it was not feasible to replace the imports of all investment goods with domestic production in even fifteen years. Therefore, in making investment decisions, there was a need for setting priorities *within* heavy-industry products based on the urgency of replacing imports of specific investment goods with domestic production and the extent of extra cost over imports to be incurred on such replacement. But there is nothing in either the second or the third plan to suggest that such considerations played any role in setting product-wise targets.

The result was that large investments got made, especially in the public sector, without regard to the per-unit cost of production at home relative to the price of imports of the same product. Citing a concrete example illustrating this point, Bhagwati and Desai write,

> In fact, . . . the later evaluations of massive public sector investments in projects such as the Heavy Electricals at Bhopal has shown that the Bhopal project, for example, was extremely low-yielding in terms of economic returns (duly adjusted to reflect social advantage) and thus either better design should have been invented or the heavy industry chosen should have been other than heavy electricals altogether (if no better design was available).'[13]

The Choice Between Public and Private Sector

Taking product-wise targets as given, the government had to decide whether a given product would be produced by the public sector, private sector or both. IPR 1956 had provided schedules listing industries in which the public sector was to be the sole producer (Schedule A), those in which the public sector was to take the lead in establishing new undertakings with the private sector supplementing its effort (Schedule B) and those in which the private sector alone was to carry out production activity (everything else). But this division was hardly sufficient to make product-level choices.

The industries mentioned in the schedules were broad categories, and the scope of each category was not well-defined. As the Dutt committee, appointed to evaluate the successes and failures of the licensing system, noted in its report,

> The category 'iron and steel', for example, not only included large integrated steel plants but also re-rolling and small

> pig-iron plants. . . . Similar ambiguity regarding other categories such as 'heavy' plant and machinery, 'heavy' electrical plant, etc., makes it difficult to examine whether licensing was in keeping with the Policy Resolution. The item mining machinery can include both heavy and not so heavy machinery. To take another example, it is not clear which of the sizes of transformers is to be treated as 'heavy electrical plant' and which falls outside that category.[14]

The committee went on to cite examples of numerous licences that were issued to private enterprises in industries classified as Schedule A industries but noted that it could not ascertain whether this was a violation of IPR 1956 or not.[15]

More dramatically, the committee found that in most Schedule B industries, the private and not public sector took the lead in establishing new undertakings. To quote the committee's report once again, 'It may be noted that in spite of the basic approach that this area would be progressively developed by the State, few public sector units were established in these industries in the period between 1956 and 1966.'[16] Industry-wise data on licences issued to Schedule B industries from 1956 to 1966 recorded by the committee show that they went overwhelmingly to private-sector enterprises. The entire development of the aluminium industry took place in the private sector. The private sector also bagged 226 out of 235 licences in machine tools, 334 out of 335 in plastics, antibiotics and other essential drugs, 36 out of 46 in fertilizers and 184 out of 199 in drugs and pharmaceuticals.[17]

The Dutt Committee did not go into circumstances leading to the entry of new private-sector enterprises in many Schedule A industries and to the dominant role assigned to them in Schedule B industries from 1956 to 1966, noting speculatively that such decisions 'must have been taken by the Government at the highest level'.[18] In the specific case of aluminium, it made inquiries but could get no documents explaining the reasons for the change from the initial decision to develop it in the public sector to relying wholly on the private sector. Answers provided by those the committee consulted were entirely speculative, such as that the industry was simple enough to be left to the private sector or that the government's scarce financial resources were better used in other industries.

The purpose behind drawing attention to these deviations from the stated policy in IPR 1956 is not to suggest that they undermined economic efficiency. If anything, the larger role assigned to private-sector enterprises in industries listed in Schedule A and Schedule B than envisaged in IPR 1956 likely added to efficiency rather than subtracted from it. What these deviations do demonstrate, however, is that in setting the original policy, the government failed to foresee the limitations that democratic polity placed on its ability to enter a diverse set of production activities within a short period. It is likely that in the process, it ended up unduly constraining the entry of the private sector into precisely the sectors it had assigned a high priority.

Industrial Licensing

The administrative ministry in charge of a given sector initiated and established public-sector undertakings (PSUs) in that sector. The ministry was expected to initiate these undertakings within the overall framework of the five-year plans. In many sectors, the Directorate General of Technical Development (DGTD), a technical body generally housed in the industry ministry, evaluated proposals for PSUs for technical soundness.[19] Sectors not covered by the DGTD, such as textiles, jute, steel, sugar, vanaspati and petroleum, had their own separate technical advisers to perform this task.[20]

From a Liberal to Progressively More Stringent Licensing Regime

The process of registering existing private undertakings, initiating and establishing new ones and authorizing them to manufacture new products and substantially expand their production capacity was significantly more complex. Soon after the Registration and Licensing of Industrial Undertakings Rules, 1952, under IDRA 1951, were made available in draft form, fears were expressed that they would scuttle private initiatives in the industry. For instance, in its 4 June 1952 edition, the newspaper *Times of India* wrote:[21]

> Adopted with the avowed objective of guiding and promoting development of industries on sound lines and ensuring efficient management consistent with national policy, the Industries (Development and Regulation) Act became effective 8 May. . . . Under the law, registration and licenses for industrial undertakings are compulsory. The draft rules now published provide a clue to the type of straitjacket into which private industry is to be forced. . . . Applications for licenses are to be scrutinized by a licensing committee composed of officials—a system which might result in the industrialists' case not receiving adequate attention.

Though these fears were not realized immediately, in the longer run, the newspaper proved prophetic. In the early years, the system worked smoothly, with applications for licences processed expeditiously.[22] In sectors where the existing capacity fell short of the target, licences were issued liberally and within a reasonable time. Licences were denied principally for products such as textiles, bicycles and sewing machines, in which the government wanted the organized industry to yield much of the space to the cottage- and household-industry sectors. For the most part, entrepreneurs knew sectors where the government was open to issuing licences and those where it was likely to deny them.[23]

As Shroff noted in his defence of the contribution of the private sector to industrial production during the first plan period, '[T]he overwhelming proportion of the increased production [between 1951 and 1956] was contributed by Private Enterprise because the few State enterprises which came into operation were mainly confined to the Sindri Fertilizer Factory, the Chittaranjan Locomotives, and the Indian Telephone Factory at Bangalore, etc.'[24] Similarly, licensed capacity in the second plan far exceeded the gap between the target capacity and existing installed capacity in most sectors. In contrast, licensed capacity in the third plan fell short of the gap between the target capacity and existing installed capacity in many products.

The growing industrial base, which increased the number of licence applications, and the adoption of strict foreign-exchange control in 1957 led to a progressive slowdown of the decision-making process. According to Marathe, licence applications increased from 1300 in 1956 to 1900 in 1961 and 2500 in 1966.[25] The scarcity of foreign exchange resulted in greater uncertainty and delays in approving import licences for machinery and raw materials. Technical authorities such as the DGTD also became more demanding on the precision and details of descriptions of machinery imports required for manufacturing the proposed product.[26]

The registration and regulatory provisions of IDRA 1951 were wide-ranging. Their reach and impact on private-sector economic activity can only be appreciated by their detailed examination.

Coverage of Undertakings by Size and Sector under IDRA 1951

IDRA applied to all undertakings in industries listed in its First Schedule except those directly owned by the central government. The act thus applied to all undertakings owned by private-sector entities, state and local governments and public-sector corporations.[27] In the legislation, 'undertakings' were defined as industrial enterprises using fifty or more workers if using power and hundred or more workers if not using power. In other words, none of the provisions of the legislation applied to undertakings with fewer than fifty workers if using power and fewer than hundred workers if not using power.

The First Schedule originally contained forty-two items but was substantially expanded by adding another twenty-eight items in 1956. Though the schedule was not exhaustive even in its expanded form, its reach was deep and wide for three reasons. First, listed items were often described in broad terms, allowing them to subsume many items not listed. For instance, an item such as a 'wireless communication apparatus' could be interpreted to include even mobile phones and tablets that did not exist at the time. Second, in numerous instances, the lists of named items were followed by the expression 'and the like,' giving the implementing agencies the freedom to include other unnamed items that could arguably be similar to those named. Finally, two explanatory notes at the end of the schedule explicitly included component parts, accessories and intermediate inputs used to manufacture several items listed in the schedule.

In its original form, IDRA 1951 exempted undertakings in the scheduled industries with less than Rs 1,00,000 in fixed assets (machinery, building and land). An amendment in 1953 replaced this provision by Section 29B, which empowered the government to exempt small undertakings, to be defined in terms of number of workers or the amount invested, from specified provisions of the Act. In 1960, the government exempted undertakings with less than 100 workers and less than Rs 1 million (10 lakh) in fixed assets from the licensing provisions of the Act under this section. In 1962, except for a few industries, the government extended the exemption to all undertakings with Rs 1 million in assets, regardless of the number of workers employed. In 1964, it raised the threshold for exemption to Rs 2.5 million in fixed assets.[28]

Though exempt from the Act's licensing provisions, these undertakings were not necessarily exempt from its registration requirement. According to an official report by a study team headed by H.C. Mathur (Mathur study team), all undertakings with Rs 5,00,000 or more in fixed assets were required to register with the central government. Remarkably, though IDRA 1951 applied to only scheduled industries, according to the study team, the registration requirement also came to be applied to unscheduled industries.[29] This meant that undertakings larger than Rs 5,00,000 in fixed assets were subject to registration requirements regardless of whether they were included in the First Schedule of IDRA 1951 or not.

Based on its case study of forty-eight registration applications, the study team stated that registration was no longer optional. Few industrial undertakings over Rs 5,00,000 in fixed assets could operate profitably without access to imports or allocations of critical inputs, such as cement and steel, whose distribution and prices were controlled by the government. Therefore, all undertakings with Rs 5,00,000 in fixed assets, whether listed in the First Schedule or not, felt obliged to register themselves. Many registration cases in the case study conducted by the study group belonged to the non-scheduled sectors.[30]

This near-universal coverage of registration requirements would not have been of much consequence had the registration process been a routine affair and could have been completed quickly. But such was not the case. In the words of the Mathur study team, 'The procedure in vogue for registration is no longer simpler than that for licensing. Registration is neither automatic nor any longer optional.' The team adds, '[T]here is practically no difference between the ways in which registration and license cases are handled. Both are judged by the same criteria of demand, installed capacity, regional distribution, import requirements, priority, and so on.'[31]

Indeed, the Mathur study team took the view that the near-compulsory nature of registration and the complexity of the registration process had left no free sector in the economy except the one consisting of undertakings with less than Rs 5,00,000 in assets. 'The Rs. 5 lakh [Rs 5,00,000] boundary for small scale industry is thus also the boundary between the free decentralized sector and the controlled (in one way or the other) centralized sector.' Furthermore, 'since foreign exchange is thought to be more easily available under Central patronage, there is the paradox of a scramble on the part of the units in the free small scale sector to climb into the centralized sector covered by registration'.[32]

Types of Industrial Licences

To fully appreciate the difficulty of doing business during this era, especially following the 1957–58 balance-of-payments crisis, we must consider different licensing requirements under IDRA 1951 and their administration. Beyond registration, the Act required the undertakings to obtain licences for five kinds of activities. First, there was the licence for a new undertaking to be issued to a new enterprise proposing to produce an article listed in the First Schedule and not qualifying for the exemptions noted in the previous section. The licence normally specified the product, scale of production, location of the undertaking and any other conditions that the licensing authority deemed appropriate. The latter could include, for example, indigenization of the product within a specified period, restrictions on imports of raw materials, export obligation and obligatory sales of a part of output at below-market prices. The original intent of the specification of scale under the Act was to establish a floor for the size of the unit to pre-empt the emergence of overly small and, therefore, technically inefficient units. But over time, the provision came to be interpreted as a ceiling on the total production capacity.

The second type of licence under IDRA 1951 was required for 'substantial expansion of capacity' by an existing undertaking. The Act defined substantial expansion as 'the expansion . . . which is of such a nature as to amount virtually to a new industrial undertaking, but does not include any such expansion as is normal to the undertaking having regard to its nature and the circumstances relating to such expansion'. Most likely, the intent behind this definition was to avoid constraining the undertaking excessively from future increases in output that might result from improved productivity or even incremental expansions of capacity to sustain normal business activity. But as Hazari stated in his report, this provision later came to be used to place a tight cap of 10 per cent on expanding production capacity.[33]

The third type of licence was required by an undertaking intending to produce a 'new article' covered by the First Schedule of IDRA 1951. The licence was required even if the new article required no new investment. Confusion arose when the new article required new investment but was classified within the same scheduled industry, such as 'other products of iron and steel'. Under such circumstances, it was unclear whether the undertaking was to apply for a licence for a new article or substantial capacity expansion.

Fourth, if an undertaking wanted to move a part or the whole of its operations to another location, it required a 'location licence'. This provision also gave rise to ambiguities that left the undertaking at the mercy of licensing authorities. For example, it was up to the licensing authorities to decide whether a location licence was required when the undertaking wanted to move only its registered or liaison office but not its production unit.[34]

Finally, the Act provided for a licence for 'carrying on business'. This licence was required when an undertaking should have applied for registration but did not do so. It was also required by enterprises exempt from the Act's provisions earlier but became subject to them subsequently due to, for example, expansion of production capacity.

Licensing Bureaucracy and Procedures

As already noted, obtaining a licence was not overly burdensome or time-consuming in the early years of its inception. But once the sterling balances, accumulated through balance-of-payments surpluses during the Second World War, ran out and the government greatly tightened the import controls beginning in 1957, administrative processes became progressively more complex, and delays in approving licences became endemic. For instance, reporting in 1964, the Swaminathan Committee noted,

> Rule 15 of the Registration and Licensing of Industrial Undertakings Rules, 1952, lays down a period of three months within which decisions should be taken on applications for industrial licences. For various reasons, this provision has in practice, remained inoperative. In fact, in respect of 8 cases selected at random for case study, the time taken ranged from 61 to 396 days, and in 6 out of the 8 cases, the period involved was more than 150 days.[35]

Beginning with the appointment of the Swaminathan Committee in 1963, the government appointed committee after committee throughout the 1960s to study the system's workings and recommend improvements. But little success was achieved in improving the outcomes.

Licensing procedures required the applicant to submit his application in the prescribed form in multiple copies to the ministry in charge of licensing, which was the Ministry of Commerce and Industry until August 1961, the ministry with jurisdiction over the product to which the application related from August 1961 to February 1964 and the Ministry of Industrial Development after that.[36] In rare cases, the ministry in charge of licensing invited applications, but the dominant practice was to consider them on a first-come, first-served basis.

Upon receipt, the ministry in charge of licensing sent copies of the application to the administrative ministry in charge of the product to which the application related; one of the DGTD, Textiles Commissioner, Jute Commissioner, Iron and Steel Controller, Coal Controller, sugar and vanaspati directorates in the Department of Food, and the technical adviser in the

Department of Petroleum; the Planning Commission; the Department of Economic Affairs; and the state in which the undertaking was located or proposed to be located. The state was expected to comment on the availability of certain inputs locally, including land, power, water and raw materials. The Planning Commission commented on the compatibility of the proposed project with plan targets and objectives. The Textiles Commissioner, Jute Commissioner, Iron and Steel Controller, Coal Controller, sugar and vanaspati directorates in the Department of Food, and the technical adviser in the Department of Petroleum provided technical evaluations of applications in their respective industries. For applications relating to products in the remaining industries, the DGTD provided a similar technical evaluation.[37] From 1963 onward, the Department of Company Affairs also came to be consulted for any adverse information on the applicant.

The administrative ministry with jurisdiction over the product to which the licence application was related served as the nodal agency for that application. It sought and collected comments from all entities involved in the evaluation process, prepared a summary and sent it along with its recommendations to the Licensing Committee. The Licensing Committee was an advisory body with the industry secretary as its chair and representatives of the Planning Commission and ministries of finance, railways, labour and concerned industries as members.[38] Representatives of state governments could be invited to serve as members as well.

On average, the Licensing Committee met once a month for two hours and often disposed of as many as twenty to thirty cases per hour. In the vast majority of the cases, it accepted the recommendation sent by the nodal ministry. It sent its recommendation to the government. The final decision was taken at the level of the minister in charge of the industry ministry responsible for the administration of IDRA 1951. The industry ministry conveyed the decision to the nodal ministry for the application, which, in turn, informed the applicant.[39]

Two considerations created additional procedural complications for the applicant: capital goods imports and foreign collaborations. In the early years, the Licensing Committee itself did the necessary scrutiny for capital goods imports. In doing so, it gave preference to projects using indigenous machinery and raw material, those producing exportable products and those saving foreign exchange by substituting domestic output for imports. Once the committee approved the industrial licence for projects requiring imports, it conveyed the decision to the Chief Controller of Imports and Exports, which issued the import licences after minimal scrutiny. But the depletion of the sterling balances led the government to appoint the Capital Goods Committee in 1957 to evaluate licence applications for capital goods imports. This change added a significant bureaucratic layer for undertakings seeking a licence requiring capital goods imports.

It can be gathered from a media report that in the early years of the licensing regime, the Licensing Committee was also empowered to give approval for foreign collaboration.[40] But procedures evolved over time, with the approval authority divided between finance and commerce ministries. In January 1959, the government additionally set up an inter-ministerial Foreign Agreements Committee for clearances on foreign collaborations in cases that fell outside the authority of finance and commerce ministries.

To minimize delays, the government began issuing a Condition Letter indicating its intention to grant the licence once the relevant agencies gave clearances for capital goods imports and foreign collaboration. After 1959, it adopted the practice of issuing the industrial licence, leaving it to the applicant to obtain clearances for capital goods imports and foreign collaboration. But this switch in practice added to delays in starting operations. Therefore, following the recommendation of the Swaminathan Committee, in February 1964, the government adopted the practice of issuing a Letter of Intent. But this letter was equivalent to the earlier Condition Letter and therefore failed to solve the problem of delays.

To lighten the burden of licensing authorities and expedite the disposal of applications, in December 1959, the government decided to delegate the decision-making authority in certain cases to the administrative ministry in charge of the products to which the licence application was related. For this purpose, it created a Free List and a Banned List. The former contained products with considerable scope for capacity expansion and the latter those with sufficient existing capacity. For products on the Free List, the ministry was authorized to issue the licence independently without sending the application to the licensing committee. But the practice was discontinued in December 1962 because the government felt it resulted in many unqualified applicants receiving licences. For products on the Banned List, the ministry in charge of the product could reject the application independently. This list was revised periodically and remained in operation until after Nehru died.

Role of the Directorate General of Technical Development (DGTD)

The DGTD served as the principal technical agency to advise the government on licensing applications and other matters related to the planning and development of industries. From 1951 to 1962, the agency was known as the Development Wing and existed as a separate office in the Ministry of Commerce and Industry. In November 1962, it was designated as the DGTD and placed first in the Ministry of Economic and Defense Coordination, then in the Ministry of Supply and Technical Development, and finally moved back to the Ministry of Industrial Development and Company Affairs.[41]

From a small group of technical officers initially, the DGTD grew into a large organization with specialized directorates dealing with different groups of industries. By the middle of 1965, it had 170 engineers and other technical personnel.[42]

It came to be responsible for advising the government on all technical matters relating to industries other than those for which separate technical agencies had been set up. The latter included textiles, jute, iron and steel, coal, sugar, vanaspati and petroleum.

For industries under its jurisdiction, the DGTD advised the government on technical matters relating to applications for industrial licences, imports of capital goods and raw materials, allocation of foreign exchange and scarce raw materials, such as cement and pig iron, fixation of production targets and foreign collaborations. It also served as a technical consultant to public-sector undertakings and autonomous and statutory organizations such as the Tariff Commission, Industrial Finance Corporation and the National Industrial Development Corporation. It kept track of the implementation of licences and collected and compiled data relating to installed capacity and actual production.[43]

Implications for Efficiency

We have already seen that the translation of broad objectives and policy into the sector- and sub-sector-level investments and then into product-level production and capacity targets had been made without applying any cost-benefit analysis or other economic principles. Nor did the planning process predicate the phasing out of production targets over time or their division between the public and private sectors on any efficiency criteria. As it turned out, translating production targets into enterprise-level investments through licensing followed a similar path. Drawing on the excellent analysis and evidence amassed by Bhagwati and Desai, several points are worthy of repetition in brief.[44]

First, all evidence indicates that no economic efficiency criteria were applied in the evaluation of the applications for licences. The DGTD was heavily staffed by engineers who may have had at best qualifications to assess the projects from a technical feasibility viewpoint but not economic efficiency. The administrative ministry, which coordinated the inputs of different authorities involved in the evaluation process, summarized the comments, formulated its recommendations on their basis and sent them to the Licensing Committee. The Licensing Committee, which took decisions at the rate of twenty to thirty applications per hour, could not have carried out its own evaluation. There is no evidence to suggest that the DGTD or the coordinating administrative ministry carried out even back-of-the-envelope economic rate of return calculations on the projects. A parliamentary committee that examined the entire process in great detail and submitted its report in 1967 concluded in bold letters thus,[45]

> The Committee are concerned to note that since the inception of the licensing system under the Industries (Development and Regulation) Act, 1951, no general principles/guidelines have been laid down which are followed for the consideration of applications for grant of an industrial license for establishing a new undertaking/expansion of existing undertaking under the Act although the Rules specifically provide for it. It is obvious that in the absence of such principles/guidelines, the merits of each application are apt to be judged on an ad hoc basis.

Second, in addition to the absence of an economic evaluation of *individual* projects, the process failed to allow for a rational choice among alternative projects. The approval process worked on a first-come-first-served basis, which implied that if well-connected entrepreneurs managed to submit applications early on and got them approved and their projects sufficed to hit the capacity target set by the planning authorities, the door to latecomers would close even if their projects would have delivered superior outcomes in terms of productivity and product prices. In his report, R.K. Hazari documented a clear dominance of the well-connected and large business houses in a large number of approved applications during the years of his examination. Concerning one business house, Birla, he made the following scathing observation:[46]

> It is difficult to evaluate the multitude of Birla applications in almost every product without a close and complete follow-up of developments after the consideration of applications by the Licensing Committee. The data in hand indicate abiding or at least persevering interest in a tremendous variety of products, interest which at times defies several deferments or rejections of applications to attain consummation in approval, interest which seeks to overwhelm the relevant authorities with multiple proposals the moment suitable opportunities offer themselves. This performance is unrivalled, and is not to be belittled or underestimated. Whether and if so, to what extent, this performance actually blocks the entry of other, existing or potential, entrepreneurs is an open question.

The parliamentary committee reporting in 1967, which looked into the issue in detail, also concluded that the bureaucratic process had failed to prioritize higher productivity projects over lower productivity ones. After reporting its detailed investigation, it went on to recommend,[47]

> The Committee feel that at the present stage of development of Indian economy, it is essential that emphasis should be placed on establishment of most competitive industrial units so that the end products are available to the public at competitive and low prices. The Committee, therefore, recommend that Government should evolve a suitable procedure for inviting applications by public notice from prospective entrepreneurs, who should be given adequate time to enclose with their applications feasibility reports indicating the capital cost, the foreign exchange components, the cost and sale price per unit

etc. so that applications may be judged on the basis of their competitiveness.

Third, exemption thresholds for excluding undertakings from licensing were based on no specified economic criteria. In all likelihood, they were set with the view to contain the burden of an excessive number of applications on the licensing authorities. But a possible fallout from it may have been the proliferation of small units exhibiting higher production costs than would have obtained in larger units requiring a licence. Furthermore, given that there was no tracking of the production capacities of these small undertakings, it is conceivable that they led to a divergence between target capacities and actual capacities created.

Finally, in addition to bureaucratic delays to which I have already drawn attention, bureaucratic processes introduced avoidable uncertainties in the economic decision-making process by the undertakings. How much capacity expansion would be considered substantial enough to require a licence, what would constitute a new product for which a separate licence must be sought even if the product is manufactured using the existing capacity, and whether an additional factory by an existing undertaking would require a licence for a new undertaking or that for substantial expansion gave rise to uncertainties that arose from the lack of clarity in the rules even taking the presence of licensing as given.

Price and Distribution Controls

In addition to investment licensing, the Nehru era was also characterized by price and distribution controls on some consumer goods and inputs. Not all goods subject to price control were subject to distribution control. Products subject to one or both controls included automobiles, scooters, commercial vehicles, cement, sugar, iron and steel, non-ferrous metals, coal, fertilizers, cotton textiles, medicines, kerosene and other petroleum products, ethyl alcohol and molasses, bicycles, cotton, and cotton yarn and textiles.

The need for distribution control arose from price control since a ceiling on the price below the free-market price meant the demand for the product exceeded its supply. The only way to clear the shortage was to let the price violate the ceiling or distribute the available supply administratively according to some prioritization of potential buyers. The question was then how those priorities were set by the government.

Upon being quizzed on this issue by a 1967 parliamentary committee, the then Secretary of the Ministry of Industrial Development and Company Affairs replied,

> The considerations are different in different cases. In the case of motor cars and scooters, for instance, it will be the shortage of supplies against a very large demand. For commercial vehicles also, partly that will be the consideration and partly the importance of it to the economy of the country. As regards ethyl alcohol and molasses, it is a question of making sure that there is no diversion from proper industrial uses to other less priority uses.[48]

These distinctions meant that no basis for discrimination among various buyers existed in the case of automobiles and scooters, so the distribution was done on a first-come-first-served basis. On the other hand, in the case of ethyl alcohol and molasses, buyers identified as having high priority were granted an allocation, while those assigned a low priority were denied it. In the former case, the process resulted in long queues with buyers having to wait for months, even years, to receive their allocation, while in the latter case, low-priority buyers did not get an allocation.

The controls brought with them the usual inefficiencies. First, unsatisfied demand due to long waits, such as that in the case of automobiles and scooters, or an outright denial of allocation, as in the case of a low-priority cement user, gave rise to the black market. For example, a used scooter came to command a higher price in the black market than the corresponding official, controlled price for a new unit. Second, shortages gave rise to corruption, with potential buyers trying to gain allocations of controlled commodities by offering bribes to officials. Third, to the extent that there was no economically rational basis for identifying priority industries for allocating controlled commodities, the system essentially benefited those lucky enough to access the commodities at the controlled prices. When the controlled commodities were produced in the public sector, and beneficiaries of official allocations happened to be from the private sector, the system effectively resulted in a loss of revenue for the former.[49] Finally, special pockets of priority allocations still got created for products such as scooters and automobiles, which were otherwise allocated on a first-come-first-served basis. For example, a separate priority quota for automobiles was created for government officials. Similarly, anyone who could get a relative abroad to pay for a scooter in dollar terms could get it allocated on a priority basis. Once again, the benefit in these cases went to the well-to-do, leading to a perverse redistribution effect.

Concluding Remarks

The government implemented its industrial policy in two steps. In the first step, the Planning Commission determined the total size of the investment, spelt out its broad sectoral allocation and set product-level production and capacity targets. In the second step, various ministries came together to translate the product-level targets into actual investments in specific undertakings in the public and private sectors. The allocation of investment to private-sector undertakings was done via the issuance of investment licences involving a complex administrative process spread over many ministries.

The discussion of the implementation process in this chapter shows that the decisions on product-level targets and undertaking-level investment allocations largely ended up being ad hoc. For example, specific choices of products and their production targets within heavy industries were not based on any economic criteria. Likewise, the choices of undertaking-level investments to achieve the production targets did not rely on any meaningful cost comparison across different applicants. Each licensing application was evaluated independently, with decisions made in the order in which the applications came. Moreover, the applications were evaluated in terms of their technical feasibility but not economic efficiency. This meant that more efficient producers who were late in making their applications were denied a licence, while the more aggressive applicants with superior knowledge of the system who could act fast got their applications approved even if they were high-cost producers. The premium was on being ahead in the queue and not being the most cost-effective producer.

Given these facts, a natural question is whether there existed an alternative strategy that would have yielded a superior outcome without compromising on the promotion of heavy industries and other objectives set out by Nehru. In answer to this question, Bhagwati and Desai argue that a superior approach, even within the constraints of the same objectives, would have been to limit detailed planning to a handful of key industries, ensure that they got the desired levels of investment and leave the remainder of the decisions to private entrepreneurs. This would have generated greater competition and economic efficiency in production. As the authors recognize, this less bureaucratic and more market-oriented approach would have required greater exchange rate flexibility. The reason is that without it, the government would have still required strict import controls to combat the shortages of foreign exchange, which would have persisted given the overvalued exchange rate. Strict import control, in turn, would have rendered a liberal investment policy ineffective since entrepreneurs would have remained dependent on the government for the allocation of necessary foreign exchange for the imports of machinery and raw materials.

Unfortunately, the government had little appetite for exchange-rate flexibility during the Nehru era. For this reason, prospects that the path suggested by Bhagwati and Desai would have been followed were dim.

This last point reveals the intimate relationship between investment and import decisions in a controlled regime. As long as a project requires imported machinery and raw materials, the decision to issue an investment licence cannot be made without ensuring that foreign-exchange resources necessary to affect those imports are available. As we will see in the next chapter, as long as the sterling balance that India had accumulated during the Second World War on account of its large balance-of-payments surpluses was not exhausted, import policy could remain liberal and did not majorly constrain investment licensing decisions. But once the sterling balances ran out, the availability of foreign exchange became a serious constraint on investment licensing decisions and made the licensing regime an order of magnitude more burdensome.

7

A Liberal Import Regime: 1882–1956

In his writings, Nehru described international trade as an instrument of imperialism and sought self-sufficiency for India. Against this backdrop, trade policy during a significant part of his tenure was remarkably liberal. Moreover, an extensive archival search of the leading newspaper of the time, the *Times of India*, produces no evidence that he intervened in implementing trade policy. At least, going by publicly available accounts, he left the trade policy implementation to his ministers and bureaucrats.

It may be hypothesized that Nehru was principally concerned with industrialization in general and building heavy industry in particular. So long as this objective occupied centre stage, he was willing to leave the details of trade policy to commerce, industry, finance and other line ministries. Rather than deploy protection as an active instrument of industrial policy, he sought to rejig the production basket according to the domestic consumption needs of the citizenry. When import controls were used, they largely resulted from the scarcity of foreign exchange, with the pattern of those controls determined through negotiations among the relevant line ministries and their respective bureaucrats. Though the domestic non-availability condition was systematically applied, especially after the accelerated depletion of foreign-exchange reserves in 1956 led to a tightening of import controls, its primary purpose was the conservation of foreign exchange and not protection.

A possible explanation for the broad support for a liberal import policy during the first ten years following Independence is the existence of a relatively low level of protection and the absence of physical controls on imports during the pre-Second World War era. The experience with a control-free flow of imports for several decades probably inclined many Indians in decision-making positions in the immediate post-Independence era favourably towards a liberal import policy.

Equally and somewhat paradoxically, trade policy measures necessitated by the Second World War prepared the ground for and trained future Indian bureaucrats in deploying the exchange and import controls that would proliferate following the balance-of-payments crisis in 1957. Wartime shortages of goods, as well as shipping space, had led the British government to introduce a strict Empire-wide exchange cum import control regime. Import licensing, open general licensing and 'essentiality' and 'domestic-non-availability' conditions, which India would deploy throughout the second half of the twentieth century, had become commonplace during the first half of the 1940s. Even many of the ill effects of licensing, such as bureaucratic delays and corruption, were visible in the immediate aftermath of the war, even before Independence.

The Bhagwati and Desai book remains the standard source of India's trade policy during the Nehru era. But while these authors provide a vivid picture of the import-policy regime as it existed in the mid-1960s, they do not provide a detailed account of its evolution. They only mention in passing that the import control regime prevailing in 1965 had its origins in the Second World War, that the policy oscillated between liberalization and tight control during the second half of the 1940s, that the period of the First Five-Year Plan (1951–52 to 1955–56) was characterized by progressive liberalization, and that the balance-of-payments crisis after the first plan led to the tightening of the import control regime. Neither they nor other authors offer a detailed account of how these policies evolved and what the political-economy factors underlying them were. I make a special effort in this chapter to fill this important gap in the literature. As a by-product, the stock-taking exercise also yields useful insights into the thinking on import policy in contemporary India. It reveals that the opinion among nearly all relevant constituencies, including political leadership, remained favourable to a liberal import policy until at least 1956. The discussions surrounding the Second Five-Year Plan and a foreign-exchange crisis eventually led to India's inward turn.

This chapter initially considers the import policy from the late nineteenth century till the beginning of the Second World War. This discussion helps us understand the more detailed discussion of the following one and a half decades. It shows that though the World War led to the establishment of a full-throttled foreign-exchange control and import licensing regime, India successfully returned to a more liberal regime from 1945 to 1956. As we will see in the next chapter, this liberal regime failed to sustain itself subsequently due to an acute foreign-exchange shortage that arose in the face of a fixed exchange rate and rising domestic prices relative to those of foreign goods.

From Free Trade to Modest Tariff Protection: 1882–1940

The key objective behind the trade policy pursued by the British government in India until the end of the First World War was preserving producer interests in Great Britain. This objective was best served by maintaining a free-trade regime in India. Fortuitously, the policy coincided with the prevailing free-trade orthodoxy among the British elite, including the ruling class. Accordingly, the British maintained a policy of no import protection in India from 1882 to the end of the First World War. Though the need for additional revenue forced the government to impose a customs duty at the general rate of 5 per cent in 1892, with a lower rate applying to machinery and other inputs, its protectionist impact was neutralized by an equivalent excise duty on the like domestic products.[1] The financial burden of the First World War led the government to raise the general rate of customs duty to 7.5 per cent from 5 per cent and that on machinery, iron and steel, and railway material to 2.5 per cent from 1 per cent. In 1919, an administrative reform led to the devolution of land revenue to provinces. This fact created a need for additional customs revenue. As a result, by March 1922, the general import duty rose to 15 per cent, and customs revenue as a proportion of the total revenue rose to 34 per cent in 1922–23.[2]

In the meantime, in 1921, India was granted fiscal autonomy, which opened the door to a tariff policy responsive to producer interests in India. For the first time, the Indian Fiscal Commission of 1921–22 recommended that an industry could be granted discriminatory protection provided (i) it had natural advantages, (ii) it would not develop without initial protection, and (iii) it would eventually be able to withstand foreign competition without protection.[3]

The Indian Fiscal Commission recommended setting up a permanent Tariff Board to investigate the claims of particular industries for protection and advise the government on implementing such protection. In the event, the government decided to set up a series of temporary tariff boards. Two Tariff Boards were appointed successively in 1923 and 1926 with overlapping years of operation. They were entrusted with evaluating the cases for protecting the steel and cotton textile industries, respectively.[4] The investigation by the first board led to protective duties on steel imports for three years beginning in 1924. However, before the expiry of these duties, the government announced a new set of duties on steel imports for another seven years.[5] The investigation by the second Tariff Board also resulted in protective duties on cotton textiles.

Between 1923 and 1939, tariff boards conducted fifty-one investigations, with thirteen industries receiving temporary protection. The protected industries included iron and steel, cotton textiles, paper and paper pulp, matches, salt, heavy chemicals, sericulture, magnesium chloride, plywood and tea chests, gold thread, wheat and rice.[6] In 1932, under the Ottawa Agreement, India also became a member of the Commonwealth preferential trade area, with India and Britain agreeing to lower tariffs on each other's products while charging higher tariffs on imports from other countries.[7] But the arrangement proved unpopular in India, leading the legislative assembly to vote to discontinue it in 1936.[8]

In 1940, Theodore Gregory, who served as Economic Adviser to the Government of India from 1938 to 1946, studied the tariff burden from 1926–27 to 1936–37. Though I have been unable to track down this study, a contemporary media report provides useful details.[9] According to the latter, Gregory found that the incidence of custom duties was the highest on goods of general consumption, followed by luxuries, raw materials and capital goods in that order. The share of goods of general consumption in total imports as well as total customs revenue fell throughout the study period. In comparison, the share of luxuries remained steady in imports but rose in the customs revenue. The share of capital goods in imports rose while in the customs revenue, it remained unchanged. Raw materials saw their share in imports and the customs revenue rise.

Estimates of import values of and corresponding custom revenues on cotton piece-goods, sugar, iron and steel, and matches allow us to compute the average ad valorem rate of custom duty on these products in 1926–27 and 1936–37. These rates work out to 19.3 per cent and 33.5 per cent, respectively. Given that the four products accounted for 41 per cent of all imports in 1926–27 and 15 per cent in 1936–37 and were among the most heavily protected products, these rates are a good indicator of tariff rates at the high end of the spectrum. Given that no other direct import controls were present then, these rates imply that the protection level before the war was still moderate. This was to change drastically with the onset of the World War, which brought an import-policy regime characterized by foreign-exchange control and direct import and export controls. This regime not only survived the war's end but became a centrepiece of the command-and-control system beginning in the early 1960s.

The Advent of Foreign-exchange cum Import Control Regime: 1940–45

The Second World War brought with it foreign exchange control and systematic direct import controls for the first time to the shores of India. Though the end of the war would lead to considerable loosening of the controls, triggered by a balance-of-payments crisis in 1957–58, the regime would revert to more or less wartime severity for at least two decades. It would see some piecemeal liberalization in the 1980s but would not begin to be genuinely dismantled until 1991.

Exchange Control

The Bank of England and the British Treasury had anticipated that disruptions resulting from the war would undermine their ability to maintain free convertibility of pound sterling into the dollar and other currencies on the gold standard at fixed exchange rates.[10] Therefore, they had begun preparing for an orderly transition to a system of exchange control in coordination with its colonies as early as April 1939. These preparations culminated in the implementation of a foreign-exchange system throughout the Empire except Canada, Hong Kong and Newfoundland at the beginning of the war on 3 September 1939.[11]

Under this system, Britain brought together the Empire countries (other than Canada, Newfoundland and Hong Kong) to form what came to be called the sterling area. Before the war, these countries had held all of their foreign exchange earnings in London in pound sterling. Each country deposited its foreign exchange earnings at the Bank of England, which credited an equivalent amount of sterling, converted at fixed exchange rates, to the country's sterling account. With sterling freely convertible at the time, the country could convert its sterling holdings back into any of the other currencies as per its requirements. But with the outbreak of the war, Britain ended the free convertibility of sterling into other currencies, and this arrangement broke down.

Under the new arrangement, Britain required each sterling area country to hand over all its export earnings from convertible-currency countries such as the United States, Japan, Canada, the Philippines, Sweden, Belgium, Switzerland and Argentina to the Bank of England, which held them in a common pool. Because the United States dollar was the most important foreign currency then, the pool became known as the Empire Dollar Pool. The country could draw convertible currencies out of this pool, but these drawings had no relationship to its contribution to it. Instead, the country was required to certify that the import for which the currency was drawn was essential and not available from within-sterling-area countries. *Essentiality* and *non-availability* conditions for imports, which would become integral to India's import control regime for nearly half a century, were thus born. Any excess contributions to the Empire Dollar Pool by a country over its drawings from it remained deposited in its sterling account. Therefore, countries such as India, which contributed much more to the Empire Dollar Pool than they drew from it, accumulated large amounts of sterling balances over the years. By the end of March 1945, India's accumulated sterling balances stood at £1022 million.[12]

The regime put in place by Britain required that drawings from the Empire Dollar Pool satisfy the twin conditions of essentiality and non-availability of the import item from within-sterling-area countries. Therefore, each member country had to adopt an import control regime. The country was allowed to define essentiality in its own way, and it turned out that as applied, it varied in strictness not only across countries at any time but also within the same country over time, depending on the quantum of foreign exchange available in the Empire Dollar Pool. Once the country gave a declaration that a particular item satisfied essentiality and non-availability conditions, the Bank of England released the authorized volume of the desired convertible currency with no questions asked.

Direct Import and Export Controls

The exchange control system in each country was reinforced by a set of export and import controls. Export controls were largely motivated by considerations directly related to the war or shortage of supply of essential items within the sterling area. India introduced the first set of controls as early as 8 September 1939 by imposing a ban on the exports of five categories of items to the enemy territories (as defined in the Defence of India Rules of 1939).[13] The categories included arms and ammunition, fuels of all kinds, means of transport and communication, and foodstuff and clothing. On 25 September 1939, the Department of Commerce announced additional export controls that applied globally. It also divided the items subject to the controls into five categories, with items in four categories restricted to alleviate wartime shortages and those in the remaining one to prevent them from reaching the enemy territories. Exports of items in one of the categories were entirely prohibited, while those in the remaining four required a licence.[14]

In March 1940, exports to countries on the American continent (excluding Canada and Argentina), Belgium, the Netherlands and Switzerland became subject to restrictions. Initially, the restrictions applied only to jute manufactures and rubber exports, but by June 1940, they became applicable to all exports to the United States and Switzerland. The restrictions were aimed at ensuring that the convertible-currency proceeds of exports ended up in the hands of the Reserve Bank of India and were eventually deposited to the Empire Dollar Pool.[15]

India introduced the first set of import controls on 27 May 1940, a solid eight months after the war had begun.[16] The government notified a list of sixty-eight items whose imports from hard-currency countries became subject to restrictions. Of these items, thirty-four were subject to prohibition, while the remaining thirty-four required a licence. In turn, the quantum of permitted imports was fixed at some fraction of the importer's imports in the pre-war base year beginning on 1 September 1938. The items placed in the prohibited category were viewed as luxuries and therefore deemed prima facie non-essential. In the case of other items, the importer was required to establish essentiality. Because the purpose of these import controls was the conservation of hard currencies, they were applied to imports from hard-currency countries only. Imports from sterling-area countries were permitted freely, at least in the early stages of the war.[17]

In the following one year, the list of items subject to import controls grew longer. An exhaustive list of items notified as being subject to import controls is not feasible, but a search of the *Times of India* archives yields a new list every few months until July 1941. A notification on adding paper, pasteboard and several chrome compounds to the import-control list was issued on 27 December 1940.[18] A much longer list of as many as fifty items was notified on 9 May 1941.[19] Cotton twist and yarn ribbons, artificial silk and staple fibre yarn, cotton piece goods and coral came under import licensing on 21 July 1941.[20]

A near absence of reports of additional lists of import items being notified after July 1941 suggests that the controls had come to cover nearly all major import items by now. Bhagwati and Desai explicitly state that the import control regime had come to embrace 'practically all imports by January 1942'.[21] As the war progressed, shipping space emerged as an important constraint on the movement of goods between countries, with the result that licensing was also extended to sterling-area countries.[22] Indeed, the shortage of shipping space also led to restrictions on exports destined to countries within and outside the sterling area.[23] The existence of widespread controls on within-sterling-area trade is also confirmed by the appearance of several media stories in 1945 and 1946 on government orders notifying the shift of within-sterling-area import items from the restricted to the open general licence section of the Import Trade Control Schedule.

A Liberal Beginning in the Post-Independence Era: 1945–56

It is tempting to conjecture that once the controls had been put in place, they would create vested interests that would come together to perpetuate them. It would also appear that Indian national leadership, which had acquired considerable influence over policymaking by this time, as exemplified by the Statement of Industrial Policy of 1945, would be sympathetic to maintaining the controls, even tightening them. Surprisingly, however, as the war made its way towards its end, India witnessed the emergence of considerable support for import liberalization. Not only did business interests seek easier access to machinery and inputs, worries about inflation also created pressure for liberalization of consumer goods imports. What is even more surprising is that the support for liberal trade policies was broad-based and was sustained until the mid-1950s. It only began to wane after the discussions on the Second Five-Year Plan moved the opinion within the leadership and among the Indian elite progressively towards greater physical control of the economy. With ambitious investment targets to build heavy industries leading to a rapid expansion of imports of machinery and inputs, poor domestic crops resulting in expanding food grain imports and exports performing poorly, the sterling balances ran out by 1957. The natural outcome was a foreign-exchange crisis. There being no political support for the devaluation of the rupee, a dramatic tightening of the import-control regime was the result.

A search of the *Times of India* archives from 1945 to 1955 reveals the existence of broad-based support for import liberalization. I offer two specific examples from the second half of the 1940s illustrating this point. Later, in our discussion of the first half of the 1950s, we will encounter more such instances.

Powerful Voices for Liberalization: Two Examples

In 1946, the *Times of India* published four editorials in quick succession exposing the ills of the control regime under the titles 'Import control excuses', 'End import control', 'Blocked imports' and 'More import muddles' on 15 May, 30 May, 20 June and 17 July, respectively.[24] A common theme of these editorials was that the import-control regime had outlived its utility, and the government needed to allow a freer flow of imports into the country. The following excerpt from the editorial of 30 May 1946 gives some flavour of the depth of dissatisfaction with import controls expressed by the newspaper:[25]

> Promises to do their best to mend their ways have been made by import control authorities since a protest against the department's corruption and inordinate delays was made in these columns. Yet the same state of affairs revealed by our correspondents shows clearly that attempts to clear up corruption and speed the disposal of applications by decentralizing control and increasing staff will not meet the case. A sound case has been established for thoroughgoing curtailment of this department's activities, if not its complete abolition. Apart from the charges of corruption and favouritism and the extraordinary policy of allowing the import Controller to do the Tariff Board's work, there is reliable evidence of unbelievable laxity in the department's work. Applications for import licenses not only remain

> unanswered for months, and even for more than a year, but they are frequently lost. Such a state of affairs implies shocking organization and it is a scandal that the import trade of a country should be at the mercy of such bungling.

As the editorial made its way towards conclusion, it turned harsher and went on to make a case for the complete removal of the import-control regime:

> At present, bad handling of the control policy is simply bolstering the black market which will not disappear until there is free flow of goods. Such a flow is also required to check inflation—a menace which has not yet been removed. When all these circumstances are taken into consideration, it will be apparent that the necessity for import control has ceased—even if it ever existed. . . . The sooner this major blot is removed from India's administration the better.

The sentiment expressed in the *Times of India* editorials is echoed repeatedly in the 'Letters to the Editor' published from May to July 1946. The authors of the letters include established importers, owners of businesses dependent on imports and private individuals with knowledge of the system.

The second example of pro-liberalization thinking relates to the then Minister for Commerce K.C. Neogy. A *Times of India* report on his speech on 26 February 1949 testifies to his enlightened thinking.[26] The report states,

> The mere fact of control over imports, the Minister said, even when liberally used, tends to restrict trade and unnecessarily to inflate consumer prices and the profit margins in imported goods. These prices are a legitimate cause of discontentment among consumers, while the high profit margins resulting from restricted imports lead to a disorganization and demoralization of trade.

Continuing to report on the speech, the story adds, 'Import restrictions were not the appropriate method of affording protection to industry, he [Neogy] added, and it would be open to other countries to retaliate and restrict exports from India.'[27]

Non-linear Progress Towards Liberalization: 1945–50

Though modest liberalization began with the winding down of the war in 1945, imports in any given year being dependent on the availability of foreign exchange that year, progress was non-linear. For India, sterling balances accumulated during the war constituted a major potential source of foreign exchange. But because the United Kingdom suffered from massive foreign debt and simultaneously suffered from large balance-of-payments deficits in the immediate post-war years, it was unwilling to release these balances freely either for imports from within the sterling area or for conversion into other currencies. Therefore, access to the sterling balances and their convertibility into hard currencies remained thorny issues between India and the United Kingdom.

Under an interim agreement reached on 14 August 1947 after heavy lobbying by India, the United Kingdom agreed to split India's sterling account into two: a No. 1 account, which India could use freely for current purchases, and a blocked No. 2 account, which could only be used to make payments for such purposes as acquiring surplus military stores, discharging pension liabilities and financing capital outflows from India to the rest of the sterling area (mainly savings and repatriation of investments of British citizens in India). The initial allocation of sterling balances in the No. 1 account was small, and only a part was convertible into non-sterling currencies.[28] Therefore, the transfer of additional sterling balances from the No. 2 account to the No. 1 account remained a prickly issue between the two sides, and India had to negotiate hard to gain access to its sterling balances.[29] It was not until sometime in the second half of the 1950s that it could draw down all its balances.

While small steps towards unwinding the import control regime were taken during 1945 and the first half of 1946 through a shift of several items from restricted categories on the Import Trade Control Schedule to the open general licence for imports from within-sterling-area countries, the process greatly accelerated in the second half of 1946. The government issued licences for imports from non-sterling-area countries liberally as long as the twin conditions of essentiality and non-availability from within the sterling area were fulfilled. In addition, it placed a handful of items on a universal open general licence, meaning they could be imported from all countries without obtaining an individual licence.

The effect of this relatively aggressive liberalization was to create massive pressure on the balance of payments, which in turn forced the government to reverse the liberalization the following year. Several items were returned from the open general licence to restricted categories. More importantly, the government replaced qualitative controls with quantitative controls by dividing imports into three categories: free, restricted and prohibited. Items in the first category were placed on the open general licence, those in the second were licensed up to a monetary ceiling and those in the third were not permitted to be imported at all.[30] From mid-1947, the government also adopted foreign exchange budgeting whereby the Ministry of Finance estimated the likely availability of foreign exchange for each half of the year and then set ceilings on its allocations to individual ministries such that their sum would not exceed the available amount. The budgeting fell into disuse by 1953 only to be vigorously revived amid the 1957 foreign-exchange crisis.[31]

Measures taken in 1947 helped ease foreign-exchange scarcity and paved the way for import liberalization from sterling-area and soft-currency countries in 1948. Initially, this was done in January by raising monetary ceilings on the imports of several consumer goods.[32] Subsequently, in July and twice in September, several items were placed on the open general licence for import from sterling and soft-currency countries.[33]

Licensing on imports from hard-currency-area countries saw some tightening in the first half of 1949 and the removal of certain items from the open general licence for sterling-area and soft-currency countries in the second half.[34] These measures brought the balance-of-payments situation under control, permitting a more liberal policy in 1950. In the first half of the latter year, the monetary ceiling on imports was raised with licences issued more liberally from sterling-area and soft-currency countries for some items and from hard-currency countries for others.[35] This liberal stance was maintained in the second half with some decentralization by delegating the licence-issuing authority to ports. The policy for this period also opened the door to importers being permitted to enter formal commitments for the six months following its term, for the January–June 1951 period.[36]

An Era of Uninterrupted Liberal Import Policy: 1951–56

In early July 1950, the government appointed the Import Control Inquiry Committee under the chairmanship of G.L. Mehta, a planning commission member, to conduct a comprehensive investigation of the import control regime and recommend improvements.[37] The committee submitted its report in mid-October 1950 and suggested several reforms to liberalize and simplify the licensing system. It recommended raising the import ceiling for the following two years to Rs 4 billion (400 crore) annually. Its other suggestions included decentralization of licensing procedures by allowing port authorities to issue licences, making the policy more predictable by avoiding frequent changes and allowing newcomers to become established importers. The committee also recommended a priority list for imports, placing raw and semi-finished materials for existing industries at the top and non-essential goods at the bottom.[38] The government's resolution of 4 January 1951 accepted the committee's recommendations with some modifications.[39]

An era of a more liberal import policy lasting till 1957 followed the recommendations of the Import Control Inquiry Committee. The liberal policy could be sustained for this relatively long stretch due to improved access to sterling balances and satisfactory export performance. The process began with a notification on 12 March 1951, which doubled the value of licences for the January–June 1951 period and extended their validity until December 1951. It also expanded the list of items on the open general licence.[40] Subsequent six-monthly import policy announcements till 1957 largely maintained this liberal stance, tightening imports in certain sectors while liberalizing in others based on the perceptions of domestic availability and essentiality of products. While maintaining a liberal stance towards imports of raw materials and machinery, the policy also remained sensitive to the needs of consumer goods imports through open general licensing for some items and issuance of import licences to established importers for others. For instance, imports of some consumer items had been tightened in the second half of 1952, but this was rectified in the first half of 1953.[41]

T.T. Krishnamachari (TTK), Minister of Commerce and Industry around this time, held a generally liberal attitude towards foreign trade. This was reflected in a speech he delivered to the Import Advisory Council on 22 May 1953, in which he stated, 'I cannot foresee our being compelled to impose drastic cuts on imports all around. On the contrary, if anything, we hope to ease the position.'[42] He went on to note that there was a need to increase imports further, given the increased demand for goods following increased development expenditure. He also mentioned that he could take this process a step further by raising import quotas on certain items after the finance minister had raised import duties on those items on 1 March 1953.

The import policy for the second half of 1953, which the government issued on 24 June 1953, liberalized imports of a range of items consisting of machinery, raw materials and consumer goods. As regards other items, continuity was maintained with the previous six-month period. An important feature of this policy was a wholesale simplification of procedures.[43] An editorial in the *Times of India* on 1 December 1953 expressed satisfaction with the policy changes in these terms, 'The Commerce Ministry has every reason to be proud of having improved its administration of import and export controls. Complaints about delays, corruption and patronage are rarely heard now.'[44]

A speech by the Minister of Commerce D.P. Karmarkar on 28 November 1953 further illustrates the strong support for a liberal import policy at the political level during this period. Speaking to the Import Advisory Council, the minister explicitly rejected the suggestion that import control should be used to protect Indian industry. He argued that this was better left to tariff regulation. Towards the end of the event, he made the case against protection as a means of industrialization in stronger terms. To quote from a contemporary media report,

> Summing up the discussions, the Minister for Commerce, Mr. Karmarkar, said that everyone was agreed that ultimately national interest had to be served by increasing national production. The Government appreciated that protection through import controls was not a scientific remedy. Psychologically too, they must develop the confidence in Indian industry that they could successfully compete with imported goods from any part of the world. The Government wanted to pursue a policy which would not be stifling to industry and at the same time introduce as much of free trade as possible.[45]

Import policy for the first half of 1954 retained much of the policy in the prior six-month period with minor tweaking. Import quotas for some consumer items were enhanced while for others, reduced. Provision was made for a larger volume of imports of industrial equipment, raw materials and consumer goods. Several liberalizing procedural changes were also made.[46] The policy for the second half of 1954 left the bulk of the policy of the first half unchanged. Its main change was moderate increases in the import quota of sixty items, including several consumer goods items, and a scaling down of quotas for thirty-five items. The policy also opened the door wider to small importers and newcomers to the import business.[47] Later, in September 1954, when the government raised customs duties on several items through the enactment of the Indian Tariff (Second Amendment) Bill of 1954, it considerably liberalized the import quotas on those items as well as some others. An interesting reason the government gave for this liberalization was to encourage the import of superior foreign products to encourage indigenous manufacturers to improve the quality of their products.[48] Unfortunately, this important connection between imports and local product quality was forgotten later when the domestic availability of a product, regardless of its quality, became the basis of a complete ban on the imports of that product.

Import policy for the first half of 1955 exhibited stability with some tweaking of licensing in the liberal direction. But it introduced one important change for the worse: for the first time, it introduced canalization of imports (meaning the concentration of all imports in the hands of a single government agency) of a few items in the 'public interest'. Items identified for canalization included silk, soda ash, caustic soda, sodium bicarbonate and muriate of potash. The Silk Board was identified as the agency to canalize the imports of silk, with agencies for the canalization of other items left for future announcements.[49] For the second half of the year, the policy remained largely unchanged. Quotas were expanded for a few items but also cut for some because domestic supply was available. The policy also opened some items to imports not previously permitted.[50]

The trend of liberalizing imports of some items and restricting others on the margin while maintaining the stability of policy in the bulk of the items continued during both halves of 1956.[51] The year saw two significant developments, however. First, the government launched the State Trading Corporation (STC) in June 1956 as the agency in complete charge of India's trade with communist countries, where governments had the sole authority to conduct foreign trade. STC also became the canalizing agency for products such as raw silk and cement, whose imports became the monopoly of the government.[52] Second, with the launch of the Second Five-Year Plan during this year, the policy for the second half of the year made an effort to better integrate import policy with industrial policy. This reinforced the emerging trend in favour of imports of heavy machinery and heavy electrical goods while also opening the door wider to items such as spare parts, machine tools and components required for the healthy growth of the industry. To its credit, the policy did not neglect consumer goods, liberalizing several items in this category.

Concluding Remarks

In this chapter, I have discussed India's import policy from 1882 to 1956, with emphasis on the last seventeen years ranging from 1940 to 1956. Until early 1920, motivated purely by self-interest, the British government followed a free trade policy with no protectionist duties imposed. With the freedom movement gathering steam and domestic industry gaining a voice in the system, the government opened the door to protection for specific industries. But even then, such protection remained temporary and modest. Only during the Second World War did the balance-of-payments difficulties faced by the British lead to the adoption of Empire-wide exchange control, which had to be reinforced by a strict import control regime. The war years brought to India import licensing and introduced the notions of essentiality and indigenous non-availability of imports as pre-conditions for issuing an import licence. The idea of open general licensing also had its birth during this era. Frequent complaints relating to bureaucratic delays and corruption in issuing licences during the 1960s and beyond could also be witnessed aplenty during this period.

The end of the war witnessed considerable support for the liberalization of import controls. Because the British pound remained subject to foreign-exchange control and India was a member of the sterling area, the rupee remained subject to exchange control. Therefore, complete dismantling of the import control regime was not an option. Instead, liberalization took the form of the expansion of open general licensing and liberal issuance of import licences for items on the restricted list. Because foreign-exchange availability oscillated between scarcity and plenty, import licensing also oscillated between tightening and loosening control. But from 1951–52 to 1956–57, with the foreign-exchange situation of the United Kingdom improving, India's access to the sterling balances, which it had accumulated during the war years through balance-of-payments surpluses, improved as well. This liberal availability of foreign exchange allowed India to maintain a reasonably liberal import regime. But the accumulated sterling balances eventually ran out, and India faced a foreign-exchange crisis in 1957. What followed is the subject matter of the next chapter.

8

A Highly Restrictive Import Regime: 1957–1964

The year 1957 proved to be a watershed year for import policy. Two factors contributed to initiating changes that eventually turned India into a near autarky. First, over the years, higher inflation at home than abroad combined with a fixed nominal exchange rate rendered domestic products progressively less competitive than their foreign counterparts. Over time, this fact led to a steady rise in import demand and stagnation in export revenues. Initially, the government maintained a liberal import policy by drawing down on the sterling balances. But a sharp decline in the sterling balances from Rs 7.42 billion in January 1956 to Rs 5.39 billion in November 1956 due to a rapid expansion in imports left B.K. Nehru, then a senior official in the finance ministry, deeply disturbed at this rapid 'hemorrhage in our foreign exchange resources'.[1] The immediate reaction of the ministry was to begin pressing brakes on imports to slow down the depletion of the sterling balances in the remainder of the year.[2]

The second development leading to the inward turn in the import policy around this time was the launch of the ambitious Second Five-Year Plan with its key goal of developing heavy industries locally. In the process, all ministries were drawn into rethinking their policies in ways that would aid the effort to give a big push to the economy in general and heavy industries in particular. For import policy, this meant a turn away from consumer goods imports to spare foreign exchange for the imports of investment goods, raw materials and components used in heavy industries and not produced domestically. Therefore, the import policy was to reorder priorities away from consumer goods towards machinery, raw materials and components not available at home.

Import Policy Tightens

These considerations led the government to take two critical steps towards tightening the import-policy regime. First, it decided to re-introduce foreign-exchange budgeting beginning on 1 January 1957.[3] Foreign-exchange budgeting consisted of placing a ceiling on the total volume of foreign exchange available for imports and administratively allocating it among its different uses in a manner I shall describe later in this chapter.

Second, the government began making its import policy progressively more restrictive. Immediately, the import policy announced for the first half of 1957 made drastic cuts in import quotas of 509 items and outright denial of licences for several items perceived as non-essential. A contemporary *Times of India* report stated, 'The import policy for January-June 1957, more restrictive than any time during the last five years, is designed to effect a saving of Rs. 30 crores [Rs. 300 million] in foreign exchange.'[4] It went on to add, 'Liquors, cigarette, toilet requisites, paper, woolen fabrics, cutlery, motor parts, species, betelnuts, fruits, tallow, lead pencils, patent and proprietary medicines and coal tar dyes are among the commodities whose imports will be cut.' These and other items impacted by the cuts testify to the long list of consumer goods whose imports had been permitted more liberally until the end of 1956. They also included musk oil, shoes, billiard accessories, golf clubs, roller skates, fish, bacon, ham, condensed milk, butter, powdered milk, fruits, cocoa, jams, jellies and fruit juices.

Until 1956, separate licences had been issued for sterling-area countries and dollar-area countries due to the greater dollar scarcity. But given the dwindling stock of sterling balances, the pound became scarce as well, and the government decided to substantially reduce the discrimination against the dollar by permitting the holders of licences for imports from sterling-area countries to utilize them for imports from dollar-area countries more liberally.[5] From the importers' viewpoint, this was a positive step since it allowed them to buy their imports from the cheapest source available regardless of the currency area of the seller.

At the end of the first half of 1957, the government aligned the import policy to the financial year. Therefore, rather than announce the next policy for the entire second half of the calendar year, it restricted it to three months spanning July to September, and followed it up by a six-month policy covering the second half of the fiscal year 1957–58 that is, 1 October 1957 to 31 March 1958.[6] Both policies adhered to the spirit of the predecessor policy for January–June 1957. The policy for July–September did away with open general licences except in the case of poultry, fish, fresh vegetables and eggs from Pakistan and, with rare exceptions, restricted new import licences to capital goods and essential raw materials. These measures translated into the established importers being denied any new licences.[7] The policy for the October–March period continued the ban on open general licences and placed a total ban on many consumer goods imports, including tobacco manufactures, woollen fabrics, bicycles, watches, fountain pens, crockery, cutlery, glassware and shaving blades. More essential consumer goods were permitted but in reduced quantities. These goods included milk foods, species, betelnuts, cinema films, sports goods, and drugs and medicines. A more liberal view was taken of imports of raw materials, spares and replacement machinery.[8]

Though these restrictive measures alleviated foreign-exchange shortages in the longer run, they were less effective in the short run. The reason was that an estimated Rs 4.35 billion worth of unutilized import licences had existed at the beginning of July 1957. As a result, the sterling balances declined by a hefty Rs 1.13 billion between the middle of June to September as against Rs 0.64 billion in the preceding three months.[9] This trend continued in the second half of 1957–58, resulting in total imports during the full fiscal year exceeding those in 1956–57.

Import policy for the first half of 1958–59 relaxed imports of parts and raw materials for some industries considered essential, such as printing machinery, agricultural tractors and photographic paper, but slashed the imports of consumer goods such as fish, fruits and milk foods. The net effect of these changes was to hold the total import expenditure at the same level as the second half of 1957–58.[10] The policy for the second half of 1958–59 also remained restrictive, with the possibility[11] of some external assistance allowing the total expenditure on imports to be raised marginally by Rs 40 million.[12]

The policy in the following three years followed the same pattern with minor tweaks. In particular, there was a further movement away from established importers to actual users, and incentives in the form of more liberal imports were introduced for exporters. The policy in the first half of 1959–60 made marginal adjustments in the composition of imports, leaving the overall size of the foreign exchange budget unchanged from the second half of 1958–59.[13] The overall expenditure on imports was kept unchanged in the second half as well, with exporters providing an incentive such that they could use the sales proceeds of additional exports to finance capital goods imports.[14] The process of incentivizing exporters continued in 1960–61 and 1961–62 with small tweaks to imports of specific products in each six-monthly policy but no fundamental change.[15]

On the recommendation of the Mudaliar Committee report on export and import policies and procedures, submitted in March 1962, import policy was made an annual affair beginning with the fiscal year 1962–63.[16] Correspondingly, import licences also became annual though foreign-exchange allocation remained a twice-a-year affair. Because of the possibility of a reduction in foreign-exchange allocation in the second half of the year, the licence holder was allowed to affect only half of the authorized imports in the first six months. He had to get the licence revalidated for the second half of the year with the possibility of reduced entitlement of imports.[17]

The policy for 1962–63 restricted the imports by established importers further by banning sixty-five new items. Though the licensing of a few items, such as coal tar dyes, newsprint and transport equipment, was subject to marginal liberalization, broadly speaking, restrictions on the imports of raw materials and machinery remained as stringent as ever.[18] Furthermore, in December 1962, a drop in the foreign-exchange reserves by Rs 500 million in the preceding twelve months led the government to ban the imports of consumer goods items such as liquor and tape recorders. Cuts were also applied to the imports of motor vehicle parts by established importers and certain items imported by actual users.[19]

Finally, the policy for 1963–64 brought some relief to established importers by expanding the list of permitted imports by them from 91 to 170 items and restoration of some of the cuts in the quotas in the previous year. In addition, the policy gave greater consideration to the needs of defence and export industries. But overall liberalization was limited, with extra foreign exchange in the first half of the year limited to Rs 10 to 20 million over what had been provisioned in the second half of 1962–63. Thus, in sum, the policy from 1957 until the end of the Nehru era remained highly restrictive.[20]

A Digression to the Devaluation Debate

During 1957 and 1958, opposition members of Parliament had repeatedly demanded an inquiry into the mismanagement of foreign exchange reserves, but the government successfully rebuffed them.[21] An interesting proposal from the viewpoint of contemporary economic thought around this time was for a devaluation of the rupee, though it found no takers beyond its proponent, B.R. Shenoy. In an article published on 5 May 1958, Shenoy reasoned that given the fixed nominal exchange rate, the higher inflation at home than abroad had left Indian exports less competitive in foreign markets and imports more competitive in the Indian market. This lack of competitiveness of the Indian vis-à-vis foreign goods had brought the balance of payments under great pressure. By making foreign exchange more expensive in rupee terms, a devaluation would restore the competitiveness of Indian vis-à-vis foreign goods and alleviate this pressure.[22]

Unfortunately, Shenoy was a lonely voice. In its editorial on 25 June 1958, the *Times of India* questioned the wisdom of devaluation, arguing that the problem of Indian exports was not price but their quality and marketing techniques. Regarding imports, it argued that devaluation would hurt by making them more expensive in rupee terms.[23] A contemporary media story reported Nehru describing 'as fantastic nonsense the suggestions by some people that the rupee should be devalued' in his monthly press conference on 3 July 1958. It quoted Nehru as further stating, 'It (devaluation of the rupee) is not going to be done whatever happens. The rupee is one of the very, very few sound currencies in the world. It is not my opinion. It is the opinion of hard-headed foreign businessmen.'[24] Nehru suggested that this was a short-run problem that the country would try to overcome by seeking loans from abroad.

As an immediate response to the foreign-exchange shortage, the proposal by Shenoy failed to elicit a favourable response from even the liberals of the day. In a contemporary piece, A.D. Shroff, one of the most ardent defenders of free enterprise and markets in the 1950s, considered the subject of the foreign-exchange crisis in detail but rejected devaluation as a viable option. He stated, 'One remedy which has been suggested in certain quarters is the devaluation of the Rupee. I for one am not yet convinced that it would be in the interest of the country in the context of the present situation to devalue the Rupee.'[25] He added, however, 'At the same time, I must sound a note of warning that dogmatism on this issue is not going to help us to solve the situation. Whilst devaluation immediately will not be in the interest of the country, if the present adverse balance-of-payments position continues for a long period, it would be sheer folly to say today that devaluation can be ruled out for all time.'[26]

In retrospect, Shroff had misread the situation. Except for the tight foreign-exchange situation, the Indian economy exhibited sound fundamentals, including healthy, even if not spectacular, growth at the time. On the export front, it had a thriving textiles and clothing industry that would have benefited from devaluation, provided the licensing authorities were willing to allow its expansion. On the import front, the regime being still relatively liberal, devaluation would have helped by raising the rupee prices of imports. Even a modest success of devaluation at the time would have helped open the door to greater acceptance of similar future exchange-rate adjustments. The situation at this time stood in sharp contrast to that in June 1966, when devaluation had to be undertaken in the thick of an economic crisis. By 1966, the import regime had become subject to bans and across-the-board licensing while the industrial structure had moved further away from light industries and towards heavy industries. As a result, devaluation failed to deliver on its promise and acquired a bad reputation as a policy instrument. That, in turn, rendered future overt exchange-rate adjustment a political liability, and the rupee continued to appreciate in real terms against the currencies of competing countries for a long time after June 1966.[27]

In hindsight, India paid a high price for its decision not to devalue the rupee by a significant margin sometime in 1957 or 1958. The only substitute for it was a highly restrictive foreign exchange cum import licensing regime. The adoption of such a regime can be justified as a necessary evil during wartime but not in peacetime, especially when a country is seeking to achieve a high rate of growth to rapidly overcome abject poverty. Apart from reduced access to imports overall, allocating foreign exchange and import licences at the individual entrepreneur level quickly becomes an administrative nightmare and damages the economy along multiple dimensions. The breadth and depth of this damage can be appreciated fully only after a detailed examination of the bureaucratic machinery involved and the process of implementation that had to be followed. As it turned out, the government came to follow a different process for approving import licences and allocating foreign exchange depending on the identity of the importer and the nature of the product.

The Import Licensing Regime[28]

The Imports and Exports Control Act of 1947 and the order issued under it delegated the power to control the flows of imports and exports to the Chief Controller of Imports and Exports (CCIE), Iron and Steel Controller and Development Officer (Machine and Tools). Because the latter two exercised jurisdiction over only a tiny fraction of imports, I restrict the discussion below to the licensing regime overseen by the CCIE.

With rare exceptions relating to non-recurring imports, the period over which licences were issued corresponded to the financial year (1 April to 31 March). Though the licences were issued for the full year, they were implemented in two six-monthly periods. The reason was that the finance ministry released foreign exchange in two tranches, one at the end of June for the first half of the financial year and the other at the end of December for the second half. The licensee was entitled to only half of the annual entitlement in the first half of the financial year, with the possibility that the entitlement in the second half could be revised downward in case there was a shortfall in the availability of foreign exchange.

Three major considerations governed the issue of a licence:

1. Availability of foreign exchange,
2. Essentiality of the item to be imported, and
3. Domestic non-availability of the item.

The Department of Economic Affairs (DEA) centrally controlled the allocation of foreign exchange for imports, as described in the next section. Essentiality was certified by a designated 'sponsoring' authority. This authority was the administrative ministry in charge in the case of public-sector undertakings, the DGTD or another specified agency in the case of private-sector undertakings not classified as small (Rs 5,00,000 or more in capital investment in 1965), and the development commissioner of the state in which the undertaking was located in the case of SSI undertakings. Finally, a domestic-non-availability certificate was provided by a technical authority, principally the DGTD but also including technical advisers in other industries and the Development Commissioner of Small-Scale Industries (Development Commissioner, SSI).

Sometime in December, immediately preceding the financial year for which licences were to be issued, the CCIE sought the recommendations of the DGTD and other technical authorities on import items that they considered essential in the forthcoming financial year. The latter sent their replies by the end of January. Based on these replies, the CCIE drafted the *Import Trade Control Policy Book*, popularly known as the Red Book. The book, published on the first day of the financial year (1 April), contained three lists: an 'open' list containing items that could be imported without licence conditioned on the availability of foreign exchange; a 'banned' list containing items whose imports were prohibited; and a 'restricted' list containing items requiring an import licence. It is the items on the last of these lists for which potential importers could submit applications for licences. Given that the list itself was issued on 1 April and it took some time to obtain import licences, it was understood that undertakings reliant on imported raw materials, components and spare parts would keep sufficient inventory from imports in prior years for the running of their operations until the licences were issued and new imports were affected.

Import licensing procedures varied according to the importer's identity and the nature of the imported product. While an exhaustive discussion of these procedures is beyond the scope of this work, we may gain a considerable appreciation for their complexity by considering them for five categories of imports, covering 90 per cent or more of the imports throughout the period. These categories are imports under the actual user licence, imports under the established importer licence, capital goods imports by private-sector undertakings, imports by public-sector undertakings and projects, and imports by state electricity boards.[29]

Imports under the Actual User Licence

Actual user licences were issued to private-sector undertakings for the imports of raw materials, components and spare parts used by them. Three broad categories of actual users may be identified for the purpose at hand:

a. Undertakings in industries listed in Schedule I of IDRA 1951 and borne on the books of the DGTD.
b. Undertakings with capital investment exceeding Rs 5,00,000 and in industries not listed in Schedule I of IDRA 1951 or listed in it but not borne on the books of the DGTD. Industries in the former included coffee, fisheries and coir, and those in the latter included textiles, jute, sugar, vanaspati, tea, petroleum, rubber, iron and steel, silk, collieries and other mines, electricity, shipping and pharmaceuticals.

c. Undertakings in the SSI category, defined as enterprises with capital investment below Rs 5,00,000 in 1965 and not borne on the books of the DGTD.

Licensing procedures for each of these actual user categories differed from one another. In the case of undertakings in category (a), as described in the next section, the DGTD received the licensing application, took the decisions on essentiality and domestic-non-availability, made the allocation of foreign exchange and forwarded the application with its recommendation to the CCIE. The CCIE almost always accepted this recommendation and, if positive, issued the licence.[30]

In the case of undertakings in category (b), applications were not routed through the sponsoring authorities but submitted directly to the regional offices of the CCIE. Sponsoring authorities varied by industry and were generally bodies in charge of the industry, such as the textile commissioner for textiles, tea board for tea, directorate of sugar and vanaspati for sugar and vanaspati, and iron and steel controller for iron and steel.[31] The undertakings had to obtain clearances for essentiality and domestic-non-availability and foreign-exchange allocation from these authorities and send the associated paperwork to the licensing authority. Though the undertakings in this category made their licence applications once a year, licences were issued for each half-year separately. Correspondingly, the undertakings had to obtain clearances from sponsoring authorities twice a year.[32]

SSI being a state subject, state governments got involved in the licensing application process for undertakings in category (c). In this case, the sponsoring authority was the director of industries in the state where the undertaking was located, while the technical authority was either the DGTD or the Development Commissioner, SSI in the central government. An undertaking seeking the import licence had to submit two separate applications. The first one was submitted to the director of industries in the state of its location for essentiality certification immediately after the publication of the Red Book on 1 April but before 31 May. The second application had to be submitted to the regional office of the CCIE with jurisdiction over the state for the import licence by 15 August. If the undertaking had already received the essentiality certificate before submitting the import-licence application, it attached it to the latter. Otherwise, the CCIE regional office waited to receive the certificate from the director of industries in the state. The CCIE regional office also consulted the technical authority (Development Commissioner, SSI, or the DGTD) for clearance on the domestic non-availability of the import item.[33] Foreign exchange allocation was done by either the technical authority or the CCIE.[34]

Imports under the Established Importer Licence

Items licensable to established importers were spare parts, tools and components required for servicing.[35] Licences for these items were granted based on quota certificates showing the value of past imports during a prescribed basic period. Once issued, the quota certificate remained valid as long as there was no change in the ownership of the importer's business or in the prescribed basic period.[36]

The established importers applied for these licences directly to the CCIE based on their quota certificates. They did not require clearances for essentiality and domestic non-availability. Licences were issued annually with the provision that only 50 per cent of the authorized quantity could be imported in the first half of the year. The entitlement for the second half was subject to downward revision if circumstances changed, especially concerning the availability of foreign exchange.[37]

Capital Goods Imports by Private-Sector Undertakings

With four exceptions, licences for imports of plant and machinery for private-sector undertakings were issued by the headquarters office of the CCIE. The exceptions were: (i) Licences for textiles and hosiery machinery were issued by the Joint Chief Controller of Imports and Exports (JCCIE) in Bombay, (ii) Licences for jute, coal mining and tea machinery were issued by the JCCIE in Calcutta, (iii) Licences for machinery imports worth up to Rs 5000 by undertakings in the SSI sector were issued by the respective regional licensing authorities, and (iv) Licences for machine tools up to the value of Rs 1,00,000 were issued by the Development Officer (Tools) in the DGTD.[38]

As in the case of raw materials, components and spare parts, imports of capital goods required prior clearance for essentiality, domestic non-availability and foreign exchange. Considering first the licence applications falling under the jurisdiction of the headquarters office of the CCIE, the essentiality clearance for them was, as usual, given by the sponsoring authority. This authority was the DGTD in the case of DGTD-borne undertakings; administrative ministries in charge of undertakings in sectors such as sugar, vanaspati, petroleum, rubber, iron and steel, silk, mines, shipping, pharmaceuticals, coffee, coir and fisheries; and the Development Commissioner, SSI, for undertakings bearing SSI classification. The DGTD provided the domestic non-availability certificate for all undertakings. Finally, foreign-exchange clearance was provided by the Capital Goods Committee or Capital Goods Ad Hoc Committee, depending on the value of imports.[39] The former was housed in the Ministry of Industry and handled applications for imports exceeding in value a specified threshold. The latter was housed in the CCIE and processed the remainder of the applications.[40]

Procedurally, applications for imports exceeding the specified threshold and, therefore, to be considered by the Capital Goods Committee, were required to be submitted to the DGTD. For undertakings borne on its books, the DGTD scrutinized the applications for both essentiality and domestic non-availability. For other undertakings, it scrutinized them for domestic non-availability only. It sent the applications rejected on one or both criteria directly to the CCIE for the final action. As for other applications, it sent them to the administrative ministries concerned. The administrative ministries considered the applications further and prepared summaries of the cases. Administrative ministries such as textiles, mines and petroleum, which served as sponsoring authorities for undertakings in their sectors, also evaluated the applications for essentiality. Each administrative ministry sent its summaries to the foreign-exchange section of the Ministry of Industry. The foreign-exchange section collected the summaries and placed them before the Capital Goods Committee, which considered the applications for foreign exchange approval. The decision of the Capital Goods Committee was conveyed to the administrative ministry, which, in turn, sent the application to the CCIE for final action.[41]

Applications for imports below the specified threshold in value were to be considered by the Capital Goods Ad Hoc Committee for foreign-exchange clearance. Because this committee was housed in the CCIE, these applications were submitted directly to the CCIE. The applicant had to furnish the essentiality certificate from the sponsoring authority and evidence of foreign-exchange-loan commitment, if any, with the application. The CCIE consulted DGTD for essentiality and domestic non-availability for units borne on its books. For other units, it consulted the latter for domestic non-availability only. In the case of SSI undertakings, essentiality was determined by the Development Commissioner, SSI. After the grant of essentiality and domestic non-availability clearances, the application went to the Capital Goods Ad Hoc Committee for foreign-exchange clearance. The final step was for the CCIE to issue the licence.[42]

Finally, applications for capital goods imports by undertakings in the textiles industry had to be submitted to the JCCIE in Bombay and those in the jute, coal and tea industries to the JCCIE in Calcutta. The sponsoring authorities for these industries, textiles commissioner, jute commissioner, coal controller and tea board, had their own technical advisers. As such, they provided clearances for essentiality as well as domestic non-availability. But for the machinery of general nature in which these authorities lacked technical expertise, clearance for domestic non-availability had to be obtained from the DGTD.[43]

Imports by Public-Sector Undertakings and Projects

Public-sector undertakings and projects got their foreign-exchange allocations from the DEA through their respective administrative ministries. But procedures varied according to the nature of imports.

For maintenance and spare parts, the DEA collected information from each undertaking through its administrative ministry on its expected foreign exchange need three or four months before the beginning of the financial year. Based on this information and its overall assessment of the availability of foreign exchange, the DEA made separate allocations for the two halves of the year for maintenance and spare parts needs of each undertaking. Within the ceiling of its allocation, the undertaking could certify essentiality and domestic non-availability of the import on its own and apply for an actual user import licence to the CCIE. The latter normally issued the licence.[44]

The DEA also assessed the foreign-exchange needs of each undertaking for raw materials, components and major assemblies through its administrative ministry three or four months before the beginning of the financial year. Based on the assessment and the availability of foreign exchange for the year, it then decided upon the allocation to the undertakings. Each undertaking was empowered to certify essentiality on its own but had to obtain domestic non-availability clearance from the DGTD. With the two clearances in hand, it submitted the application for an actual user licence to the administrative ministry, which obtained approval for foreign exchange from the DEA and forwarded the application to the CCIE. The latter issued the import licence.[45]

The same procedure also applied to obtaining the import licence for machinery and plant. The DEA first made a foreign-exchange allocation, and the undertaking or its administrative ministry could certify essentiality. It then obtained domestic non-availability clearance from the DGTD and foreign exchange approval from the DEA. The final step was to submit the application to the CCIE. Unlike private-sector undertakings, public-sector undertakings did not have to get clearance from the Capital Goods Committee for foreign exchange.[46]

Imports by State Electricity Boards

Unlike other public-sector undertakings and projects, the DEA made no unit-wise allocation of foreign exchange for state electricity boards and projects. Instead, based on prior information collected from the boards, it placed a bulk allocation at the disposal of the Ministry of Irrigation and Power. For each import, a state electricity board had to first get an allocation of foreign exchange from the ministry, obtain essentiality and domestic-non-availability clearances from the Central Water and Power Commission and then get the final approval for foreign exchange from the ministry. It then sent the application for the licence to the CCIE through the commission.[47]

Allocation of Foreign Exchange

In describing the licensing procedures in the previous section, I have referred to the allocation of foreign exchange for each licence approved. The allocation of foreign exchange to the licensee was the last step in the otherwise more complex and elaborate exercise by the DEA aimed at preparing six-monthly foreign-exchange budgets for periods from 1 April to 30 September and 1 October to 31 March. The starting point in this exercise was estimating the expected quantum of foreign exchange in the relevant six-month period. To this end, every six months, the DEA carried out an 'Availability Exercise' involving a rough calculation of foreign exchange likely to accrue from various sources over the remaining years of the five-year plan. The sources of foreign exchange included receipts from exports of goods and services, investment income from abroad, net foreign investment and foreign loans and grants. Subtracting from the total foreign-exchange accruals so estimated, the payments due on import commitments already made and those expected on imports of invisibles such as travel, transportation and debt service yielded the net foreign exchange available for fresh imports over the remaining plan period. Taking into account the pattern of utilization of import licences in the immediate past and expected future needs, the DEA worked out the limit up to which the public and private sectors could make fresh import commitments during the six-monthly period concerned. This limit served as the overall ceiling on the new foreign-exchange commitments during the period.[48]

The next step in the process, conducted at the beginning of each six-month period, was to collect information on anticipated foreign-exchange demands of public-sector undertakings and projects from the administrative ministries and those of private-sector undertakings from the Economic Adviser, Ministry of Industry. The latter, in turn, collected the information from the DGTD for DGTD-borne undertakings and other sponsoring authorities such as textiles and jute commissioners, silk board, CCIE, coffee and tea boards, food ministry and mines and metals ministry for other private-sector undertakings. Based on this information and the availability of foreign exchange and after making provisions for the imports of food grains, defence items, fertilizers and petroleum, oil and lubricants (POL), the DEA made the following allocations at the end of June for the first half of the financial year and at the end of December for the second half:[49]

1. A bulk allocation went to the Economic Adviser, Ministry of Industry for downstream allocation to private-sector

undertakings for importing raw materials, components and spare parts other than iron and steel.

2. An allocation went to the Iron and Steel Controller for downstream allocation to public- and private-sector undertakings for the imports of iron and steel; and
3. Separate allocations went to each administrative ministry in charge of public-sector undertakings and projects for imports of raw materials, components, spare parts and equipment.[50]

These allocations did not provide for the import of capital goods by new or existing private-sector undertakings. As described in the previous section, approvals for foreign exchange for capital goods imports by private-sector undertakings were given via a separate channel by the Capital Goods Committee or Capital Goods Ad Hoc Committee. Foreign exchange for these imports was sourced primarily from foreign loans, investment by a foreign collaborator or government loans.[51]

Three steps were involved before the bulk allocation to the Economic Adviser, Ministry of Industry reached individual private-sector undertakings, which were the actual users of the imported raw materials, components and spare parts.[52] In the first step, the bulk allocation was distributed among different sponsoring authorities, such as the DGTD, textile and jute commissioners, silk board, CCIE, drugs controller, food ministry, and mines and metals ministry. In the second step, the sponsoring authority distributed its allocation among different industries. In the final step, the foreign exchange earmarked for a given industry was allocated among different undertakings within it.

The Economic Adviser, Ministry of Industry, himself initiated the first step by working out a tentative distribution of his bulk allocation among different sponsoring authorities based on past usage and other relevant information available at the time. These distributions were then discussed at an inter-departmental meeting attended by the representatives of the Ministry of Finance, Ministry of Petroleum and Chemicals, Ministry of Mines and Metals, the Planning Commission,

DGTD and CCIE and chaired by the Secretary, Industry. The final decision on distributing the bulk allocation of the foreign exchange among various sponsoring authorities was made at this meeting.[53]

The DGTD-borne undertakings, for which the DGTD served as the sponsoring authority, constituted the vast majority of private-sector undertakings. As such, the DGTD received the largest share of the Economic Adviser's bulk allocation. It additionally received foreign exchange allocations from the Iron and Steel Controller for steel imports by undertakings on its books and from the Mines and Metals Ministry for mineral and metal imports by them. Its next step was to apportion its total allocation among industries for which it was the sponsoring authority. The last and final step was unit-wise allocation within each industry. One of the directorates within the DGTD performed this task.[54]

As of 1965, the DGTD was divided into two wings, a chemical wing and an engineering wing. These two wings together consisted of eleven divisions, divided into fifty-three directorates. Each directorate had one to three development officers and several assistant development officers. Each development officer was in charge of a group of industries, with each industry comprising several manufacturing units.[55] The unit-wise allocations of foreign exchange were made at this level.

A private-sector undertaking wishing to import raw materials, components or spare parts addressed its application to the CCIE and submitted it to the coordinating directorate in the DGTD. The directorate sent the application to the unit's sponsoring directorate. As discussed in the previous section, this directorate cleared the application from essentiality and domestic non-availability angles. If one or more import items fell under the jurisdiction of the other directorates or sponsoring authorities outside the DGTD, they had to be consulted for essentiality and domestic non-availability clearances.[56] Once the application received these clearances, the directorate recommended an allocation of foreign exchange to it, taking into account the overall allocation to the industry. It sent the application to the coordinating directorate, which, in turn, forwarded it to the CCIE, the agency responsible for issuing the import licence.[57]

Other sponsoring authorities receiving foreign-exchange allocations from the Economic Adviser, Ministry of Industry had their own technical advisers who oversaw the distribution of those allocations among private-sector undertakings within their jurisdiction. One of these sponsoring authorities, the Metals and Mines Ministry, made a bulk allocation to the DGTD for downstream allocation to undertakings under its jurisdiction for imports of minerals and metals. The Iron and Steel Controller, which received an allocation directly from the DEA as described in (ii) above, performed the same task regarding undertakings under its jurisdiction. Additionally, it made a bulk allocation to the DGTD for downstream allocations to undertakings under its jurisdiction for iron and steel imports.

I have already discussed the process of foreign-exchange allocation for capital goods imports by private-sector undertakings and imports of raw materials, components, spare parts and equipment by public-sector undertakings in the context of import licensing in the previous section. Therefore, we can now turn to a discussion of the pitfalls of the system and its efficiency implications.

Pitfalls of the System and Its Efficiency Implications

Drawing on contemporary sources, most notably the two reports by the Mathur study teams, Bhagwati and Desai provide a detailed dissection of both the direct shortcomings of the complex bureaucratic regime and its deleterious economic efficiency effects. Therefore, my discussion of these issues below is less detailed than theirs and has a different emphasis.[58]

Allocation of Foreign Exchange a Purely Bureaucratic Process

In all, four steps were involved in preparing and implementing the foreign-exchange budget. The first step involved estimating the total foreign exchange available during the relevant six-month period. The remaining three steps concerned the allocation of this foreign exchange down to actual importers.

The DEA was largely groping in the dark to estimate the available foreign exchange. The task required not just the knowledge of potential revenues from exports and aid but also the ability to predict the payments coming due during the six months on imports affected under licence issues in the past. But the DEA lacked the necessary data to predict such payments. The problem was discussed in detail by the 1968 parliamentary committee report on foreign exchange. Quoting a study team set up by the Administrative Reforms Commission, it stated, 'Thus, for lack of adequate knowledge during any given period, the foreign exchange budget cannot prevent sudden increases or decreases in payments unrelated to the value of licenses issued during that period.'[59] The study team lamented that 'forecasts based on an inadequate data have limited operational utility' and that the foreign-exchange budget became 'a series of intelligent guess-work due to the imperfect data available to the administration'.[60]

Once the DEA had settled with its estimate of the available foreign exchange, its next step was to allocate it between public and private sector undertakings and among different public-sector undertakings. Given that foreign exchange remained scarce throughout the period, it stands to reason that it would be allocated among competing alternatives to maximize return on it. From whatever little information on the criteria for this allocation is available, it can be safely concluded that neither the relative efficiency of public- and private-sector undertakings nor of different public-sector undertakings played any role in decision-making. The DEA made its decisions based exclusively on the needs expressed by the administrative ministries in the case of public-sector projects and undertakings and by different sponsoring authorities in the case of private-sector undertakings. There is no indication in the contemporary reports that the administrative ministries and sponsoring authorities relied on anything other than recent history to assess the needs of the undertakings under their respective jurisdictions.

The third step in the process was the distribution of the bulk allocation made by the DEA to the Economic Adviser, Ministry of Industry among different sponsoring authorities of the numerous private-sector undertakings. Once again, neither the past performance nor any well-defined criteria prioritizing various authorities formed the basis of the allocation. This is the only conclusion we can draw from the brief description of the process provided by the Mathur study team, which had looked into the question. To quote it,[61]

> The task of distributing this [bulk allocation of foreign exchange by the DEA] to various heads is then taken up by the Economic Adviser on the basis of past performance and other relevant considerations obtaining at the time. He prepares a tentative distribution list against each demand which is then discussed at an inter-departmental meeting taken by the Secretary (Industry). The meeting is attended by representatives of the Ministries of Finance, Commerce, Petroleum and Chemicals, Mines and Metals, the Planning Commission, Directorate General of Technical Development and Chief Controller of Imports & Exports. In this meeting the allocations are finalized, . . . [and] the Directorate General of Technical Development receives his allocation of foreign exchange.

In Appendix III of the report, the study team lists twenty-six industry heads with their corresponding sponsoring authorities, among which the allocations had to be made at this stage. The

DGTD, with jurisdiction over all engineering and chemical industries, was the largest among the sponsoring authorities. Each of these heads, in turn, represented large groups of industries. Bhagwati and Desai reproduce a list of 123 industries under the head of engineering industries alone. Furthermore, each of the 123 engineering industries is further divided into several sub-industries. For instance, machine tools and small tools, the first of the 123 industries on the list, is divided into 19 sub-industries. A similarly large number of industries and sub-industries existed under the head of chemical industries. No economically meaningful criteria could have been applied to the allocation of foreign exchange among this large number of industries and sub-industries. Unsurprisingly, Bhagwati and Desai characterize the problem as 'Orwellian', with the authorities having to rely on a history of some kind or resorting to ad hoc priority criteria to arrive at industry-wise allocations. When cuts had to be made in allocations due to the overall scarcity of foreign exchange, they applied proportionately equal cuts across industries.[62]

A similar situation characterized the fourth and final step involving unit-wise allocations within each industry. Based on its case studies, the Mathur study team found no single criterion for this allocation, and the criteria differed across directorates within the DGTD.

> In some cases the norm prescribed is utilization of the foreign exchange in the *past* periods while in some others the criterion is the production in the *current* year. In some cases, consumption of indigenous raw material is the norm while in others, allocation may be justified on the grounds of the industry being 'priority industry'. In some cases, it was found that the firms were given foreign exchange even without conforming to the norms.[63]

The final point is that in so far as it can be ascertained, virtually no attention was paid to the allocation of foreign exchange between capital goods on the one hand and raw materials, components and spare parts on the other. The decision on allocating capital goods imports by private-sector undertakings was delegated to the Capital Goods Committee or the Capital Goods Ad Hoc Committee and was entirely outside of the foreign-exchange budget exercise of the DEA.

Too Many Small-Value Licences

Equity considerations mandated that foreign-exchange needs of small entrepreneurs receive adequate attention. On the one hand, the low productivity of these entrepreneurs meant that foreign exchange allocated to them was not put to the most productive use while on the other, their large numbers and small-value import licence applications meant that they ended up clogging the licensing administration for the allocation of a small proportion of the total foreign exchange. Two specific types of applicants in this category were the small-scale undertakings seeking actual user licences and small established importers.

In 1963–64, the CCIE issued 86,119 actual user licences valued at Rs 4.1 billion. Of these, 17,879 licences valued at Rs 132 million were issued to SSI undertakings. Therefore, 20.76 per cent of the actual user licences were issued to applicants accounting for just 3.25 per cent of the value of all actual user licences.[64] One-third of these licences were valued at only Rs 15,000 or less.[65]

Since SSI development happened to be a state subject, the procedure for issuing licences applicable to them became more complicated than that for the larger units. The sponsoring authority certifying the essentiality of imports by these undertakings had to be a state agency, while the technical body certifying domestic non-availability was the DGTD. As a result, unlike in the case of larger undertakings, import licence applications by these undertakings had two separate masters. Adding to this complication was their spatial dispersal across the breadth and length of the country. The Mathur study team described the challenges posed by these undertakings to the allocation system in these stark terms:

> The task of applying a control mechanism like import licensing in this sector, therefore, is inherently difficult and calls for more than ordinary administrative skills and courage. The tackling of such a vast number of scattered applicants, both old and new (verified or otherwise), through the various levels of industrial organizations in the State and at the Center, and the concomitant work-load, duplication of effort, multiple scrutiny, etc., involved are so time consuming and such a fertile ground for mal-practice that we feel that the procedure here, which is at present more complicated than in the case of the large-scale sector, requires drastic simplification, even if that involves unusual degree of administrative and financial decentralization.[66]

The story is only slightly better in the case of established importers. Of 30,000 licences issued to these importers in 1963–64, approximately 90 per cent were valued at Rs 15,000 or less. These licences accounted for only 25 per cent of the annual allocation to established importers, a small proportion of the total foreign exchange allocation. Of the 90 per cent of licences valued at less than Rs 15,000, 85 per cent (76.5 per cent of all established importer licences) were valued at Rs 5000 or less.[67]

The Mathur study team judged the costs associated with the administration of small-value import licences so high that it recommended that the government discontinue its practice of requiring the licence holder to have her licence endorsed for the second half of the year in the case of all licences worth Rs 15,000 or less. Emphasizing the importance of this reform in his transmittal letter accompanying the report, Mathur stated,

> One of our most important recommendations is about licensing (without any mid-year endorsement) for the entire

sector of established importers and small-scale units and for those in the non-SSI sector holding licenses valued up to Rs. 15,000. This will spare about 40,000 odd licensees from thronging the licensing and sponsoring offices all over the country in order to get their licenses endorsed for the second half. In terms of man-days saved for the trade and the Government Departments as also the facility in import, negotiations, planning, etc., we are convinced that this will bestow a phenomenal benefit to all concerned.'[68]

Slow Pace of the Approval Process

The decision-making process was slow in all its aspects. Several factors contributed to the delays. First, once the total number of applications that the system had to handle crossed a threshold, the usual organizational diseconomies of scale set in. Centralized systems of delivery can work well on a limited scale. But as the scale expands, congestion takes its toll, making a decentralized system more efficient.

Second, the design of the decision-making process within the Indian bureaucracy added to the delays. By design, files within a department begin at the level of the junior-most officer and move up in the hierarchical order. Such a system automatically slows down the decision-making process since the file must pass through many levels of bureaucracy within each department before it reaches the final authority. Furthermore, when interdepartmental consultations are required, which is the case most of the time, the process of hierarchical movement of the file is repeated in each department. In the Indian system, there is also a tendency to consult multiple departments sequentially rather than simultaneously.

Third, delays were also caused because bureaucratic steps were introduced without evaluating their costs relative to the benefits. The requirement of endorsement of even small-value licences for the second half of the year, whose abolition the Mathur study team recommended, is a case in point. Indeed, the reports by the Mathur study team carried innumerable suggestions for how the entire process could be speeded up by eliminating many unnecessary steps in the decision-making process.

Finally, delays were also added by rising corruption in the system. Files would get 'stuck' even at the desks of junior-most officers to extract bribes. As this tendency grew, honest applicants and those too new to know when, to whom and how much to bribe became victims of the resulting delay.

By the mid-1960s, long delays in the approvals of licences had already become endemic. To begin with, like the financial year, the licensing year began on 1 April, with the Red Book issued on that date. But given the lag in the availability of reliable data on foreign exchange, the DEA did not take the first step towards the allocation of foreign exchange until June for the first six-monthly period and until December for the second six-monthly period. For private-sector undertakings, the first recipient of the DEA allocation was the Economic Adviser, Industry Ministry, who, in turn, apportioned it among the sponsoring agencies. Though the applicants were required to submit their applications between 1 April and 31 May, the sponsoring agencies began processing them only after they received their foreign-exchange allocation, sometime towards the end of June in the case of the DGTD.[69]

The Mathur study team did in-depth case studies of the time taken for the approval of licences for applicants of different categories. Findings of the case study relating to actual user licence applications for raw materials and components by undertakings borne of the DGTD illustrate the magnitude of delays in the approval process.[70] In the 154 cases studied, it took the DGTD, on average, 104 days from the date of allocation of foreign exchange to finalize its recommendations to the CCIE. As many as 4287 applications for licences during the 1964–65 licensing year were still pending in the DGTD on 15 February 1965. In 36 out of the 154 cases studied, the sponsoring directorate had to consult one or more other directorates, mostly for domestic non-availability clearance. In thirteen of these cases, it consulted two or more directorates. It did so sequentially rather than simultaneously when consulting two or more directorates. The consultations took an average of 15.2 days per directorate consulted.[71]

Predictably, the time taken to approve licences for capital goods requiring clearance for foreign exchange by the Capital Goods Committee or Capital Goods Ad Hoc Committee was significantly longer than in the case of licences for raw materials and components. Applications in the former category had to be first submitted to the DGTD and cleared for essentiality and domestic non-availability before being sent to the Capital Goods Committee for foreign exchange approval. Only after these three clearances did the application go to the CCIE. The case study by the Mathur study team revealed, 'In the case of applications falling within the purview of the C.G. [Capital Goods] committee, the average time taken for final disposal was 405 days; nearly half of this time was before the application came to the CCIE office with the recommendation of the C.G. Committee.'[72] Applications reviewed by the Capital Goods Ad Hoc Committee were submitted directly to the CCIE. As a result, they received approval in less time at 177 days.[73]

The assessment of the approval process for capital goods imports by the Mathur study team was less than flattering. It stated, 'We appreciate the position that, as against applications for raw materials, those for capital equipment require greater scrutiny and, therefore, comparatively longer time for disposal. However, we feel that the time actually taken in the disposal of such applications as revealed by results of case-studies is considerably more than what is necessary.'[74] The team noted numerous procedural flaws, including duplication of work at the individual and committee levels and avoidable movement of papers from office to office, often multiple times. It also offered suggestions for remedying these flaws and reducing approval time.

Undertaking-Level Costs and Inefficiencies

The system generated several costs and inefficiencies at the level of an individual undertaking. First, each undertaking needing imported raw materials and components to maintain production had to deploy personnel who would follow up with various government agencies to ensure that the import licence was issued each year and that foreign exchange allocation was made every six months. In addition, there could be financial costs in the form of bribes at various points. Insofar as the larger undertakings were better informed and better connected and sought the imports on a larger scale, the incidence of these costs was disproportionately on smaller undertakings.

Second, with the licence granted to the actual user, every undertaking had to individually search foreign markets, negotiate prices and have the imports shipped in relatively small and individualized packages. The system thus eliminated any scope for scale economies that arise from intermediation by wholesale importers who could minimize search costs, do due diligence to ensure quality, negotiate better prices on their bulk purchases and have them shipped at significantly lower per-unit cost. Once again, these costs were disproportionately higher for the smaller undertakings.

Third, the fact that the licence was issued to the actual user and that there was considerable uncertainty concerning the approval of the licence and renewal of allocation of foreign exchange in the second six-month period meant that inventory costs were significantly higher than would have been the case in a more rational system. If wholesale importers had been permitted, the overall inventory level would have been significantly lower than in a system requiring each undertaking to hold its own inventory. And the inventory level had to be yet higher because of unanticipated delays or even denials of imports. When the undertaking ran out of imported raw materials or components, it had to either discontinue production or use poorer-quality domestic substitutes, resulting in lower-quality products, higher costs or both.

Finally, in many cases, the quantity of imports permitted to an actual user was based on the installed capacity. This fact meant that the only way to expand the production of a profitable item requiring imported raw materials was to add further capacity, even if unused capacity existed. The result was an investment in unproductive capacity.

Sector-Level Inefficiencies

Import licensing also produced several inefficiencies at the level of the sector. First, strict enforcement of the domestic non-availability condition served as a signal to producers that they could effectively get the authorities to impose tight restrictions on, even discontinue, the imports of products that could qualify even remotely as substitutes for what they produced. This fact led to a yet more restrictive import regime than was justified, with applicants denied import licences on the grounds of domestic availability when, in fact, the items they sought to import were not available. This feature of the system also gave rise to an extreme form of import substitution since potential producers could get the authorities to curtail or discontinue the imports of any product that they offered to produce at home regardless of their production cost vis-à-vis the price paid for imports.

Second, this form of protection also worked to impart an extreme form of anti-export bias to the economy, for it moved scarce resources, especially capital, progressively into import-competing sectors. The fact that exporters were obliged to use domestically produced inputs and raw materials whenever such substitutes were available placed them at a further disadvantage in the world markets. For one thing, domestically produced substitute inputs were invariably of a lower quality than their imported counterparts. Moreover, a large import premium (defined as the difference between the wholesale market price of an import and its landed price inclusive of import duty) existed on nearly all imports. Therefore, as the actual user, the exporter paid a significantly lower price for an imported input than its domestically produced counterpart. Both factors contributed to the reduced competitiveness of Indian exports in the world market. For example, the denial of fabric imports to apparel exporters was partially responsible for the erosion of India's competitiveness in the world apparel market.

Third, insofar as the government was willing to give investment licences, the import regime paradoxically created a bias in favour of industries using imported as distinct from domestically produced inputs, including capital goods. As just noted, as an actual user, a producer paid the landed price plus import duty for an imported input, which was significantly less than what she would have paid for its domestically produced counterpart. This fact made industries that used machinery, raw material and components not produced at home more attractive than those for which these inputs were domestically available.

Fourth, the import regime, complemented by the investment licensing regime, eliminated nearly all competition. Once domestic production of a product had begun, competition from abroad was largely eliminated since a potential importer of the same product faced a high bar when it came to demonstrating to the licensing authorities that the product was not available domestically. At the same time, the investment licensing regime contributed to the elimination of domestic competition. Incumbent firms could often use their excess capacity as evidence of insufficient demand to block the approval of licences to potential entrants. There were also cases of incumbent firms applying for investment licences they did not intend to use to prevent future entrants from getting approval for their licence applications. The licensing authorities were prone to deciding on new licences based on the capacity already approved rather than actually installed. Finally, in sectors where inputs had to be imported, limits on the volume of imports of those inputs eliminated competition even through an expansion of output by the existing undertakings. An implication of this lack of competition was the creation of monopoly profits, which led the government to impose price and distribution controls with concomitant efficiency costs.

Finally, at least in industries requiring imported inputs, the import regime undermined within-sector efficiency through at least two mechanisms. One, it denied efficient firms the ability to outcompete inefficient ones. Import-allocation systems operated on 'fairness' and 'equity' criteria rather than efficiency. As a result, neither was the allocation to an efficient firm expanded nor to an inefficient one reduced. Two, the actual user condition meant that if a firm faced a shortage of an imported input and another had an unused allocation of the same, the former could not buy it from the latter. The system thus ruled out an efficiency-enhancing exchange.

Concluding Remarks

In this chapter, I have discussed in detail the highly restrictive import regime that evolved in the wake of the foreign-exchange crisis India faced once the sterling balances, accumulated during the Second World War, ran out. A prudent step at this point would have been a sizeable devaluation of the rupee. A higher inflation rate in India than in its trading partners, combined with a fixed nominal exchange rate, had left the rupee substantially overvalued. This fact meant that, over time, average rupee costs and prices of domestically produced goods had risen relative to their foreign counterparts. This situation automatically made imported goods more attractive to Indians and Indian goods less attractive to foreigners. Devaluation was the effective remedy to correct this misalignment of domestic and foreign prices. Unfortunately, there was no political support whatsoever for this remedy. The result was the return to the wartime tight foreign-exchange-control regime as the only option. Along with it came the tight import control regime.

I have deliberately provided a detailed discussion of approval processes for import licences and foreign exchange allocation. The purpose behind this exercise has been to bring out, especially to young readers, the gross irrationality of the bureaucratic regime India created to administer the economy and to pave the way for the following discussion on its pitfalls and efficiency implications. The discussion of processes reveals that the foreign-exchange cum import-licensing regime required not only the creation of specialized bureaucracies such as the CCIE, DGTD and the Capital Goods Committee but also the participation of nearly all administrative ministries and several state agencies. With the decision-making process characterized by slow speed and uncertainty, efficiency took the back seat.

The regime had serious costs in terms of efficiency at the level of the undertaking as well as the sector. Each undertaking had to devote considerable resources to follow up with different ministries and departments to ensure it got its import entitlements and foreign-exchange allocation. It also had to search for the sellers of its imports in the foreign markets, negotiate the prices and arrange transportation. Given the delays and uncertainty associated with the approval of import licences and foreign-exchange allocation, the undertakings had to maintain larger inventories than under a market system.

The bureaucratic allocation system made no distinction between efficient and inefficient undertakings with import entitlements of inputs governed entirely by the installed capacity and production history. This fact meant that the more efficient undertakings had no chance of out-competing the less efficient ones. With the entry of new undertakings constrained through investment licensing and output expansion of existing undertakings capped by restrictions on imports of raw materials and components, the competition was virtually eliminated. In many cases, the resulting high profits brought price and distribution controls with their own harmful efficiency effects.

An alternative to import control would have been export promotion. But this course was not followed. As we will see in the next chapter, as long as the sterling balances remained plentiful, India remained wedded to wartime export licensing and export taxes on the major exports. Though the need to promote exports was progressively recognized after the sterling balances ran out, available instruments proved grossly inadequate in the absence of devaluation. A more liberal foreign investment policy, pursued during the Nehru era, helped on the margin insofar as new investments were concerned, but its contribution remained limited due to the insufficient appetite of foreign investors to invest in the Indian market.

9

Export and Foreign Investment Policies

This chapter briefly discusses India's export and foreign-investment policies during the Nehru era. Exports were the principal recurring source of foreign exchange though foreign investment also contributed to the kitty. An interesting contrast between policies in the two areas, however, was that whereas exports were subject to widespread restrictions, the foreign investment regime remained liberal.

Export policy, which I consider first, has been thoroughly analysed by Manmohan Singh and Bhagwati and Desai.[1] Completed as early as 1962 and published in 1964, the book by Singh is especially impressive in its mastery of data, analysis and policy prescriptions. It exhibits a thorough grasp of the limitations of restrictive export policies pursued by India during the 1950s and rightly recommends a devaluation of the rupee complemented by export taxes on a few selected commodities for which the world demand exhibited low price elasticity. Devaluation was something that Shenoy had advocated in 1958 and remained an eminently sensible measure even in 1962. But lacking any political constituency, the recommendation went wholly unnoticed.[2]

For their own discussion of export policy during 1951–61, Bhagwati and Desai rely heavily on Singh's work. They go further, however, by extending the analysis till the 1966 devaluation of the rupee. Given the existence of these detailed accounts, I choose to be brief in my own discussion of the export policy during the Nehru era. Instead, I pay greater attention to the earlier history since, as in the case of import policy, it proves helpful in understanding what followed.

The First Half of the Twentieth Century

Prior to the Second World War, restrictions on exports were rare. The only significant export duties were those applied to raw jute and jute goods. The rationale for these duties was that India was the sole supplier of these products and therefore held a monopoly position in the world market.[3] As in the case of imports, across-the-board physical controls on exports had their origins in the Second World War. Media reports on the imposition of export restrictions on mica and coffee can be seen to appear as early as 1940.[4] By the middle of 1942, a quota system restricting the exports of textiles had also been put in place.[5] By mid-1943, shipping-space constraints had led to the spread of controls to nearly all exports. A July 1943 communication by a committee of FICCI to the government is reported to have stated, 'The difficulties of Indian exporters are increasing day by day, and if no action is taken by Government to alleviate these difficulties, the Indian exporters will find themselves totally eliminated from the export trade of their own country.'[6] By the end of the war, export taxes on a wide spectrum of products had also come to exist. This development was a natural response to the differences between the prices of exportable goods at home and abroad that had come to exist due to export controls. The government decided to convert a part of this difference into revenues for itself through taxes.[7]

As the war drew to a close, an effort to relax export controls was made through a series of notifications. While these notifications carried long lists of items from which export controls were withdrawn, they left out nearly all the major export commodities of India, including jute and cotton textile manufactures, tea, coffee, vegetable oilseeds and oils, raw cotton and coffee.[8] Unsurprisingly, when the government appointed the Export Promotion Committee under the chairmanship of A.D. Gorwala in July 1949 to make recommendations for 'stepping up exports so as to achieve balanced trade', its first major recommendation was to substantially liberalize the export controls.[9] Part II of the report, which provides general recommendations to promote exports, begins by noting,

> It is somewhat paradoxical that, while the Government has been aiming at export drive, elaborate machinery to exercise control over the majority of exports exists. The present export control notification has been inherited from the days of the war when there was need to restrict the volume of exports for a variety of reasons, many of which no longer hold good.[10]

In a penetrating statement immediately following this observation, the report proceeds to question the wisdom of these restrictions:[11]

> The effect of restrictions on exports is to give a higher priority to the demand of the internal consumer and let overseas buyer have only the surplus. A country with a favourable balance of trade such as we used to have in the past may perhaps be able to afford such a policy. When, however, there is a large adverse balance of trade it is a mistake to imagine that export control can help in assuring a better standard of living for the people. If we conserve indigenous production for internal consumption, in order to balance our trade we must necessarily curtail imports severely. In either case internal consumption has to be cut. The real question is one of weighing the importance of the goods that are allowed to be exported against the essentiality of the imports which must be cut on account of the fall in the country's exports. When we have to depend on imports to supply us with food and fertilizers, raw materials and machinery, the necessary foreign exchange for which is not being earned by our present

> level of exports, clearly the case for reducing as far as possible all restrictions on our export trade is overwhelming.

The report, divided into three parts and spanning sixty-four pages, is full of wise analysis and sound recommendations, both general and commodity specific, of which any modern-day trade economist can be proud. For instance, at a time when primary products seemed to dominate the export basket, it points to the centrality of exports of manufactures noting, 'One of the most undesirable features of the present export control is that a large number of manufactured goods are still subject to control.' It goes on to add,

> If we are to achieve a balance in trading once again, we must rely on a considerable expansion in the exports of our manufactures. In the long-term interests of the country's foreign trade, manufactured goods as a class must be freed from export control and indeed it should be our policy to encourage such exports in every possible way.'[12]

The report then points out the folly of export restrictions imposed by many ministries based on the fact that the inputs used in those exports were wholly or partly of imported origin. It reasons, 'We are of opinion that except in respect of goods which come from hard currency countries, there is no reason to place any obstacles on re-export, . . . No one will export goods which he has imported from outside unless he makes a profit on such exports.' It recommends, 'Our general view, therefore, is that there is no need to have export restrictions on any commodity simply because it happens to be partly or wholly of imported origin.'[13] The report cites the interesting example of Swiss watches to clarify its point,

> We are aware that clocks and watches are mostly of hard currency (Swiss) origin. Watches however have to be imported at the cost of hard currency, not primarily because we must

> have them, but because the Swiss insist that if we take other things from them which we really need, we must also take some watches, the export of which forms part of their traditional pattern of trade. In our view, it is desirable that these watches should be exported so that the hard currency spent on them may not mean a total loss of foreign exchange but only of hard currency, soft currency being obtained in substitution.[14]

The report calls out the fallacy, common among Indian policymakers at the time, that a country does a favour to the importing countries by exporting its products to them.

> Our export policy has suffered to a great extent from this fallacy . . . Our attitude throughout is very different from that of other countries who attach importance to exports. They give every possible inducement to the customer to buy. We seem to proceed on the basis that it really does not matter very much whether the customer buys or not.[15]

Predictably, the report also leans against export taxes. 'It may be said, as a general rule, that to tax exports is to reduce exports. Hence it is that the great exporting countries of the world have hardly ever had a tax on exports.'[16] The report recognizes that removing export duty in every case may not be advisable and recommends their retention on jute manufactures, given the country's monopoly over them. But it categorically rejects the use of export duties to raise revenue.

> It should be realized that to rely on export duties as a stable source of revenue is most unsafe and indeed opposed to every canon of fiscal prudence. To put a tax on some exportable commodity in order to meet a budget deficit is to injure the export trade and thus inflict much more damage on fiscal system than the revenue brought in by the tax can repair.[17]

Finally, the report makes a reasoned case for the drawback of duty paid on inputs used in exports and cites the example of the United Kingdom.

The report goes beyond export restrictions and duties and suggests how India could ensure that the quality of its exports matched what the exporters promised their buyers. It recommends the enforcement of quality standards of the importing countries, standardization of packing of commodities such as tea and cotton piece goods, and reliance on arbitration clauses in the contracts when the latter specify quality standards. The report also makes detailed recommendations on what we call export facilitation in today's terminology, including priority to export products in transportation to ports, cutting delays in customs clearances and shipment, and congestion at the docks. Finally, the report recommends the creation of an organization within the government dedicated to collecting commodity-specific data and information on exportable products at home and abroad and tracking restrictions on Indian exports in the importing countries.

In sum, the report of the Export Promotion Committee is comprehensive and full of wise suggestions, many of which remain relevant even today. In the event, the report got hardly any traction with the government. Instead, it was IPR 1948 that dominated the policy discourse at the time and set the direction of policy. Consequently, export controls and duties on major commodities remained in place through most of the 1950s.

The Planning Era: 1951–66

Bhagwati and Desai describe India's export policy during the first three plans succinctly thus:

> Indian export policy has evolved over the period from indifference, pessimistic neglect, and, for several major items, even a constellation of measures amounting to positive

> discouragement, to growing encouragement via escalating subsidization (culminating in the 1966 devaluation) and promotional measures undertaken by the Government. These two periods *broadly* correspond to the first two Five-Year Plans (1951–56 and 1956–61) and the period thereafter.[18]

Regarding the first period, they go on to observe that export controls, which started during the Second World War, were continued for jute manufactures until 1958, for tea, vegetable oilseeds and oils, and raw cotton throughout the decade of 1951–60, and for cotton textiles until 1953. In addition, export duties were applied either throughout the decade or a substantial part of it on jute manufactures, tea, raw cotton, manganese ore and different kinds of oils.[19]

Commodity-wise analyses by Singh and Bhagwati and Desai show that domestic policies were particularly detrimental to export outcomes. While Pakistan subsidized its exports of jute manufactures and emerged as a successful rival, India continued to impose export duties on them. A similar scenario occurred in tea, with Sri Lanka and some African countries investing in developing exports while India applied export controls and duties. In cotton textiles, the government explicitly adopted policies that hampered the expansion and modernization of machinery and led to the poor and stagnant quality of textiles at a time when rivals, especially Japan, were constantly improving quality to win a larger share of the world market. In coffee, the Coffee Board explicitly adopted policies promoting domestic consumption, undermining exports.

A plausible hypothesis is that the near exhaustion of the sterling balances by the end of 1956 would have led to a major shift in policy in favour of export promotion. But while we come across instances of government exhorting the industry to step up exports, official documents highlighting the need for export promotion and media publishing articles favouring exports, concrete policy actions remained half-hearted until as late as 1962–63.[20] Rather than confront the balance-of-payments challenge by measures aimed at boosting export revenues, by and large, the government chose to rely on progressively tighter import controls and foreign aid and loans.

The Ministry of Commerce and Industry set the target of raising the total annual exports to Rs 7 to 7.2 billion in 1958 from the average of Rs 6 billion from 1955 to 1957. Measures adopted to reach this target till early February 1958 included setting up nine export promotion councils, the drawback of import duties and a rebate of excise duties, assistance for the supply of raw materials to exporting industries, quality control, rail movement facilities, export risk insurance, publicity of Indian goods abroad, trade agreements for more balanced trade, the setting up of the State Trading Corporation and strengthening of the commercial services in Indian missions abroad.[21] Many of these measures had existed earlier in one or the other form. As such, they failed to produce significant results.

For example, in a 1959 article, Shenoy argued that the monetary benefits of these measures to the producers of export goods viewed as a whole had been negligible, leading to continued stagnation in exports.[22] In the article, he also reminded that during the first three years of the second plan, the government had already drawn a massive Rs 6.34 billion on currency reserves to finance imports. Consequently, by June 1959, the currency reserves had fallen to Rs 1.14 billion.

Shenoy reasoned that tightening imports further to meet the foreign-exchange challenge would only undermine the growth objective. Therefore, stepping up exports was the only rational course open to the country. Exports were, however, hamstrung by the higher domestic prices on average relative to those prevailing abroad. As a solution, he suggested two policy measures: devaluation of the rupee to align the foreign prices with domestic ones and restraint on money creation to avoid future misalignment between the two sets of prices.

Neither of the recommendations by Shenoy resonated with policymakers at the time and, unsurprisingly, went unheeded.

Nevertheless, having fallen sharply in 1958–59, export earnings gradually recovered in the following three years, returning to their 1957–58 level in 1961–62.[23] Even this modest recovery resulted principally from increased exports to Eastern European countries attributable to bilateral trade relations forged at the governmental level. With exports still at their 1957–58 level, inflows of foreign capital either through aid or loans abroad limited and import needs continuing to rise, given the ambitious goals of the third plan, the threat of serious balance-of-payments difficulties in the forthcoming years loomed.

Recognition of this threat led the government to introduce several measures aimed at export promotion, first in 1962–63 and then in 1963–64. Simultaneously, the government strengthened some of the existing export incentives introduced in earlier years. The budget for 1962–63 increased excise duties on several commodities, including tea, to restrain domestic consumption. Export duties on several commodities, including tea, were reduced as well. In May 1962, the government set up a Board of Trade to regularly review export promotion policies in consultation with industry. Positive steps to make exports more attractive included:[24]

- The increase in the corporation tax on companies from 45 to 50 per cent introduced in the 1962–63 budget was not applied to earnings from exports.
- The scheme of the drawback of import duties on inputs used in exports was extended to cover new items such as cocoa, cocoa powder, chocolate, butter and radio components. The procedures for obtaining drawbacks and import entitlements against exports were also simplified.
- The 50 per cent freight concession on railway freight granted for the movement of export consignments was extended to jute goods.

- Restrictions on the exports of several commodities were relaxed, and the ban on some 100 items was removed altogether.
- A series of steps were taken to enforce quality standards to facilitate the marketing of goods abroad.
- Measures were also taken to help exporters secure shipping space and reduce ocean freight.
- The Reserve Bank of India was authorized to give accommodation to commercial banks for up to 180 days regarding finance granted by these banks to exporters to improve the existing credit facilities for exporters.
- It was decided to prioritize licensing to expand existing capacity and create new capacity in industries with export potential.

Measures introduced in 1963–64 included:[25]

- Government withdrawal of the ban on the exports of several commodities and liberalized export quotas for others, including raw cotton, oil cakes and handloom fabrics
- Creation of a Marketing Development Fund to assist with export publicity and promotion
- Enactment of a law ensuring compulsory quality control and pre-shipment inspection
- Establishment of a Minerals and Metals Trading Corporation to oversee the growing volume of state trading in ores
- Setting up of new export promotion councils in basic chemicals, pharmaceuticals, soap and finished leather and its manufactures
- A general rebate of 25 per cent in the railway freight for sixty-five engineering industry products booked for export from any station to any port

Bhagwati and Desai provide a more detailed and systematic account of the export promotion measures during these years. They particularly emphasize the import entitlement scheme under which eligible exporters were provided import licences which fetched them handsome profits on account of domestic prices of the licensed products exceeding the corresponding foreign prices by 70 to 80 per cent. The licences issued grew in value rapidly in the early 1960s, with the implicit subsidy adding up to approximately half a billion rupees by 1963–64.[26] With the exchange rate misaligned by a wide margin and domestic prices continuing to rise, these promotion measures proved too little too late. Eventually, faced with the balance-of-payments difficulties and a food crisis, the government could not resist the pressure from the United States and was forced to devalue the rupee in June 1966.

Export Performance and Policies

In 1947, India enjoyed a share of 2.5 per cent in total world exports. The share fell to 2.1 per cent in 1951, 1.4 per cent in 1956, 1.2 per cent in 1961 and 0.9 per cent in 1966.[27] At least in hindsight, especially given what the experiences of countries such as South Korea, Taiwan and Singapore in the 1960s and 1970s revealed, this loss of the global markets had much to do with India's own policies. Rather than take a commodity-wise approach to explain the failure as done by Singh and Bhagwati and Desai, I limit myself to a handful of broader points.

First and foremost, India's basic approach to industrialization already had a strong anti-export bias. India was a labour-abundant country, and its comparative advantage was in labour-intensive commodities such as textiles, footwear and other light manufactures. But it started industrialization with some of the most capital-intensive industries, such as steel and machinery. The chances that India could become competitive in the global marketplace in these products relatively quickly were almost nil. Simultaneously, India used the instrumentality of investment licensing to deny the expansion and modernization of the factory sector in products such as textiles to protect small-scale and cottage-industry producers of the same products. The result was that India failed to take advantage of space vacated in the export market for cotton textiles by the United States and the United Kingdom during the 1950s. While India's share in this market stagnated, Japan's share rose from 13.2 per cent in 1951 to 18.1 per cent in 1960.

Second, the fixed nominal exchange rate in the face of a higher inflation rate relative to those prevailing in competing countries led to the progressive erosion of competitiveness of even products India had already been exporting. With the rupee overvalued, domestic sales of exportable products became more profitable than exports. This factor contributed to the loss of export-market shares across the board. It also undermined the competitiveness of the new products in sectors such as engineering and chemicals in which India had invested during the 1950s and beyond.

Third, the denial of imports of higher-quality and lower-price inputs in favour of domestically available substitutes hurt the quality and cost of production of products that India could export. This factor was especially relevant to labour-intensive light manufactures such as apparel, textiles, footwear, bicycles and sewing machines.

Finally, explicit export restrictions and taxes on many commodities also contributed to the loss of market share in the long run. For instance, quantitative restrictions were applied to products such as jute manufactures, tea, vegetable oilseeds and oils, and raw cotton, while export duties were applied to jute manufactures, tea, raw cotton, manganese ore and different kinds of oils either throughout the decade or a substantial part of it. It was thought that India had market power in many of these products because of its large share in the world markets for them. But the strategy failed because, in the longer run, these restrictions led to the emergence of new sources of supply and a shift into substitute products. For example, in the tea market, restrictions by India made it easier for Sri Lanka and several African countries to establish themselves as alternative suppliers. Likewise, paper bags emerged as substitutes for jute bags for packaging at least some of the products.

Foreign Investment Policy

Though Nehru left the formulation and implementation of trade policy to his juniors, he took direct responsibility for formulating foreign investment policy. He was acutely aware that his biggest challenge was growth or, in his language, rapid expansion of production. Just as he recognized the importance of domestic private capital for promoting this objective, he saw merit in wooing foreign capital.

At Independence, domestic private business, as well as socialists and communists among the political class, had been opposed to the entry of new foreign capital. Indeed, they also wanted the nationalization of enterprises held by foreign entities. As a result, IPR 1948 had walked a fine line between shutting the door tight and opening it wide to foreign capital. It extended the guarantee against nationalization of private enterprises for ten years, including those owned by foreign entities, and recognized that foreign-invested enterprises had a role to play in bringing 'industrial techniques and knowledge' but proposed to bring legislation to regulate the 'conditions under which they may participate in Indian industry'. It also noted that exceptions apart from the proposed legislation would 'provide that, as a rule, the major interest in ownership and effective control, should always be in Indian hands'.

Not only did the government not enact the proposed legislation, exactly a year after the adoption of IPR 1948, Nehru took a major step towards opening the door to private foreign capital much wider. In the Prime Minister's Statement to the

Parliament on the participation of foreign capital in India on 6 April 1949, he announced several steps extending protection to existing foreign-owned enterprises and welcoming new foreign capital. Because this statement served as the essential policy towards foreign capital throughout the Nehru era, it is important to spell out its main contents.[28]

First, Nehru conferred the national treatment on the existing foreign-owned enterprises in India and promised a friendly environment to future entrants. He said,

> In the first place I would like to state that the government would expect all undertakings, Indian and foreign, to conform to the general requirements of their industrial policy. As regards existing foreign interests, Government do not intend to place any restrictions or impose conditions which are not applicable to similar Indian enterprise. Government would also so frame their policy as to enable further foreign capital to be invested in India on terms and conditions that are mutually advantageous.

As a second policy provision, Nehru assured foreign enterprises regarding the repatriation of profits abroad. 'Second, foreign interests would be permitted to earn profits subject only to regulations common to all. We do not foresee any difficulty in continuing the existing facilities for the remittance of profits, and Government have no intention to place any restriction on the withdrawal of foreign capital investments . . .'

Nehru's third assurance related to fair compensation in case of a takeover of a foreign enterprise. 'Third, if and when foreign enterprises are compulsorily acquired, compensation will be paid on a fair and equitable basis as already announced in the Government's statement of policy.'

In the fourth provision, Nehru sought to ensure that his statement would not conflict with IPR 1948. In it, he reiterated that, as a rule, the majority ownership and effective control of enterprises would remain in Indian hands. He added, however, that this did not amount to closing the door on majority ownership and control in foreign hands. 'Obviously, there can be no hard and fast rule in this matter. Government will not object to foreign capital having control of a concern for a limited period, if it is found to be in national interest and each individual case will be dealt with on its merits.'

The fifth and final provision in the statement related to the temporary employment of foreign personnel if Indians with similar qualifications were unavailable. Though the government attached vital importance to the rapid Indianization of personnel, noted Nehru, it 'would not object to the employment of non-Indians if requisite qualifications are not available [locally] . . .'

Though domestic private business interests viewed this policy as a threat to them and vocally opposed it, the government stayed the course.[29] A press note issued in September 1949 clarified that the country was open to both majority ownership and effective control of enterprises. The note stated,

> The Government of India no longer think that a majority non-Indian interest in ownership, and in some cases effective control, can be regarded as *ipso facto* detrimental to the interests of the country. It is therefore proposed not to insist too strongly on majority control residing in Indian hands in the formative stage of industries.[30]

Later, on 28 February 1950, Finance Minister John Mathai took extra care to reiterate the importance of foreign capital to India when presenting the 1950–51 budget. Drawing a sharp distinction between debt and equity capital and emphasizing the role played by the latter in enhancing the productivity of domestic capital, he noted,[31]

> I consider that foreign capital is necessary in this country, not merely for the purpose of supplementing our own resources,

> but for the purpose of instilling a spirit of confidence among our own investors. I would like to make just this proposition that any considerable assistance in the way of capital from foreign countries must hereafter be looked for not in the shape of fixed interest-bearing loans and bonds, but in the shape of equity capital on the basis of joint participation on strict business consideration without any political strings attached to it.

Mathai also assured potential foreign investors that the end of colonialism did not mean the end of a secure environment for their investments:[32]

> The difference between the position today and the position in the 19th century is this: In the 19th century, when foreign capital went out from advanced countries to underdeveloped countries . . . colonialism provided the necessary sense of security to the foreign investor. Today, since colonialism has disappeared, the only way in which the same sense of security could be imparted is by friendly agreement. Therefore it is necessary that we should consider providing reasonable conditions of security and fair treatment for those who are willing to take the risk of investing their money in this country. The statement that the Prime Minister made last year still represents our policy in this matter and I believe that the terms and conditions outlined in the statement ought to provide reasonable security to foreign investors.

Over time, the government progressively relaxed restrictions on the repatriation of investments, encouraged foreign firms to enter industries reserved for the public sector, such as machine tools and fertilizers, and granted oil companies a substantial extraterritoriality as an inducement to set up refineries. By 1953, there was general recognition that the policy regime governing foreign capital matched 'almost exactly' the code published by the International Chamber of Commerce in the United States.[33]

In the second half of the 1950s, the foreign-exchange crisis of 1957–58 served as another catalyst for foreign investment liberalization. The Indo-US convertibility agreement was signed in September 1957 to attract American investment into India. The agreement guaranteed facilities for remittances of profits of American investment in India at the prevailing exchange rate. Previously, such a facility was available only in respect of investments made after 1950.[34] India also adopted a more relaxed attitude towards granting majority ownership to foreign investors in joint ventures. For example, CEAT Tyres of India Ltd was licensed in February 1958 with 60 per cent ownership by the Italian company and 40 per cent by the Indian public.[35] The government also invited foreign firms to take up the more profitable parts of industries reserved for the public sector, such as drugs, aluminium, heavy electrical equipment, fertilizers and synthetic rubber. Corporate taxes on income and royalties saw cuts in the 1959–60 and 1961–62 budgets. Double taxation avoidance treaties were signed with several creditor countries, including Sweden, Norway, Denmark, West Germany, Japan and the United States.[36] In February 1961, India also established the Indian Investment Centre with branches abroad to assist and advise Indian industrialists on strategies to attract foreign private capital and to inform foreign business entities on investment opportunities in India. As a part of the latter function, the centre was to promote knowledge and understanding in the major capital-exporting countries on conditions, laws, policies and procedures relating to investment in India.[37] In sum, throughout the Nehru era, India maintained an open policy regime towards foreign capital.

Concluding Remarks

In this chapter, I have discussed the export and foreign investment policies during the Nehru era. As long as the sterling balances remained plentiful, India remained wedded to wartime export licensing and export taxes on its major exports. Exports were seen as a means to dispose of residual output after domestic needs had been met. Until the sterling balances ran out, policymakers not just neglected exports but actively restricted them through export controls, export taxes on the major commodities and anti-export domestic policies. The result was that India lost the opportunity to capture a sizeable portion of the space in the cotton textiles export market created by the withdrawal of the United States and the United Kingdom during the 1950s. Japan instead took that space despite its higher wages relative to India.

Though the need to promote exports was progressively recognized after the depletion of the sterling balances left the balance of payments in a continuous state of fragility, available instruments proved grossly inadequate in the absence of devaluation. The instruments included the removal of export controls, reduction in export taxes and outright export subsidies of various kinds. But given India's fiscal needs for investment, fiscal resources available to exercise these instruments were limited. Eventually, in June 1966, India was forced to devalue the rupee, but it proved too little too late and also ill-timed since two back-to-back droughts at the time sent the economy into a tailspin and robbed the policy action of much of its power in the short run.

In contrast to import and export policies, India pursued a remarkably liberal foreign investment policy during the Nehru era. The explanation for it is much the same as that for the accommodation of private domestic capital: rapid expansion of production. Motivated by his socialist instincts, Nehru was keen on expanding the share of the public sector in the ownership of resources as rapidly as possible. But he was keener still on growth to eradicate India's 'appalling' poverty. Whenever Nehru saw a conflict between the expansion of the public sector and growth, he opted for the latter. Therefore, it is no surprise that he accommodated domestic private business interests and adopted a policy that would encourage private foreign capital to locate in India. In doing the latter, on occasion, he even had to fight the domestic private business interests that feared the competition from more efficient foreign capital.

My focus in this part of the volume up to this point has been on the policy regime, its implementation and qualitative analysis of its efficiency implications. I have generally abstained from the discussion of the actual outcomes. Did the government succeed in achieving what it had set out to achieve? Did the economy produce sufficient growth to make a material difference in poverty? Was a significant dent made in the economic structure to turn the economy from agricultural to industrial? These are some questions I turn to in the last chapter in this part of the book.

10

Growth, Industrialization and Poverty

The ultimate test of any development strategy is its outcome in terms of growth, structural transformation, poverty and social sectors such as education and health. Though I have touched on some aspects of outcomes in these areas when discussing the policies, they require a fuller, more focused treatment. I undertake this task in the present chapter. I shall turn to the profound long-run implications of the path chosen during the Nehru era in the next and last part of the book.

Growth

While the Herculean effort made by the government to mobilize the nation's savings and convert them into effective investments had its dividends, the objective of increasing GDP by 200 to 300 per cent in ten years, set by the National Planning Committee of 1938, was missed by a wide margin. From 1951–52 to 1963–64, GDP grew at an annual average rate of 4.1 per cent. This rate was a significant improvement over the 1 per cent rate achieved during the first half of the twentieth century but too little to make a dent in poverty.[1] With the population rising annually at 2.1 per cent, per-capita GDP rose only 2 per cent per year during these years. Given the low initial per-capita income, this increase was too small to push even a small proportion of the population above any reasonable poverty line. Indeed, given the poor performance of agriculture and the concentration of industrial growth in the large-scale, capital-intensive industry, it is unlikely that even a slightly faster growth would have successfully brought the fruits of growth to the bulk of the population. Scope for poverty reduction through income redistribution was also lacking: given the low income, whatever revenues could be raised got used up in augmenting public-sector investment and financing other administrative expenses, leaving little room for initiating anti-poverty programmes.

Figure 10.1 shows the evolution of GDP and per-capita GDP at constant 2011–12 prices during the thirteen years under study. It sets the value of each indicator at 100 in the year 1950–51 and plots its evolution over time. From 100 in 1950–51, GDP rose to 168 and per-capita GDP to 130 thirteen years later in 1963–64. The GDP growth rate was 4 per cent in the First Five-Year Plan (1951–56), 4.5 per cent in the second plan and 4 per cent in the first three years of the third plan. The critical Second Five-Year Plan produced only a small increase in the growth rate over the predecessor plan, and even that could not be sustained. Over the full five years of the third plan, the growth rate fell to 3.5 per cent. Moreover, by the end of it, the economy had arrived at the doorstep of a balance-of-payments crisis, which forced a devaluation of the rupee in June 1966.

Composition of Output and Employment across Broad Sectors

Table 10.1 reports the growth rates in agriculture (including forestry and fishing), industry and services (including construction). During the thirteen years, agriculture grew 2.4 per cent annually, industry 6.6 per cent and services 4.6 per cent. While agriculture can be said to have performed satisfactorily in the first ten years, it practically entered a crisis during the last three. Though 1964–65 was a good year for the sector, it was followed by two back-to-back droughts. This debacle in agriculture was substantially responsible for the balance-of-payments crisis that culminated in the devaluation of the rupee in 1966.

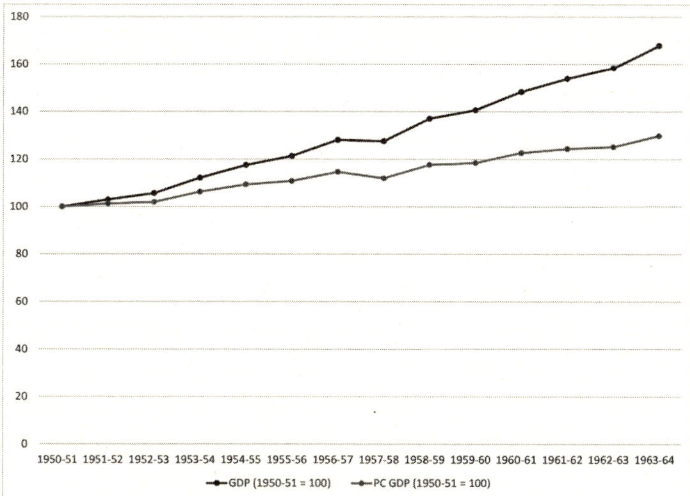

Figure 10.1: Evolution of GDP and per-capita GDP at constant 2011–12 prices

Source: Author's construction using data downloaded from https://dbieold.rbi.org.in/DBIE/dbie.rbi?site=statistics

In contrast to agriculture, industry did see a modest acceleration in the second and third plans. Because planning had focused on the industry, this acceleration could be viewed as its success. The growth pattern in services largely mirrored the growth in industry, though at a lower rate.

Table 10.1: Growth Rates in Agriculture, Industry and Services

Period	Agriculture, Forestry and Fishing	Industry	Services
1951–64	2.4	6.6	4.6
1951–56	2.9	5.6	3.9
1956–61	3.3	6.6	4.6
1961–64	0.1	8.3	5.5
1961–66	–0.3	6.9	5.2

Source: Author's calculations using data downloaded from https://dbieold.rbi.org.in/DBIE/dbie.rbi?site=statistics

NSO estimates

Figure 10.2 depicts the evolution of the three sectors over time. Similar to Figure 10.1, it sets the production level in each sector in 1950–51 at 100. By 1963–64, output in industry more than doubled, while in agriculture, it expanded only 35 per cent. Services fell in the middle with 78 per cent growth during the thirteen years. The differences in growth led to a considerable shift in the composition of output away from agriculture and towards industry and services.

Table 10.2 shows the percentage shares of the three sectors in 1950–51, 1955–56, 1960–61 and 1963–64. From 57.7 per cent in 1950–51, the share of agriculture in GDP fell to 49 per cent in 1963–64. The industry share rose from 11.6 per cent to 16.7 per cent, and services from 30.7 per cent to 34.5 per cent over the same period. Planners could view these shifts as signs of progress in industrialization and the transformation of the economy from an agricultural to an industrial one. But the transformation in the people's lives was far less than these output shifts might suggest.

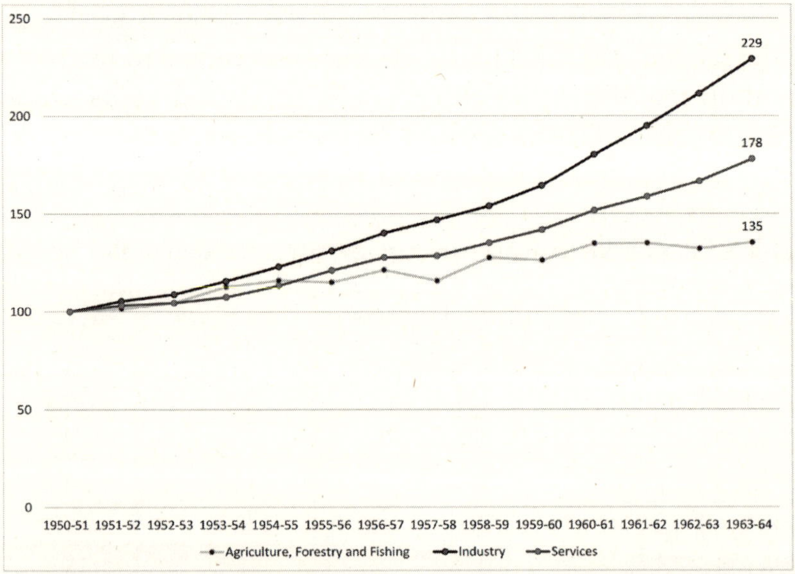

Figure 10.2: Evolution of agriculture, industry and services

Source: Author's construction using data downloaded from https://dbieold.rbi.org.in/DBIE/dbie.rbi?site=statistics

Table 10.2: Sectoral shares in GDP at constant 2011–12 prices

Year	Agriculture, Forestry and Fishing	Industry	Services
1950–51	57.7	11.6	30.7
1955–56	55.9	12.8	31.3
1960–61	53.5	14.4	32.1
1963–64	49.0	16.7	34.4

Source: Author's calculations using value added in agriculture, industry and services at constant 2011–12 prices available at https://dbieold.rbi.org.in/DBIE/dbie.rbi?site=statistics

In particular, shifts in the workforce across sectors were far smaller than in output. This fact is shown in Table 10.3, which divides the economy into slightly different broad sectors than Table 10.2: primary, secondary and tertiary. The major difference is that whereas the classification in Table 10.2 places construction in services, the one in Table 10.3 includes it in the secondary sector. The other difference concerns electricity and water, which are included in industry in Table 10.2 but in the tertiary sector in Table 10.3. The estimates in the table are based on the census, which takes place only once in ten years. Hence, I report the shares for 1951, 1961 and 1971.

As can be seen, the share of agriculture in the workforce at approximately 72 per cent hardly moved between 1951 and 1971. Within agriculture, the share of cultivators initially rose from 50 per cent in 1951 to 52.8 per cent in 1961 but drastically fell to 43.4 per cent in 1971. Correspondingly, the share of agricultural labourers fell between 1951 and 1961 but rose significantly in the following decade. The rise in the share of agricultural labourers suggests a worsening of fortunes within agriculture.

Table 10.3: Occupational distribution of workforce: 1951 to 1971

Sector	1951	1961	1971
I Primary Sector (1+2+3)	**72.1**	**71.8**	**72.1**
1. Cultivators	50	52.8	43.4
2. Agricultural labourers	19.7	16.7	26.3
3. Livestock, forestry, fishing	2.4	2.3	2.4
II. Secondary Sector (4+5+6)	**10.6**	**12.2**	**11.2**
4. Mining and quarrying	0.6	0.5	0.5
5. Manufacturing	9	10.6	9.5
6. Construction	1	1.1	1.2
III. Tertiary Sector (7+8+9)	**17.3**	**16**	**16.7**
7. Trade and commerce	5.3	4	5.6
8. Transport, storage and communication	1.5	1.6	2.4
9. Other services	10.5	10.4	8.7

Source: Excerpted from Kwait (undated)

Like agriculture, manufacturing and industry also saw their shares in the workforce more or less stagnate. The share in manufacturing rose from 9 per cent in 1951 to 10.6 per cent in 1961 but fell to 9.5 per cent in 1971. The share of industry as a whole largely mirrored this pattern. The share of the tertiary sector fell from 17.3 per cent in 1951 to 16 per cent in 1961 before rising to 16.7 per cent. It is unlikely that there was a major shift in the occupational structure, even within manufacturing, since industrial growth was concentrated mainly in the highly capital-intensive sectors. Much of the industrial and services workforce remained in the household and cottage industry sector with little access to capital.

Structure of Organized Industry

As planners intended, the structure of organized industry shifted decisively towards heavy industry, which was highly capital-intensive. Within the organized sector, labour-intensive light manufactures suffered. Table 10.4 illustrates this trend by tracing the evolution of the output of some of the major products during the first two plans.

Table 10.4: Index of industrial production (1950–51 = 100)

Group	1955–56	1960–61	Per cent Change
General index	139	194	39.6
Cotton textiles	128	133	3.9
Iron and steel	122	238	95.1
Machinery (all types)	192	503	162.0
Chemicals	179	288	60.9

Source: Planning Commission 1961, 39, Table 7 (Third Five-Year Plan)

The machinery sector exhibited the fastest growth, expanding five-fold during the decade. Growth in this sector was especially rapid during the second plan. The chemical industry had grown more than iron and steel in the first plan. But it fell behind the latter in the second plan. Reflecting the shift in policy in favour of heavy industry, iron and steel grew 95.1 per cent, overshadowing chemicals. Cotton textiles experienced the slowest growth during the decade, expanding just 33 per cent in ten years. At 3.9 per cent, growth was particularly disappointing during the second plan period. Policy priorities set by the planners in the second plan had begun to decisively push the industrial structure towards capital-intensive sectors.

Agriculture: Food Grain Production

Agriculture was subject to benign neglect during the Nehru era. Food grain production failed to keep pace with the demand, which had been rising due to the growing population. Any increase in the output may be attributed largely to an increase in the cultivated area (Figure 10.3).

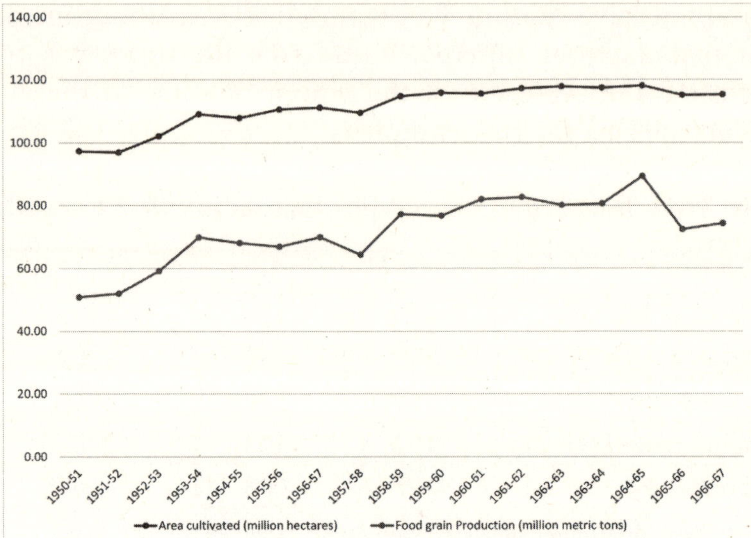

Figure 10.3: Area cultivated and food grain production from 1950–51 to 1966–67

Source: Author's construction based on *Agricultural Statistics at a Glance 2012*, Table 4.5(a), p. 61, Directorate of Economics and Statistics, Department of Agriculture and Cooperation

Progress in irrigation barely kept pace with the area cultivated, with the proportion of cultivated area irrigated rising from 18.1 per cent in 1950–51 to 19.8 per cent in 1963–64 (Table 10.5). The increase in productivity was also modest, from 522 kg per hectare to 687 kg per hectare.

Fluctuations in agricultural productivity suggest that agriculture remained subject to the vagaries of the weather. Good weather resulted in an upward jump in output per hectare (for example, from 580 kg in 1952–53 to 640 kg in 1954–55), and drought led to a fall in it (for example, from 706 kg in 1961–62 to 680 kg in 1962–63). Luckily, for the most part, droughts lasted only one year. But this good luck saw its first reversal one year after the death of Nehru, with two back-to-back droughts occurring in 1965–66 and 1966–67. Total food grain output drastically fell from 89.36 million metric tons in 1964–65 to 72.35 million metric tons in 1965–66 and 74.25 million metric tons in 1966–67. This experience led Nehru's successor, Prime Minister Lal Bahadur Shastri, to initiate steps towards the Green Revolution. Though Shastri passed away in January 1966, his successor, Prime Minister Indira Gandhi, sustained his effort towards raising agricultural production.

Table 10.5: Area, yield, output and area irrigated: 1950–51 to 1966–67

Year	Area cultivated (million hectares)	Food grain production (million metric tons)	Yield in kilogram per hectare	Per cent of cultivated area irrigated
1950–51	97.32	50.82	522	18.1
1951–52	96.96	51.99	536	18.4
1952–53	102.09	59.20	580	18.1
1953–54	109.07	69.82	640	18.1
1954–55	107.86	68.03	631	18.4
1955–56	110.56	66.85	605	18.5
1956–57	111.14	69.86	629	18.2
1957–58	109.48	64.31	587	19.3
1958–59	114.76	77.14	672	18.7
1959–60	115.82	76.67	662	18.8
1960–61	115.58	82.02	710	19.1
1961–62	117.23	82.71	706	19.1
1962–63	117.84	80.15	680	19.8
1963–64	117.42	80.64	687	19.8
1964–65	118.11	89.36	757	20.2
1965–66	115.10	72.35	629	20.9
1966–67	115.30	74.23	644	22.2

Source: *Agricultural Statistics at a Glance 2012*, Table 4.5(a), p. 61, Directorate of Economics and Statistics, Department of Agriculture and Cooperation

Export Performance

A fixed nominal exchange rate, combined with rising prices at home relative to abroad, a domestic policy that actively discouraged the production of labour-intensive products—products in which India had a comparative advantage on account of its cheaper labour—in the organized sector, and barriers to exports including licensing and duties together resulted in the extremely poor performance of exports. Though world exports had seen healthy growth during these years, the same was not true of India's exports (Figure 10.4). The result was a steady decline in India's share in world exports from 2.5 per cent in 1947 to 0.9 per cent in 1966 (Figure 10.5). This share did not begin to recover until after the 1991 reforms.

Yet another commonly used measure, the exports-to-GDP ratio, also points to a progressively deteriorating performance of exports. From the peak of 6.8 per cent in 1951–52, this ratio fell to a paltry 2.9 per cent in 1965–66 (Figure 10.6). This near collapse of exports and continuing pressure on imports due to rising demand for imported raw materials, components and machinery resulted in the balance-of-payments crisis and devaluation in June 1966.

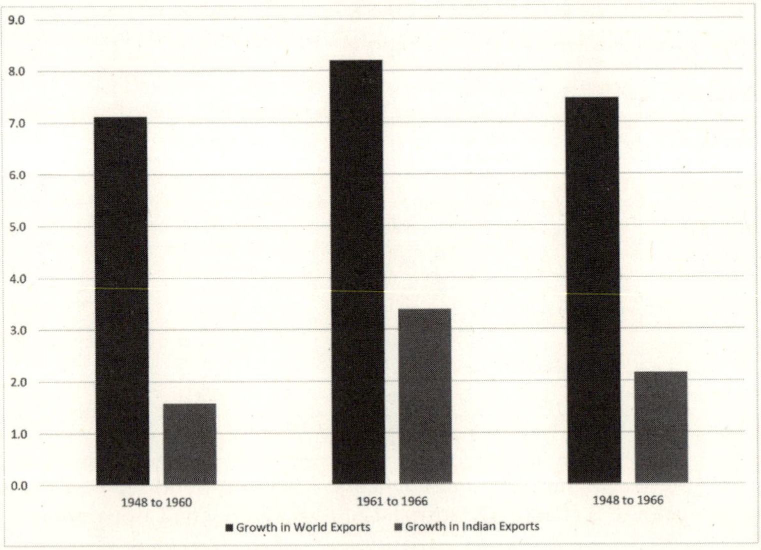

Figure 10.4: Export growth in India and the world: 1948 to 1966

Source: Author's construction based on export data in Bhagwati and Desai 1970, Table 18.1, p. 370

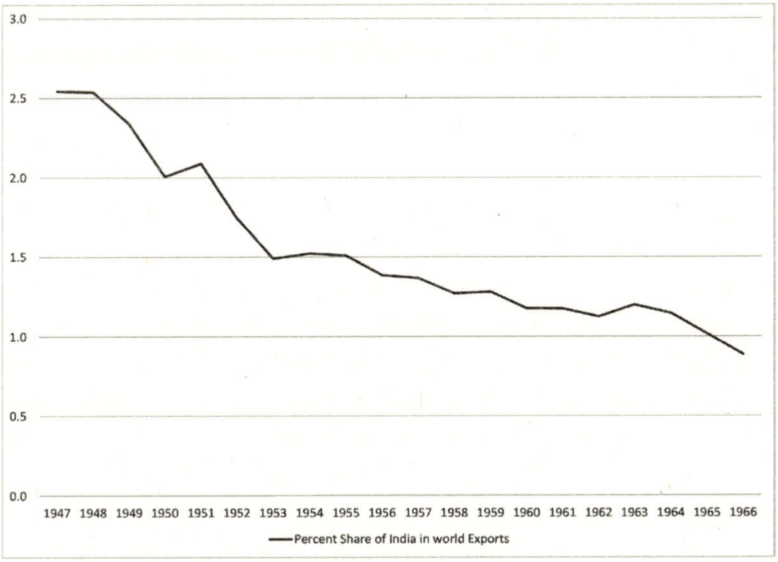

Figure 10.5: India's share in world exports: 1947 to 1966

Source: Author's construction based on the export data in Bhagwati and Desai 1970, Table 18.1, p. 370.

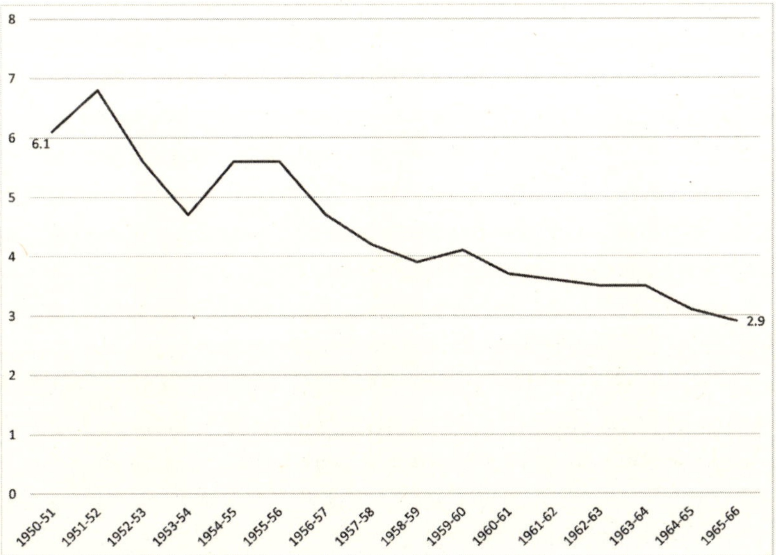

Figure 10.6: Exports as a percentage of GDP: 1950–51 to 1965–66

Source: Author's construction using data from the RBI Handbook of Statistics 2012, Table 1 for GDP and RBI Handbook of Statistics 2005, Table 145 for exports and imports

A study of the commodity structure of exports and its evolution offers further insight into why exports performed poorly. In Table 10.6, I have reported percentage shares of different commodities in merchandise exports in 1951–52, 1955–56, 1960–61 and 1965–66. Nearly all items listed in the table can be classified as traditional exports (jute manufactures, tea, cotton piece goods and manufactured leather) or primary products (minerals, unmanufactured tobacco, raw cotton and raw wool). In 1951–52, these items accounted for 65.9 per cent of all exports. This share declined steadily in subsequent years but remained high at 55.4 per cent in 1965–66. Though significant export subsidies were given in the 1960s to non-traditional exports, most notably engineering goods, their shares in the total exports remained too small to register an independent presence, as can be seen in Table 10.6.

India steadily lost ground in the world market of its top three exports, jute manufactures, tea and cotton piece goods. With its large shares in jute manufactures and tea markets, India had tried to exercise its market power by imposing export taxes on them. But over time, this led the importing countries to look for substitute products and other sellers and previously uncompetitive potential suppliers to become competitive. Pakistan emerged as a competitor in jute manufactures, and Sri Lanka and Kenya in tea. In cotton piece goods, with the United States and the United Kingdom exiting the export market during the 1950s, India was well positioned to expand its share in the latter. But with domestic policies positively discouraging its production in the organized sector, Japan took the entire space vacated by the two countries.[2] Despite several decades of experience in this sector, India lost an important opportunity to capture a market that promised both the creation of good jobs and the generation of valuable foreign exchange.

Table 10.6: Composition of exports during 1951–66: Selected years

Item	1951–52	1955–56	1960–61	1965–66
Jute manufactures	37.0	19.6	20.8	22.7
Tea	12.9	18.1	19.5	14.3
Cotton piece goods	7.2	9.4	9.1	6.9
Vegetable oils	3.2	5.7	1.3	0.5
Iron ore	0.1	1.0	2.7	5.2
Manganese ore	2.2	1.8	2.2	1.4
Mica	1.8	1.4	1.6	1.4
Unmanufactured tobacco	2.2	1.8	2.3	2.4
Coffee	0.1	0.2	1.1	1.6
Cashew kernels	1.2	2.1	3.0	3.4
Manufactured leather	3.4	3.7	3.9	3.5
Spices	4.0	1.5	2.6	2.9
Coir yarn and manufactures	1.4	1.5	1.4	0.1
Raw cotton	1.9	4.9	1.1	1.2
Lac	2.0	1.9	1.0	
Raw wool	0.7	1.6	1.2	
Others	18.6	23.7	25.0	32.5

Source: Bhagwati and Desai 1970, Table 18.3, p. 372.

Import Performance

The government had been able to maintain a somewhat liberal import policy as long as it had a comfortable pool of foreign exchange reserves on account of the sterling balances. The situation greatly deteriorated in 1956–57, leading to considerable tightening of import licensing. But because of the backlog of unused licences issued earlier, imports continued to expand briskly until 1957–58. Following this year, the trend shifted downward, with the import-to-GDP ratio declining from 7.8 per cent in 1957–58 to 5.1 per cent in 1965–66. Figure 10.7 depicts these developments.

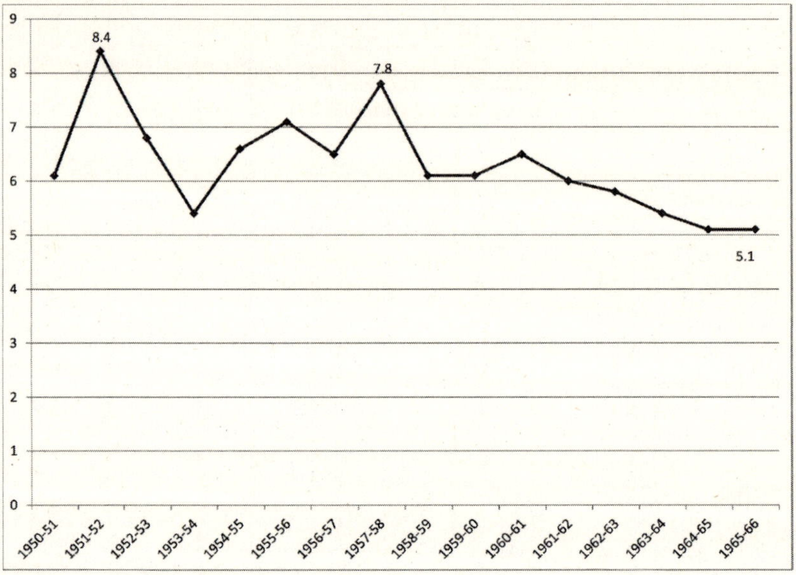

Figure 10.7: Imports as a per cent of GDP: 1950–51 to 1965–66

Source: See Figure 10.5

It is instructive to relate the movements in imports to the movements in foreign-exchange reserves. Accordingly, Figure 10.8 depicts the evolution of foreign-exchange reserves from 1951 to 1965. It can be seen that the reserves began to deplete sharply beginning in 1956. Though the government reacted by reintroducing foreign exchange budgeting, it could not stop the depletion immediately due to the existence of unused import licences issued earlier. As a result, foreign-exchange reserves continued to decline at a fast pace in 1957 and, at a reduced pace, in 1958. Between the end of 1955 and 1958, the reserves had fallen from $1881 million to $772 million. In the following years, foreign-exchange reserves remained precarious, and import licensing became progressively tighter. The composition of imports also shifted, with the imports of all but the most essential consumer goods, such as food grains and life-saving medicines, prohibited. The bulk of the free foreign exchange was reserved for raw materials, components and spare parts essential to keep running the existing factories. Machinery imports relied predominantly on the foreign exchange made available by foreign investors, aid and foreign credit.

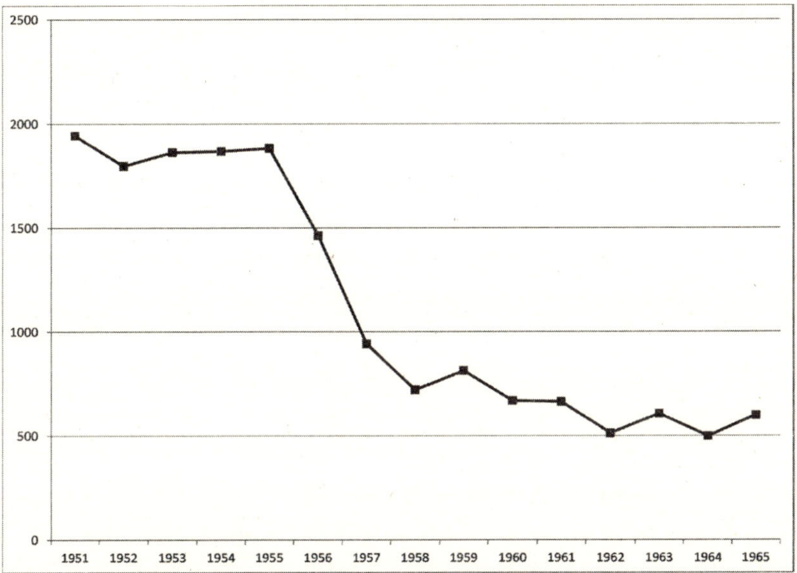

Figure 10.8: Foreign exchange reserves at the end of the year in million dollars: 1951 to 1965

Source: Bhagwati, Jagdish and T.N. Srinivasan 1975, Table 1–11

A key objective behind the heavy-industry approach was eliminating the dependence on imported machines to undertake new investments. But item-wise import data suggest that this dependence was not reduced over time. Indeed, we know from our discussion of the import licensing regime that its acute shortage mandated that the foreign exchange generated by exports be predominantly reserved for the imports of raw materials and components in order to utilize the existing production capacity as fully as possible. To the extent possible, the government was keen to find additional foreign-exchange resources through aid, loans abroad and foreign direct investment to finance the imports of machinery. Therefore, actual machinery imports remained heavily constrained and well below their demand. There is little doubt that these imports would have been far larger had exports been doing well to generate enough foreign exchange. But even then, the quantum of machinery imports remained elevated, and by the mid-1960s, India was further from achieving self-sufficiency than in 1950. Even iron and steel, a particular focus of the government's self-sufficiency drive, saw imports rise at least in nominal value.

Table 10.7 shows the imports of the major commodities during the first and second plans and the first four years of the third plan in nominal rupees. Machinery and locomotive imports saw a major expansion from Rs 1160 million in the first plan to Rs 2650 million in the second plan and then to Rs 3530 million in the first four years of the third plan. Iron and steel imports rose from Rs 340 million in the first plan to Rs 960 million in the second. Assuming proportionately the same level of imports in the fifth year as the annual average imports during the first four years, the five-year equivalent imports of iron and steel in the third plan would have been Rs 975 million. Though in real terms, this number would likely be less than that in the second plan, it still would be large and certainly exceed that in the first plan. The pursuit of a heavy industry approach to industrialization was unsuccessful in moving India towards self-sufficiency.

One final point on the composition of imports is that consumer goods imports fell to insignificant levels following the balance-of-payments crisis in 1957–58. In 1956–57, non-food consumer goods imports amounted to Rs 1475 million, accounting for 13.7 per cent of all imports.[3] In 1958–59, these imports fell to Rs 639 million and amounted to just 6.2 per cent of all imports.[4] By the third plan, the proportion fell to negligible levels. As one official source puts it, '. . . imports of consumer goods other than cereals and cereal preparations were reduced to the barest minimum during the Third Plan period. Imports of this category constituted only 1.1 per cent of the total imports during the Plan period.'[5]

Given that India relied largely on progressively tighter import licensing in the late 1950s and not on high customs duties, there emerged very large premiums over the tariff-inclusive price in the domestic market on the imported products. Bhagwati and Desai studied this question in detail and reported premiums (the difference between the domestic price and the tariff-inclusive price as a percentage of the latter) exceeding 100 per cent for many commodities. In Table 10.8, I reproduce a subset of the items and associated premiums in the chemical and engineering sectors they reported. The authors report even larger premiums over c.i.f. import price for some consumer goods, such as 260 to 620 per cent for lead pencils, 291 to 387 per cent for pens and 162 to 270 per cent for radios.

Table 10.7: Imports of principal commodities: 1951–66

			Rs million
Item	1951–52 to 1955–56	1956–57 to 1960–61	1961–62 to 1964–65 (4 years only)
Food grains	1200	1600	1960
Fertilizers	30	110	150
Cotton	770	450	540
Jute	250	50	50
Mineral oils	730	800	890
Chemicals, drugs and medicines	340	530	560
Metals other than iron and steel	200	350	520
Electrical goods and apparatus	160	190	200

Machinery and locomotives	1160	2650	3530
Iron and steel	340	960	780
Vehicles	410	610	580
Others	1710	2500	2050
Total	7300	10800	11810

Source: *Economic Survey 1965–66*, Government of India, p. 37

Table 10.8: Import premia in excess of tariff duty (percentage of tariff inclusive c.i.f. import price)

Item	1961	1962
Chemicals		
Hydro-sulphate of soda	30	212
Sodium	129	155
Sulphadimidine h.p.		55
Calcium	60	74
Titanium dioxide (rectile)	36	117
Engineering		
Shock absorbers, Jeep	75	146
Shock absorbers, Landmaster	103	150
Carbons (1): 12 x 300 mm	54	42
Carbons (2): 14 x 300 mm	42	44
House service meters (1) a.c. 10 amps	19	19
House service meters (2): a.c. 20 x 40 amps	66	66
Files: bastard 12 inch	301	250
Files: flat bastard 12 inch	297	256
Files: round bastard 12 inch	282	166
Electric motors a.c. 0.5 h.p.	19	19
Electric motors a.c. 0.5 h.p.	25	25
Piston assembly Land-Rover	139	139
Piston assembly Packard	184	228

Source: Bhagwati and Desai 1970, Table 16.5

These large premiums encouraged entrepreneurs to seek access to imported machinery, raw materials and components even if their equivalent domestically produced counterparts were available. Tariff inclusive c.i.f. price of the former being an order of magnitude lower than those of the latter, this outcome was inevitable. The premium also encouraged corruption since the importer and the officials granting import licences could split the handsome value of the premium between them.

Poverty Alleviation

The ultimate goal of all development efforts was reducing and eliminating poverty. But by all accounts, little progress was made on this front. In the debate on a no-confidence motion against the Nehru government between 19 and 22 August 1963, a lively argument ensued between Nehru and socialist leader Rammanohar Lohia. The argument was later labelled the '*teen anna pandrah anna*' (3 annas and 15 annas) debate.[6] Lohia argued that 270 million Indians, amounting to 60 per cent of the population, lived on just three annas (less than a quarter of a rupee which equalled 16 annas) per day. Nehru contested Lohia's estimate and stated that the average income of the population in question was more like 15 annas per day. Lohia disagreed with Nehru and contended that the only effect of the plans was to enrich a few each year. To quote him,

> Two or three lakh [2,00,000 to 3,00,000] persons grow rich every year. It is the only effect of the Five-Year Plans and a major portion of the increased national income is siphoned off for that purpose. In my opinion there are 50 lakh rich people at the moment and 3 lakh people are becoming rich every year. During the last 12 to 15 years 3 lakh people have been becoming rich. The British Government functioned with the support of 3 lakh people and the present Government is run by 50 lakh people.'[7]

When we consider the benign neglect of agriculture except in the first plan, the focus of industrialization efforts solely on heavy industry, no transition of the workforce out of agriculture into industry and services, denial of access to either capital or superior technology to cottage and household industry where the vast majority of non-agricultural workforce was employed, and the inflation fuelled by deficit financing, the essential point of Lohia would seem to be valid. Income increases were concentrated in the organized industry, which employed a tiny proportion of the workforce.

The evidence based on the household expenditure surveys conducted during the years under consideration supports this view. It is difficult to be confident about the quality of these surveys since they were conducted when resources were meagre. But if one is to resort to empirical evidence, this is the best we can do. Using the surveys, economist Gaurav Datt calculated rural, urban and overall poverty nationally almost annually, beginning with the period spanning August 1951 to November 1952.[8] He pegs the poverty line at a modest Rs 49 per person per month at prices prevailing from October 1973 to June 1974 and identifies the proportion of the population with expenditure below this threshold.

Figures 10.9 to 10.11 depict rural, urban and national-level poverty based on these estimates. They also show exponential trendlines for rural, urban and overall poverty. While urban poverty exhibits a rising trend, rural poverty has a barely visible declining trend. Poverty in rural and urban areas combined is almost entirely flat.

If we accept these trends as reflecting reality, a legitimate question is why urban poverty would have risen. Even if expenditure levels of the urban poor did not rise, why would they fall? Very likely, this change resulted from inflation. Increases in incomes in the organized industry partially financed by money creation led to rising prices of consumer goods. But nominal wages and income per person in the cottage and household industry sector, where the urban poor were employed, did not keep pace with these price increases.

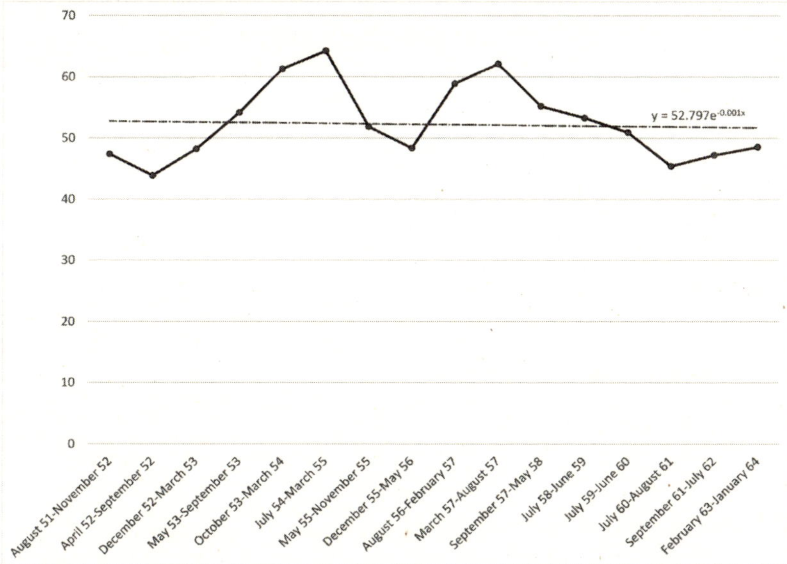

Figure 10.9: Evolution of rural poverty during the Nehru era

Source: Author's construction using poverty estimates by Datt 1998

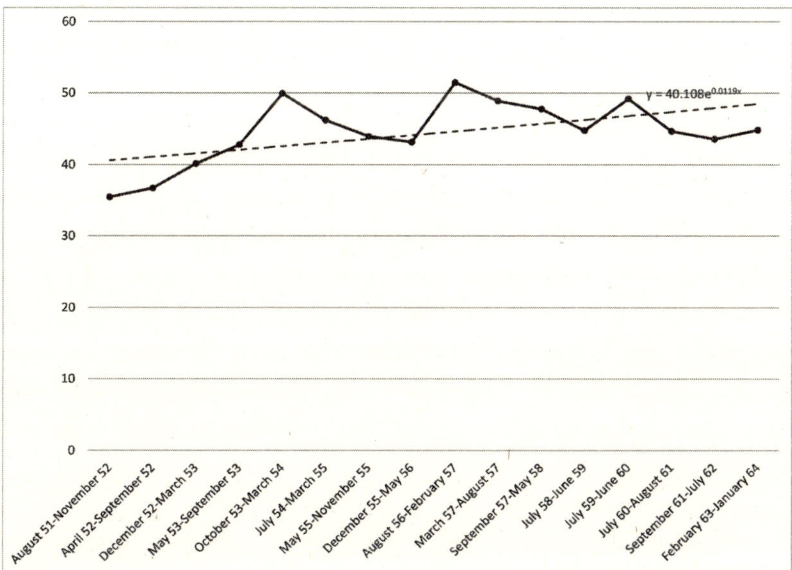

Figure 10.10: Evolution of urban poverty during the Nehru era

Source: Author's construction using poverty estimates by Datt 1998

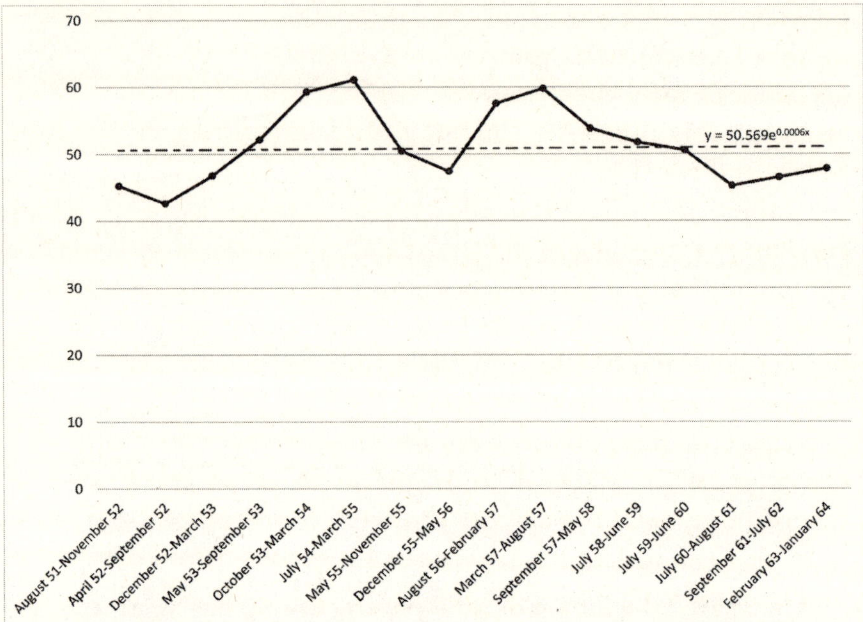

Figure 10.11: Poverty in India (Rural + Urban)

Source: Author's construction using poverty estimates by Datt 1998

Education

One final area of interest from the viewpoint of assessing outcomes is education, especially the schooling of children aged fourteen or less. With the government keen on developing capital-intensive industries and relatively low levels of income and savings rate, only limited resources could be spared for investment in education. Because the development of heavy industry also required investment in engineering, management and research institutions, resources left for school education shrank further.

An important directive principle of state policy in the Constitution stipulated that 'The State shall endeavour to provide, within a period of ten years from the commencement of this Constitution, for free and compulsory education for all children until they complete the age of fourteen years.' But attaining this objective remained a distant dream in the mid-1960s and was not achieved till the mid to late 2000s.

Table 10.9 reports the total enrolments and gross enrolment ratios at different levels of education just before the commencement of the first plan (1950–51) and in the terminal years of the first three plans. Though significant expansion took place at all levels of education over the fifteen years, the country remained very far from achieving the goal set by the directive principles of state policy. Even for children over six and under eleven years (in grades 1 to 4), the gross enrolment ratio had reached only 69.2 per cent in 1965–66. For students aged more than eleven and less than fourteen (in grades 5 to 7), the ratio had reached only 35.6 per cent.

Low inherited levels of literacy combined with slow progress in improving access to schools resulted in very low literacy levels in the immediate post-Independence decades. As per Census figures, the literacy rate for the population seven years and older was 18.3 per cent in 1951, 28.3 per cent in 1961 and 34.5 per cent in 1971. These low literacy rates stand in sharp contrast to those in South Korea. For example, according to Kwan S. Kim, 'There was an educational revolution primarily based on individual initiatives during the 1950s which paved the way for the industrial revolution, boosting the 30 per cent literacy rate in 1953 to 80 per cent ten years later. By 1970, the country's literacy rate was one of the highest in the world.'[9] Other countries in the region, such as Singapore and Taiwan, had similarly high literacy rates by the end of the 1960s.

Table 10.9: Total enrolments and gross enrolment ratios (GERs) at different levels of education

Education level	1950–51	1955–56	1960–61	1965–66
Total Enrolment in million				
Grades 1 to 4	13.65	17.38	24	37.09
Grades 5 to 7	3.23	4.59	7.46	12.55
Grades 8 to 10	1.51	2.37	3.68	6.13
Grades 11 and 12	0.28	0.5	0.85	1.4
College and University	0.26	0.44	0.65	1.1
Gross Enrolment Ratio*				
Grades 1 to 4	37.8	42.6	54.6	69.2
Grades 5 to 7	13	16.5	24.3	35.6
Grades 8 to 10	6.5	9.3	13.1	19.1
Grades 11 and 12	1.9	3.1	4.9	7
College and University	0.7	1	1.4	2.1

*Enrolments as a percentage of the total population in the relevant age group

Source: Compiled from estimates in Government of India 1966a, 161 (Table 7.5), 167 (Table 7.6), and 300 (Table 12.1)

While primary education for the masses in India failed to receive adequate attention, higher education did better than in comparator countries. In the early decades, India produced more engineers, managers, doctors and scientists than any other developing country. In this sense, the dualism in industrialization, whereby a small part of the industry saw the emergence of modern capital-intensive factories while the vast swaths of it remained traditional, was mirrored in dualism in education levels. At the high end, a small section of the population acquired skill levels comparable to those prevailing in the Western economies, but at the low end, even basic education failed to arrive.

Some authors attribute India's lacklustre economic performance during the 1950s to 1980s to its slow progress in spreading literacy. But this plausible-sounding proposition is highly suspect. Though the faster spread of literacy was a desirable social goal in its own right, it could have made no real difference to the growth rate. Literacy contributes to growth by facilitating skill creation. But skill creation in India during the first few post-Independence decades was hampered principally by the heavy-industry strategy, which left the cottage and household industry sector, where most of the non-agricultural workforce earned its living, without access to almost any capital. Literacy can help a worker acquire skills only if she has some minimum level of capital to work with, which was lacking. Put another way, even at the low rate of literacy, in absolute terms, there existed a sufficiently large number of educated individuals for enterprises capable of utilizing their services. The problem was that such enterprises were conspicuous by their absence. Except for the few operating in the organized sector, enterprises lacked the capital to modernize their production processes.

A Critical Examination

GDP and per-capita GDP growth rates at 4.1 per cent and 2 per cent per annum from 1951–52 to 1963–64 were significantly higher than 1.03 per cent and 0.24 per cent, respectively, achieved during 1900–01 to 1946–47. This fact has led some observers, notably Nayyar (2006), to claim a victory for Nehru's socialism. But as Deena Khatkhate (2006) has pointed out, such a conclusion is unwarranted. To quote him,

> During the latter [pre-independence] period there was no autonomous economic policy geared to the interests of a nation. The objective functions were different. It was a colonial policy, addressing the interests of the home country. Any policy, statist or otherwise, with India's interests at the centre, would have achieved better results than under a colonial regime.

My own past assessment of the Nehru era has been relatively favourable due to some growth acceleration and a more liberal policy regime relative to what came later under Prime Minister Indira Gandhi.[10] Until the balance-of-payments crisis, trade policy remained liberal, the direct-foreign-investment policy was significantly more liberal throughout the era, and the instinct for nationalization was restrained. But my research for this volume has led me to rethink my original assessment and take a more critical view of the economic strategy adopted by Nehru. The industrialization strategy centred on heavy industry and the strict adherence to a fixed nominal exchange rate undermined the potential benefits of the liberal elements in the economic policy regime along several dimensions. Even at the cost of some repetition, it is useful to bring together various aspects of the damage done to the economy by this strategy.

First, for a country with extremely limited capital, the strategy allocated it all to a handful of highly capital-intensive industries. The result was the division of industries into two extremes: at one extreme, there were industries with nearly all of the country's capital but little labour, and at the other extreme, there were industries with all the country's labour but no capital. As Friedman rightly pointed out in his short note on his maiden visit to India, efficiency required India to be somewhere between these two extremes.[11] Indeed, the limited capital would have been deployed far more efficiently if much of it had been allocated to precisely those industries that were denied any access to it, and almost none of it had been allocated to the ones to which it was allocated almost entirely. India's comparative advantage at the time was in labour-intensive manufacturing, and therefore, they should have been the vehicles of industrialization until it had accumulated a lot more capital. Instead, it started at the opposite extreme, where its costs relative to its trading patterns were the highest.

Second, an immediate outcome of this allocation of capital was that the vast majority of the population was excluded from the development process. Apart from the small elite workforce employed in heavy industry, the remainder stayed in agriculture or cottage and household industry. With almost no investment, little productivity improvement took place in these sectors. Paradoxically, the country's most abundant resource—labour—remained as underutilized as before the launch of planning. The strategy also deprived India of effectively exploiting the readily available technologies in light manufacture. The exclusion thus undermined growth, which in turn undermined the fight against poverty.

Third, the conceptually flawed division of industries into large- and small-scale ones missed the basic economic fact that all industries can be operated at varying production scales, and per-unit costs depend on the chosen scale. For example, one could build small-, medium- or large-scale steel mills just as one could set up small-, medium- or large-scale textile mills. The flawed conception, in turn, rendered the scale of the enterprise as a crucial choice variable for minimizing per-unit production costs irrelevant. Because capital had to be spared for the capital-intensive heavy industries, enterprises in the labour-intensive light industries were confined to the cottage and household enterprise sector and thus forced to operate at a small scale. And because the total volume of capital was limited and diversification was sought even within the heavy-industry sector, the enterprises in the latter could not be built on the scale matching their counterparts in the more capital-abundant industrial economies either.

Fourth, several decades of experience had placed the Indian textile industry in a leading position at Independence. In 1948–50, India enjoyed an 11.3 per cent share in the world cotton textiles exports, the same as Japan. In the 1950s, the United States and the United Kingdom, which accounted for 15 per cent and 17.5 per cent of textile exports in 1948–50, partially withdrew from this market. Unfortunately, India was unable to take advantage of the space so created. Consequently, its share in world exports dropped to 10 per cent during 1958–60 whereas that of Japan rose to 17.5 per cent.[12] Two key factors responsible for the decline in India's share were increased profitability of textiles in the domestic market relative to the export market and barriers to expansion and modernization necessary to improve product quality to the world standards. The former resulted from higher inflation at home than abroad in the face of a fixed nominal exchange rate. The latter followed from the government's desire to protect the cottage and household industry sector. As Bhagwati and Desai pointedly stated, 'The reasons for the stringent restrictions imposed on the installation of automatic looms were that (1) retrenchment of current employees would become necessary and (2) protection of labour-intensive methods was considered more economical to a labour-surplus economy.'[13]

Fifth, the experience of East Asian tigers in the 1960s and 1970s and of China subsequently demonstrated that skill upgradation in the early stages of development takes place in manufacturing with workers working with modern machinery. As the economy progresses, it moves into more complex products using machines requiring higher levels of skills. Alongside, workers initially unskilled become semi-skilled, those semi-skilled become more skilled, and the more skilled become highly skilled. In India, only a handful of workers lucky enough to find employment in heavy industries had the opportunity to acquire skills. Most remained employed in the cottage and household industries, which continued to produce strictly for local markets using traditional technology. As a result, little skill upgradation took place.

Sixth, with a large part of the revenues allocated to heavy industry, the government was already short on funds for investment in education and health. But even a significant proportion of these meagre funds were absorbed by engineering and management institutions since the development of heavy industry required advanced engineering and management skills. The result was a greater scarcity of funds for school education and investment in health. In his critique of India's development strategy, Bauer makes this telling observation regarding the implications of heavy industry strategy on expenditures on education:

> The preoccupation with investment expenditure, especially in heavy industry, has resulted in the neglect of government functions essential to Indian development. This is particularly true of education. The development expenditure on education in the Second Plan is between one-third and two-fifths of that on large and medium industries in the public sector. The development expenditure on elementary education is about one-half the cost of each of the three steel plants planned in the public sector; it is less than the corresponding figure in the First Plan, despite the rise in prices, increase in population and doubling of total planned outlay.[14]

Seventh, the combination of priority to heavy industry and the fixed nominal exchange rate proved fatal to the country's export performance. India could achieve competitiveness in the export markets in hardly any manufacturing activities and, over time, even lost market share in textiles, which had shown great promise at Independence. Ground was lost even in primary product exports due to rising prices at home relative to abroad and the fixed nominal exchange rate. As a result, the share of exports in GDP fell from 6.1 per cent in 1950–51 to just 2.9 per cent in 1965–66. Though some engineering and chemical goods exports began to appear in the 1960s, they had to be heavily subsidized and, in any case, remained too small to make a major dent in India's export revenues.[15]

Eighth, policy-induced failure of exports, which culminated in the balance-of-payments crisis of 1957–58, led to yet greater tightening of import controls and, consequently, investment licensing. If foreign exchange was scarce, not all machines required to set up new factories or raw materials and components necessary to run existing factories at full capacity could be imported. That meant a tightening of import licensing as well as investment licensing. Along with it came all the inefficiencies of running a vast and complex system of allocating foreign exchange and investment funds. Long delays and ad hoc decision-making inevitably followed with all kinds of inefficiencies plaguing the industrialization process.

Concluding Remarks

The reorientation of economic policies with Indian rather than British interests at their centre and the massive effort at industrialization in both private and public sectors successfully catalysed industrial growth at the average annual rate of 6.6 per cent during 1951–64. This growth spurred demand for many non-traded services and helped accelerate their growth as well. The net result was GDP growth at the annual average rate of 4.1 per cent during the thirteen years ending on 31 March 1964.

Unfortunately, however, the heavy-industry-centred industrialization created a dualistic structure of the economy consisting of a small, highly capital-intensive modern industrial enclave on the one hand and a vast swath of unorganized sectors consisting of agriculture and small and cottage industry on the other. The bulk of the workforce remained outside the modern industrial sector and hence was excluded from sharing the fruits of whatever growth occurred. As a consequence, poverty saw almost no decline. At the same time, the strategy also failed to take advantage of the country's large workforce, which resulted in sub-par growth. Because the workforce continued to be employed in the cottage and small industries, which were denied access to capital, it experienced little productivity growth.

The choice of a heavy industry strategy had other deleterious effects on the allocation of resources. With heavy industry absorbing a large proportion of scarce capital, social sectors such as education and health failed to receive their deserved share.

And within education, the needs of heavy industry required the creation of engineering and management institutions and undermined the progress in primary education.

The harmful effects of the chosen strategy did not remain confined to the Nehru era. On the contrary, the most damaging effects of the choices made during the 1950s were to unfold in the following decades. The indoctrination of nearly all influential constituencies in socialism within a democratic polity during this era had placed India on a path from which it found itself impossible to retreat for many decades. I turn to this critical theme in the last part of this volume.

Part III

The Lasting Impact

11

The Political Leadership I: 1950–84

I noted in the introduction that between the two foundational projects that Nehru initiated at Independence, the political one establishing a democratic rule with universal suffrage was a resounding success while the economic one involving the pursuit of a mixed economy with the aim of achieving self-sufficiency was an unqualified failure. In the end, the combination of socialism, which was integral to his economic model, and democracy proved deadly. Like India, China, too, had adopted a socialist model of development beginning in 1949. Like Nehru, its leader Mao Zedong promoted heavy industry to the neglect of light industry in the early years with even worse economic outcomes.

But given China's authoritarian regime, his successor Deng Xiaoping could switch course at a faster pace after he passed away than was the case in India in the post-Nehru era. Within a decade, Deng could replace the autarkic and centrally controlled policy regime with one progressively open to trade and foreign investment and reliant on decentralized markets. That switch in policy regime allowed China to take full advantage of the country's vast labour resources and technology available for the taking. Given his unquestioned authority, neither old ideologues nor entrenched economic interests could prove decisive in their pushback against his near-total abandonment of the economic regime that Mao had put in place.

In contrast, given its democratic structure, India found it impossible to make a similarly rapid transition. For one thing, ideological entrenchment produced successors of Nehru who themselves saw the solution in more rather than less of what Nehru had put in place. And when the country did have the good fortune to be gifted with leaders keen to move away from what Nehru had bequeathed, they were blocked or slowed down by the entrenched political, ideological and economic interests. Consequently, switching course from the Nehru Development Model has proved a significantly more difficult and long-drawn battle for India.

This argument, of course, sheds no light on the democracy versus authoritarianism debate. Anyone concluding in favour of authoritarianism from these observations must remember that if potential gains from pro-growth policies can be reaped rapidly under an authoritarian regime, the potential damage from anti-growth policies under such a regime is equally swift and deeper. China's own experience under Mao in the past and Xi Jinping currently bear witness to this fact. The limited point, for which we will see ample illustrations in the following pages, is that a vibrant democracy such as India provides considerable space for dissenting voices at all levels. This feature, consciously built into the system, implies that any change is slower but has the approval of the people at large and, therefore, is durable.

The dominant socialist themes that grew their roots under Nehru included the priority to heavy industry in development, the progressively larger role of the public sector, the pursuit of self-sufficiency, reliance for employment on small, cottage and household industries, and the pursuit of income and wealth equality. During the Nehru era, these ideas became entrenched in the psyche of the population in general and the decision-making elite in particular. With each succeeding generation inheriting these ideas from its predecessor, their dominance continued long after Nehru was gone. That, in turn, placed India on a more or less deterministic path on which the essential

Nehru model remained the economy's foundation. Despite growing evidence of India's poor economic performance and considerably superior growth and poverty outcomes in the countries that had opted for market-friendly and outward-oriented policy regimes, change was slow in India and remains so till today. Though the internal and external events did weaken the influence of socialist ideas, the process was slow.

Short of a popular uprising in favour of it—a rare occurrence—a major shift in policy in a democratic country requires initiative by the political leadership of the day. Such initiative may not always be sufficient to bring about change, but it is necessary. Even within the narrow confines of political leadership, the top decision-making authority—normally the prime minister in a parliamentary democracy—must be committed to the change. For it is the top leader who has the power to place the proposal for change on the table and rally support in favour of it.

With minor exceptions, until at least the end of 1984, India's prime ministers remained committed to the ideology and development model pioneered by Nehru. Lal Bahadur Shastri, who served as prime minister for nineteen months immediately following him, gave primacy to agriculture over industry but did not fundamentally challenge the ideas and system he had inherited. His successor, Indira Gandhi, the daughter of Nehru, turned out to be more socialist than her father. Except for 1977–79, she remained at the helm till 1984. As a result, the basic Nehru model remained unchallenged until her son, Rajiv Gandhi, succeeded her. As we will see in the next chapter, Rajiv Gandhi was the first prime minister to have escaped indoctrination in socialist ideas.

Jawaharlal Nehru: No Retreat until the End

I begin with an investigation of whether Nehru himself had second thoughts on any aspect of the economic policy regime he had chosen during his long tenure as India's prime minister. That the answer to this question is unequivocally negative is demonstrated by his long speech in the Lok Sabha in August 1963, less than a year before his death. The occasion was the debate on a no-confidence motion tabled against his government by the opposition parties. The debate lasted four days, from 19 August to 22 August 1963, and as many as forty-one parliamentarians spoke for or against the motion.

The Critique by Minoo Masani

Among the speeches delivered by the opposition members of Parliament, the one that stands out for its trenchant critique of Nehru's economic strategy was delivered by Minoo Masani, a member of the Swatantra Party, known for its advocacy of free enterprise. It is worthwhile to quote Masani at some length to give the flavour of what the staunchest critic of Nehru's policies thought before turning to the latter's response for insights into his thinking at the time.[1]

Masani began with a frontal assault on the philosophy underlying Nehru's economic strategy. He stated:

> I venture to say that while the objective was noble, . . . the method was hopelessly wrong—the method of Statism, of State capitalism, of believing that the people could do nothing, that Government must do everything for them, the carrying on of that *ma-baap sarkar* [mother-father government] mentality of the British raj, which has been the bane of this country during the past fifteen years.

He then attacked the instrumentality of planning in arriving at the production decisions. He asked,

> Who decided how the balance of the sectors will go? Is it not the people of India who by their consumer preference, by deciding what they want to buy and what not to buy, have the

> right to decide? Do you want to have economic democracy in this country, or do you want six or eight people sitting in Delhi, like the Government planners in Moscow, to dictate to the people what they should produce and what they should not produce, what they shall buy and what they shall not buy?

Masani next took to task the sinking of the national resources into inefficient heavy-industry enterprises in the public sector. Reminding that the share of the public sector in the total investment had risen from 46 per cent in the first plan to 54 per cent in the second and was estimated at 61 per cent in the third, he added

> And what return do we get on the capital that is being extracted from us by taxation and pumped into State enterprises like steel and other industries? The finance minister in his Budget speech of February, 1962 . . . admitted to the House that the average return on Government enterprises had dropped from 0.5 per cent to 0.3 per cent, but he encouraged the House by giving it good cheer that in the coming year it would rise to 0.4 per cent! If any industrialist or businessman tried to float shares on the market and offered those whose money was wanted 0.5 per cent, he would be considered insane. And yet our national capital is being wasted on projects, sunk in projects, which do not give us any return at all.

As a concrete example, he cited Hindustan Steel, calling it 'the biggest white elephant'. By 31 March 1962, the government had invested Rs 6.64 billion in it, but it had yielded a total loss of Rs 401 million.

Masani then targeted price controls. 'Then we come to controls—the main bane of our economy,' he stated. 'It is said we should stop prices rising by putting on controls. If I may say so, that is flying in the face of the laws of economics. Nothing can stop prices rising if the supply and demand position warrants it.' He added, 'Prices, like water, will find their own level, and no amount of juggling will stop the laws of hydrodynamics or the law of economics from having play.'

Taking to task the bureaucratic power and corruption that inevitably flowed from the controls, he noted,

> What, Sir, is a control? A control is giving an official, even a small one, the power of life and death over a peasant, a shopkeeper or a businessman. Human nature being what it is, is it a matter for surprise that our public life is now riddled with corruption? I am not putting on any cloak of moral superiority. We are all the same under the skin, whatever party we may belong to. But the danger is that when you combine economic and political power in the same hands, you are creating opportunities for corruption that should not be created. I would not entrust anybody, including my own party, with the unlimited power that you give to the bureaucracy and politicians to exercise controls.

Later in the speech, Masani returned to the theme of controls and corruption, this time invoking none other than the Father of the Nation, Mahatma Gandhi. He noted,

> Corruption, as Mahatma Gandhi said, is the result of controls. Every control leads to corruption. So long as you do not wind up the system of controls and red-tape in which you have tied India, you will not get rid of corruption. Gandhiji saw that, and it is still true. Gandhiji also saw that when the Congress Party, when it became the Government, became the rulers of the people instead of being the servants of the people, the people would turn against them.

Drawing the bottom line, he said, 'So, one comes to the conclusion that all this talk of socialism, however well-intentioned it may have been, has been a cover for setting up state capitalism and bureaucracy benefiting a new class and exploiting the mass of people.'

Nehru's Defence

Nehru's response, though aimed at the entire Opposition, took on more frontally the critique of his economic strategy and philosophy by Masani.[2] His response testifies to his full ownership of ideas he had championed in the 1950s and earlier. After expressing his disappointment at the 'absence of a larger [alternative] vision' in the Opposition members' speeches, he went on to defend his heavy-industry approach to industrialization as a means of achieving self-sufficiency. He said,

> Shri Masani gave expression to his views about economic affairs, and I am astounded that any intelligent people should talk in the way he did. There is no sense in it, no understanding of the modern world of economics as it is understood today. He said: why have a steel plant? A more astonishing remark it has not been my bad fortune to listen to. What does he expect? We should not have that, [then] we should have small industries? I am all for small industries. We should have what is called no capital-intensive works that take up too much capital and therefore we should advance like this? Where do machines come from for the small industries? We can get them from Germany, Japan, Russia, wherever you like, and pay heavily for them, go on paying for them? Is this anyone's conception of industrialization of this country? No country has been industrialized in that way.

Returning virtually to the language used and arguments made in *The Discovery of India*, published almost two decades earlier in 1946, Nehru went on to add,

> You cannot advance, industrialize this country, without an industrial base, and an industrial base means basic industries

> and mother industries, heavy industries and the like. As soon as that is established, smaller industries flow from them, and the rate of progress is fast. If you do not establish that, well, you remain tied up not only not advancing fast, but you are tied up to other countries who are economically dominant over you, who can prevent your growth, who can lower down the rate of progress. You are not economically free completely.

Turning to a defence of socialism, Nehru reminded that the Constitution had provided the necessary background even if it did not explicitly mention it.

> Later this parliament definitely adopted the ideal of socialism, and the Planning Commission too. If any hon. Member in the opposite side criticized us for not having gone fast enough on the road to realize socialism, I would accept that criticism; we have not gone fast enough. . . . But I am convinced that there is no choice for India, party or no party; no party whatever it may feel can stop this march to socialism in this country, to democratic socialism.

Nehru then went on to extol India for simultaneously adopting democracy and planning.

> We are perhaps the only country . . . where an attempt has been made to put this idea of social democracy and try to achieve it by planning. Planning has taken place in other places; [but] they are not democratic places. Other countries which are democratic have not accepted planning. But the combination of the two is rather unique.

Thus, Nehru remained convinced that the path he had chosen for India was the right one. Indeed, by the time he passed away on 27 May 1964, his view of socialism with its attendant features of heavy-industry-led industrialization, progressive expansion of the public sector and a push for self-sufficiency had been accepted and adopted by a broad spectrum of the political class. The critique by Masani was an exception, and if asked, few among the ranks of the Opposition would have endorsed it. At one point in his long speech, Masani himself explicitly approved of public-sector enterprises as long as they competed with private-sector enterprises on a level playing field. He stated,

> It is not true that some of us do not believe in State enterprises. We stand for a mixed economy. We stand for a mixed economy of private and State enterprise working side by side to serve the needs of the community, but this must be on a basis of free and equal competition, of allowing the consumer to decide whether he wants to buy these goods or those goods, and not State monopoly capitalism which is becoming increasingly the pattern of our socialist economy here.[3]

Two days later, when Morarji Desai spoke and chided Masani for having admitted 'the necessity of socialism' and expressing belief in 'a mixed economy,' the latter fully owned up to the same stating, 'I have always believed in a mixed economy.'[4]

Lal Bahadur Shastri: A Champion of Agriculture but . . .

Against this state of political play, it should come as no surprise that at least in his public pronouncements, Lal Bahadur Shastri, who succeeded Nehru on 9 June 1964 and ruled for a brief period of nineteen months, remained committed to the Nehru Development Model. While some authors have suggested that his public pronouncements notwithstanding, he made far-reaching changes to the policy regime, others have said that he would have made such changes had he lived longer. In the former category, we can cite political scientist Francine Frankel who has written, 'During the brief twenty months of Shastri's tenure, a series of undramatic initiatives in economic policy that went virtually unnoticed at the time cumulatively altered the entire approach to India's development strategy.'[5] In the latter category, we may refer to economist I.G. Patel who had served in senior policy positions under Nehru, Shastri and Indira Gandhi. He writes in his memoir, 'He [Shastri] was too shrewd to give an impression that he was out to undo the work of Pandit ji [Nehru]. But I have no doubt that that is precisely what he would have done if he had lived longer.'[6] Later in the memoir, when referring to Shastri's decision to devalue the rupee less than two weeks before his untimely death, he states, 'I have no doubt that if he [Shastri] had lived longer, devaluation would have come earlier, and been managed more smoothly, accompanied or followed by far-reaching reforms.'[7]

Elaborating on her proposition, Frankel adds,

> Among the results of decisions taken during this period were the eclipse of the Planning Commission as a policy-making body; a shift from controls to incentives as major instruments of development planning; a reorientation of public investment from basic industries to agriculture; a new agricultural strategy to concentrate modern inputs in irrigated areas of the country; and an enlarged role for private domestic and foreign investment in the development of the industrial sector.[8]

While one can accept her points that Shastri shifted some of the decision-making power from the Planning Commission to line ministries and gave agriculture its long overdue priority in policy as well as investment, it is a stretch to argue that the changes he made led to a fundamental departure from the Nehru Development Model or set the system irreversibly moving in that direction. Whether we consider the public sector or regulation of the private sector via investment and import licensing, and price and distribution controls, there was little change either during his rule or soon after. As regards the planning commission, it did lose some of its clout in policymaking to line ministries, but it remained a central player in the system till at least the early

1990s, exerting significant influence on investment allocation through target-setting.

Even regarding agriculture, given the massive and recurrent food shortages that threatened starvation deaths around this time, the shift in priorities in its favour was inevitable. This same shortage also compelled Indira Gandhi, his successor, to sustain the shift, notwithstanding her major push to otherwise expand the scope of socialist policies. Events following Shastri's death also bring into question Patel's speculation that Shastri would have undone the Nehruvian regime much earlier, provided he had lived longer. The balance of political forces at the time was overwhelmingly against such a change.

To expand on these themes, begin with Shastri's public pronouncements. His speeches betray no desire to move away from Nehru's socialism. In his first address to the nation upon assuming office on 9 June 1964, he emphatically promised to stay the course on economic (and foreign) policy. He said,

> There comes a time in the life of every nation, when it stands at the crossroads of history and must choose which way to go. But for us there need be no difficulty or hesitation, no looking to right or left. Our way is straight and clear—the building up of a socialist democracy at home with freedom and prosperity for all . . .[9]

Three months later, responding to a no-confidence motion in the Lok Sabha, he underlined the importance of planning. 'Whether it is agriculture or industry,' he said, 'they have all to be viewed under the shadow of our Plans. . . . Insofar as planning is concerned, I need not repeat that it is absolutely essential for our country. If there is no Plan or no Planning Commission there will be chaos.'[10]

A month later, in October 1964, the National Development Council (NDC) of the Planning Commission met to discuss the Memorandum on the fourth plan. Shastri expressed his support for all major aspects of Nehru's development strategy in his speech to the council. He said,

> I should like to say here a word about the relative roles of the private sector and the public sector. Our objective, as you all know, is socialism. This does mean an immense growth of the public sector. In regard to the private sector each plan sets out what the private sector will do and what the public sector will do. Failure in either sector affects the Plan and creates imbalances in the economy.[11]

Then, going even further than Nehru on the role to be played by the public sector, he added,

> In the context of rising prices and the difficulties which the common man has to face about basic consumer goods, it would be necessary that some of the consumer goods industries also are developed in the public sector. It seems to me that the Government should also set up textile mills, sugar factories and plants for the manufacture of cement, drugs and medicines; only then can we be assured that the shortages which we have been experiencing in the recent past will not become chronic.[12]

Shastri then acknowledged the continued importance of heavy industry. 'Heavy industries, will, of course, continue to be the backbone of our economic development,' he said. 'Steel and machinery must be produced in larger quantities. Care has, of course, to be taken, as I have had occasion to emphasize in the past, that we secure the utmost out of the investment which we make in heavy industry in the shortest possible time.'[13] He expressed particular concern with the efficiency of heavy industry. 'Planning of heavy industries for the Fourth Plan has to be on the basis of performance,' he noted. 'Only then will planning become more real and more accurate.'[14]

The area in which Shastri genuinely differed from Nehru was his greater concern for agriculture. For a man who had himself grown up in poverty and, as such, had an instinctive empathy for the poor, the concern that everyone must have access to food in adequate volume was a natural one. He not only aired his concerns publicly but expended much effort and political capital on introducing price incentives to increase food grain production and create infrastructure for the procurement and distribution of food grain. The establishment of the Food Corporation of India and the Agricultural Price Commission was a part of this effort.[15]

Shastri's early keenness to increase the share of agriculture in the total investment turned into urgency by the time the NDC met a second time in his tenure in September 1965. He expressed this urgency in his inaugural speech to the members, thus,

> We have also to see that in the first year of the Fourth Five Year Plan, we give our fullest attention to agriculture. . . . I do not say that other things must be cut down. For example, in the first year, if we try to complete all the industrial projects we have in hand and which have not been completed by the end of the Third Five Year Plan, we can concentrate on those projects. . . . But what I had suggested, and would suggest today, is that we should be prepared to make any sacrifice in the first year of the Plan with a view to providing adequate funds for agriculture.[16]

Though these changes did not translate into reality in the form suggested both because Shastri passed away four months later and economic circumstances originating in two back-to-back droughts led to the postponement of the launch of the fourth plan till 1969, they testify to Shastri's willingness to keep large investments in industry temporarily on hold to solve India's food problem.

Granting that priority to agriculture was a matter of conviction for Shastri, it remains true that even absent such conviction, internal and external forces mandated the course he chose. Internally, the country had experienced stagnant or declining food grain production during the first three years of the third plan, necessitating imports of food grain in the order of 11 to 12 million tons over the three years. While the fourth year saw a significant jump in output, the fifth, 1965–66, turned out to be a drought year. Consequently, food grain imports in 1965 alone touched an unprecedented 7.5 million tons.[17] By September 1965, when the NDC met, the country was already amid a food crisis. Therefore, a shift in priorities in favour of agriculture was inescapable.

Because these food grain imports came principally from the United States, they gave the latter considerable leverage over policy in India. Being unhappy about what he considered a neglect of agriculture, United States President Lyndon Johnson had been pressing India to rejig investment priorities towards this sector and away from heavy industry. There was thus also credible external pressure for the shift.

As regards the devaluation, domestic politics was wholly against it. But the external pressure for it proved binding. Foreign-exchange shortage due to the poor performance of exports had increased foreign aid requirements, giving the World Bank considerable leverage over Indian policies. Unsurprisingly, it had been pressing India to devalue the rupee as one of the key conditions of additional aid around this time. According to an account provided by Patel, less than two weeks before passing away, Shastri had authorized his finance minister to negotiate the magnitude of the exchange-rate adjustment with the International Monetary Fund (IMF). It is on the strength of this decision that Patel hypothesizes in his memoir that had Shastri lived longer, India would not have had to wait for far-reaching reforms as long as it did.[18]

But this inference is difficult to sustain given what transpired within the following year. Shastri died on 11 January 1966 from a heart attack and was succeeded by Indira Gandhi (IG). The opposition to devaluation she encountered illustrates the hostility any leader pushing for liberalization would have faced at the time. Nearly all senior members of her cabinet and the entire senior leadership of Congress rose in revolt against devaluation. She even wavered at the last minute and had L.K. Jha, the head of her secretariat, contact B.K. Nehru, Indian ambassador to the United States, to withhold the announcement of devaluation. But Nehru replied that India had already gone too far to turn back and risked losing international credibility and access to aid if it did not devalue. At that point, IG decided to bite the bullet and had her finance minister announce the decision on 6 June 1966.[19]

Once devaluation was announced, politicians, media persons and economists condemned it nearly unanimously. With rare exceptions, even the handful who had expressed approval of the step when consulted privately by the prime minister or her office before its announcement turned against it. Frankel describes the ferocity of the criticism thus:

> Attacks on devaluation cut across ideological lines. Opposition leaders, including those in the conservative Swatantra party and the Jan Sangh, could find neither 'sound economics nor honorable politics' in the decision. Even the major industrial and business groups were sceptical, welcoming the step only if it paved the way for the complete dismantling of government regulations and controls over the economy.

She continues, 'The left perceived more sinister results. *Link*, the pro-CPI [Communist Party of India] weekly newsmagazine, denounced the decision to devalue as a "craven surrender" to the United States that dealt the final blow to Nehru's strategy of economic independence built on rapid industrialization and agrarian reform.'[20]

Given this harsh and near-universal criticism, it is difficult to imagine that the outcome would have been any different had Shastri been the one to embark upon the measure. Perhaps he would have navigated the politics more deftly, and his enhanced political stature in the wake of the victory in the 1965 war against Pakistan would have muted, even silenced, some of the critics. But it is inconceivable that even he could have turned the political opinion to favour devaluation. Faith in the Nehru Development Model and passion for socialism still ran deep in the rank and file of Congress and many in the Opposition. Even more implausible is the suggestion that Shastri would have embarked upon a major liberalization programme aimed at the eventual dismantling of the Nehruvian edifice.

Indira Gandhi: The Ultimate Socialist

Events during the three years following devaluation demonstrate that socialism remained a powerful political force in late 1960s India. IG had owed her elevation to the prime minister's office to Congress bosses heading the organizational wing of the party and known as the 'Syndicate'. There was no obvious successor to Shastri who could have won a majority of Congress parliamentary party votes on his or her own. As such, the Syndicate wielded the power to choose the next prime minister. For them, the natural candidate would have been Morarji Desai, who shared their more conservative economic philosophy. But they feared Desai was too strong-willed and ambitious to share power with them. For a number of reasons, they saw a more suitable candidate in IG and opted for her.[21]

Battling the Syndicate with Socialism as Her Sword

The party bosses had entirely misread IG. As future events revealed, she was a woman of iron will and had no intention of doing their bidding. Soon after the 1967 national and state elections in which Congress fared rather poorly, differences between her and them came out in the open. In the ensuing struggle, which lasted approximately two years, she scored a decisive victory over them. The interesting fact from the viewpoint of the argument in this chapter is that the key weapon IG used to defeat her opponents—the nationalization of the fourteen largest banks—represented a major advancement of the socialist agenda. Jubilation and celebrations in the streets of Delhi that followed the announcement of this measure testify to the popularity of socialism at this time. A few months later, when the Congress was split between an IG faction and a Syndicate faction, recognizing IG's newfound popularity, a sufficiently large majority of Congress members of Parliament threw in their lot with her so that, with the additional support of a few other parties and independents, she was able to retain a majority in the Parliament.

That socialism had continued to find support across a wide spectrum of politicians at this time is illustrated by the fact that though the Syndicate has often been described as conservative and right-of-centre and IG as socialist and left-of-centre, their positions on economic policy, if any, were minuscule. Indeed, going by their policy choices, they can both be characterized as more socialist than Nehru. This claim is supported by the fact that the Ten Point Programme, adopted unanimously by the All-India Congress Committee (AICC) in June 1967, was unambiguously more socialist in its content than Nehru's socialism. It included social control of banks, nationalization of general insurance, state trading of exports and imports, state trading of food grains, abolition of princely privileges, and curbs on monopolies and concentration of economic power.

A conservative by the definition of the day, Desai had been in the Syndicate camp. As a compromise between IG and the Syndicate, he was appointed deputy prime minister and finance minister following the 1967 election. As such, it is he who took the steps to implement the first two items in the Ten Point Programme. In December 1968, he took the lead in the passage of the Banking Laws (Amendments) Act of 1968 to gain social control of banks. In parallel, he also initiated steps to bring similar legislation for general insurance.

The argument that the support of the Syndicate for the Ten Point Programme indicates the continuing faith in and popularity of socialism may be countered by contending that this may have represented nothing more than a political compromise on the part of the Syndicate to reposition itself after the poor showing in the 1967 elections. Of course, a counter to this argument is that in June 1967, IG still lacked sufficient following within the party to force the Syndicate to accept her agenda. But even if valid, the political-compromise argument only testifies to the central position socialism continued to occupy in Indian politics. Political survival mandated a movement towards rather than away from socialism.

Ultimately, the Syndicate lost to IG precisely because its socialism failed to go far enough and fast enough. Right from the time the Ten Point Programme was adopted by the AICC, a group of young socialists known as the Young Turks and loosely organized as the Congress Forum for Socialist Action (CFSA) had argued that the programme did not go far enough. In particular, some had argued in favour of outright nationalization rather than just social controls of banks. In the following two years, they aggressively pushed for the nationalization of banks and immediate implementation of various measures promised in the Ten Point Programme but Desai successfully limited action to the Banking Laws (Amendments) Act of 1968.[22] For her part, IG maintained a strategic silence and chose not to come to the rescue of conservative members of the Syndicate when attacked by the members of the CFSA. She also began to consult the Syndicate, including the Congress president, less and less on government matters. All these factors contributed to widening the divide between IG and the Syndicate.

The tensions finally came to a head when in July 1969, the Congress was confronted with having to choose a candidate to contest the election for the position of the President of India left vacant on account of the unexpected death of President Zakir Hussain. Both IG and the Syndicate knew that in an open conflict between them, the President would play a critical role in choosing the prime minister. Therefore, they wanted to be sure that the candidate was not someone partisan to the other side. Sensing that she lacked the necessary votes in the Congress Parliamentary Board (CPB) at the Bangalore AICC session during 10–12 July 1969, IG went on an all-out offensive. After the CPB had voted her long-time foe Neelam Sanjiva Reddy as the presidential candidate, she announced to the press that her preference was Vice President V.V. Giri, who was already the acting President. Giri himself announced (perhaps with the tacit approval of IG) his independent candidacy.

IG immediately relieved Desai as the finance minister, took charge of the ministry and, on 19 July 1969, had the acting President Giri issue an ordinance nationalizing the fourteen largest private banks. Within two weeks, she got the Parliament to replace the ordinance with a parliamentary act. The nationalization made IG an instant hero and greatly emboldened her. In the presidential election, she decided to side with her two senior colleagues who had publicly called for a vote based on conscience (which meant voting for Giri). When the votes were counted on 20 August 1969, Giri won by a paper-thin majority.

A split in the Congress followed in November 1969. IG inherited the larger of the two factions, with 220 members in the Lok Sabha, which fell well short of the majority. But she could bridge the gap with the support of independents and other parties, including the two communist parties. In 1971, she called for early elections and, with her newfound popularity, scored a spectacular victory. Her party won 352 out of 518 seats in Lok Sabha. The two communist parties, taken together, won another 48 seats while the rival Congress faction was reduced to just 16 seats.

A Rapid March to the Left

The years 1969 to 1976 saw India rapidly march to the left, with most changes concentrated between 1969 and 1973. The nationalization of banks was quickly followed by the

Monopolies and Restrictive Trade Practices (MRTP) Act of 1969 in December. The Act gave the government wide powers to regulate large undertakings or groups of inter-connected undertakings defined as those with Rs 200 million or more in assets. These undertakings became known as the MRTP firms and were subject to additional licensing restrictions, including confinement of all new investments to a narrow set of highly capital-intensive industries identified as the 'core' industries.

The government promulgated an ordinance nationalizing general insurance in May 1971. New restrictions on exports and imports were introduced, with the list of canalized items greatly expanded. The coal and oil industries were nationalized in 1973. The Foreign Exchange Regulations Act (FERA) of 1973 placed tight restrictions on foreign exchange transactions and, with a handful of exceptions, capped the foreign equity share in a corporation resident in India to 40 per cent. Small-scale industries (SSI) reservation, originally introduced in 1967, was expanded from the original 47 items to 177 items by 1974. A new chapter, Chapter V.B, was added to the Industrial Disputes Act of 1947 in 1976. It made laying off workers nearly impossible for factories with 300 (revised to 100 in 1982) or more workers. The same year, the Urban Land Ceiling Act of 1976 was enacted. It imposed formidable restrictions on the ownership of urban land. The marginal personal income tax rates reached over 90 per cent in the early 1970s. Through the Constitution (Forty-second Amendment) Act of 1976, IG also changed India's official title in the preamble to the Constitution from 'sovereign democratic republic' to 'sovereign socialist secular democratic republic.' Socialism was thus formally incorporated into the Constitution and, going by the Supreme Court verdict in the 1994 S.R. Bommai v. Union of India case, is now a part of the basic structure doctrine.

Opportunist, Pragmatist or Socialist?

A common belief is that when IG came to office, she had no strong views for or against socialism and that her ultra-socialist policy agenda was driven by her advisers, most notably P.N. Haksar. The latter was a committed socialist with a communist past. He joined IG as the head of her office in May 1967.

For example, historian Ramchandra Guha has written, 'Mrs. Gandhi had rarely invoked the word "socialist" before 1967, although it was one of the four pillars of her father's political philosophy' and that 'the prime minister was, so to say, non-ideological—an attribute not shared by her advisers. The chief among these was the principal secretary, P.N. Haksar.' Describing Haksar's views on economic and foreign policies, Guha adds, 'His political views were those of the left wing of the British Labour Party, circa 1945—pro-state and anti-market in economic affairs, pro-Soviet and anti-American in foreign policy.'[23] Political scientist Sudipta Kaviraj takes a similar view of IG stating, 'To the Congress bosses she was a good candidate precisely because her symbolism of Nehru was in a sense false; she could, in their eyes, benefit from her connection with Nehru without any inheritance of his reformism.'[24] Patel is more categorical when he asserts, 'There was nothing basically ideological about Mrs. Gandhi. Everything was as it suited her at the time.'[25]

In my view, this narrative underestimates the extent to which IG felt committed to socialism well before P.N. Haksar joined her office. No doubt, like any other successful politician, she had a pragmatic and opportunistic side. But this did not exclude subscribing to the socialist ideology. While she rarely aired her views publicly, as someone who had actively participated in the freedom movement, spent decades by her father's side, served on the Congress Working Committee and held the party's presidency, she had plenty of exposure to socialism. Frankel explains why the Syndicate chose her to succeed Shastri in these words,

> She had a 'progressive' image in the party, having supported the younger activists in their efforts to organize Socialist Forum

> groups since the late 1950s. She was, indeed, accessible to leaders of the left opposition parties, maintaining friendships since her student days in London with men such as Bhupesh Gupta and Mohan Kumaramangalam, who later cast their political fortunes with the CPI [Communist Party of India]. Like her father, she was reputed to be a firm proponent of planning, somewhat suspicious of private enterprise, and well disposed toward the Soviet Union.

Frankel adds, 'The Syndicate was, nevertheless, uneasy. Its most conservative member, S.K. Patil, found Mrs. Gandhi's reputation for left-leaning views unpalatable.'[26]

To be sure, Haksar played an extremely active role in decision-making while he served in the office. But one can scarcely neglect that it was IG who chose to bring him to her office, likely precisely because she knew of his unflinching commitment to socialist ideology. She had found L.K. Jha, whom she had inherited from Shastri as the head of her secretariat, to be 'too far right of her views'.[27] Therefore, once the devaluation episode and the 1967 elections were behind her, she set out to replace him with someone whose views were better aligned with her own. Given that she had known Haksar well, he was a natural choice for the job. Indeed, it is probable that she had him marked for the job within months of taking office. Just two months after becoming the prime minister, she had officially visited the United States. On a stopover in London, she had picked Haksar as a part of her team. Haksar had been serving as India's deputy high commissioner in London at the time.[28]

Haksar had been a frequent visitor to the home of IG and her husband, Feroze Gandhi, in London in the late 1930s.* From 1934 to 1939, the Communist International had been promoting the idea of establishing 'popular front' governments in Europe to fight Hitler, Mussolini and their allies. Haksar's own

---

* Katherine Frank places the timing of these events in early 1941 when Indira Gandhi and Feroze Gandhi briefly lived together before their marriage in 1942.

baptism into communist ideology took place around this time, and neither he nor IG could remain untouched by the popular front idea. Ramesh puts the matter in these terms,

> He [Haksar] remained a 'popular frontist' all his life. He was wedded—as indeed was Indira Gandhi—to this mode of thinking about progressive political alliances. It was this political outlook imbibed in England in the late-1930s that led Haksar to welcome communists into the Congress fold and that encouraged Indira Gandhi to keep them on her side between 1967 and 1977.[29]

A final point in support of the hypothesis that IG followed her own instincts on matters of policy is that much of her policy agenda was driven by the Ten Point Programme. While Haksar actively advised IG on the design of strategy and timing of action, he played no role in formulating the Ten Point Programme. Such important policy measures as social control of banks, nationalization of general insurance, end to privy purses and privileges of princes, state trading of exports and imports, state trading of food grains, and curbs on monopolies and concentration of economic power had already been on the Congress party agenda with IG's full support when Haksar arrived on the scene.[30] The only major modification to this agenda was the replacement of social control of banks with nationalization. Some of her policy actions, such as the laws on urban land ceiling and the addition of chapter V.B to the Industrial Disputes Act, came after Haksar had left her office.

Morarji Desai: Nothing Conservative about Him

On 25 June 1975, IG declared an internal emergency under which she acquired the power to rule by decree. However, approximately nineteen months later, on 18 January 1977, she decided to call fresh elections. In the following elections, she and her party were decisively defeated by the Janata Party, formed by merging several Opposition parties, including the Syndicate faction of the original undivided Congress. Desai became the prime minister on 24 March 1977. But due to internal squabbles, the Janata Party failed to serve its full term. The Parliament was dissolved early, and fresh elections were held in January 1980, in which IG was voted back to office with a clear majority.

Desai has been uniformly described as a conservative who favoured the private sector. Parties that had come together to form the Janata Party shared a dislike of all that IG stood for. They also included the Swatantra Party and Jana Sangh, with the former being overtly pro-free-enterprise and the latter, a party of traders. Given these facts, it was reasonable to expect the Desai government to steer the economy away from Nehruvian socialism. Yet, going by the industrial policy statement announced by the government on 23 December 1977, there is little indication that it had any intention of bringing about a significant change to economic policy. True, it tried to shift the emphasis in favour of small-scale enterprises, which were devoted predominantly to producing consumer goods. However, this was not a deviation from the Nehruvian policy framework since encouraging these enterprises as an instrument of employment generation had been integral to the latter. The statement also introduced some liberalization of imports but, once again, whenever the foreign-exchange situation permitted it, this had been the policy under Nehru.

The government increased the role of the so-called small-scale industries (SSI) enterprises principally by expanding the list of items reserved for exclusive production by them.[31] The list had been originally introduced by the IG government in 1967 and contained 180 items when the Janata government came to office. The latter added 324 items on 23 December 1977 and another 303 items on 26 April 1978. The additions led to the list expanding to a total of 807 items. The policy statement also froze the mill and power-loom sector capacity for textile production, stipulating that no new capacity would be licensed.

Beyond this modification, which can also be viewed as a natural extension of the policy inherited from IG, the policy statement did not propose any significant change of course. It continued to recognize the importance of heavy industry stating,

> In general, the areas for large industries will be—(a) basic industries which are essential for providing infrastructure as well [as] for development of small and village industries, such as steel, non-ferrous metals, cement and oil refining; (b) capital goods industries for meeting machinery requirements of basic industries as well as small-scale ones; (c) high-technology [items] needing large-scale production, . . . such as fertilizers, pesticides and petrochemicals; (d) other industries . . . considered essential for the development of the economy such as chemicals and machine tools.

The policy statement endorsed the public sector as a countervailing power to the growth of large business houses and as an instrument of socializing the means of production in strategic areas. It provided for the expansion of the public sector not just in the field of basic and strategic industries but also in consumer goods industries to ensure essential supplies. The public sector was also to help develop ancillary units and other small industries. The policy statement thus proposed to expand rather than restrict the role of the public sector in the economy.

The policy statement promised to further tighten the controls around the large private business houses and enterprises. To this end, it proposed to enforce the provisions of the Monopolies and Restrictive Trade Practices Act of 1969 with fewer exceptions allowed than under IG. It also promised to reduce the access of large private enterprises to public financial institutions to force them to raise a higher proportion of their funds themselves. To this end, it expressed the government's intention to tighten the debt-equity norms.

The statement retained the IG-era policy of keeping the majority ownership and effective control of foreign-invested enterprises in Indian hands. It stated that the government would enforce strictly the provisions of FERA in this regard. As a result, the exit of foreign multinationals that began under IG continued. Two cases, extensively covered in national and international media, were of Coca Cola and IBM. Both proposed compromise plans but the government remained firm. In a contemporary report, *Time* magazine noted,

> India's ruling Janata Party, in vigorously enforcing the nation's 1973 Foreign Exchange Regulation Act, is pressing hard for at least partial Indian ownership of foreign companies operating in the country. A total of 57 foreign firms have decided to close down their Indian plants rather than meet demands for some degree of Indian ownership. One company under pressure: Coca-Cola, which has all but stopped making Coke in India. The company had been ready to reach an agreement on mixed ownership, but rejected India's demand for the formula for Coke's syrup, a secret that is supposedly locked in a Georgia bank vault and known to only ten people in the world.'[32]

The only promise for liberalization in the policy was regarding imports. It proposed to rely less on quantitative restrictions and more on tariffs to regulate imports. This concession was driven principally by an improvement in the foreign-exchange situation, partly due to remittances from the Middle East following the oil crisis and partly due to an improvement in export performance following the reduced overvaluation of the rupee. By way of concrete result, this provision in the policy statement led to a small expansion of the open general licensing list.

In a critique published within less than a month of the announcement of the policy statement, economist Deepak Lal pointed to three major weaknesses in it. He elaborated on the third of them thus, 'The third major shortcoming of the Janata's industrial policy reflects the limited extent to which it has succeeded in escaping from the general mode of thinking popularized by the Nehru model of development.' He argued that the major flaw of the Nehru model was to intervene in economic decision-making through direct bureaucratic control rather than manipulating prices. He pointed out that the Janata government seemed to grasp this flaw when favouring tariffs over quantitative restrictions to regulate foreign trade. He added, however, 'It is therefore surprising that when it comes to industrial policy the Janata party, including Mr. Charan Singh, still seem enmeshed in the mode of thinking associated with the Nehru model.'[33]

The cumulative result of the pursuit of a policy aimed at expanding the public sector by successive governments was that by the early 1980s, the central government had more or less acquired control of the 'commanding heights' of the economy. Frankel offers the necessary empirical evidence to ground this conclusion:

> About 45 per cent of output in organized industry was accounted for by the public sector, as well as banks and other long-term lending institutions. As of 1981–82, India's eight largest firms were in the public sector, as were 24 of the top 30 in terms of total capital employed. Overall, the public sector enjoyed a 3:1 advantage over the private sector in paid-up share capital, and a 4:1 advantage in the value of sales.[34]

Indira Gandhi Returns: A Liberal This Time Around?

Because the only force unifying the disparate constituent parties of the Janata Party was their shared opposition to IG, they could not hold together for long. Non-stop internal squabbles among them almost from the beginning led to the Desai government's downfall on 19 July 1979. The President invited Charan Singh to form the government and prove his majority. But, unable to muster a majority, Singh resigned after only three weeks in office. With no other coalition able to muster a majority, the President dissolved the Parliament and called for fresh elections. With Singh serving as the interim prime minister, elections were held in January 1980, returning IG to office once again with a two-thirds majority in the Lok Sabha.

While these political battles were being fought in India, neighbouring China was experiencing political developments of much bigger consequence. Mao Zedong died in 1976, and Deng Xiaoping succeeded him. The latter quickly grasped that the heavy-industry-led development reliant almost exclusively on the public sector and near total central control over economic activity had failed to serve China well. Taking advantage of the near complete authority vested in him, Deng began to make far-reaching changes to the economic regime. Those changes began restructuring the Chinese economy towards greater export orientation and specialization in labour-intensive products. As the 1980s progressed, the country achieved growth rates in the 8 to 10 per cent range. By the mid-1980s, textiles and apparel had emerged as China's two major exports.

In India, as the end of the 1970s approached, dissatisfaction with the performance of the economy in general and industry in particular was growing. But with almost the entire political class having its roots directly in the Nehru era, predictably, the consensus in favour of a serious departure from the economic policy framework of that era was nowhere to be seen. IG, who returned to office in January 1980, issued a new industrial policy statement on 23 July 1980. Unsurprisingly, with differences in shades but not substance, it represented a reiteration of her policy before losing office to Desai.

At the outset, the policy statement reaffirmed its faith in the MRTP Act of 1969 and the Foreign Exchange Regulation Act of 1973, which the earlier IG government had enacted.[35] It called for the rehabilitation of faith in the public sector, promising to evolve an effective operational management system in the public-sector undertakings. As regards the private corporate sector, the policy statement provided for it to develop in consonance with the targets and objectives of national plans and policies while promising to curb the growth of monopolistic tendencies or concentration of economic power and wealth in a few hands. It promised, however, not to place avoidable restrictions on the fullest use of the existing industrial capacity, particularly in the case of the core industries or industries directly linked to them. The statement also underlined the government's commitment to the SSI sector, raising the investment ceiling on them from Rs 1 million to Rs 2 million.

One area in which the policy statement differed from the policies IG had pursued from 1966 to 1977 was exports. It provided for sympathetic consideration of requests for setting up 100 per cent export-oriented units, expansion of existing units solely for purposes of exports and allowing higher production to fully exploit emerging export opportunities. It further promised to consider favourably proposals for units deploying advanced technology and sufficiently large in scale to achieve competitiveness in the world markets.

While the industrial policy statement thus made no promise of liberalization, in reality, the IG government did take some baby steps towards it. These steps are related to both imports and industrial licensing. Import liberalization took place by trimming the list of banned items, expanding the Open General Licensing (OGL) list and reducing the canalization of imports. Industrial licensing was liberalized through the expansion of licensed capacity via various measures, enlargement of the scope of new investments by the MRTP firms, a hike in the threshold below which a licence was not required and opening the manufacture of telecommunications equipment to the private sector.[36]

These liberalizing steps have led political scientist Atul Kohli to assert that 'the trend toward the liberalization of the economy was initiated, not by Rajiv Gandhi, but by his mother, Indira Gandhi'.[37] He connects this liberalism in economic policy to what political scientist James Manor has described as her 'rightward' shift in politics during her last phase spanning January 1980 to October 1984.[38]

This is a questionable interpretation of the evidence. For one thing, these were very small steps introduced through purely bureaucratic actions and without any change in the policy framework or public pronouncements. As such, they were like safety valves releasing the excessive pressure generated by an expanding economy. Despite tight controls, accumulated investments over three decades had created a large enough industrial base that entrepreneurs progressively demanded greater capacity expansion.

More importantly, though marginally bigger in magnitude, the liberalizing steps were quite similar to those IG herself had taken in 1975 and 1976. In this sense, she was not walking a new path. As I noted in my 2008 book, these steps represented a 'piecemeal retreat, begun in 1975, from the highly restrictive regime that she had herself put in place'.[39] Two factors had led her to initiate the retreat in 1975 and 1976. One, even the slow-paced industrialization during the first twenty-five years of planning had created sufficient business interests that sought access to imported inputs to fully utilize the production capacity they had already created and an easing of investment licensing to add to that capacity. And two, various factors combined to relax India's foreign-exchange constraint. That, in turn, made some import liberalization feasible. As such, 1975–76 witnessed the introduction of automatic import licensing on certain items and the reintroduction of the OGL list. With the foreign-exchange situation remaining favourable, additional liberalization took place in 1976–77 and during the Janata years.

The upshot of this discussion is that no cracks had appeared in the Nehru Development Model until October 1984, when IG was assassinated. Indeed, with several major steps in the leftward direction taken by IG during 1969–76 and her liberalizing steps only partially reversing them, the policy regime remained more restrictive than at the time of Nehru's death. This fact was acknowledged by influential economics commentator of the time, Prem Shankar Jha, in a 1982 column devoted to the analysis of some of the liberalizing steps by IG. In the concluding paragraph of the column, he wrote,

> The relaxation of price controls on cement and steel is thus the last albeit the most important of reforms the government has undertaken. But all of these are only tentative first steps towards a more *laissez-faire*-oriented economy. By and large the economy remains hedged by controls on pricing and investment, subject to severe credit constraints, and to high corporate taxation . . . Nearly every one of the steps taken so far involves a relaxation and not an outright removal of a control.[40]

Concluding Remarks

The impact of the Nehru Development Model did not remain confined to the Nehru era. Being grounded in the enticing philosophy of socialism, its practice while Nehru lived unleashed ideas that became integral to the thinking of the influential politicians who survived him. Though a conservative wing within the Congress had existed even under Nehru, differences between it and the more radical socialist wing were only of shades and not substance. By 1964 when Nehru died, no mainstream politician was prepared to publicly challenge the essential elements of the Nehru model. For example, Shastri, who is considered by some as lacking enthusiasm for heavy industry, never made any mention of it in his public utterances.

After the unexpected death of Shastri, a power struggle did break out between the more radical socialist daughter of Nehru, Indira Gandhi, and the conservative wing of the Congress, which held sway over the organizational wing of the party. But in the end, the former came out victorious by painting the latter as the friends of big business. Clearly, socialism had continued to have popular appeal. Once firmly in the saddle, by advancing a socialist agenda that went much further than

Nehru, IG positively added to her popularity and scored a massive electoral victory in 1971.

That the grip of socialist ideas on nearly all political parties remained intact throughout the 1970s is illustrated by the fact that when in 1977, good fortune placed the reins of the nation jointly in the hands of nearly all who opposed IG, the policies they pursued were hardly distinguishable from hers. They dismantled none of the major anti-growth policies she had put in place. It is difficult to escape the conclusion that having learnt their trade while Nehru led the nation, they had remained socialist at heart and approved of the policy regime he and his successors had put in place.

By January 1980, when IG returned to office, the socialist regime had peaked. In the following five years, she did take some measures to loosen the grip of licensing on investment and imports and to weaken the hold of price controls, but those measures cannot be characterized as a fundamental change of heart. She made no fundamental change to the policy framework, and the policy regime remained far more constraining than at the time of Nehru's death.

Yet, India's fortunes were about to take a turn for the better regarding economic policy. The assassination of IG on 31 October 1984 was to fortuitously bring her son, a young, new-generation leader with the ambition to take the country into the twenty-first century, to the helm. He had been an airline pilot through much of his professional career and had deliberately chosen to keep away from politics. As such, he carried none of the baggage that had burdened his predecessors, especially his mother.

12

The Political Leadership II: 1985–2023

Genuine cracks in the wall of socialism began to appear only in 1985. Over time, these cracks grew larger though it is arguable whether they will ever lead to its total collapse. The process has been gradual, reflecting the country's democratic polity. The result is that after almost four decades of the initial cracks, the public sector continues to have a heavy presence in manufacturing, while private industry remains saddled with overregulation. Complex labour and land laws remain unreformed. Worse still, import-substitution industrialization has seen a comeback.

Rajiv Gandhi: A Leader without Socialist Baggage at Last

Rajiv Gandhi (RG) succeeded Indira Gandhi after she was assassinated. RG was a reluctant entrant to politics and the first prime minister without the baggage of socialism. He had studied first at the elite Doon School in Dehradun and then at the University of Cambridge in the United Kingdom. He was unsuccessful in completing his engineering degree at Cambridge and, returning to India in 1966, became a member of the Delhi Flying Club. In 1970, he joined the state-run Indian Airlines as a pilot and remained with it till 1980. During these years, he kept his distance from politics. But in 1980, his younger brother, Sanjay Gandhi, who had been an active partner of their mother in politics, unexpectedly died in a plane accident. At the urging of his mother, RG then entered politics rather reluctantly. He contested the election from his brother's constituency and became a member of Parliament in 1981. Even then, he spent the following year organizing the Asian Games. As such, he entered the prime minister's office with minimal political experience and no prior commitment to socialism.

In an article published less than six months after RG assumed office, influential journalist Girilal Jain described him and others around him as having preoccupations different from those of their predecessors. 'They have not been influenced,' he wrote, 'either by Mahatma Gandhi or by Jawaharlal Nehru's anti-imperialist and socialist commitments. They are modernizers who call themselves pragmatists.'[1] To sharpen the contrast with the conventional Indian politicians, Jain mentioned two members of RG's innermost circle, Arun Nehru and Arun Singh, describing them as 'top executives in two multinationals before they took to politics'.

Later in his Radhakrishnan Lectures, Bhagwati attributed RG's tilt in favour of markets to 'an intuitive grasp of the costs that the vast control apparatus, in particular, was imposing on the country.' Elaborating on the point, he stated:[2]

> Rajiv Gandhi, a former pilot with the Indian Airlines, was the first Prime Minister to have done honest work outside politics. He thus had seen for himself, and through his friends, the system that he sensibly deplored and would seek to change. It really makes all the difference how you see the control system, whether from the lens of the one who runs it or of the one whom it runs over. The wise Nobel laureate economist Arthur Lewis, adviser to Hugh Gaitskell, is supposed to have gone up to Thomas Balogh, later adviser to Prime Minister Harold Wilson, and said: 'Tommy, the difference between your socialism and mine is that when you think of socialism you think of yourself as behind the counter whereas when I think of socialism I think of myself as being in front of it.'

Advocacy of Liberal Policies

One way to gauge how little baggage RG brought to the office is through his speeches in his first year as prime minister. In a collection of 133 speeches by him between 31 October 1984 and 31 December 1985, the word 'socialism' appears only thirteen times.[3] Of them, six references are in the historical context of India's post-Independence development policy. Of the remaining seven, the earliest one is in a speech delivered partially as a tribute to his mother the day after her mortal remains were consigned to the Himalayas. His reaffirmation of 'adherence to socialism and planning' in this speech can be taken as nothing more than a show of respect for his mother.[4] The last six references are in the context of his policy, and each time, he has used the term explicitly in the sense of removal of poverty. Not once, across the entire collection of speeches, has he used it in the sense of social control of the means of production.

For example, in his free rendering of the May Day address on 1 May 1985 in Hindi in Dhanbad, RG asked for and provided his own definition of socialism in these terms: 'We must, however, ask ourselves now what socialism means. If it means that to bring all to the same level, we drag everyone down, that is not going to benefit anyone. My view is that socialism really means that equality has to be achieved by bringing up those who are now depressed.'[5] A month later, on 1 June 1985, he restated this definition in a speech delivered at Ferguson College, Pune. He began by asking, 'We have promised a socialist system in our Constitution. What do we mean by socialism?' He answered, 'We want to see, that in our system, we help the weakest people in our society. We have to see that our economy is such that it helps the weakest lifting them up to a level from which they are self-sustained.'[6] Finally, speaking to the National Development Council of the Planning Commission on 8 November 1985, he reiterated this same definition to his planners: 'Development must be accompanied by equity and social justice—by removal of social barriers that oppress the weak. This is the essence of our concept of socialism.'[7]

RG's early speeches also indicate a willingness to expose industry to foreign competition. Delivering the inaugural address at a seminar on the electronics industry organized by the All India Manufacturers Organization on 21 February 1985, he told his audience, 'I feel, for example, that protection should be only one sort, preferably only fiscal protection and not licence protection, which means that you will have to be more efficient.'[8] Hinting at the big policy changes he was poised to bring about, he added, 'You will find this Government moving faster than you are moving. The problem will not be the Government constraints or Government restrictions or the time taken by Government but with "Can you keep up with what we are doing?"'[9]

Even more pointedly, inaugurating the National Conference on Engineering Export on 22 March 1985, RG complained about the poor quality of Indian products, attributing it to a lack of competition. 'The quality of our products,' he noted, 'really leaves very much to be desired. One of the problems is that we have been selling to a captive market. We are selling really in an absolutely seller's market. Such a market is not responsive to quality.'[10] He added, 'Ultimately you will be called upon to compete not with each other but with other industries in the world. And we must prepare today for that day.'[11] Later in the speech, he referred to the continued use of outdated technology, blaming it on import substitution. He said,

> With import substitution, we have been able to develop our own technology and to be equal to any other country's technology in certain fields. But sometimes this has gone astray. It has been brought to my notice that on occasion, parts that may cost a few dollars and are not of strategic

> importance are costing us thousands of dollars because we are substituting them with local manufacturers.[12]

As a solution, he rightly advised, 'You must be able to increase our export earnings so that we shall be able to have this freedom to be able to import a few items which might make our products much cheaper, much more competitive and much more efficient.'[13]

In this speech, in a first for a prime minister, RG also raised the issue of industrial sickness whereby many enterprises had become permanently unprofitable but were kept alive through their government takeover and infusion of taxpayer money. He noted,

> This [industrial sickness] is something which is dragging us down. We are not going to put up with sickness. And this will be very clear to you in the coming weeks. We shall make it very expensive to go sick and you must also respond by seeing that industry does not go sick or does not go towards sickness. Certain industries must die. We cannot pretend that all industries which are going on for the last 300 years must carry on into the 22nd century.[14]

Less than a month later, on 15 April 1985, RG addressed the 'Roundtable on India' organized by the European Management Foundation. In the early part of this address, he played up India's progress, telling his audience that the basic thrust of the country's policies was 'growth with equity and social justice'.[15] Later on, he spoke about the new import-export policy that had just been introduced, 'At this stage of our development, it is not feasible to open up our industries to free competition from all industries abroad. . . . At the same time, we are, in certain areas, opening up to foreign competition so that our industries might face the pressure and perform under that pressure.'[16] He then added,

> We look for self-reliance, not autarchy. In India we today need to interact with the world market, with world industry and we realize that too much protection can be damaging to our industries. We look for improved technology, for domestic requirements, for better competitiveness, for better quality in our products, and above all, for a more efficient production process.'[17]

Once again, this was the first time that any prime minister explicitly and publicly repudiated Nehru's goal of self-sufficiency while also bringing to the centre stage the goals of achieving higher product quality and superior production efficiency. This emphasis on quality and efficiency was in contrast to the Nehru model, which relied solely on investment as the growth driver.

Backing Rhetoric with Action

In his first year, RG fully backed up his rhetoric with policy action. He promised wide-ranging reforms in the 1985–86 budget and rapidly implemented them during the year. These reforms are detailed throughout the *Economic Survey 1985–86*, especially in the fiscal policy, industrial policy and foreign trade chapters. A quick look at this document demonstrates the depth and breadth of these reforms. It can be safely inferred from the actions in 1985–86 that had RG been able to maintain this pace of reforms during the remainder of his term, the more far-reaching reforms of 1991–94 would have already been in place, and the trajectory of India's economy would have been very different.

Socialists Strike Back

But RG neither had the authority of Deng Xiaoping of China nor the political savvy of Prime Minister Narasimha Rao, who entered office in 1991 and successfully navigated some far-reaching reforms. With the remainder of the political class still exhibiting continuity with the past, opposition to his policy agenda quickly emerged. As early as 4–5 May 1985, when he placed his draft economic policy resolution in front of the Congress Working Committee for eventual ratification by the AICC, his party members mounted a full-scale opposition, arguing that it represented a break from socialism that his mother and grandfather had championed.

According to the brief account of the episode provided by Kohli, the draft resolution had contended that 'in the process of continued development, the policy instruments relevant to one stage cannot be treated as permanently sacrosanct. Nor are they ends in themselves.' Many senior party members saw this kind of language as representing a shift away from the longstanding development strategy of self-reliance and socialism and vehemently opposed the draft resolution. Eventually, a compromise was forged whereby the resolution, as ratified by the AICC, recommitted RG and the Congress to socialism, but it also accepted all the policy changes that the government had introduced till then.[18]

In his public address to the AICC on 4 May 1985, while RG reaffirmed faith in socialism and the capture of the commanding heights of the industry by the public sector, he also went on to take 'a dig at the "socialists" in the party by saying that socialism did not mean spreading poverty or perpetuating it. Socialism, he said, meant the socio-economic upliftment of the masses'.[19] By restating this definition of socialism in the speech, RG was presumably sending the message to his opponents that he still intended to move away from those aspects of socialism which undermined growth and the fight against poverty.

The Slowdown in Reforms

Though RG continued to advocate the cause of openness in trade, competition and production efficiency in his speeches till at least the end of 1985 and was able to implement nearly all the economic reforms he had announced in the 1985–86 budget, further progress in this direction saw a considerable slowdown.

As a quick look at the *Economic Survey 1986–87* reveals, additional liberalizing steps during his second full fiscal year were, at best, limited and evoked none of the euphoria in the business community that the predecessor budget had. The rare pro-liberalization commentators such as Nani Palkhivala and Prem Shankar Jha expressed disappointment with the budget. Speaking at a meeting hosted by the Forum of Free Enterprise, the former opined that the 1986–87 budget was a budget of consolidation with political tranquilizers but by no criterion a growth-oriented budget.[20] The latter contrasted the sustained rise in the stock prices following the 1985–86 budget with the slump in them after the presentation of the 1986–87 budget and observed, 'The behavior of the share prices sums up the profound sense of disappointment that the budget has evoked in industry and among at least one school of economists.'[21]

By 1987, RG's speeches had begun to sound lukewarm towards liberalization and played up the public sector. Thus, for example, delivering the inaugural address at FICCI on its Diamond Jubilee celebration in mid-May 1987, he sounded a caution against excessive liberalization. He stated,

> If we suddenly totally deregulate and allow new industry to come in at any capacity-size, with other efficiencies built in, those that we have ourselves kept stifled because of our rules, because of our licensing laws, will find it very difficult to stay alive in such a rapidly changing environment. So, while we do want to bring about a change, we would not like the change to be so sudden so as to create a shock in the established industries. We must give them time to change over to the new system.[22]

Earlier, in January 1987, he had spoken of the public sector in glowing terms at a conference in New Delhi on public enterprises. Describing the sector as an instrument and 'the cutting edge of our development,' he had stated,

> In the first stage of our development, the public sector has brought in, an industrial, technological ethos in the country. . . . Today, it is very easy for us to criticize it and say 'this is wrong and that is wrong.' But we must go back thirty years, to the early fifties, when the first public sector enterprises were coming up and remember what those PSU [public sector undertakings] managers had to face in terms of labour, in terms of qualified manpower. Then you will see what we have achieved and how far we have come. This is the real achievement of the public sector.'[23]

Echoes of this essential message could also be heard in his address at FICCI in mid-May. Invoking the 'mixed-economy' and 'commanding heights' metaphors of the Nehru era, he reminded his audience,

> We have a well-defined mixed economy. The public sector has a major role in many key areas, in our core industries, in many of our basic industries. It is at the commanding heights of our economy and we would like that not just to continue but we would like to build on that and give the public sector an even stronger position.[24]

After 1987, if not sooner, RG also adopted the theme of continuity in policy, thereby relegating liberalizing reforms to the background. Defending a largely business-as-usual 1987–88 budget on the Parliament floor in March 1987, he said,

> Some Members talked about direction in the Budget. Let me reiterate that direction is not something which we would like to give annually in every Budget. Direction is something that Pandit ji gave in the '50s which we are continuing today. Direction is what Indira ji gave in the '70s and '80s which we are continuing today. It is the basic policy which has been developing from the freedom movement throughout our Independence.[25]

Towards the end of the speech, he returned to this theme, adding, 'The Budget gives stability and it continues in the direction that the Congress has given the nation since before Independence, that it has continued giving the nation during these forty years of Independence.'[26] The same theme also appeared in his address at FICCI in May 1987. Referring to the policies of the preceding forty years, he noted,

> We should not be in a rush to push them out or throw them out; but at the same time, with the new circumstances and new challenges, we have to link these past policies with the future. It was for these reasons that in 1985 we enunciated certain parameters of change for our industry. But the parameters that we had set then, were to be within the continuum of our traditional policies. . . . The overall strategy is unchanged—a mixed economy with a strong emphasis on self-reliance.

It is evident from this sampling of his utterances that by 1987, RG had yielded to the anti-reform forces in his party. Rather than speak of taking India into the twenty-first century, he now came to embrace continuity. Unlike Prime Minister Narasimha Rao, who, in 1991, would use the rhetoric of continuity as the shield of protection against critics of reforms, such talk now reflected the reality of policy. During these remaining years of his tenure, he also became politically extremely weak on account of corruption charges and various political misadventures. As a result, save in the area of international trade, little further progress in liberalization took place while he ruled.

The Door to Liberal Ideas Opens

The continuing stranglehold of socialism on the political leadership within Congress thus set back the first genuine effort at liberalizing reforms. Had RG been politically savvy and retained his popularity in the last three years, he may have regained the initiative over his opponents, but lacking the necessary political experience, he could not do so. Even so, not all was lost for at least two reasons. First, the fact that RG himself was keen on efficiency, competition and openness to trade broke the taboo surrounding the discussion of liberalization. These discussions gained momentum within the government, with pro-liberalization actors gaining ground. Second, piecemeal liberalization of the external sector through the expansion of open general licensing, the shrinking role of canalization of imports and export promotion measures continued throughout his tenure. The appointment of a pro-reform governor at the Reserve Bank of India, R.N. Malhotra, by RG also yielded dividends since he allowed the rupee to depreciate significantly, thereby giving a hand to exports. These and earlier liberalizing measures, especially those introduced in 1985–86, yielded dividends with the growth rate from 1988–89 to 1990–91 averaging a solid 7 per cent. This experience strengthened the hand of those pushing for greater liberalism in policy.

As the 1980s came to a close, three events helped turn the political atmosphere more accepting of liberalization. First, it became progressively clear that, after three decades since the days of Nehru, the world was a changed place and that India's policy regime was leaving it further and further behind. The favourable effect of even the limited reforms by RG on the growth rate in the late 1980s suggested that liberalization offered a way out of this trap. Second, China, which was even more populous and, on top, a communist country, had emerged as an astonishingly fast-growing country after Deng Xiaoping began opening it up. As such, the argument that the accomplishments of the earlier fast-growing countries consisting of Singapore, Hong Kong, Taiwan and South Korea had few lessons for India due to them being either city-states or small compared to India lost validity. Finally, the Soviet Union, which had inspired Nehru's pursuit of socialism and planned development, collapsed. The collapse gave greater credibility to the argument that inefficiencies engendered by planned development in the Soviet Union were also responsible for the poor performance of the Indian economy.

V.P. Singh and Chandra Shekhar: Two Short-Lived Governments

With his popularity taking a major hit in the last three years of his tenure, RG failed to win a majority in the parliamentary elections held in November 1989. V.P Singh, who had served as his first finance minister and had presented the ground-breaking 1985–86 budget, succeeded him. Singh had broken away from the Congress in 1988 and formed his own party called the Janata Dal. Lacking majority votes, his party formed a minority government with outside support from the Bharatiya Janata Party (BJP) and the left parties.

With the liberal ideas becoming somewhat more acceptable, on 31 May 1990, the Singh government released the Industrial Policy Statement, 1990. Arguably, this policy statement went three-fourths towards dismantling industrial licensing. For example, it eliminated the requirement for an investment licence for all ventures requiring Rs 250 million or less in investment in assets. According to a contemporary media report based on the press conference given by the then industry minister Ajit Singh, this provision was expected to eliminate the need for a licence for 60 to 65 per cent of new investments.[27] The policy also included provisions for the withdrawal of licensing on certain priority industries and opening a set of sectors to foreign investment.

Unfortunately, however, the Singh government failed to take follow-up steps to implement this policy and, within months of its announcement, in November 1990, lost the support of the BJP, resulting in its ouster.[28] While the media had widely covered the policy statement in early June 1990, and I have described it in detail in my 2008 book, it has received surprisingly little attention in the post-1990 writings on industrial policy in India.[29] Even though the Singh government failed to implement the policy, it represents an important link to the Industrial Policy Statement 1991, which went much further and effectively ended investment licensing altogether. As per the media reports, there was little opposition to the 1990 policy except by the left parties, most notably the Communist Party of India. This fact points to greater acceptance of further liberalization of industrial licensing policy by 1990.

After the fall of the Singh government, a minority government, supported from outside by the Congress, came to office. It was headed by Chandra Shekhar, one of the Young Turks from the early Indira Gandhi era. Shekhar had left the Congress during the Emergency Rule and joined the Janata Party. But with the Congress withdrawing its support by early March 1991, his government, too, was short-lived. Fresh elections were called in the absence of any leader succeeding in mustering a majority of votes in the Parliament. During the election campaign that followed, RG was assassinated, leading to the emergence of P.V. Narasimha Rao as the president of the Congress. He led the party to victory in the election and became prime minister on 21 June 1991.

P.V. Narasimha Rao: A Decisive Turn to the Markets

When Rao came to office, India was in the thick of a balance-of-payments crisis. Foreign exchange reserves had dried up almost entirely, and the country was staring at a possible default on its external obligations. A default was unthinkable for India, and therefore Rao's immediate first step was to physically fly out the gold held by the Reserve Bank of India as collateral to London and meet the payments owed abroad. Simultaneously, he moved ahead to set the economic house in order and open the credit lines from the IMF and the World Bank while also returning the economy to a sustainable growth path.

With Dr Manmohan Singh (MMS), the technocrat serving as the finance minister and representing the face of his economic reforms, Rao acted decisively and at a speed never previously witnessed in India. Within a month, he had devalued the rupee in two successive steps by 18.3 per cent from Rs 21.2 per dollar to Rs 25.8, ended licensing on all imports except consumer goods, removed many export restrictions, ended investment licensing, trimmed the list of industries reserved for the public sector, majorly opened India to foreign direct investment and imposed strict fiscal discipline on the government. In the subsequent years, he broadened the reform process, extending it to the financial sector, opening telecommunications and civil aviation to private players, making the rupee convertible on the current account and bringing the top tariff rate down to 50 per cent by 1995–96 from 355 per cent in 1990–91.

Pushback on Reforms and Their Successful Navigation by Rao

Compared with some of the recent politically challenging reforms, the first set of reforms by Rao may be described as low-hanging fruits. But seen from the vantage point of 1991 India, they were nothing of the sort. The speed and scope of those reforms in the first month surprised even the most ardent advocates of reforms. Despite progressively greater recognition of the need for a movement away from trade, investment and price controls in the previous decade, the political class as a whole still saw their wholesale removal as a betrayal of Nehru. This fact was reflected in the exclusion of some of the complementary reforms from the industrial policy.[30]

Continued faith in the controlled regime on the part of the political class also manifested itself in the resistance to and all-around criticism of the proposed reforms by not just Opposition parties but also many within Congress. Jairam Ramesh, who had worked closely with Rao during the critical first ten weeks of the latter's tenure, provides an overview of the unfolding of these events.[31] More detailed criticisms of the reforms and their defence by Rao can be found in the Lok Sabha debates that took place on the trust vote (12 and 15 July), the motion of thanks (16 to 19 July), and the demand for grants relating to the Ministry of Industry (21–23 and 26 August).

The devaluation was announced in two successive steps on 1 and 3 July 1991, and trade policy reform on 4 July 1991. Because of the sensitivity of these reforms, no prior consultation was done with either the party or the cabinet. When it came to industrial policy, as industry minister, Rao himself was in charge of it. Given the far-reaching changes he sought, he decided to get prior cabinet approval for it. Accordingly, he got the ministry to prepare a cabinet note on the proposed policy and presented it to the cabinet on 19 July. Ramesh summarizes the proceedings in the cabinet thus,

> Expectedly, there were fireworks in the cabinet on 19 July. Many ministers objected both to the substance and style of the note on industrial policy reforms. Some felt that we were abandoning the Congress's ideology while some others felt that a strong case had not been made for these far-reaching changes. The predominant view was that the cabinet note appeared too damning of the past.[32]

In a replay of events witnessed by RG when he began introducing pro-market reforms, the hand of socialism had returned to strike at the central plank of Rao's reform package.

But Rao was not Rajiv Gandhi. From the beginning, he had played his hand with great care. His first act upon becoming the prime minister was to appoint MMS as his finance minister. MMS had worked in senior policy positions in the government since 1971 and was widely viewed as an establishment person and someone with full faith in Nehru's socialism. Only six years earlier, as the deputy chairman of the Planning Commission, he had incurred the wrath of RG by pushing back on the latter's pitch for urban-centric development in the seventh-plan period (1985–86 to 1989–90). RG had later denounced MMS and his senior colleagues at the Planning Commission as a 'bunch of jokers'.[33] MMS thus enjoyed the image of someone on the side of the longstanding policies of the country. On 25 June 1991, Rao appointed A.N. Verma as his principal secretary. Verma had served as industry secretary in the V.P. Singh government when the latter had mooted the Industrial Policy Statement 1990. Probably in the light of that earlier policy, Rao was aware that Verma would be in sync with his reform programme.

Having spent more than twenty years in Andhra Pradesh state politics and served as a senior minister in both Gandhi and RG cabinets in the 1980s, Rao was a seasoned politician. Having enjoyed the full confidence of the two prime ministers (more on this below), he came to the office with an intimate knowledge of political pulls and pushes characterizing liberalization measures they had sought to introduce. He had command over five Indian languages, was widely read, had a thorough understanding of Nehru and was given to deep introspection during his years of political exile.[34] These attributes equipped him to navigate the political minefield he was required to tread while implementing his reform agenda.

To placate his cabinet colleagues after they expressed deep reservations about his proposed industrial policy, Rao appointed a Group of Ministers (GoM) to take a second look at it. A meeting of the GoM the following day revealed deep apprehensions on the part of the ministers on several features of the policy. To address those apprehensions, Rao had his team prepare a long preamble to the policy providing the historical context beginning with Nehru, linking the proposed policy to the seventh plan under RG and reiterating commitment to self-reliance, small-scale enterprises, abolition of monopoly, the rightful role for the public sector and protection of labour. The preamble concluded by emphasizing the need for efficient use of the available resources and describing the policy as 'continuity with change'. With the addition of the preamble, the cabinet note sailed through the cabinet on 23 July.[35] It was tabled in the Parliament the following day before MMS presented his historic budget.

Once announced, the devaluation, trade policy package and industrial policy were all subject to thorough criticisms in and outside the Parliament, with politicians, economists, influential media critics and the business community joining the chorus. One would have expected the business community to stand in full solidarity with the reforms, but it only wanted to be freed of the shackles of investment licensing while being spared the competition from abroad through liberalization of trade and foreign investment.[36] But Rao, supported by Singh, stood his ground. The duo pro-actively defended the reforms, offering well-reasoned arguments.

Explaining Rao's Conversion to Liberalization

The fact that Rao could successfully defend the reforms is not surprising. What is more puzzling is that unlike most of the politicians of his generation, especially within the Congress, he was determined to bring about far-reaching changes. Admittedly, the constituency for liberalization had been gaining ground, but if the grip of socialism practised by Nehru and his daughter on the vast majority of the influential politicians of the day remained strong, how did Rao escape it? After all, he was only four years younger than IG and had been a loyal member of the Congress since the late 1940s.

One possibility is that Rao did not believe in the reforms and embraced them under pressure from the IMF and the World Bank. Though this view has its subscribers, it fails to pass muster because the Indian economy had recovered quickly following the July 1991 reforms, with foreign-exchange reserves returning to a satisfactory level within a year. At that point, the IMF and the World Bank no longer had any clout left, and Rao could have returned to business as usual.[37] He could have even reversed some of the reforms he had announced till then. But he stayed the course and continued to advance the cause of reforms, entering new areas such as financial-sector liberalization and private-sector entry into telecommunication and civil aviation.

The inescapable conclusion is that Rao had used the occasion of the balance-of-payments crisis to place India on the path to liberalization by conviction and not compulsion. As such, the evolution of his thinking in this direction requires an explanation. Unfortunately, at most, we have limited and indirect evidence of his belief that the time was ripe for India to change course in favour of a more liberal policy regime.

For example, Rao's visits to the United States in the 1970s and his observation of the changes in China may have influenced his thinking. He had visited the United States in 1974 and again in 1979 and had been favourably impressed by its progress. According to Sitapati, already in 1974, he had returned from the United States with electronic equipment and stories of American technological prowess. 'So enamoured was he by the United States that he even delivered lectures in Telugu on three occasions, telling his perplexed audience of American industrial success.'[38] In the 1980s, as foreign minister in Gandhi's cabinet, Rao closely watched the changes Deng had been bringing to China. To quote Sitapati once again, 'Deng opened the economy to domestic and foreign enterprise in late 1978, and Rao was primed to watch China abandon Maoism for the Market, all the while paying lip service to the glories of the first chairman of the Communist Party of China.'[39]

While these observations may help understand what influenced Rao's thinking on economic policy, they remain hopelessly insufficient to derive anything conclusive about it. Rao himself did not speak or write about it. Indeed, through experience, he had most likely concluded that political survival would be best assured by refraining from airing publicly anything that conflicted with the views of the party's leadership of the day. And he was hardly wrong in adhering to this practice. Had Sonia Gandhi, RG's widow, known what Rao would do upon being given the reins of the Congress in 1991, she would have never invited him to helm the party upon her husband's death.

Therefore, the only option left to us is to look for clues in what Rao wrote and spoke after he became the prime minister. Having reached the top and then retired, Rao was no longer encumbered by the compulsions of political survival during this phase of his career. At the same time, two possible sources of risk remain in relying on his post-1991 speeches and writings. One, they may have been (ghost) written by his advisers and staff members. And two, even if he authored them, they may contain misrepresentation with the view to preserve one's image and legacy.

Going by the views of those who have known or studied Rao closely, the risk on either of these counts is minimal. On the first issue, Ramesh says, 'For the most part, Rao was the author of whatever he spoke and wrote; he may have received inputs from here and there, but like Nehru before him, he was an original and crafted his own speeches.'[40] On the second issue, Sitapati quotes Gopalkrishna Gandhi, a former Governor of West Bengal, as saying, 'He was too shy of his own truths to put them straight, but he was too honest to hide them. He was too proud to be a hypocrite.'[41] Ramesh expresses a similar view somewhat differently, noting that he was self-effacing and not given to 'projecting a machismo of any kind'.[42] At the same time, says Ramesh, he was acutely conscious of his own abilities. Having read or listened to many of Rao's speeches and watched some of his television interviews, I agree. The bottom line is that in explaining why he turned out to be a different kind of politician than his contemporaries in the Congress, we can rely on his own utterances expressed verbally or in writing.

The first source worth a look is journalist Shekhar Gupta's conversation with Rao on the TV show, 'Walk the Talk', which aired on 8 May 2004, approximately seven months before the latter passed away. It is worthwhile to reproduce the transcript of a three-minute portion of the interview to give the full flavour of Rao's thought process.

Gupta: You were a lifelong socialist. Or you were brought up in a Nehruvian milieu. When did you conclude that this has to change, the world has changed? Was it in the first couple of weeks? Was it a chat with Manmohan Singh?

Rao: Nehru was a person who said something about his not being a Nehruite. Gandhi was a person who said very strongly that I am not a Gandhiite. Becoming 'ite' becomes something frozen. Gandhi was never static, nor was Nehru. Why did Nehru leave the whole of agriculture in the private sector? Not many people realize it. He said it in so many words that if you are talking of socialism, don't misunderstand, it is not something being imported from abroad, it is being evolved under our own conditions. So, that should suffice as a permanent answer in favour of what Nehru wanted to do and what we are trying to do.

Gupta: So, for you it was not such a big instinctive shift, it was not like Deng Xiaoping changing [the] Chinese economy?

Rao: Not for me. No, you have to read my presidential speech of Tirupati in 1992. In fact, I traced from Nehru to what I was doing and no one could say that it is a sudden shift or sudden U-turn. You *cannot* afford U-turns in this country. You cannot.

Gupta: So, how do you make a U-turn without making a U-turn? That is special Narasimha Rao art.

Rao: No, no, it is not like that. It's not like that. If you understand that where you were standing is itself in motion, the turning becomes easier. You are NOT static; that is what I have just told you. You are not static; you are never static. Look at what Gandhiji has done, look at what Panditji has done, a little more carefully.

Gupta: So, you never had a feeling that you were leaving something behind, that a faith with which you had gone on for forty years, you are now junking that and moving on to a new path?

Rao: Well, I didn't feel that. I thought we are only growing up. I can't possibly make do with the clothes I wore fifty years back.

We can identify three key elements in Rao's thinking from this conversation: (i) The world is constantly evolving ('where you were standing is itself in motion'); (ii) We are continuously evolving ('You are not static. . . . Look at what Gandhiji has done, look at what Panditji has done); and (iii) In India, you cannot afford an abrupt change; the change has to be piecemeal ('You *cannot* afford U-turns in this country. You cannot.'). Once these three elements in Rao's thinking are accepted, and his role in the liberalization efforts under Indira Gandhi and Rajiv Gandhi is considered, the mystery around his evolution into a leader different from his contemporaries is largely resolved.

The source of the history of Rao's involvement in the liberalization efforts under IG and RG is a forty-six-page unpublished paper titled 'Two Crucial Years: India under Shri P.V. Narasimha Rao's Stewardship' that he wrote about himself in the third person in 1993.[43] In the portion relevant to the present argument, Rao explains why the Congress Parliamentary Party elected him as its leader. After referring to his experience of having served in almost all key ministries except finance and having been a close associate of both IG and RG, he states, 'Another reason why he was regarded as a natural successor to Indiraji and Rajivji was that he was not only acquainted with their thinking but had also been *involved in the formation of their new ideas on how to carry the country to a new stage in its development.*' [italics added]. Rao then proceeds to elaborate on this point:[44]

> When Indiraji returned to power in 1980, she had to devote herself to the difficult task of pulling the country out of the morass in which the 1977–79 Janata interregnum had landed it, and return it to the path of national advance which it had taken under the leadership of Mahatma Gandhi and Jawaharlal Nehru and which had been endorsed by the nation in successive general elections. But she had also come to realize from her long experience at the helm of the nation that having reached the stage and level of development already, the country needed fresh thinking and innovative practice. That is where Narasimha Raoji's sagacious advice proved useful and she did initiate some new ideas and measures. The young Rajivji pursued these ideas and practices with youthful boldness and greater vigour, and elaborated his thinking in terms of concrete time-bound measures in the election manifesto for the 1991 mid-term poll. Narasimha Raoji has helped him in drawing up the manifesto and has come to realize in the period since the Congress went out of office, the economic situation in the country has so deteriorated that immediate remedial measures were needed.

Reading this paragraph in conjunction with the three elements of his philosophy, we may reasonably infer that as early as 1980, Rao had concluded that India had reached a 'stage and level of development' that the right next step was to begin unwinding the controlled regime. If we take the above paragraph at face value, he rendered this advice to both IG and RG. That he was in a position to render such advice to the two leaders is confirmed by his biographer Sitapati. Regarding his relationship with Gandhi, Sitapati writes, 'He was also, by 1982, one of Indira's most trusted advisors, along with Pranab Mukherjee and R. Venkataraman. Party papers and government files from other ministries would be redrafted by him.'[45] Sitapati further quotes the late President of India, Pranab Mukherjee, as stating that Rao was the first person that IG would consult on any major issue. In the case of RG, one piece of circumstantial evidence is that whereas he eased out most of his mother's senior cabinet colleagues, replacing them with his younger friends, he not only kept Rao in a senior cabinet position but also let him choose his own ministerial portfolio. Once again, Sitapati writes that according to Mukherjee, RG considered Rao indispensable for his ministry.[46]

Once it is accepted that during the 1980s, Rao was already favourably inclined towards liberalization, his actions in 1991 fall into place. Upon taking charge, he was keenly aware that he faced a situation requiring a quick response. He was also convinced that at its stage of development, India needed to move in a liberal direction. Finally, Rao recognized the limits of how far he could go at the time. He could take a turn but not a U-turn. For more, he would have to wait and see if future developments offered such an opportunity.

This broad diagnosis is further supported by the speed at which Rao took advantage of the crisis. He took the oath of office on 21 June 1991 and recruited MMS as his finance minister the same day. Four days later, Rao appointed A.N. Verma his principal secretary. Most remarkably, on 22 June, in an address to the nation that lasted only ten minutes, he provided a crystal-clear road map of almost all his reforms that would unfold in the following month. The only component of the package missing from the address was the one that could not be revealed in advance: the rupee devaluation. Sitapati confirms that Rao had himself drafted this speech.[47] In the portion of the address relevant to economic policy, Rao pointed to the urgency of action and the need for fiscal restraint. 'The economy is in a crisis,' he told the nation.

> The balance of payments situation is exceedingly difficult. Inflationary pressures on the price level are considerable. There is no time to lose. The Government and the country cannot keep living beyond their means and there are no soft

> options left. We must tighten our belt and be prepared to make the necessary sacrifices to preserve our economic independence, which is an integral part of our vision for a strong nation.[48]

Having thus prepared the ground for an austere budget, he expressed his determination 'to address the problems of the economy in a decisive manner', and went on to outline for the nation what he intended to do:[49]

> This Government is committed to removing the cobwebs that come in the way of rapid industrialization. We will work towards making India internationally competitive, taking full advantage of modern science and technology and opportunities offered by the evolving global economy. Utmost efficiency will be fostered. We cannot tolerate waste, inefficiency and indifference to quality, in the public or any other sector. We also welcome foreign direct investment, so as to accelerate the tempo of development, upgrade our technologies and to promote our exports. Obstacles that come in the way of allocating foreign investment on a sizeable scale will be removed. A time-bound programme will be worked out to streamline our industrial policies and programmes to achieve the goal of a vibrant economy that rewards creativity, enterprise and innovativeness.

This single paragraph compellingly shows that Rao came to office with full appreciation that the economy suffered from gross inefficiencies, poor product quality and a lack of competitiveness in the world market. He knew that rapid industrialization required the removal of 'cobwebs' from its path, attention to exports, significant opening to foreign investment and streamlining of industrial policies. These themes reverberated in his speeches in the following weeks and months. Three of these speeches, all delivered within the first year of Rao's rule, are worthy of discussion.

In a speech delivered at the Federation of Export Organizations on 7 October 1991, Rao described the evolution of policy from Nehru onwards, explaining how changes not possible at one point in time can become possible at another. 'He [Nehru] did not shut India out of the world,' Rao told his audience. 'At the same time, he did not throw India to the turbulence of the world before India was ready to integrate. Now, we are ready to integrate and, therefore, we are integrating.'[50] He added,

> Ten years ago, we would not have been able to get this consensus. Anyone would know, Manubhai would know if he had introduced these things when he was the commerce minister, he would have been stoned, it would not have been possible. Today it is possible because we have come of age, Indian economy has come of age.[51]

The logic underlying this argument exhibits remarkable consistency with the answers Rao gave Shekhar Gupta more than a decade later, supporting the hypothesis that his actions in 1991 were more likely the result of prior introspection than overnight transformation or pressures from outside agencies.

The second speech worthy of consideration in the present context is the one Rao delivered in the Lok Sabha on 26 August 1991 in response to criticisms of his reforms during the debate on the demand for grants in respect of the Ministry of Industry. Rao delivered this speech extempore, and it testifies to his excellent grasp of basic economic principles despite never having studied economics or held the finance ministry. The speech also speaks to his conviction for taking India into the modern age. I focus on six different points Rao made in it.

First, responding to the allegation that the new policy had been either dictated from outside or lacked continuity with the past industrial policies, Rao reminded that it had emanated directly from the Congress manifesto. 'The Party promised to tackle the problem through vigorous export promotion, effective import substitution and increasing productivity and efficiency in the economy, among other things,' he stated.[52] He noted that in the industrial sector, the manifesto had promised to pursue a policy that would 'lead to encouragement of entrepreneurship, simplification of the regulatory system, bringing in new technology and increasing competitiveness for the benefit of the common man'.[53]

Second, Rao challenged those contending that he was reversing what Nehru had bequeathed. Referring to the Industrial Policy Resolution 1956, he reminded that its basic objective was to speed up industrialization in the country and that it provided for the development of industries of basic and strategic importance in the public sector. The resolution additionally provided for the public sector entry into industries where the private sector was unwilling to come forward. Rao argued that the new policy also allowed the public sector to invest along these lines. What was different now was the state of finances. On the one hand, nearly one trillion rupees worth of investment in the public sector had failed to generate the expected return, which could be ploughed back for its further expansion, while on the other, the government lacked enough resources independently to appreciably expand it.

Third, Rao reminded the house that in the changed times, the Indian industry could not escape competition with the rest of the world and had to become efficient. 'Industry in India has to compete with the industries in other countries,' he said, serving notice to those seeking protection for an indefinite period. He added,

> And if we think that we can live all alone in this country or can live in an isolated way, this, I think, is not correct, is not going to be possible. All other countries with centralized economies, are now relating to, and entering the world economy in a big way. We have already entered the world economy in a big way. . . . And that is why, we have to be competitive.

> That is why, we have to think of cost effectiveness. That is why we have to think of the latest technology.[54]

Fourth, having thus connected cost-effectiveness to the latest technology, he confronted head-on Nirmal Kanti Chatterjee of the Communist Party of India (Marxist), who had spoken before him and argued that liberalization was already leading to the replacement of labour by machines with consequent losses of jobs. For example, he argued that liberalization had given rise to the production of washing machines. Each washing machine cost Rs 10,000. With Rs 10,000 in fixed deposit, one could earn Rs 100 a month, which could then be used to provide part-time employment to someone to wash clothes.[55] Rao's first counter to this argument was that it ignored the jobs created in washing machine production. But what he said next was the crux of the matter and something that probably few of his contemporaries would have seen with his clarity. If you take the displacement of employment in washing clothes as the criterion to formulate policy, he reasoned,

> . . . then you will remain a country of maid-servants only. This is the point. You are condemning our women folk to life of drudgery permanently. That is where diversification is necessary. That is why we have not given them any education so far. Let her be educated. She will refuse to do the washing, the moment you educate her.[56]

Then, elevating the argument to a higher philosophical level, he added,

> We want to modernize: we want to be a modern society: we want to be a society in which every member has a certain quality of life. . . . Whatever the price to be paid, we will have to modernize, we will have to become competitive: we will have to rub shoulders with others. There is no other way.[57]

Fifth, Rao turned to the question of opening the economy to multinational corporations (MNCs). Rather than be apologetic, which is what most politicians of the day defending the opening of the economy to them would have done, Rao took on the critics frontally. 'About multinationals, I really don't know why this fear of the multinationals is still haunting us. I would like to submit to the House that what we consider multinationals in the past as a big monster coming from outside is no longer a monster . . .'[58] Offering the economic rationale for allowing MNCs, he said, 'We are inviting MNCs for the sake of taking their technology, for the sake of employment, for the sake of better competitiveness.'[59] Then, turning the knife a little, he retorted, 'The only thing I cannot understand is . . . why we should be squeamish about inviting foreign investment. Nothing else is the reason except an inferiority complex. We seem to feel inferior to the others who are coming in or whom we are inviting.'[60]

Finally, Rao took up the question of ending the restrictions on large firms and industrial houses as defined under the Monopolies and Restrictive Trade Practices (MRTP) Act of 1969. He reminded the house that the idea had been conceived more than two decades earlier. Past governments had tried to implement it in the only manner possible, but it had not worked. He then made a subtle economic argument for the abolition of the restrictions, which, at most, a tiny fraction of the economists of the day in India could have made. 'Any pre-entry restrictions will not work and they will only stifle industry,' he said, adding,

> They will not give any fillip to industry, if there are restrictions before you enter the industry. So, it has been decided . . . that no pre-entry restrictions are desirable. . . . We expect that this policy will bring in greater freedom, greater and unfettered freedom to the growth of industry and that is what we want today.[61]

The third and final speech I briefly refer to is Rao's presidential address on 16 April 1992 at the AICC session in Tirupati.[62] In this speech, Rao brought together many of the ideas he had expounded in his 26 August speech to argue that his path was well within Nehru's vision of a socialist India. He noted that laissez-faire and communism formed two extremes. The former was premised on the idea that the pursuit of individual welfare maximizes the collective welfare of society, and the latter on the exact reverse. Rao said that rather than embrace either extreme, inspired by Buddha, Nehru had chosen a 'Middle Way' that sought to balance individual and common good. He, Rao, remained committed to that Middle Way; his policy changes represented a response to the changed circumstances, but they constituted a Middle Way (not a U-turn).

In the Tirupati address, Rao focused on three big policy areas in which his government had made major changes: foreign trade, foreign investment and the public sector. Much of what he said on the last two subjects was largely a restatement of what he had said in his 26 August speech. But his exposition of foreign-trade policy was much deeper and sharper in this speech and, therefore, worthy of elaboration.

Nehru had sought self-sufficiency concerning foreign trade. His decision to go for basic industries first was based on the assumption that this would allow the country to produce machines so that it would not have to depend on imports for future investments. By opening the economy to foreign trade, Rao moved away from this aspect of Nehru's policy framework. But in the address, he tried to reconcile the differences between his and Nehru's foreign-trade policy by replacing the terminology of self-sufficiency with self-reliance. This terminology gave him the space necessary to resolve the contradiction between the operative part of Nehru's foreign trade policy—establishment of basic industries in the initial stage of development—and his own.

'Our concept of self-reliance so far,' Rao stated, referring to the Nehru era, 'has included an emphasis on building up basic industries within the country and on import substitution. The priority given to basic industries was one of the great contributions of Nehru.' But it was time to review that policy. Questioning the wisdom of import substitution for its own sake, he reminded the audience that no country insisted on making everything by itself. It is not that a country is incapable of producing everything, 'but it finds it more economical, in its circumstances, to buy a number of things from others who make them.' Therefore, 'the criterion of self-reliance today has to be not whether you can make whatever you need, but whether you can pay for whatever you need.' Going a step further, he applied the concept of self-sufficiency to defining the limits to foreign debt, stating that 'we should be indebted only to the extent we have the capacity to repay.' As a final defence of his shift in the policy, he fell back on the Indian tradition reminding the audience that this was 'also in perfect conformity with the Indian tradition and ethos. Therefore, while we are re-defining self-reliance, we are not abandoning the basic principle.'[63]

In sum, the inescapable conclusion from a careful evaluation of the available evidence is that though Rao belonged to the generation of politicians who cut their political teeth in an era in which socialism held sway, he was markedly different from nearly all of his contemporaries. Unlike the latter, he appreciated that the world was continuously evolving and that changing circumstances required nations to evolve and adapt. He sought pathways to move forward in an evolving world rather than freeze in time.

The economic failures of India in the 1960s and 1970s had likely led Rao to begin thinking about feasible pathways to a change for the better early on. After Indira Gandhi had relieved him of the position of chief minister of Andhra Pradesh in January 1973, he had plenty of free time to introspect till she made him the foreign minister in January 1980. In the interim, he had only served as a general secretary of the Congress from October 1974 to sometime in 1976 and as an Opposition member of Parliament from March 1977 to January 1980. Neither of these duties was overly time-consuming, giving him time to read, write and, especially, introspect about his own experiences in Andhra Pradesh and the post-Independence history of India. These were also the years during which he made two visits to the United States and observed Deng begin opening the Chinese economy to foreign investors.

Rao got his first opportunity to contribute to the small movements towards liberalization under Indira Gandhi when she introduced her liberalizing measures. This opportunity grew bigger under Rajiv Gandhi, who came to office without baggage and pursued liberalization with greater vigour. The pushback RG got from his own party members may have given Rao a glimpse of the limits to the change that can be implemented at a point in time. Luckily, when he came to the office, the situation was more favourable for liberalizing measures for two reasons.

First, the country faced a balance-of-payments crisis. In Rao's own words, as spoken in the *Walk the Talk* interview with Shekhar Gupta,

> We had come against a blank wall. There was nothing more to do. You see, you had no money, you were going to become a defaulter within two weeks and you can imagine what it means for India to become a defaulter. . . . Once you become a defaulter, your entire economy, your honour, your place in the comity of nations, everything goes haywire. And you have really no face to show.

As such, substantive action was required, and the opponents had less room to push back.

Second, since 1985 when RG was deluged with criticisms in response to his liberalizing measures, there had been progress towards their greater acceptance. One concrete piece of evidence is the near absence of a pushback that V.P. Singh faced against his Industrial Policy Statement of May 1990. A.N. Verma, who had been the industry secretary when Singh mooted his policy, brought with him first-hand knowledge of the experience with the 1990 policy in his capacity as Rao's principal secretary. And, with a long political career behind him, Rao himself came to the office well-equipped to navigate his path through the troubled political waters.

We thus have a robust explanation of why Rao turned out to be different from his contemporaries and how he successfully placed India on its journey towards a market economy. One final point concerns Rao's decisiveness or lack thereof. Based on his working style during the early years of his political career, first as a minister and then as chief minister in Andhra Pradesh, it has been said that he was given to indefinitely postponing decisions. But this is not generally true of him. As Sitapati describes in his biography, Indira Gandhi had specifically charged him with implementing land reform as the chief minister of Andhra Pradesh. On this task, he acted so decisively and at such speed that many of his friends from the landed aristocracy became his enemies and eventually became the cause of his downfall. I find myself in agreement with the anonymous source whom Ramesh describes as 'one of Rao's closest aides' and quotes as stating, 'I don't believe he [Rao] was indecisive; he was deferential to authority or to positions where the ultimate responsibility for decisions lay, but where he was assured that the position was his to hold, he was quick to decide.'[64] As prime minister, Rao was his own master and anything but indecisive.

The Post-Narasimha Rao Era

It is not an exaggeration to say that even though in his own mind Rao may have believed that he had stayed within the boundaries of socialism that Nehru had drawn, he had opened the door to a change that had seemed highly unlikely, if not impossible, just five years earlier. As late as 1990, after listening to a highly upbeat and inspiring speech on the economic prospects of India at the World Bank by the then Indian Ambassador to the United States, Dr Abid Hussain, I had written to him that with the vested interests unwilling to let go of the licence-permit raj, the economic potential of India would remain unrealized. Hussain responded that he was confident that the Indian middle class would force the change. In less than two years, he had proved at least half right: while it is debatable whether the middle class forced it, the change did become a reality.

Rao's reforms led to a robust positive response from the Indian economy. This response had two positive implications for the future of economic policy. One, it made a reversal of the reforms already in place less likely. And two, it made the path to additional liberalization by a future reformist government smoother. The flip side of the coin was that socialism still dominated the psyche of a large section of the political class. Therefore, there was no guarantee that future leadership in the top office would be reformist. Moreover, even with a reformist government in place, as it enters the territory of more contentious reforms, anti-reform forces will acquire salience.

Rao lost the parliamentary election held in 1996. Three short-lived coalition governments, lasting 16, 324 and 332 days, respectively, followed. These years witnessed some relatively modest and uncontentious reforms, notably in personal income taxation and customs duty. Then, in March 1998, Atal Bihari Vajpayee of the Bharatiya Janata Party (BJP) came to office and remained there till May 2004. Despite being composed of numerous parties with diverse interests, the Vajpayee government successfully implemented reforms in various areas. It even took the daring step of privatizing several public-sector enterprises. Though not entirely free of socialist thought, the BJP has been generally critical of Nehru's policies. As such, it is not surprising that Vajpayee carried forward the reform process at a brisk pace. It deserves noting, however, that it faced resistance in certain areas from the coalition partners and Opposition parties. For example, it had promised to reform the labour laws but had to withdraw the proposal for it. Likewise, it had to shelve its plan to privatize two public-sector oil companies due to opposition in the Parliament.

Just when it had appeared that progress on reforms was unstoppable, the BJP-led coalition lost the parliamentary election in May 2004, paving the way for a Congress-led coalition known as the United Progressive Alliance (UPA). The UPA ruled for the following ten years until May 2014. The Congress was now headed by Sonia Gandhi, widow of Rajiv Gandhi. Although she appointed MMS the prime minister, she herself remained the power behind the throne. It turned out that she had none of the liberalizing instincts of her husband and, instead, shared the socialist thinking of her mother-in-law, Indira Gandhi. Socialism, thus, had a comeback, though in a much milder form.

The only notable reforms the MMS government undertook in its first term were the continuation of trade liberalization until 2007–08 and the gradual trimming of the list of items reserved for small-scale enterprises. Beyond these measures, the reform process came to a standstill. Matters got worse in the second term when the MMS government enacted at least two legislations reminiscent of 1970s socialism: the Right to Education Act of 2009 and the Land Acquisition Act of 2013. The second UPA term also witnessed a highly activist environment ministry that held back the environmental clearances on most infrastructure projects. High levels of social spending, financed by large fiscal deficits, became the hallmark of the government. As a consequence, economic performance suffered. The last half of the second UPA term saw a perceptible decline in the growth rate, high inflation and large current-account deficits. As such, whereas it had inherited a vibrant economy from its predecessor government in May 2004, it bequeathed a weak one to its successor government.

In May 2014, the BJP returned to power with Narendra Modi as the prime minister. He proved a highly popular leader and returned to the office in 2019. He remains the country's prime minister at the time of writing and is considered the favourite to win a clear mandate in the 2024 parliamentary elections. After initial hiccups, the Modi government resumed the process of reforms with some major politically challenging steps such as the Insolvency and Bankruptcy Code of 2016, the Goods and Services Tax and a major cut in and simplification of the corporate profit tax. It also enacted four labour codes to replace more than two dozen existing labour laws, but they remain to be implemented except for a small portion of the Code on Wages, 2019. Once implemented, the labour law regime would become considerably more employment-friendly. The Modi government has also resumed the privatization programme under which it has successfully transferred the ownership of the national carrier Air India to Tata Sons.

The record of the Modi government has not been without blemish, however. In particular, it has revived import-substitution industrialization (ISI), which remains popular among its rank and file. The popularity is not the least because some of the original icons of the BJP, such as Deen Dayal Upadhyay, were contemporaries of Nehru and steeped in the socialist thinking of the day. To be sure, the current pursuit of the ISI is not anything like the one India had pursued until 1991, when the government would offer to ban the imports of any product that an entrepreneur wished to produce domestically. Today, export expansion remains an explicitly stated objective of the government, and the level of protection is modest by pre-1991 standards. Nevertheless, the belief that a country can simultaneously expand total exports while shrinking its imports is not only damaging to the efficiency of the allocation of resources but also conceptually flawed.

Concluding Remarks

The hold of socialism on the Indian leadership remained firm for decades after the passing away of Nehru in 1964. Setting aside some baby steps by Indira Gandhi during 1980–84, the first genuine attempt at a retreat from socialism was made by none other than her son, Rajiv Gandhi, who had been untouched by politics almost all his life and therefore carried no baggage of socialism. RG had gone to college in the United Kingdom and was an airline pilot for the entirety of his professional career before joining politics in 1980. The death of his younger brother in 1980 led his mother, prime minister Indira Gandhi, to urge him to enter politics to assist her. Then, in 1984, Gandhi herself was assassinated, and at the young age of forty years, RG unexpectedly found himself in the chair of the prime minister of India.

RG was a modern man and genuinely wanted to launch India into the twenty-first century. He embarked upon a major liberalization programme in his first year as prime minister. To his disappointment, he found that much of the leadership within his own party, which had spent most of its political life under Nehru or Indira Gandhi, opposed a major shift away from the policies in place. Their pushback dramatically slowed RG's liberalization programme in his second year. Then, in his last three years, RG saw his own political capital and popularity rapidly erode, ending any hope of reviving the liberalization programme. Though the first experiment in the retreat from socialism thus ended without yielding immediate results, it triggered a dialogue for change at the political and bureaucratic levels.

The real change in the direction of economic policy came one and a half years after RG exited office in December 1989. He lost the mandate in the parliamentary election held in late 1989, giving way to two successive, short-lived coalition governments. With no party able to muster a majority to form another government, elections were called in March 1991. In the election campaign that followed, RG was assassinated, bringing the more senior Narasimha Rao to the prime minister's office. Rao had worked as a senior minister in the cabinet of Indira Gandhi during her 1980–84 term and RG during his 1984–89 term. He had been involved in and had closely observed the liberalization experiments of both of them.

Moreover, India was amid a balance-of-payments crisis when he came to the office. As a result, he turned out to be the right man in the right place at the right time. Drawing on forty years of political experience, he carefully navigated liberalizing reforms, nudging India towards a market economy.

Given India's democratic polity and the continuing grip of socialist philosophy on the political class, the change was slow under RG and Rao and remained so under their successor governments. While liberalization received a major boost under Vajpayee during 1998–2004, it reached a near standstill under the UPA during 2004–14, only to be revived by Modi in 2014. Under him, liberalization has returned, with the government successfully implementing some of the most contentious and long-overdue reforms.

Though democratic polity and the slow change of mindset of the political class have been the most critical elements in this slow progress towards a market economy, other factors have also played a role. In particular, the intellectual class, including economists and influential media commentators, has clung to the old ideas for too long and evolved just as slowly as the political class. On balance, they have strengthened the hand of politicians opposed to the change. Institutions, including the bureaucracy, the erstwhile Planning Commission and the legal system, too have been slow to evolve on account of entrenched interests and slow evolution of thinking in favour of a movement away from the socialist past. Finally, even the business community in India has been less than fully enthusiastic about liberalization. These themes constitute the subject matter of the next two chapters.

13

Institutions and the Business Community

Political leadership is the most important force in determining whether the major economic decisions will be made administratively or left to the market and how far the public sector would enter production activity. But the leadership does not operate in a vacuum. The institutions, business community and policy analysts also have a role in influencing the outcome.

In this chapter, I focus on the role played by the institutions and business community. Institutions consisting of the bureaucracy, the Planning Commission and laws and judiciary first played a supportive role in building the edifice of socialism, and once entrenched, became a source of resistance to change. To be sure, there were players in different pockets of the institutions, especially bureaucracy, that recognized the deleterious effects of the control-ridden regime in the later decades, but they were a small minority and, in any case, lacked the means to initiate a major change on their own. They could only play a facilitating role after the political leadership had initiated the change. With each change, the numbers of such actors and their power to bring about the next change grew.

The role of the business community was more complicated than institutions. Its interests would have been best served without the government mobilizing a large and rising proportion of savings for investment in the public sector or regulating the private sector with a heavy hand. But at least in the years immediately preceding and following Independence, it realized that the consensus in favour of a dominant role for the public sector and protection of small, village and household enterprises was so strong that its best bet was to carve out a part of the industry for itself. Accordingly, in the early post-Independence era, it became a full partner of the government, lending it full support in building the planning edifice in which heavy industry was assigned the highest priority, the government assumed the principal responsibility for its development and the private corporate sector became heavily regulated through a system of investment and import licensing. It was only after the passing away of Nehru that the business community gradually began articulating demands first for better administration of licensing and then for its removal. But its influence was minimal beyond achieving procedural changes to licensing administration and import liberalization to the extent permitted by the availability of foreign exchange. All it could accomplish was making the political leadership and the bureaucracy aware of its travails. The actual change it sought had to await the arrival of political leadership that saw the affairs as it did.

Institutions

The subject of institutions is vast, and a book chapter can scarcely do justice to it. Therefore, I confine myself to bureaucracy, the Planning Commission and the legal framework. These three components of institutions played an important role initially in creating the socialist regime and later in its preservation. Even after the top leadership had decided to replace the licensing regime with a price mechanism, these institutions were slow to change and impeded the transition to a market economy.

Bureaucracy

Through its role in policymaking and implementation, the bureaucracy has been integral to the advancement of the socialist agenda of successive governments. The top civil service of India, known as the Indian Administrative Service (IAS), has played a particularly important role in this regard. The IAS is the post-Independence successor to the colonial-era Imperial Civil Service, more commonly known as the Indian Civil Service (ICS). The ICS represented the top layer of the civil service under the British. Just before Independence, there were 980 ICS officers, of which 468 were Europeans, mainly British, and the rest Indian. With rare exceptions, ICS officers of European origin returned to their home countries, while those from India were divided between India and Pakistan.

As a group, the ICS officers were highly Westernized, with many having studied in Britain during an era in which socialism was a popular creed on that country's university campuses. As such, they broadly shared the philosophy of and passion for socialism with their political counterparts, including Nehru and many of his cabinet colleagues. The early recruits to the IAS from India, whether directly or through examination, also came from an elite, English-speaking background and quickly adopted the culture and values of their ICS counterparts.

Until at least 1960, written examinations and verbal interviews for selecting new IAS officers were conducted exclusively in English. With government-run schools using Hindi or other regional languages as the medium of instruction and private, English-medium schools out of reach for ordinary Indian families, the service remained effectively closed to the latter. Indeed, even after the written examinations began to be offered in Hindi, with the verbal interview continuing to be conducted in English and accounting for a substantial part of the overall final grade, the selected candidates continued to come overwhelmingly from elite families. Only gradually, as the number of private schools employing English as the medium of instruction increased and more and more families could afford to send their children to them, did the children of ordinary Indian families begin gaining entry into the service.

The shared background of the service members in the early decades also facilitated the adoption of socialism as a shared ideology within and between generations of officers. To the extent that each new generation of IAS officers looked up to the preceding one for inspiration and guidance, it inherited the latter's values, culture and ideology. This transmission process was particularly smooth during several initial decades because of the shared social background of the officers. Despite the entry of young men and women from diverse social and economic backgrounds in recent decades, there has remained a high degree of cohesion and continuity among the officers. As a result, it has been more insular and slower to change than its counterparts in politics.

Conventionally, the top two or three layers of Indian bureaucracy have almost entirely been drawn from the IAS. These are also the layers that work closely with ministers in respective ministries. As a result, these officers have a significant influence over policymaking. They generally draft legislation originating in their respective ministries. They also write the rules and regulations associated with the laws under the purview of their ministries or departments. Even though the Parliament debates, reviews and modifies the draft legislation, the original drafts play an important role in shaping the outcome. The rules and regulations are tabled in the Parliament and are therefore implemented verbatim as drafted by the bureaucracy. Because the legislation generally leaves out many details, the rules and regulations effectively determine how the laws are translated into action. There are also issues on which legislation may be silent. In such situations, the rules and regulations play the role of legislation. The senior-level IAS officers, thus, have considerable policymaking authority in India.

The top bureaucracy also played an important role in shaping the policy regime through administrative actions at critical junctures. An excellent example is the introduction of foreign exchange budgeting in 1957 amid the balance-of-payments crisis that year. A bureaucracy sympathetic to market forces could have tried to inform and persuade the political leadership to seriously consider devaluation as the solution. Instead, its instinct was to resort to tighter direct control on the use of foreign exchange. The finance ministry lost no time centralizing foreign exchange allocation across its different uses in the Department of Economic Affairs. That single act resulted in a serious tightening of not just the import-control regime but investment licensing as well since the decisions on investment licences now became contingent on the availability of foreign exchange for the import of capital goods required by the applicant.

The bureaucracy has also exercised influence over policy through committees appointed to study specific issues preceding action. It usually has representation on such committees and also oversees their administration. Sometimes the entire committee membership, including the chair, may be drawn from it. When a committee takes multiple years to complete its work, the government in office may become due for election before it submits its report. In such situations, the bureaucracy carries forward the work begun by one government to the next. The same situation may also arise if a committee appointed by one government recommends further work but its term ends before such work is completed. A brief consideration of the history behind the Monopolies and Restrictive Trade Practices (MRTP) Act of 1969 sheds light on the bureaucracy's critical role along these lines.[1]

In October 1960, concerns raised by the Opposition members in the Parliament led the Planning Commission to appoint a committee to investigate how different income groups had shared the wealth that the post-Independence economic growth had created. One specific concern the parliamentarians expressed was whether a concentration of economic power had accompanied this growth. In its report, submitted in February 1964, the committee pointed out that the concentration of economic power in the private sector was indeed 'more than what could be justified as necessary on functional grounds'. It recommended gathering 'more comprehensive and detailed information' for 'devising adequate corrective measures'.[2]

As a follow-up, the government appointed the Monopolies Inquiry Commission in April 1964 with the mandate 'to enquire into the existence and effect of concentration of economic power in private hands'.[3] The commission confirmed the existence of such concentration, noting, 'for numerous reasons, big business was at an advantage in securing licences for starting new industries or for expanding the existing capacity'.[4] It concluded, 'The system of controls in the shape of industrial licensing . . . has restricted the freedom of entry into industry and so helped produce concentration.'[5]

These reports and discussions around them led the Planning Commission to ask R.K. Hazari of the University of Bombay to conduct a study of the working of industrial licensing. In his interim report, Hazari found that medium and large enterprises had a higher approval ratio in licensing applications, which had risen over time.[6] Discussions of the Hazari report in the Parliament led to the appointment of the Industrial Licensing Policy Inquiry Committee (Dutt Committee), which confirmed and reinforced the findings by Hazari.

Nine years had passed between the appointment of the first of the four committees and the conclusion of the last one. Bureaucracy kept the subject alive during these years. Given the tight grip of socialist ideology, none of the four committees dared ask whether the critical question at this juncture was why so little wealth had been created or the connection of the concentration to the focus on heavy industry. It so happened that around this time, political considerations led Indira Gandhi (IG) to dramatically expand her socialist agenda. She threw her weight behind the Ten Point Programme that the Congress Forum for Socialist Action had been promoting in the Congress Working Committee. The programme included the promise of an assault on the concentration of economic power. With the work of the Dutt Committee at hand, IG decided to deliver on this promise through the enactment of the MRTP Act of 1969. The Act further stifled industrial growth and, therefore, wealth creation by excluding the most successful firms from investing in many sectors.

If bureaucracy thus played an active, supportive role in policy, it was central to allocating investment, imports and critical domestically produced inputs such as steel and cement down to the enterprise level in both public and private sectors. At one level, despite many delays and inefficiencies, its overall success in administering the elaborate plans designed by the Planning Commission proved to be the undoing of India's economy. Had it lacked the ability to effectively implement the vast network of controls through elaborate allocations of inputs, either the markets would have gotten greater play de facto or the pressure to switch the policy regime in their favour would have built up sooner. But it managed to design systems to accomplish these tasks sufficiently effectively to sustain the system for many decades.

Bureaucracy acquired enormous power over business activity as policy-induced interventions and controls grew. In the public sector, it came to preside over a significant and rising proportion of industrial output with little market pressure of the kind that the managers of private-sector enterprises faced. Public-sector undertakings also became a source of lucrative post-retirement employment for senior bureaucrats. In the private sector, it exercised tight regulatory control, opening avenues to personal benefit through outright bribery or in-kind quid-pro-quo exchange of favours. Bureaucracy as a whole thus complemented the politicians in delaying a switch to the market economy.

It is sometimes argued that if political leadership has the will to make a change, bureaucracy cannot be a barrier to it; it must execute what its political masters demand. In its extreme form, this argument says that the bureaucracy shares no part of the blame for the undue delay in reforms. This claim is partially valid at best. While the bureaucracy rarely responds to the demands for change by its political masters in the negative, it is known for following the tactic of slowing down action on it. Over the years, it has placed so many regulatory layers that hardly any substantive change is possible without removing many of those layers. Invariably, these layers fall under the jurisdiction of several different ministries. Moreover, bureaucratic procedures within each ministry are elaborate, with the file proposing the change having to travel through many levels before reaching the minister or the department head, the final approval authority. When asked why there had been no action, bureaucracy can report progress on a subset of hurdles and promise action on the remaining steps 'soon'. This gradual process sometimes results in the expiry of the government's term before the final steps are complete. The matter then ends up in cold storage, or the process begins all over again if the successive government desires.

Socialist thought and the vested interest created by its practice have left many pockets of the Indian bureaucracy reluctant towards reform till today. Four specific examples may be cited in this context. First, as a legacy of the socialist era, nearly every ministry in India controls several public sector undertakings. Nearly every one of these undertakings yields returns worse than its private-sector counterparts, and many run in perpetual losses. There is no rationale for most of these undertakings to remain in the public sector.

The Modi government had adopted a policy of privatization of many public-sector undertakings (PSUs) beginning in early 2016. By late 2016, the cabinet had approved a list of undertakings to be privatized. But the Department of Disinvestment and Asset Management (DIPAM), responsible for translating the policy into action, failed to privatize a single PSU for many years. Successive secretaries heading DIPAM exhibited no interest in carrying out the government's mandate. Equally, ministries or departments in charge of PSUs identified for privatization have vehemently opposed privatization because they find the undertaking useful vehicles for post-retirement jobs, hiring workers and staff whom they cannot hire on the government payroll and incurring other expenses that would not be permitted on the government account. Only in 2021, did an exceptional Secretary, DIPAM, finally initiate the process, bringing the long-awaited privatization of Air India, the national carrier notorious for incurring mega losses every year and piling up a mountain of debt, to a closure.

Second, the practice of protectionism for decades in the socialist era has left the Ministry of Commerce almost permanently opposed to import liberalization. The Department of Revenue, which has not met a source of revenue it does not like, becomes its accomplice in the crime. Socialist-era vocabulary, including domestic availability, non-essentiality and phased manufacturing programme, continue to come back in the policy discourse and even practice.

The disproportionately large number of anti-dumping duties India imposes on imports best illustrates the point. These duties result from a purely bureaucratic process controlled by the mandarins of the Ministry of Commerce and, therefore, a good indicator of their (as opposed to the politicians') protectionist instincts. In 2019, India had just a 2.5 per cent share in the world merchandise imports. But as on 30 June 2020, it had as many as 243 anti-dumping measures in force. Only the United States, which accounted for 13.3 per cent of the world imports in 2019, had a larger number of anti-dumping measures in force. Even China, which had a hefty 10.8 per cent share in the world merchandise imports in 2019, had only 156 anti-dumping measures in force. Bureaucrats in the ministry are also known for taking a highly protectionist position in negotiations for bilateral free trade agreements and multilateral agreements under the auspices of the World Trade Organization.

Third, bureaucracy in the Ministry of Labour and Employment has been squarely focused on protecting the interests of the existing formal-sector workers at the expense of job creation. It has steadfastly resisted the reform of labour laws. After the Modi government decided to proceed with the reform of these laws, it took the ministry a long time to draft the new labour codes. More glaringly, it has been five years since the Parliament enacted the new codes, but they remain largely unimplemented. The result is that despite the passage of thirty years since the launch of the reforms, the old labour laws, of which several key ones had been enacted even before the adoption of the Constitution, remain in force today.

Finally, the education sector has remained entirely immune to reforms. It is a well-known fact that with rare exceptions, government schools today fail to deliver even a minimum acceptable level of education. Cognizant of this fact, almost all bureaucrats in the top layers of bureaucracy in the central and state governments send their children to private schools. Yet, adhering to the socialist-era ideology, they overwhelmingly argue that it is the duty of the government not just to finance but also to provide education through government schools. They remain steadfastly opposed to reforms that would give parents a greater say in choosing schools for their children. Bureaucracy has also opposed the reform of the Right to Education Act, which gives recognition to schools based solely on input norms such as the availability of a sports field, a boundary wall around the school and pupil-teacher ratio. Such criteria threaten to close down the numerous low-budget private schools that predominantly serve children from low-income families and deliver better educational outcomes than their much better-funded government-sector counterparts in the area.[7] These schools have principally mushroomed since reforms began to deliver more rapidly rising incomes because the public-sector schools offer poor education.

To end the section on a positive note, however, it is important to remind readers that the above discussion focuses on the central tendency of the bureaucracy. Its purpose is to underline that, as a whole, the Indian bureaucracy has been too slow to shed the socialist ideas of the past, and, as a result, progress on reforms has been far slower than has been politically feasible. This discussion says nothing about specific bureaucrats. To be sure, Indian bureaucracy, in general, and the IAS, in particular, have produced several highly efficient and reformist officers. Without such officers, the economic reforms that have taken place since 1991 would have been impossible. In the next chapter, I will highlight the critical role played by some liberal-minded economists inside the government in promoting reforms. As I will document there, an anomalous feature of the economics profession in India has been that reform-minded economists have been overwhelmingly resident inside the government. On average, economists in Indian academia have been slower to shed socialist-era economic thought than their counterparts inside the government.

The Planning Commission

Multiple early efforts by Nehru between 1946 and 1950 to establish a planning agency to coordinate economic policies across different ministries did not bear fruit on account of opposition by Patel.[8] Even when Nehru succeeded and the Planning Commission was established on 15 March 1950, Patel and his conservative associates saw to it that its role was strictly advisory, with the decision-making power vested in the ministries and the cabinet. After the death of Patel in December 1950, conservatives continued to exert considerable influence under the leadership of Purshottamdas Tandon, who had successfully defeated Nehru's candidate Acharya J.B. Kripalani for the presidency of the Congress in September 1950.

The draft outline of the first plan, published in mid-1951, had a strong conservative flavour to it. In the words of Francine Frankel, the outline 'limited the government's role to the creation of social capital and financial incentives for the expansion of private enterprise'.[9] It assigned the highest priority to agriculture and rejected a proposal to place a ceiling on the size of the existing holdings to redistribute land. It placed the greatest emphasis on adopting improved practices to increase food grain production, such as introducing irrigation and applying chemical fertilizers. It did not matter that this strategy favoured the larger farmers since they were positioned to take the greatest advantage of it. With its focus on growth, even at the cost of increased inequality and the assignment of a dominant role to the private sector, this blueprint was contrary to Nehru's conception.

The loss of control of the party apparatus to the conservatives and half-hearted efforts by Nehru to contain the rising clout of the latter led many socialists and Gandhians, including Kripalani, to defect from the Congress. When two of his ministers also defected at the end of July 1951, Nehru felt an existential threat. He resigned from the Congress Working Committee and the Central Election Committee to assert his authority. This act had the desired effect. By far the most popular leader among the masses, his leadership was indispensable during the soon-to-be-held general elections. Therefore, Tandon had no choice but to resign and pave the way for Nehru's election as president in September 1951.

The final version of the first plan, published in December 1952, fully reflected Nehru's thinking. It clarified the government's intention to tightly regulate the private sector and assign the public sector the dominant role in developing heavy industry. In agriculture, reversing the past stand, the plan recommended ceilings on the ownership of land by an individual. It dropped the technology-based approach, which focused on boosting the output of large farmers through investment in irrigation and chemical fertilizer. Instead, it tried to reconcile growth and equity by proposing a strategy to boost small farmers' agricultural output. The strategy relied on more effective use of traditional labour-intensive techniques through the instrumentality of Community Development projects.

From this point on, Nehru's view dominated the plans and the Planning Commission. In turn, as the work on the second plan got underway, the status and power of the commission saw a dramatic rise. Its word on economic policy effectively became the prime minister's word. As Frankel puts it,

> The demarcation originally envisaged between the advisory functions of the Planning Commission and the decision-making responsibilities of the central government grew blurred. . . . Nehru's unique position in the government and the Congress party was central to this transformation. As prime minister, he often requested Cabinet approval for recommendations he had already endorsed as chairman of the Planning Commission. In most cases, none of his colleagues had sufficient prestige or popular standing to challenge his advice effectively. The same situation prevailed in the Working Committee and the AICC. Congress party leaders who complained bitterly in private about the prime minister's 'doctrinaire' socialist views were among his most vocal supporters at the open annual sessions of the party.[10]

Nehru also boosted the commission's power by giving its members ministerial status. He further linked it with the government by having the cabinet secretary double as the commission's secretary and the finance ministry's chief economic adviser as economic adviser to the commission. Nehru also appointed some key ministers as members of the commission. He met with the full commission once or twice a month and was present at all its important meetings devoted to policy formulation. Frankel once again writes, 'From 1955 to 1964, Nehru's pivotal position permitted a handful of men to determine national economic and social policy and methods of development.'[11]

During these years, the commission's members whom Nehru chose came from a group of no more than twenty individuals who were committed to his brand of socialism. Because the appointments of the members were open-ended in terms of the length of tenure, they often served for several years. With its superior capacity over states in terms of economic expertise, data gathering and mustering teams of statisticians and researchers, the commission was also able to get them to adopt its priorities. The fact that it provided financial assistance to the states gave it an extra edge.

Under Nehru, the commission became the lightning rod of socialist ideas that, at times, were challenged by the ministries concerned. The case of the search for remedies for rising food prices during the early years of the second plan illustrates the point. As the second plan got underway, the fall of food grain output due to poor monsoons led to a 50 per cent increase in food prices between October 1955 and August 1957. Convinced that hoarding activities by traders had been driving this increase, the Planning Commission had been pushing the ministry to assume social control over the wholesale trade in food grains. It recommended that the food ministry build a sufficiently large buffer stock to emerge as the dominant trader in the economy by the end of the second plan.

The then Minister of Food, A.P. Jain, took exception to the suggestion and attacked the commission for neglecting the price incentives to farmers in the Lok Sabha. Characterizing the policy of low agricultural prices as regressive, he reasoned that the farmers' response to them would be to cut food grain production. Privately, Jain went so far as to compare the creation of marketing cooperatives to compulsorily collect the surplus from farmers and redistribute it to the consumers to the strategy that Stalin had pursued in Russia and Mao in China.[12] Until late 1957, he resisted the commission's pressure to introduce state trading in food grains. Later, when such resistance became difficult, he only agreed to procure food grain in selected states on a limited scale without replacing private traders with a state-trading agency.

Driven by food shortages, prices continued to rise in 1957–58, and the Planning Commission continued to insist on monopoly procurement of food grains and price controls at all levels of the distribution process by the food ministry and the states as the solution. The ministry rejected the recommendation, arguing that static production levels, higher income generated by development outlays and rising population growth rather than hoarding were behind the price increase. It suggested scientific practices rather than organizational changes as the foremost instrument of increasing agricultural productivity and surpluses. In particular, it pressed for larger outlays on improved seeds, pesticides and especially fertilizers, and remunerative prices for rice and wheat as the solutions. In the end, the ministry found the solution to the food grain shortage in wheat imports under PL 480 and rice imports at commercial terms in the short run.

The struggle on the socialist agenda between Nehru and the Planning Commission on the one hand and ministries and conservatives within the Congress on the other continued as the 1950s gave way to the 1960s. For example, in 1962, a ruling by the Supreme Court on the Kerala Agrarian Relations Act of 1961 effectively struck down all existing land ceiling laws. To rescue these laws, Nehru proposed a constitutional amendment the following year. But the amendment failed to pass because many Congress MPs refused to support it.

In a similar vein, around this time, rising prices had led the Planning Commission to once again press the concerned ministries to undertake a more vigorous price control and procurement policy. Under the Essential Commodities Act of 1955 and the Defence of India Rules, Finance Minister Morarji Desai enjoyed wide powers to impose such controls. But despite promising the commission an active price policy, the only commodity he imposed price control on was kerosene. Likewise, food minister S.K. Patil agreed to regulate only sugarcane's supply and price, insisting that the only effective solution to the food crisis lay in incentives for a larger production volume. Specifically, he advocated higher guaranteed prices for farmers and generous provision of funds via loans for investment in tube wells and minor irrigation projects.

These conflicts defined the relationship between the Planning Commission and the ministries when Nehru died. With Shastri taking the helm, power began shifting away from the Planning Commission to ministries. At the first meeting with the commission in June 1964, Shastri pitched for the highest priority in allocating resources to agriculture. He appealed for a 'common man's plan' that would immediately increase the availability of food, clothing and shelter. Accomplishing this task, in turn, required increased attention to minor irrigation, fertilizers and medium- and small-scale industries. In the words of Frankel, 'Taken together, the changes he favoured suggested a reduced role for detailed planning in the development process; but something less than a major departure from established goals and methods of development.'[13]

Some of the administrative and procedural changes Shastri made also worked towards weakening the power of the commission. He replaced the commission members' open-ended tenure with fixed-term tenure with the possibility of renewal. He also severed the direct link between the cabinet secretariat and the commission by discontinuing the practice of the cabinet secretary doubling up as the secretary to the commission and appointing a separate secretary to the latter. Finally, he also strengthened his own office by creating the position of secretary to the prime minister and appointing L.K. Jha, an officer with considerable economic expertise, to it. This approach was in contrast to Nehru, who had used senior officers from the commission, such as Tarlok Singh and Pitambar Pant, as his personal secretaries. Thus, the new arrangement severed the close link between the prime minister's office and the commission and created independent economic expertise in the prime minister's office. According to Frankel, 'Within a short time, Jha became the most influential official adviser in the government. Equally important, through his close personal ties with other senior civil servants, especially in the finance ministry, he played a major role in re-establishing the influence of the bureaucracy in the formulation of economic policy.'[14]

Rather than rely primarily on the commission on policy matters, he encouraged independent inputs from his cabinet colleagues.

The shift in power from the commission to the ministries was best illustrated by how the government dealt with the food crisis of the 1960s. The commission insisted that the problem was hoarding by traders and suggested price controls and state trading as the solutions. In contrast, the food ministry believed that the solution lay in incentives to increase food production. Regarding state trading, it only agreed to purchase food grains at market prices and use the stocks created to stabilize the prices.

In parallel, in the ongoing discussions on the fourth plan, the food ministry advocated higher outlays on yield-enhancing inputs such as fertilizers, pesticides and irrigation. The commission opposed them, arguing that this would increase disparities between commercial farmers and the mass of subsistence cultivators and deprive the industry of much-needed investment. Shastri sided with the food ministry in this debate and appointed a committee under Jha to suggest a road map. Jha and his committee took the view that measures such as price controls, monopoly procurement and state trading advocated by the commission made sense only in a crisis, and the real solution lay in increased food production. This approach, in turn, required price incentives to commercial farmers and much larger investment outlays on improved inputs, such as seeds and fertilizers. In what was an eventual victory for the food ministry, the government set up the Agricultural Price Commission and Food Corporation of India and introduced high-yielding varieties of seeds along with the use of complementary inputs such as fertilizers, pesticides and irrigation to bring about the Green Revolution.

The 1965 India-Pakistan war, the death of Shastri in January 1966, two back-to-back droughts in 1965–66 and 1966–67, and the accompanying economic crisis culminating in the June 1966 devaluation of the rupee combined to result in a holiday from the five-year plans for three years and further weakened the position of the Planning Commission vis-à-vis the ministries. In September 1967, Indira Gandhi appointed D.R. Gadgil, a professional economist, as the commission's deputy chairman. He had been critical of the political character of Nehru's Planning Commission and believed that it should be a purely technical and advisory body.

Gadgil's appointment was followed by the report of the Administrative Reforms Committee (ARC) in March 1968, which designated the commission as exclusively an expert advisory body, with responsibilities 'only for formulating the objectives, laying down priorities, indicating sectoral outlays, fixing basic targets and approving main programmes'.[15] The ARC explicitly excluded the commission from implementing the programmes, which were to be the sole preserve of the ministries concerned. It also cut the commission's staff in accordance with its truncated role. Soon after, the central assistance for plan outlay to the states also came to be based on the so-called 'Gadgil formula', which eliminated any role for bargaining between the states and the commission.

The five-year plans resumed in 1969–70 after three years of plan holiday. Except for two other two-year breaks during 1978–80 and 1990–92, they continued until the twelfth plan ended in 2016–17. With ministries and the prime minister assuming the charge of policymaking, the commission's powers were considerably reduced during these years relative to what it enjoyed under Nehru. Nevertheless, within the broad policy framework set by the ministries, it significantly influenced the allocation of investment across sectors through target-setting, at least until the 1991 reforms were launched.

Until the launch of the 1991 reforms, the commission also remained a defender of the economic order established by Nehru and advanced by IG. The point is best illustrated by a 1985 episode involving RG and the commission's senior leadership. According to C.G. Somiah, the then secretary of the commission, after listening to the presentation by the commission staff on the approach to the seventh plan, RG expressed serious disagreement with it and wanted the plan to be completely recast. He offered his vision to lead India into the twenty-first century, advising the commission 'to plan for the construction of autobahns, airfields, speedy trains, shopping malls and entertainment centers of excellence, big housing complexes, modern hospitals and healthcare centres'.[16] Somiah further states that RG 'concluded his speech with a grin, suggesting that we should change our mindset in drafting the seventh Five Year Plan'.[17]

RG was thus keen to change course in a major way. But the commission pushed back. Dr Manmohan Singh, the then deputy chairman of the commission, held an internal meeting to discuss the way forward.

> The broad consensus that emerged was that the Prime Minister was urban-centric without any knowledge of the socially and financially backward condition of the vast population living in the rural areas. It was decided that in the next meeting we would try and educate the Prime Minister about the hard realities of the widespread poverty prevailing in the country.[18]

Thus, the commission did not even entertain the possibility that RG may have had a point. After all, it had been thirty-five years since the planning process had begun, and the country had failed to make any dent in its massive poverty problem. Was it not a time for introspection into whether the approach adopted since the second plan may have been fundamentally flawed? But so convinced was the leadership of the institution's direction that such questions did not even occur to it. It simply dug its heels in and effectively pronounced RG as being naïve and needing to be educated by it.

With the abolition of licensing on investment and imports of capital goods and intermediate inputs in 1991, the commission effectively lost its power to guide the allocation of investment among different sectors. With entrepreneurial decisions rather than licensing authorities now determining the sectoral investment allocations henceforth, little rationale remained for formulating five-year plans. Yet, with the political leadership still unused to thinking of administering the economy any other way and the commission an influential body, five-year plans continued to be written. The seventh plan ended in 1989–90, and after a break of two years due to the economic crisis, planning resumed in 1992–93 with the launch of the eighth plan. The last plan was the twelfth and launched in 2012–13. Halfway into this plan, a new prime minister, who came to the helm in May 2014, exhibited the courage to announce the closure of the Planning Commission in his first Independence Day address on 15 August 2014. Though the Twelfth Plan was notionally completed in 2016–17, the announcement to close the commission effectively ended planning.

Laws and Judiciary

Heavily influenced by the history of industrialization in Great Britain, the Nehru government proceeded to usher in India a social revolution well before the economic revolution. The Industrial Disputes Act of 1947, the Factories Act of 1948 and the Minimum Wage Act of 1948 were all put in place even before the country had adopted its own Constitution. Many more labour laws were enacted in the early 1950s. The result is that the Ministry of Labour and Employment currently lists forty laws under its jurisdiction that remain in force.

The thrust of these laws has been mostly on protecting the existing formal-sector workers who constitute a tiny proportion of the total workforce. The laws positively discourage the creation of new formal-sector jobs by undermining the profitability in the labour-intensive sectors and nudging enterprises towards more capital-intensive technologies. It is widely accepted that the effect of these laws has been to hold back the expansion of employment opportunities in the formal sector. Though pro-market reforms began in 1991, no government was willing to take the political risk of reforming these laws until the Modi government finally enacted four labour codes to replace more than two dozen existing labour laws. These four codes, enacted in 2019 and 2020, contain provisions that would make the labour market more flexible and encourage the creation of new jobs in the formal sector. Unfortunately, however, four to five years after their passage by the Parliament, the four codes still await implementation.

Similar laws in other areas have added to the delays in the transition to a market-oriented economy. For instance, the Urban Land Ceiling and Regulation Act of 1976 and associated state-level laws have been known to have contributed to the ultra-high land prices in the larger cities in India. Yet, it took nearly two decades after the launch of the 1991 reforms to repeal these laws. Moreover, while the laws were operational, a significant proportion of the available urban land got tied up in litigation between the owners and the government. With the ongoing litigation, these parcels of land remain off the market.

The return of a socialistically-oriented Congress-led government during 2004–14 resulted even in enacting some new laws reminiscent of the Nehru-Gandhi era. For example, the Land Acquisition Act of 2013 makes land acquisition by the government for the industry extremely difficult. With no system of granting land titles in force in India, it is common for specific parcels of land to be under dispute. As a result, without the government giving a hand in acquiring those parcels on behalf of the industry, it is very difficult for private industry to assemble a large tract of contiguous parcels of land. But the new Land Acquisition Act makes such acquisition extremely difficult.

Another recent law that discourages the growth of budget private schools is the Right to Education Act of 2009. These schools had been rapidly springing up in response to poor education delivery in the public schools in low-income urban and rural neighbourhoods. But by specifying very high input norms for formal recognition, this law raises the costs to a level that the schools cannot cover at the fees their students can afford.

Turning to the judiciary, during the heydays of socialism, it also exhibited a bias in favour of protecting the interests of the existing formal-sector workers over those of their employers, thereby undermining the expansion of the formal-sector workforce. According to a family member of a former judge, who had an illustrious career serving in the Supreme Court during the 1970s and 1980s, in cases pitching the workers against corporations, the judge invariably ruled in favour of workers irrespective of the facts of the case. He argued that with corporations having deep pockets, social justice was better served by protecting worker interests under all circumstances.[19]

A dramatic example of how such litigation and its outcome could be burdensome for even a large firm in a capital-intensive sector with a low share of labour costs is provided by Sanjeev Sanyal. Describing the case of a worker whom a corporation terminated upon having been repeatedly found sleeping on the shop floor, he writes,[20]

> In August 1983, Nakate was found at 11:40 a.m. sleeping soundly on an iron plate in the factory in Pune where he worked. He had committed three previous misdemeanours but had been let off lightly. This time his employer Bharat Forge began disciplinary proceedings against him, and after five months of hearings, he was found guilty and sacked. But Nakate went to a labour court and pleaded that he was a victim of an unfair trade practice. The court agreed and forced the factory to take him back and pay him 50 per cent of his lost wages. Both parties appealed against this judgment (Nakate wanted more money). The case dragged on through the judicial system for another decade and in 1995 another court awarded Nakate more money because he was now too

> old to be rehired. Bharat Forge eventually had to approach the Supreme Court and in May 2005 – more than two decades after the original incident – the apex court finally awarded the employer the right to fire a worker who had been repeatedly caught sleeping on the job.

This case is not an isolated one. T.U. Mehta, who had served as the chief justice of a high court, analysed many judgments on cases involving the termination of service by employers given by Indian high courts and the Supreme Court. His conclusion from the review was stark. He wrote,

> Some judges are overwhelmed by the view that the only object and purpose of the Industrial Disputes Act is to take a view favourable only to labour, ignoring other facts and circumstances as also the necessity of preserving industrial peace. It is sometimes forgotten that the problem confronting industrial adjudication is to promote two-fold objectives:
>
> 1. security of employment of the workers; and
> 2. preservation of industrial peace and harmony so that industry can prosper and employment can increase. Any lopsided view, that to favour labor is the only goal of the statute is counterproductive in as much as it ultimately harms the cause of labor itself.[21]

In a recent paper, Santanu Sarkar studied the challenges to verdicts of dismissals and discharges by the Supreme Court and high courts in cases falling under one specific act, the Industrial Disputes Act (IDA) of 1947. Until 1971, this Act did not have a provision for a challenge to dismissals and discharges in the labour courts or industrial tribunals. The provision was first introduced in December 1971 by inserting Section 11A in the Act. Sarkar finds that in the handful of the cases that were brought to the judiciary between 1950 and 1970, prior to the insertion of this section, courts generally upheld the employer's right to dismiss or discharge workers, especially if the right had been exercised after the conduct of fair and proper inquiry. But after the introduction of Section 11A in IDA, in cases brought to them between 1971 and the mid-1990s, courts provided a high degree of protection against dismissals and discharges to workers. To quote Sarkar,[22]

> Post emergency, the country found its highest office of judiciary taking huge pro-labour stances. This started from mid-70s. Courts favoured the marginalized to gain justice in a number of important cases. . . . By early 80s there has been a sea change in the judiciary's appeal to common man exemplifying a rise in judicial activism. Capital and market forces trailed in the courtrooms. Rulings were no longer the tool of oppression by the capitalist to control the proletariat in class struggle. The saga continued for more than a decade in which the provenance of judicial activism amongst the honourable judges of the SCI [Supreme Court of India] triumphed over the dictums held by the lower courts.

Interestingly, the top court effectively travelled in the same direction as the government, not just during the era in which socialism was at its peak but also after the latter embarked upon economic reforms, at least in disputes over worker dismissals under IDA. Despite expanding the space for entrepreneurs through policy reforms in many areas, the government has found the reform of labour laws challenging. Here, decisions by the Supreme Court have come to play a positive role in promoting liberalization. Sarkar finds that the decisions by the Supreme Court have begun to recognize the need for expanding the space for corporations. He writes,

> LCs [Labour Courts] and HCs [High Courts] continued offering pro-labour rulings [during 1990 to 2010], but the SCI began to change from its earlier position. The apex court was no longer non-interfering. The same SCI that cooperated

> with the lower courts in resolving policy decisions until a year ago began to set distinctive judicial doctrines. It quashed bulk of orders where the LCs interfered with the findings of the domestic enquiry. SCI reduced the power of the LCs and its jurisdiction instigated limitations to the implementation of Sec-11A by LCs.

Business Community

At least in the early years of planning, the business community had accepted socialism as a part of the overall ethos within which it had to operate, even if it may have had no belief of its own in the ideology. But as the stranglehold of the licensing regime tightened, it began getting restless. Towards the end of the Nehru era, it began seeking procedural changes aimed at removing bottlenecks and eliminating unnecessary delays in the final decision on applications. Gradually, it began demanding the partial removal of controls and, by the early 1980s, their complete removal. It articulated these demands mostly through industry associations, though occasionally, a particularly influential individual industrialist such as J.R.D. Tata also took it upon himself to voice the industry's concerns.

Traditionally, India has had numerous industry associations, with many of them well-known to followers of industry news by their acronyms. A few notable associations with India-wide reach include the Confederation of Indian Industry (CII), Federation of Indian Chambers of Commerce and Industry (FICCI), Associated Chambers of Commerce and Industry of India (ASSOCHAM), All India Manufacturers' Association (AIMA), Indian Chamber of Commerce (ICC) and Indian Merchants' Chamber (IMC). Though the CII is perhaps the most prominent among these associations today, this development is relatively recent. The association which played a pivotal role in representing the industry voice on liberalization before the 1991 reforms is FICCI. It often gave voice to the concerns of the business community as a whole at its annual sessions that have regularly taken place in the month of either March or April. Accordingly, in describing the policy role of the business community after Independence, I rely on the resolutions adopted by industry leaders at these annual sessions.

The powerful business leaders who participated in the deliberations of the National Planning Committee during 1938–40 had come to accept the primacy of heavy industry in the early stage of industrialization and the dominant role of the public sector in its development even before Independence. Recognizing the determination of the political leadership to adopt a mixed-economy model, these business leaders considered it prudent to carve out a section of the industry for the private sector rather than militate against the entry of the public sector in production activity. Accordingly, the Bombay Plan for India's development in the first fifteen years, authored by eight leading industrialists and published in two parts in 1944 and 1945, ended up having much in common with the Second Five-Year Plan of the government. Later, when the government introduced the Industrial Policy Resolution of 1948, the business community embraced it without serious reservation. When the Draft Plan-frame of the second plan came up for discussion in the summer of 1955, however, contrary to the Bombay Plan, FICCI leaned against the dominant role assigned to the public sector.[23] But by the time the draft second plan was released in February 1956, its opposition had been considerably muted.[24]

With the control regime, including investment licensing working smoothly, there is little evidence of the business community calling for any liberalizing steps during the 1950s. Only in the early 1960s did prolonged and systematic delays in decisions on licence applications lead it to call for procedural changes to speed up the decision-making process. At this stage, however, it made no demands to end licensing in one or more sectors. At a meeting in March 1962, attended by some of the leading industrialists of the time, FICCI adopted a resolution stating that the 'administrative machinery must be streamlined at various levels in order to remove the procedural difficulties, expedite decisions and coordinate polices'.[25] In May 1962, the federation sent a communication to the government urging a fresh, thorough examination of the existing industrial and import licensing procedures.[26] In March 1963, in the backdrop of the India-China War of October 1962, it once again passed a resolution calling upon the union government to lend greater flexibility to its IPR 1956. In particular, it repeated its call to remove inordinate administrative delays and inefficiencies, reminding that they constituted disincentives to industrial progress.[27] These repeated calls for procedural reforms finally led the government to appoint the Swaminathan Committee, with the president of FICCI as one of the members.[28]

The appointment of the Monopolies Inquiry Commission in 1964 with the mandate to recommend measures to investigate the concentration of economic power and recommend measures to combat it led to fears of the imposition of yet more restrictions on industrial activity within the business community. Accordingly, FICCI fought back, sending the commission a memorandum arguing that a review of the legal and administrative regulations revealed that these latter had already been keeping in check the forces that gave rise to either monopoly or concentration of economic power.[29] The memorandum reasoned that the regulations such as the Industries (Development and Regulation) Act of 1951, capital issue controls and import licensing had already limited the freedom of individual enterprises. Accordingly, the government needed to focus on rolling back pervasive restrictions to stimulate economic activity instead of imposing more restrictions. In the event, the federation was unsuccessful in persuading the commission, which recommended the creation of a permanent commission with the power to investigate and curb restrictive and monopolistic practices. Luckily, the government took no immediate action on the recommendation, though another committee, and five years later, it did enact the

MRTP Act of 1969, which led to several additional regulatory layers on the large firms and big business houses.

By 1965, a food crisis had been brewing due to poor food grain crops. On top of this, exports had been performing poorly, creating a severe shortage of foreign exchange and, therefore, dependence on aid, including for food. These facts allowed the United States and the World Bank to intervene in policy. Early in the year, a special World Bank Mission under the leadership of Bernard R. Bell arrived to conduct a six-month study on economic policy. In its report, submitted to the bank authorities in October 1965, the mission recommended assigning a significantly higher priority to agriculture and, to this end, allocating a substantially larger proportion of financial resources to it. Insofar as industry was concerned, this reordering of priorities implied a restraint on expanding the public sector and enhanced role for the domestic private enterprise and foreign private capital. The policy package to achieve these shifts included relaxation of licensing on investment and imports, and devaluation.[30]

This context provided the Indian business community an opening for a push for greater economic space for itself yet again. Accordingly, at its three-day annual session in March 1966, FICCI adopted a resolution calling for a thorough review of all controls and regulations shackling industry and trade.[31] The following month, on the occasion of the departure of the planning minister to Washington D.C. for talks with the World Bank, it issued a 600-word statement calling for the relaxation of price and distribution controls and licensing procedures to foster higher economic growth.[32] Ten days later, the federation followed up with a note entitled 'Economic Planning—Lessons for the Future' circulated to members of the Parliament. In it, the federation once again leaned against industrial licensing, price controls, company law, capital issue control and similar restrictions.[33]

In June 1966, the government did announce a package of liberalization measures, including a large devaluation of the rupee. In this context, in October 1966, when the then industry minister met the Central Advisory Council of Industries to announce the government's intention to further liberalize its industrial licensing policy, J.R.D. Tata used the occasion to offer a trenchant critique of the prevailing socialist regime. He urged the government to 'make an unprejudiced, factual and objective assessment of our economic progress or lack of it during the past fifteen years and of the effectiveness or deficiencies of the means and methods we have adopted up to now in shaping our economic destinies'. According to a contemporary *Times of India* report, he went on to underline that there was no room for dogma or religion when it came to economic and technological problems, 'as in our case, the destiny of 500 million people is at stake'. He added that socialism had taken different forms in different parts of the world. In India, it had been largely based on the Soviet Model, 'characterized by total planning, rigid controls, emphasis on heavy industry and particularly monumental projects and the determination of making the public sector the dominant one at all costs'. He then rhetorically asked whether there were no lessons to be drawn from the fact that countries in the West or in the East which had adopted the Indian form of socialism had made the least economic progress while those like Japan, Korea and Taiwan in the East and Germany, France and Italy in the West had achieved a far greater rate of growth and widely distributed prosperity. However, such timely critique and warning fell only on deaf ears.[34]

The liberalization package announced in 1966, especially devaluation, proved highly unpopular. Nearly all who had a serious voice in the system saw it as capitulation by the government to the World Bank and the United States. The reaction left a deep impression on IG, who became averse to liberalization for years. In the subsequent years, she reversed most of the liberalizing measures she had taken. By 1969, she was on course to implement a highly populist and popular socialist agenda, including the MRTP Act and further tightening of controls, especially on larger firms and big business houses. The business community proved utterly powerless to resist this movement towards greater control over private industrial activity.

An interaction between IG and leading industrialists in March 1970 illustrates how little influence the latter had over the former's policy choices. The interaction took place at FICCI's annual conference, at which many members of the cabinet, members of Parliament, senior government officials and leading business figures were present. According to a contemporary report in the *Times of India*, deliberately choosing to avoid using the word 'socialism', IG began by asking the business community to cooperate with her in building up a future, 'not for some sections of the people, but for all'. She then explained that price controls, licensing regulations and anti-monopoly laws were not aimed at it and turned down all its demands for liberalization. The *Times of India* report states, 'Mrs. Gandhi made no concessions to industry. In fact, she went about rejecting almost every plea made by the president of the Federation, Mr. Ramnath A. Podar, in his opening address. She would not relax controls, nor give up the move for State takeover of imports and exports. In her view, these were necessary to reconcile the interests of different sections of society and avoid "conflict and confrontation that might generate chaos".'[35]

In the 1970s, FICCI continued to call for liberalization of policies, such as price and distribution controls, investment licensing and restrictions on non-competing inputs and capital goods imports at its annual sessions. But it rarely lent its voice to external liberalization that would bring competing foreign goods or investors to the shores of India. In March 1972, it used 'self-reliance' as the theme of its annual conference and brought out a pamphlet under the same title in which it called upon the government to do away with licensing on all investments exceeding Rs 50 million as long as the foreign exchange component was less than 10 per cent.[36] In December 1974, it once again brought out a pamphlet that suggested the reform of capital issue control, the MRTP Act, licensing-related controls and the laws on strikes and lock-outs as remedies for the looming threat of recession in many industries.[37] In October 1977, a federation-appointed committee of industrialists took advantage of the occasion of a new government in office to make numerous liberalizing suggestions, including dismantling price controls, restructuring of licensing policy, reduction in the corporate profit tax to 50 per cent and liberal excise-duty rebates for new enterprises.[38] This process of seeking improvements in the licensing and other regulations continued in 1978 and 1979.[39]

The advent of the 1980s saw the business community grow significantly more restless with the regulatory regime that severely constrained its investment and production activities. Its demands for deregulation grew in both breadth and depth during IG's last term (1980–84). Soon after she returned to office, FICCI submitted a paper titled 'A minimum program of economic action' to her government. The paper had a wide sweep covering industrial relations, industrial infrastructure, price policy, industrial control, bank credit, taxation and foreign trade. It urged the government to do away with industrial licensing altogether after reserving a few industries for the public sector and some others for the small sector. It also opposed canalizing international trade in certain items through government agencies. Furthermore, it sought liberal imports of foreign technology, relaxation in credit controls, reduction in corporate profit and personal taxation and the abolition of the wealth tax.[40] The themes relating to the need for liberalization of technology imports, import and investment licensing and price controls figured once again two years later in the address delivered by A.K. Jain, president-elect of FICCI.[41] The following year, at its annual session in April 1983, the federation adopted a resolution on 'steps for accelerating industrial progress', which called for radical changes in the industrial regulatory framework, including the MRTP Act, the Industrial (Development and Regulation) Act, price controls and industrial licensing.[42] Finally, the annual session of FICCI in April 1984 witnessed industrialist S.K. Birla point the finger at 'a pampered, over-protected labour force combined with a highly politicized trade union movement' as the source of low productivity.[43]

The business community was thus yearning for wide-ranging liberalizing reforms when RG succeeded his mother as prime minister at the end of October 1984. Therefore, it is no surprise that it reacted to the unexpected burst of liberalization measures in the 1985–86 budget nearly uniformly with delight. A contemporary *Times of India* story summarized the business community's reactions in these upbeat terms, 'Trade and industry circles have acclaimed the budget proposals for 1985–86 as imaginative, bold, realistic, forward looking and growth oriented.'[44] Echoing many other business leaders quoted in the story, the president of ASSOCHAM said,

> The finance minister has shown many initiatives with emphasis on growth, savings, reduction of corruption and social welfare. The raising of MRTP application limit [from Rs 200 million to Rs 1 billion in assets], delicensing of certain industries, steps to speed up merger of sick units, fiscal restructuring and lower import duty on capital goods will stimulate economic growth.

As it turned out, the reforms of 1985–86 were not sustained except in the area of international trade, returning the business community to its usual exercise of periodically demanding—without any expectation that such demands would be heeded—the liberalization of investment and import restrictions in the remainder of the 1980s. Already in mid-March 1986, in anticipation of its annual meeting, FICCI was floating a draft resolution titled 'Towards accelerating entrepreneurial growth', in which it called for de-licensing and broad-banding of more industries, modification of the definition of 'inter-connection' and 'associated persons' in MRTP legislation, time-bound approval of projects and abolition of price and purchase preferences in government procurement policies in favour of state-owned enterprises. FICCI continued to air these demands in the remainder of the 1980s. At the end of the decade, when the V.P. Singh government floated its industrial policy of May 1990, FICCI president S.K. Birla put his entire weight behind it, stating, 'if licensing goes tomorrow morning, then we are all for it.'[45] He also rallied behind foreign-investment liberalization, arguing that India had been starved of capital. 'India needs a bare minimum of $1 billion of foreign investment per year, instead of the present $200 million.'

Ultimately, the business community got most of its wishes when, in July 1991, the then newly elected prime minister Narasimha Rao took advantage of a balance-of-payments crisis and abolished the investment licensing almost entirely, as well as import licensing on the capital and intermediate inputs. It is remarkable that for three long decades, the business community had been the only substantial constituency that had consistently sought this liberalization despite being ignored equally consistently by the decision-makers. Though some observers also credit the middle class for its role in bringing about liberalization, it is difficult to find any direct evidence for it. Indeed, as we shall see in the next chapter, economists and policy analysts from within the country, who largely came from the middle class, supported the government's socialist policies and rarely championed the cause of liberalization.

While it is true that considerations of profitability and its very existence placed the business community on the right side of the economic-policy debate, it would be a mistake to conclude that it remained wholly untouched by socialism in its collective thinking. There are at least three reasons for this assertion. First, it rarely made a frontal assault on socialism. In this respect, a business leader like Tata was an exception. Most others were quite comfortable operating within the socialist regime as long as they could get their licences for investment and imports. During the 1950s, when these licences were more or less available on demand, hardly any business leaders cautioned against the economic devastation that socialism would bring. Even in the early to mid-1960s, when the business community began to complain, its complaints were limited to procedural difficulties and not the licensing system per se. Indeed, some among them were quite comfortable exploiting their asymmetric knowledge of and access to the bureaucratic system to pre-emptively obtain multiple licences to block the entry of potential competitors. Even after the 1991 reforms, the business community has been insufficiently vocal in raising concerns over many socialist-era anti-growth policies. This point applies, for instance, to the complex and inflexible labour laws and bankruptcy law, which remained unreformed for more than two decades after 1991.

The second area in which socialism has left the Indian business community permanently impacted is in its choice of industry. For decades, the socialist-era policies kept successful business enterprises confined to highly capital-intensive sectors through the instrumentality of investment licensing. From the beginning, the government had denied them licences for establishing large-scale units to manufacture the mass of labour-intensive products that small-scale, village and cottage enterprises could produce. Later, beginning in 1967, these products came to be formally reserved for manufacture by small-scale enterprises. The business community almost never raised its voice against this exclusion of large-scale enterprises from labour-intensive products. Instead, it accepted such exclusion as given and, over time, came to be hardwired to keep away from investing in them. The result is that hardly any successful entrepreneur today displays interest in manufacturing these products. Leading industries in India remain either those using a large volume of capital per worker, such as petroleum refining, machinery and chemicals, or those employing highly skilled labour, such as information technology (IT), IT-enabled services and finance. This fact has meant that industry and services have failed to generate enough jobs for those with limited skills. The result is that nearly 45 per cent of India's vast workforce remains in agriculture, even three decades after the 1991 reforms. This outcome contrasts with authoritarian China, where once Deng Xiaoping decided to change course, the economy quickly restructured in favour of labour-intensive industry and services, pulling a significant part of the agricultural workforce out of agriculture into the latter sectors.

Finally, the business community in India has remained unduly protectionist in its stance. During the post-Second World War era, the business community had been a force for trade liberalization in non-socialist countries. But despite having left socialism behind three decades ago, the Indian business community has not turned into a pro-trade-liberalization force. Understandably, entrepreneurs facing competition from imports in the home market would lobby for protection everywhere. But one expects the entrepreneurs exporting their products to actively support liberalization and engage in negotiations that lead to the opening of partner-country markets. Yet, it is rare to see even the export-oriented enterprises from India actively support negotiations that lead to greater liberalization.

Concluding Remarks

After political leadership, economic institutions play the most important role in bringing about policy change. Insofar as institutions evolve more slowly than political leadership, it stands to reason that they slow down the change sought by the latter. The Indian experience bears this fact out. The central tendency of the major institutions, including bureaucracy, the planning commission and law and judiciary, has been to slow down the implementation of the change sought by the political leadership through legislative action. Many actors within the institutions, especially bureaucracy, have partnered with the political leadership to speed up change, but the balance remains in favour of the slowdown.

The business community has been one of the rare forces within socialist India that has rallied for a change in favour of greater room for market forces from below. Unfortunately, its ability to influence the political leadership has been minimal. As long as the grip of socialist ideology remained strong, the political leadership remained hostage to the idea that private business was a necessary evil that had to be held down lest it concentrated economic power in its own hands. As a result, as long as socialist ideology remained dominant, the business community had almost no impact on policy choices.

In democracy, the group best placed to bring about change in economic policy is that of policy analysts, most prominently, economists. Because they do not stand to profit directly from the change, they can speak with greater credibility in favour of the overall benefit of society. Unfortunately, however, policy analysts in India have been predominantly subscribers of the socialist ideology. As such, they have been instrumental in delaying rather than speeding up the change. This theme constitutes the subject of the next chapter.

14

Economists and Other Policy Analysts

Economists and policy analysts can influence economic-policy outcomes at various levels. Those directly employed in the government can influence their other bureaucratic colleagues and politicians. They serve on important committees appointed to recommend solutions to specific policy problems. Reports of these committees can effectively strengthen the existing regime or inject new ideas for change. Economists and policy analysts outside the government can influence the thinking of politicians and bureaucrats through their writings, speeches and media interviews. But they also influence broader public opinion. As educators in academic institutions, they shape the thinking of future generations.

The Early Decades: 1950–80

As I have already discussed, at the time of the launch of the second plan, there was consensus among economists from within India as well as outside in favour of the strategy giving priority to heavy industry in the investment plan, the pursuit of self-sufficiency in international trade, assigning a prominent role to the public sector and reliance on the cottage and household enterprises for employment. Dissenting voices were rare and, with one exception, focused on the potential inflationary impact of the large fiscal deficits and the neglect of agriculture. The exception was Milton Friedman, who, in a brief memorandum written in November 1955, questioned nearly all elements of the strategy adopted in the second plan. But, as Friedman himself wrote in 2000, the memorandum was 'circulated in the government, leaked in part to the press, and not heard again . . .'[1] In the voluminous contemporary literature I have reviewed while writing the present volume, I found a reference to it only in the book authored by P.T. Bauer (more about which immediately below).

The Early Academic Critics

Between 1960 and 1970, I find just three substantial critiques of the development model India had adopted: the short book by Bauer just mentioned; a collection of essays by Shenoy, which he had written between 1964 and 1968; and the book by Bhagwati and Desai.[2] Like Friedman, both Bauer and Shenoy were members of the Mont Pelerin Society devoted to advocating freedom of expression and free-market economic policies. In the 1960s, their brand of economics was yet to gain acceptance even in the Western world, including the United States and the United Kingdom. As such, it is no surprise that the contributions by Bauer and Shenoy found no takers in an India dominated by socialist thought.

P.S. Lokanathan, easily among the top dozen Indian economists of his generation and the first director general of the National Council of Applied Economic Research in New Delhi, reviewed Bauer's book in *India Quarterly* and found no merit whatsoever in it.[3] He began by noting that the purpose behind the book was to dissuade the Western governments from offering aid to what were then called underdeveloped countries. Noting that Bauer began by pointing out that destructive criticism was a useful exercise provided the criticism was valid, Lokanathan stated that what followed in the book was 'an excellent example of what useful criticism ought not to be'. Criticizing Bauer for attacking India's focus on heavy industry, he reminded that this prioritization reflected India's desire to achieve a rapid growth rate over a short period. Therefore, he reasoned, it was incumbent upon Bauer to 'work out the implication for growth of an alternative pattern of priorities in order to show that the current scheme does not promote rapid development'. This Bauer had not done. Lokanathan's bottom line was, 'There is much prejudice and hostility in this appraisal which leads to the perverse conclusion that Indian economic policies are unlikely to promote a rise in living standards and that genuine objective of the government is to introduce a dictatorship of the left.' Recognizing that Lokanathan represented the mainstream Indian economic thought of his day, Bauer and Indian economists were on very different wavelengths.[4]

Shenoy could find a more sympathetic reviewer in Bhagwati who shared some of his views on the inefficiencies that the tight controls on imports, extensive planning, expanding public-sector production and wholesale licensing of private investments had produced. But even from him, Shenoy could get only a qualified nod. Bhagwati began by complimenting him for being 'among the few economists to notice and condemn the inefficiency of the import control regime (Parts III and IV) and the wastefulness of the detailed control of industrial licensing and production, when, in fact, it was fashionable and personally rewarding to do otherwise'. He went on to note that 'his [Shenoy's] fears of big plan outlays, and of the shift to heavy industry in the second plan (Part I), while exaggerated and not as well formulated as they could be, have been proven by events to have been not altogether unjustified'. But in concluding the review, Bhagwati turned critical stating that 'when all his strengths have been noted, and these include exceptional intellectual integrity and a feel for relevant economic problems, the fact remains that his overall view of Indian economic policies is flawed seriously by his antipathy to planning *per se*'.[5]

As this concluding quote from Bhagwati's review of Shenoy hints, Bhagwati and Desai took a more sympathetic view of Indian planning than both Bauer and Shenoy, acknowledging its need under the prevailing Indian conditions. But they recommended a considerable narrowing of its scope. They suggested in-depth planning of a few priority sectors, prohibition on further capacity expansion in certain non-priority sectors and reliance on markets in the remaining sectors. They also recommended replacing import licensing with tariffs and a more flexible approach to the exchange rate. From today's vantage point, these recommendations constituted a modest correction in favour of greater reliance on the price mechanism without abandoning the planning framework. But even this modest course correction failed to find almost any takers within India.

The conclusion that emerges from a reading of half a dozen contemporary reviews of the book by Indian economists—many of them leading scholars of the Indian economy—is that while there was some acceptance of the criticisms of the planning regime by Bhagwati and Desai, no one was willing to endorse even a movement in the direction suggested by them let alone substantially endorse their specific recommendations.[6] Yogendra K. Alagh, who had earned his doctorate in economics from the University of Pennsylvania, was the most sympathetic to price-based instruments as a replacement for the direct controls, but towards the end of the review, even he turned sceptical, asking rhetorically,

> Can market forces be relied upon for automatic and easy correction towards desired economic objectives in the suggested context? Can such forces be relied upon, for example, to ensure that productivity advantages consequent on scale expansion will be reaped? In case they are so relied upon, won't the limited size of the market raise the issue of public policies towards monopolies? What about the issue of foreign collaboration?[7]

In another review, Phiroze Medhora rejected the recommendations by Bhagwati and Desai outright. He pointed out that Bhagwati and Desai had noted the well-known inefficiencies of the economic system and proposed a new economic policy consisting of reliance on the market mechanism for investment and import decisions. But 'the attempt to revert to a *laissez-faire* regime, with reliance on market regulatory devices, is hardly likely to bring about the desired rates of growth or the required changes in the industrial structure necessary to maintain such growth rates.' Medhora asserted, 'A conscious system of physical planning, operated in a rightly determined economic context, is the only means of achieving this objective.'[8]

Even Manmohan Singh, who was the chief economic adviser in the Ministry of Finance at the time and was to play a leading role in implementing the Rao-era reforms that would go much further in replacing physical controls with price-based instruments than what Bhagwati and Desai had recommended, yielded no space to the authors. He hailed the book as a 'truly outstanding contribution to the analysis of planning techniques and instruments of control' but injected all kinds of doubts when it came to the evaluation of the authors' policy recommendations.[9] He reasoned,

> The system of direct controls as it has evolved in this country has many wasteful features, but that is hardly a [sic] convincing evidence that the country would necessarily have been better off under a different system. That the present system of planning in India scores badly when compared with the working of an idealized price system is hardly sufficient proof that the country ought to dismantle direct controls.[10]

Singh concluded his review, cautioning that 'it would be much too presumptuous to claim that modern neoclassical economics has answers to all the economic problems in all parts of the world and that an efficient framework is always one based on the principles of economic liberalism'.[11]

This sampling of reviews of the three major works favouring a movement towards yielding greater space to markets, published between 1960 and 1970, illustrates the degree to which Indian economists remained committed to the reliance on the command-and-control system during the decade. The commentaries on Bhagwati and Desai, the latest of the three studies, are especially revealing. Even compared with the reforms the Rao government implemented in a single stroke in a single month in 1991, their recommendations were modest. But such was the ethos of the early 1970s that Indian economists uniformly leaned against them.

Economists within the Government

Turning to the direct role of economists in shaping policy, economist A.M. Khusro, who had an illustrious career working in academic institutions and numerous government bodies, has written that in 'crucial development policies the economists' role has only been marginal. Most of them have come to fit the analyses to the events, that is, after the policy had been formed and implemented.'[12] He points out that apart from the work they did as holders of senior positions in various governmental bodies such as the Reserve Bank of India, the Planning Commission and the Ministry of Finance, 'it is through the reports of important commissions and committees . . . that the work of many an economist has influenced policies and development programmes.'[13]

A close look at the work of the four committees culminating in the enactment of the MRTP Act of 1969 suggests that at least during the 1960s, economists who served on government committees, whether from outside or within the government, were more or less aligned in their thinking with the bureaucrats. They largely helped preserve or strengthen the controlled regime rather than weaken it. Since I have already discussed the context of the appointment of the four committees in the discussion of the bureaucracy, here I focus more centrally on the role of the economists in them and their key recommendations.[14]

The first of these committees, appointed in 1960 and reporting in 1964, was chaired by Mahalanobis. Though not an economist by training, he played the role of one and was widely viewed as such. In addition, six out of the eight other members of the committee were eminent economists, some from within and others from outside the government. The committee noted the significant concentration of economic power in the larger private companies and an increase in it over time. It identified planned development and financial assistance rendered by public institutions such as the Industrial Finance Corporation and the National Industrial Development Corporation among the contributors to the increase in the concentration. Regarding measures countering the concentration, the committee recommended expanding the public sector, regulating large companies through licensing and price and distribution controls, and offering various incentives to new and small entrepreneurs. While noting that making recommendations for further corrective measures was outside its remit and required more comprehensive and detailed information, the committee went on to state that 'an extension of the scope and intensity of countervailing measures' would be a part of the solution.[15]

As a follow-up, the government appointed the Monopolies Inquiry Commission with the mandate to inquire into the extent of concentration of economic power in private hands and their consequences and recommend legislative and other corrective measures. The commission did not have representation of any outside economists, but it had I.G. Patel from within the government as one of the four members (not counting the chair). Patel is regarded as one of the most brilliant economists to serve in the Government of India. He later served as the Governor of the Reserve Bank of India during 1977–82, director of the London School of Economics during 1984–90, and was the first choice of Prime Minister Narasimha Rao to be his finance minister in June 1991. The commission also consulted eminent economists outside the government, including Lokanathan and S.K. Muranjan.

In its report, the commission confirmed the substantial concentration of economic power and pointed to the planned economy as a 'potent factor' contributing to it. It noted that investment licensing, controls on capital issue and import controls had all worked to produce this concentration of economic power.[16] 'We are convinced,' it noted, 'that the system of controls in the shape of industrial licensing however necessary from other points of view, has restricted the freedom of entry into industry and so helped to produce concentration.'[17] Though the commission offered some (mostly feel-good and impractical) non-legislative remedies, such as refusal by political parties to accept funds from industrialists and an end to bureaucratic corruption, the main remedy it suggested was legislative.[18] It recommended the creation of a permanent commission with the power to investigate and curb restrictive and monopolistic practices.

Reports by the Mahalanobis committee and the Monopolies Inquiry Commission led the Planning Commission to appoint economist R.K. Hazari to study the operation of industrial licensing in the context of the objectives of the industrial policy, which, among others, included avoidance of monopoly and concentration of economic power. In his interim report, Hazari found that large and medium enterprises enjoyed a higher approval ratio in licensing and that this share exhibited a rising trend.[19] A key remedy to curb the concentration of economic power he suggested was to deny the ten or fifteen largest industrial houses and their associates any further capacity addition in certain traditional industrial activities.[20]

Debate on the interim report by Hazari in the upper house of the Parliament in May 1967 led the industry minister to announce his intention to appoint a committee for a more thorough examination of the subject. The result was the appointment of the Industrial Licensing Policy Inquiry Committee (Dutt Committee). Including the chair, this committee had four members, of which one was an economist who served on the faculty of the Indian Institute of Public Administration at the time. Another member, though an engineer by training, was a member of the Planning Commission. From various lists of entities in the report, it cannot be inferred that the committee consulted other economists.

A key conclusion the committee drew was that the licensing system had worked in such a way 'as to provide disproportionate share in the newly licensed capacity to a few concerns belonging to a few Large Houses. . . . The result has been that the licensing system has not contributed adequately to the attainment of the social and economic objectives.'[21] As one of the important remedies, the committee recommended dividing the industries into three groups: a 'core' group of basic, strategic and critical industries that would be open to the large firms and big business houses, a middle group of industries that would be off limits to them and a group of industries that would be either open exclusively to small and medium enterprises or banned altogether. The implication of this recommendation was to confine the large firms and big business houses to the 'core' group of industries. After the MRTP Act was enacted, this indeed became the government's policy.[22]

At least in hindsight, it is difficult not to be disappointed by the total lack of application of basic economic logic to the problem addressed by the four committees. It was the choice of the development model that lay at the heart of the concentration of economic power. In making heavy industry the focus, the country had chosen an exclusionary development model. If steel factories were to be built, they had to be large and highly capital-intensive to be efficient. The same went for power, fertilizers and machinery plants. Given the small size of the economy, there was no escape from the concentration of capital and economic power in a few large firms if heavy industry was to be developed upfront. Remarkably, no economist contributing to these committees' work recognized this essential problem.

Equally naïve was to look for a solution to a problem created by controls in yet more controls. But that is precisely what the Dutt Committee recommended, and the government subsequently implemented through the instrumentality of the MRTP Act. Rather than solve the problem of concentration of economic power, confining the large firms to core industries was only going to result in either a disproportionately large investment in these industries or siphoning off of investment by them into the prohibited middle group of industries through the creation of business entities that could not be traced to them. The regulation also meant that the efficient firms investing in the middle group would eventually grow large and be bumped into the core group. The regulation was thus designed to exclude the most efficient entrepreneurs from contributing to the middle group of industries except for a limited period.

A little more than two decades after the release of the Monopolies Inquiry Committee report, its economist member Patel was to state in a public lecture at the University of Cambridge, 'I have never understood why even expert committees have hesitated to recommend a virtual bonfire of the industrial licensing system with a small negative list of industries such as armaments and dangerous drugs or chemicals where a prior permission might be warranted.'[23] Yet, so strong was the consensus around restraining the large firms and big business houses at the time that no economist working in India called for dismantling the licensing system for the following two decades. Indeed, as the 1960s came to a close and the 1970s rolled in, inspired by the memorable 'Garibi Hatao' (remove poverty) slogan of Indira Gandhi (IG), opinion among the most vocal economists moved towards more, not less, government control.

The Deepening of Socialism and the Rise of 'New Economics' in the 1970s

At the start of the 1970s, the government further tightened the controls on private economic activity and began expanding the scope of the public sector through nationalizing banks, insurance, oil and coal. On this count, there was now even more reason for economists sympathetic to markets to push back. But searches of archives of the *Times of India* and *Economic and Political Weekly* from 19 July 1969, the day bank nationalization was announced, till the end of 1975, do not yield a single article by economists critical of the nationalizations. Indeed, the only prominent figure reported as being critical of the expanding ambit of socialism is Nani Palkhivala, a lawyer known for his pro-free-enterprise views, in the *Times of India*. Scathingly, Palkhivala stated,[24]

> Our Constitution aimed at making India the land of opportunity; our politicians have converted it into a land of opportunism. They have made socialism the opiate of the people. 'Socialism' has become a word comprehensive enough to cover the entire spectrum of economic folly—a plethora of harmful state controls, periodic bouts of nationalization, and the pursuit of policies which ensure unemployment and economic regression.

Whereas Nehru had firmly held that India's 'appalling poverty' could not be overcome without a manifold increase in production, by the early 1970s, some analysts, including journalists and economists, had come to subscribe to the view that the real problem was not production but its distribution. Some of these analysts drew inspiration from Pakistani economist Mahbub-ul-Haq, who had worked at the United Nations and claimed in a much-celebrated article, provocatively titled 'Let Us Stand Economic Theory on Its Head: Joining the GNP Rat Race Won't Wipe out Poverty', that China had eradicated the worst forms of poverty within less than two decades. 'What's more,' he argued, 'it was my impression that China has achieved this at fairly modest rates of growth, by paying more attention to the content and distribution of GNP.'[25] With India moving yet deeper into socialism and political rhetoric dominated by IG's famous 'Garibi Hatao' rhetoric, Haq found a ready constituency among the left-leaning intellectuals in the country. The result was the emergence of a small cottage industry under the self-congratulatory rubric of 'New Economics', which coalesced around the idea that attention ought to shift from production to redistribution.

Perhaps because it suited her politics at the time, IG indirectly endorsed the Haq view in the famous speech she delivered on 25 March 1972 to FICCI. 'Growthmanship which results in undivided attention to the maximization of GNP can be dangerous,' she said, 'for the results are almost always social and political unrest. Therefore, increase in the GNP must be considered only as one component of a multi-dimensional transformation of society.'[26]

This scepticism towards growth got incorporated in the draft fifth plan, which allocated a sizeable proportion of the total plan outlay to a 'national programme of minimum needs' at the expense of investment. Though four years later, when the final version of the fifth plan came out, the programme for minimum needs was quietly dropped with the conventional pattern of allocation of the outlays restored, the scepticism towards growth as the primary instrument of poverty reduction acquired deeper roots among Indian economists and other policy analysts.[27]

For some economists, scepticism originated in the Mahalanobis Model, which had formed the basis of the second and subsequent plans.[28] An important implication of the model was that future consumption was maximized by investing more in capital goods in the early years of development and, therefore, by sacrificing some consumption in those years. It followed that more consumption and possibly a larger reduction in poverty in the early years was feasible, provided one sacrificed future long-term growth. Of course, as the experience of the East Asian tiger economies demonstrated, high growth rates in the early years were perfectly compatible with a large-scale poverty reduction provided the country specialized in and exported labour-intensive manufactures in exchange for capital-intensive ones. Based on the assumption of capital as the only factor of production, the Mahalanobis Model had entirely neglected the gains from the fuller use of the labour force. India sacrificed growth and poverty reduction during the several post-Independence decades by underutilizing its labour.

Even though the mainstream economists wrote critically of the New Economics, implicitly or explicitly, they came to question the importance of growth, arguing that it was a necessary but not sufficient condition for poverty reduction. This scepticism remained ingrained in the majority of the Indian commentators till quite sometime after the reforms had been launched and successfully delivered accelerated growth. Some of this scepticism expressed itself in the refusal to accept the evidence that growth had helped bring down poverty in all sections of society, including the Scheduled Castes and Scheduled Tribes. It was partially as a response to this continuing scepticism that Bhagwati and I wrote the book *Why Growth Matters: How Economic Growth in India Reduced Poverty and the Lessons for Other Developing Countries*.[29] Only in the last one and a half decades has the position of growth as the foremost instrument of poverty reduction been restored in the discourse in India.

The Door Opens to the Liberal Economists within the Government: 1980–90

The arrival of the 1980s, especially after RG came to office, had seen increased political receptivity to liberalizing reforms. This change led to the emergence of occasional voices in favour of reforms among economists and journalists from within India as well. As far as economists in this category were concerned, with rare exceptions, they resided within the government and expressed their ideas principally in government reports and internal papers. The list of these economists included, most prominently, Abid Hussain, Vijay Kelkar, C. Rangarajan, Montek Singh Ahluwalia, Raja Chelliah, Shankar Acharya and Rakesh Mohan. As government employees, they obviously could hardly champion the reforms publicly. Indeed, even internally, their actions were circumscribed by the boundaries drawn by the political leadership. But within the ministries or departments they served, they could still steer the policy towards a shift away from controls on the margins while helping change the minds of their colleagues and the political leadership. More importantly, when the political leadership offered the opportunity for a bigger change, they were well placed to seize it.

Two Outstanding Examples

Two examples illustrate the influence of these economists in ushering in liberalization in the 1980s. Towards the end of her term, IG had appointed a committee 'to suggest rationalization and improvements, wherever necessary, in export policies' and 'appropriate changes and rationalization of import policies for the conservation of foreign exchange and the promotion of efficient import substitution' with Abid Hussain as the chair. The terms of reference also allowed the committee to consider any other aspects related to these subjects. Led by Hussain, the committee took full advantage of the flexibility provided by the terms of reference. Seen in the context of the prevailing ethos, it made bold recommendations for trade liberalization. It recommended de-escalation of protection through withdrawal of licensing on many products, lower or no tariffs on others, drastic cuts in the list of products subject to canalization of imports, selectivity in import substitution and an end to the overvaluation of the rupee in real terms.[30] Much of the trade liberalization that took place till the end of the decade can be viewed as flowing from the recommendations of this committee.

The second example is a narrower one but with long-term implications. In 1986, the government appointed a committee under the chairmanship of Kelkar on the pricing of drugs. This committee suggested the criteria for excluding and including drugs from the list subject to price controls. Based on these criteria, it recommended excluding several drugs from such controls. The committee also recommended the relaxation of the prevailing strict controls on the profitability of drugs. Subsequently, the Drug Price Control Order (DPCO) of 1987 implemented both recommendations. It reduced the number of drugs subject to price controls from 370 to 142. The order also changed the pricing rule for drugs remaining subject to price controls to permit significant upward adjustments, thereby increasing their profitability and output. The liberalization proved instrumental in developing the pharmaceutical industry, including vaccines which the DPCO of 1987 had removed from the controlled list.[31]

It may be asked how some of the economists working inside the government managed to escape the influence of socialism that was otherwise pervasive all around, including in the bureaucracy. The answer is that each of those named above had spent a considerable number of years either studying or working as economists in the United States or Asia, exposing them to the power of markets and outward-oriented policies. Hussain had joined the IAS at an early age in 1951 but had spent the years 1974–81 heading the industry division at the United Nations Economic and Social Commission on Asia in Bangkok. During those years, he had been a student of and a witness to the rise of the East Asian tigers. The others had all spent several years as professional economists in the United States, where markets are at the centre of education and research in economics. The trajectories of these economists differed from their predecessor generation, represented by I.G. Patel and Manmohan Singh, who had been educated in Great Britain, where socialism remained a powerful force at the academic institutions.

The Scarcity of Reform Champions outside the Government

While at least some economists within the government were thus keen to seize the opportunities for liberalization, there remained a dearth of forceful champions of it among academic economists from within the country. They either remained wedded to the socialist-leftist economic thought or indifferent to policy. Regarding proactive advocacy of an end to the controls and embrace of markets from within the country, it is difficult to go beyond two economist journalists: Swaminathan Aiyar and Ashok Desai. They alone wrote favouring a shift to pro-market policies without reservation. One additional economic journalist, Prem Shankar, consistently welcomed the liberalization measures by IG and RG in his writings but did not forcefully advocate them.

Among outside Indian economists, Bhagwati and his frequent co-author T.N. Srinivasan remained the principal forceful proponents of liberalization.[32] Deepak Lal was also firmly in the liberal camp, but, like Shenoy before him, he was viewed as ideologically driven in the prevailing Indian ethos. Indeed, in the 1980s, even the writings of Bhagwati and Srinivasan had gained acceptance only among some of the more liberal economists, such as Hussain and Kelkar, who were all serving inside the government. As regards the academic economists in India, leftism ruled the roost. So much so that even Amartya Sen, who lamented the lack of attention to social sectors while giving a pass to India's anti-growth policies, got his share of criticisms from India's far-left economists.

An article by Sen in the *New York Review of Books* (NYROB) titled 'How is India Doing' and comments by two Indian economists on it offer insight into where the economics profession in India stood on big policy issues around this time. At the beginning of this article, Sen pointed to the positive achievement in 'speeding up of Indian economic expansion from, at best, just about 1 per cent at the time of independence, to 3 to 3.5 per cent, and then to 4 to 6 per cent'.[33] He argued that this achievement could not be dismissed on the usual pretext that India's performance had become internationally respectable only recently. He then vehemently criticized India for its 'sadly unimaginative and breathtakingly conservative' approach to social services.[34] Comparing India to Sri Lanka and China, he concluded that it had performed poorly in areas such as primary education and nutrition.

In the article, Sen was critical of India for its efforts to accelerate growth further without a significant expansion of social spending simultaneously. Specifically, he came down heavily on the government for striking a deal for a large loan with the IMF that 'seems to involve a pattern of development that includes a further move in the direction of the no-nonsense South Korean model and that will have the effect of excluding ambitious programmes of social services'.[35] The article assumed that growth could bring no direct gains to the poor without expanding social spending. It also refrained from making any reference to the counter-productive role played by the dominance of the public sector and the tight control of the private sector through the complex licensing regime.

As already noted, ironically, attacks on the article came not from the right but from the far left. Sen had blamed the lack of attention to social services on 'the elitist character of Indian society and politics' in his article.[36] He had reasoned that the leadership of parties, whether from the extreme left or extreme right, came from an elite background.

Rejecting this explanation in a letter to NYROB, Ashok Mitra, an economist and Marxist politician in India, argued that:

> Sen's glib assertion that 'much of the leadership of all political parties in India—from the extreme right to the extreme left—comes from an elitist background' is not of much help for understanding the phenomenon: a rightist party like the one led by Mrs. Gandhi—who is on record that elementary

> education is not that important for economic growth—would stall literacy programmes, while the leftists would place the maximum stress, along with land reforms, on such programmes.[37]

For Mitra, even IG, who had pushed socialism much farther than Nehru and had made a valiant effort to implement land reforms in the early 1970s, was not leftist enough!

Another Marxist economist, Ranjit Sau, chose to comment on Sen's article in the leading Indian magazine *Economic and Political Weekly*. He attacked Sen for suggesting that India had not only done well regarding GDP growth but was also witnessing an acceleration in it. He statistically tested the hypothesis of a positive trend in the growth rate and rejected it. He concluded that Sen was, therefore, in error in suggesting that India was on a path of accelerating growth rate.[38] In the light of his other writings, the comment by Sau implied that a government that represented the interests of the lower middle class and rich peasantry could not be expected to deliver on either economic growth or social goals.[39]

Reforms Spawn New Reform Champions: 1991–2004

The 1980s thus did not produce any proactive champions of reforms in the public space from among economists and fewer than the number of fingers on a palm from among journalists. But the post-1991 reforms brought about what may be described as a dramatic change in this scenario. The announcement of the first set of reforms in July 1991 emboldened the few who had previously written favouring a dismantling of the licence-permit raj. They now wrote more aggressively, defending the Rao reforms and asking for more. Others, who felt uneasy about the controlled regime but were hesitant to express it publicly, could now muster the courage to come out of their shells. The change was reflected in the surprisingly large number of op-eds and news stories in full or partial support of liberalization that came out in the *Times of India* alone during the first few months following the announcement of the reforms. J.R.D. Tata, who had once been the driving force behind the Bombay Plan of 1944 and through it gave the nod to the reservation of the commanding heights of the industry for the public sector and extensive regulation of the private sector, came to the defence of the reforms at the advanced age of eighty-seven. In an article aptly titled 'Berlin Walls Should Fall' to reflect the contemporary context, the veteran industrialist went after critics who attacked the New Industrial Policy (NIP) on the grounds that it represented a betrayal of Nehru. Scathingly, he wrote, 'I am saddened though not surprised to find that several critics of the NIP have denounced this as anti-Nehruvian, which only shows how little they knew of the dynamic mind of Pandit Nehru which, faced with the havoc created in the economy, would have been the first among the first to salute the NIP.'[40]

The advent of Rao's reforms also spurred economists in and outside India into subjecting the crisis and reforms to deeper analysis. The first major book on the subject came from economist bureaucrat Bimal Jalan in which the author admitted to having had faith in the unlimited capacity of the State to intervene in the interest of society and to not having paid 'adequate attention to . . . the economic consequences of excessive bureaucratic intervention'.[41] In a review, though Deepak Lal described the book as Jalan's expiation of past ways of thinking and Jalan's conversion to economic liberalism as only partial, the book was a symptom of what would come in the following years and decades. [42]

More forceful and justifiably triumphant was the book *India in Transition: Freeing the Economy* by none other than Bhagwati. Based on the author's Radhakrishnan Lectures delivered at the University of Oxford in the first week of June 1992 and published in 1993, the book elegantly described the early history of Indian economic development, tracing the low growth achieved during the four decades to the extensive bureaucratic controls, inward-looking trade and foreign investment policies, and a substantial public sector.[43] He then systematically linked the reforms Rao had implemented to these factors and outlined what more needed to be done.

Yet another book to appear in the early 1990s was Ashok Desai's *My Economic Affair*. Having served as the chief consultant in the Indian Ministry of Finance during the critical years of 1991 to 1993, he offered an early insider's account of the reforms in the book. Soon after, Vijay Joshi and Ian Little published two books in quick succession, one in 1994 focusing on the political economy of India's macroeconomics and the other in 1996 detailing how far the reforms had progressed, how much further they needed to go and in what direction.[44] Having returned to academia in the fall of 1993 and reclaimed my freedom to write publicly, I also wrote my first long article on India's reforms in 1994 under the title 'India: A New Tiger on the Block?' At a time when almost no one believed that 7 per cent growth was possible for India, I concluded the article thus, 'Will India accomplish in the next decade what China did in the previous one? Although it is overly optimistic to respond affirmatively, a 6 to 7 per cent annual growth rate in India cannot be ruled out. The world should not be surprised if, in a decade's time, it sees another tiger on the block.'[45]

Pushback on reforms soon after their enactment by Rao came from none other than Amartya Sen in his joint book with Jean Drèze, *India: Economic Development and Social Opportunity*. Elaborating on Sen's central theme in his NYROB article and drawing on more detailed work by Drèze on issues such as child mortality and sex bias, the book documented India's failures along social dimensions and chided the policymakers and policy analysts for neglecting it. It lamented that:

> the debates on such questions as the details of tax concessions to multinationals, or whether Indians should drink Coca Cola, or whether the private sector should be allowed to operate city

> buses, tend to 'crowd out' the time that is left to discuss the abysmal situation of basic education and elementary health care, or the persistence of debilitating social inequalities, or other issues that have a crucial bearing on the well-being and freedom of the population.[46]

Reviewing the book in the *Economic Journal*, Bhagwati described the authors' narrative as being marred by a reluctance to acknowledge the importance of the economic reforms underway and criticized the book for taking 'even a sneering attitude towards them'.[47] Commenting on the quoted excerpt, he lamented, 'Much is wrong here. No one can seriously argue that there is a crowding out when the articulation of Indians is manifest in multiplying newspapers, magazines, and books and expression of a whole spectrum of views on economics and politics; . . .' Characterizing the reference to Coca-Cola as a 'cheap shot' against multinationals, he added, 'it also betrays the assumption that Coca Cola is drunk by the elite or the Westernized middle class, not by the many poor. It is more likely however that the former derive their caffeine from espresso coffee as well whereas the poor are the ones who must depend on Coke instead.'[48]

Sen and Drèze were hardly alone in expressing scepticism towards reforms. As the 1990s ended and the 2000s unfolded, critics began questioning the reforms for three reasons. One, the acceleration in growth during the Nehru era had been proportionately larger than in the wake of the 1980s and 1990s reforms; two, growth during the 1980s and 1990s resulted from a pro-business tilt of the Indian state beginning with Gandhi during 1980–84 rather than the post-1991 reforms; and three, reforms and accelerated growth had failed to bring poverty down. At the intellectual level, all three claims were refuted by pro-reform economists.[49] Nevertheless, it hardly meant that the battle for reforms had been conclusively won.

The Narrative Changes Yet Again: 2004–14

Indeed, anti-growth interventions put in place over the long period of four decades being too numerous, the process of reforms within India's contentious democratic polity being slow and recurring bouts of relapses of policy into dirigisme, the road to such a victory is a long one. For example, in the 2004 parliamentary elections, the ruling reformist government lost the mandate, paving the way for the emergence of the United Progressive Alliance (UPA) led by the Congress. The new government not only lacked conviction for reforms but was also focused exclusively on the expansion of social spending and implementation of what may be called a socialist legislative agenda.

The ten-year UPA rule that followed delayed not just the economy's transition to markets but also the country's intellectual transition in that direction. The dominant narrative once again turned sceptical of reforms. The government's focus primarily on redistributive policies and disdain for carrying the economic reforms forward, especially during its 2009–14 term, strengthened the hand of those opposed to reforms and relegated the pro-reform voices to the background. Many pro-reform voices that had emerged during the prior one-and-a-half decades receded into the background. During these ten years, there were, at best, a handful of voices among economists and journalists speaking against socialism-infested legislations such as the Right to Education Act of 2009, the Land Acquisition Act of 2013 and the National Food Security Act of 2013.

The Pro-reform Narrative Triumphs Again: 2014–22

The intellectual tide began turning once again after the economic performance took a turn for the worse in the years 2012–13 and 2013–14, and Narendra Modi of the BJP decided to launch his bid for the highest office in the country in the 2014 parliamentary elections on the back of a strongly pro-reform platform. By coincidence, two books happened to appear around this time, one by Bhagwati and Panagariya advocating the view that economic reforms and growth were the only effective means to eradicating poverty and the other by Drèze and Sen arguing that reforms and growth had, at best, a secondary role to play and what was required was a focus on social spending.[50]

In July 2013, influential commentator Niranjan Rajadhyaksha wrote an article titled 'Gandhi vs Modi is Sen vs Bhagwati' with the opening lines, 'Bhagwati versus Sen may not have the same resonance as Modi versus Gandhi, but behind the political fight scheduled for 2014 is a duel of economic ideologies.'[51] Rajadhyaksha went on to write, 'Indeed, if Sen and his long-time collaborator Jean Drèze are supporters of the entitlement-led public schemes launched by the Congress-led United Progressive Alliance government, then Bhagwati and his long-time collaborator Arvind Panagariya are admirers of what they call the Gujarat model.' Gujarat model was a metaphor Bhagwati and I had used for a strategy based on outward orientation and growth, which Modi had pursued in Gujarat during his long tenure as the state's chief minister. In the following months, a 'Modi vs Gandhi' debate around the above two books ensued, filling the pages of Indian newspapers.

In the end, the decisive victory of Modi in the election proved most critical to restoring the reform and growth narrative to the dominant position. The return of Modi in 2019, also on a reform-oriented platform, has helped place the narrative on yet firmer ground. During the nine years of Modi's rule (at the time of writing), the group of pro-reform economists has grown bigger, with the advocacy of reforms becoming mainstream. Few commentators now question the importance of growth. Indeed, increasingly, growth has become the litmus test of the success of the government's policies.

Working at financial institutions such as JPMorgan, Goldman Sachs, erstwhile Credit Suisse, Nomura and HSBC, many younger economists and financial analysts have lent their voices to advancing and sustaining reforms, especially in the area of macroeconomics. Even the think tanks such as the National Council on Applied Economic Research and Indian Council for Research on International Economic Relations (ICRIER) have begun to lend their voices to the cause of reforms. Economists regularly write questioning reversals of liberalization in areas such as international trade and call for speedier privatization of public-sector undertakings and banks. Even in social programmes, pro-reform economists' prescription of cash instead of in-kind transfers has gained much traction with policymakers.

Concluding Remarks

Despite setbacks such as the one under the UPA rule, the constituency for and the influence of pro-reform economists, journalists and other policy analysts has grown. Advocacy of reforms is no longer the lonely struggle it once was for those who have engaged in it for a decade or longer. Even so, one specific disturbing feature of this evolution stands out. Pro-market commentators residing in India are predominantly those who have spent substantial time in the United States or Asia, either studying or working as professional economists. Even within this group, former economist bureaucrats account for a sizeable proportion. Locally trained professional economists with a consistent record of advocacy of pro-market reforms are rare. Indeed, I am hard-pressed to think of anyone fitting this description other than Govinda Rao, best known for his contributions in the area of Indian public finance in general and for leading the effort to bring services centrally into the tax net in particular. Underlying this phenomenon is the fact that the educators in the academic institutions in India continue to be staffed predominantly by teachers who themselves acquired their education during the era dominated by socialist thought. Left or left-leaning faculty in economics uniformly dominate Indian institutions of higher education, whether they be public or private.

15

An Afterthought

I have already provided a summary of the volume in the introduction, and it will not serve much purpose to repeat the exercise. Instead, I end this volume with a discussion of the question of whether we can think of a scenario in which the course of Indian economic history would have turned out to be different. My argument in the volume is that post-Nehru, India was on a deterministic path. There was little prospect of a change of course before 1991. Externally, the change had to wait for the socialist regime in the Soviet Union to end in total failure and for China to dramatically improve its economic performance after it opened up its economy. Internally, there had to be an economic crisis to give the leader at the helm the opportunity to bring about change.

Though a movement towards piecemeal liberalization had been underway in the late 1980s, absent the balance-of-payments crisis, it is doubtful that even Rao could or would have moved as decisively as he did in 1991. Most likely, he would not have gone beyond the adoption of a version of the May 1990 industrial policy mooted by V.P. Singh under such circumstances. It is all but certain that there would have been no devaluation of the rupee, in which case import licensing on the capital goods and intermediate inputs would have remained intact as well, with trade liberalization proceeding only at the pace set in the second half of the 1980s.

We may go a step further and plausibly argue that India was on this deterministic path even before Independence. Nehru had embraced socialism by the late 1920s and had successfully committed Congress to some measures of his future policy agenda in the Karachi Resolution adopted by the party in 1931. They included a high level of protection for industrial workers and state control of key industries and services, mineral resources, railways, waterways, shipping and other means of transport. Later, as the chairman of the Congress-appointed National Planning Committee, Nehru successfully built consensus among key stakeholders on planning, self-sufficiency, development of heavy industry and protection of cottage, village and small industries. Being the youngest among the top leaders in the freedom movement, he was the only top leader in the freedom movement to survive till the mid-1960s. This fact guaranteed him not only the position of the prime minister of free India for several years but also left him with no equals. Even if Patel had become the first prime minister, Nehru would have succeeded him after his death. Historical events had thus begun to conspire in favour of the Nehru Development Model two and a half decades before the second plan became a reality.

What, then, is the scenario under which the outcome could have been different? An interesting possibility to explore in answer to this question is whether the outcome could have been different had Patel been in command of the policy during the first several years following Independence. To make the exploration interesting, even if entirely hypothetical, we may ask how different the outcome would have been had the age profiles of Nehru and Patel been switched. Under this scenario, Nehru would have been the older of the two and departed from the scene in December 1950, while Patel would have been younger and lived till May 1964. In such a case, Patel would have been the prime minister beginning in December 1950, if not sooner. What kind of economic development model would Patel have adopted under such circumstances?

Unlike Nehru, Patel did not articulate his vision of development in detail. He expressed his views on this subject sparingly and generally in the context of specific pressing problems of the day. He was not a part of the deliberations in the National Planning Committee, which had held extensive discussions on the post-Independence architecture of the economic-policy framework during 1938–40. Much of what can be gleaned about his views is contained in the speeches he delivered after Independence, especially during 1948–50.

In January 1948, India was barely emerging out of the post-Partition communal riots. The atmosphere in the industry was vitiated, with workers in Calcutta and Bombay resorting to strikes to seek higher wages and better terms of employment. Patel, who saw production as the foremost need of post-Independence India, visited both cities during the month to persuade the workers and industrialists to cooperate. Speaking to a half-million-strong audience of workers in Calcutta on 3 January 1948, he said, 'For an all-out industrial effort which is necessary in order to promote India's industries, support from labour is indisputably necessary, but labour has fallen on evil days. Its organizers know only one thing and believe only in one method. That is to prop up their leadership by strikes.'[1] He reminded the workers that 'if they killed industries, labour itself would cease to exist' and went on to advise that the road to reaping the just reward went not through strikes but arbitration. 'Let them look around for guidance. Other countries have advanced industrially. In America there is no labour problem. In England there is a Socialist Government but it does not have to use force or resort to firing. Labour responds to its calls patriotically.'[2]

During the same visit to Calcutta, Patel also shared his thoughts on industry with a group of industrialists at the Calcutta Club on 5 January 1948. In this speech, entitled 'Produce and Distribute Equitably', he tried to allay the fears of his audience on the possible nationalization of industries and enterprises. The speech also gives some flavour of his disapproval of socialism in the context of contemporary India. Patel told the industrialists,

> We have now to settle down to the task of reconstruction. . . . In the task ahead we have to take labour and capital with us. If we fail to do so, we are doomed to disappointment. I have no doubt whatsoever that the conflict between labour and capital, and may I say, also the Government at this stage would be nothing but ruinous to the country. . . . We must remember that Socialism in England came after England had advanced considerably on the road to industrialization. I am convinced that any promotion of a conflict between labour and capital at this stage would deal a disastrous blow to India's industrial future.'[3]

Lest the industrialists take his disapproval of the conflict between labour and capital as an approval of the exploitation of the workers, Patel went on to tell them explicitly that the disapproval simply reflected his preference for arbitration over strikes as the means to the resolution of the conflict. Turning to the subject of the nationalization of industries, he said, 'The cry of nationalization is being entered into merely to cause panic. If you get panicky, you fall into the trap. You should yourself realize that industry is to be established before it is nationalized. India is yet industrially in an infant stage.'[4] He reminded the industrialists that despite having a Labour government and a high degree of advancement of industrialization, England had not gone for nationalization at a fast pace. By joint efforts of labour and capital and government, it had been successful in increasing production. 'On the other hand in India,' he added, 'we seem to believe in the miracle that labour should produce less and get more money. The result is strikes which retard production. Less production means more misery and privations. We have got to break this vicious cycle.'[5] As he proceeded towards the conclusion of the speech, he said, 'All the three parties, Labour, Capital and Government, have common interests and common outlook in many fields. We must act with mutual consultation.'

On 20 January 1948, Patel spoke to a large crowd of workers in Bombay. In the speech titled 'Labour is at the Crossroads', he revisited some of the themes he had articulated in Calcutta. Emphasizing the importance of production first, he said,

> The future depends on whether we step up production of food, cloth, iron, steel, cement and other essential articles both for the civil population and defence needs. This is necessary not only for banishing hunger and disease from the country but also for consolidating the freedom which we have won after so many years of struggle.

He then went on to exhort the workers to 'take the right road and contribute all energies to strengthen the country'.[6]

Coming down heavily on the socialists for misguiding the workers into resorting to strikes to press their demands, Patel advised,

> If the Socialists are bent upon snatching the leadership, there is no objection to handing it over to them. After all our mission [of ending the colonial rule] has been accomplished. We do not want to hand over a ruined concern but a going concern for constructive progress, not for wrecking the future of the country. The Socialists threaten to break away from the Congress. The doors are open. But I would urge them not to mar the progress of the young nation which has after all got the rare opportunity to mould itself according to its dreams and desires after many hundreds of years.[7]

Patel then asked the workers 'to keep away from this strike fever, since "produce or perish" is the crucial question facing us at this juncture. . . . I, therefore, advise you that if you want more wages you should increase productivity and step up production.'[8]

The theme that is common to many speeches by Patel during 1948–50 is that raising production is the foremost national objective, and doing so requires cooperation among industrialists, workers and the government. He repeatedly exhorted workers to avoid strikes and deliver high productivity and industrialists to share the fruits of production equitably with workers. Simultaneously, on the government's behalf, he reassured the industrialists against nationalization and workers for their fair share in production. Entirely missing from all speeches that I have reviewed is any reference whatsoever to the public sector as a producer. Whether he refers to heavy industry or light industry, the context is that of the private sector. Seen against the backdrop of his explicit disapproval of the socialists and nationalization, this last fact offers a clear signal that a Patel-led government would not have espoused the entry of the public sector as a producer.

Two remaining features of the Nehru policy framework concern the role of heavy industry and priority accorded to self-sufficiency as an objective. Regarding heavy industry, Patel spoke approvingly of increasing the production of steel and chemicals but was also comfortable with India importing machinery as long as foreign exchange for it was available. For example, in a speech at a conference of businessmen, industrialists and labour leaders on 11 November 1949, he stated,

> Increased production would enable us not only to meet the demands of the consumers but also to substantially cut down our imports, thereby saving valuable foreign exchange for other more pressing needs, chief of which would be the import of capital goods which we would require for old or new undertakings. A few industries in which I feel increased production is possible and must be achieved are: steel, cotton textiles, sugar, electrical goods, chemicals, machine tools, paper and cement.[9]

Patel thus took no strong position on focusing new investments squarely on heavy industry, especially machinery. As long as the domestic production of certain goods could ease up the foreign-exchange situation, he was comfortable importing machinery.

Patel exhibited stronger conviction in favour of achieving self-sufficiency though more from a nationalist viewpoint than as a means to keep imperialism at bay. Unlike Nehru, he also did not advocate giving priority to heavy industry to achieve self-sufficiency. To quote him once again from a speech delivered on 29 January 1950,

> The swarajya we have gained is not the real thing. Real swarajya we can have by producing in our country what we need. For this we will have to change our habits. . . . We have to pledge ourselves not to use imported goods. Of course, if there is anything not produced in our country, but required in the national interest to produce more wealth, like machinery, it will have to be used. . . . Our industrialists and other capable people should try to manufacture the machinery we now import and make our economy self-reliant.[10]

Stated in this manner, machinery production at home was a part of the self-sufficiency objective but did not enjoy priority over other industries. Equally important, he singled out 'our industrialists and other capable people' to produce machinery and not the government.

A subject of some importance in considering Patel's thinking on the economy is agriculture. This sector occupied a significantly more important position for him than Nehru. He argued that India needed to expand agricultural production to achieve self-sufficiency in food, provide employment and free up foreign exchange for the import of machinery. In a speech delivered to the chief ministers of the states on 26 April 1950, Patel noted that many had expressed admiration for the work that had been done in India, 'but that work would not last unless we have enough food in the country to feed our people'.[11] He went on to add, 'Machinery will not solve the problem because millions of idle hands who have no work cannot find employment on machines. India's planning must necessarily differ from the planning of highly developed and industrialized countries. India is primarily an agricultural country and in a country as thickly populated as India is, idleness is the greatest disease.'[12] Recognizing that defence needs necessitated the development of the industry as well, he concluded, 'We have to plan both for industry which is immediately necessary and for agriculture which is of primary importance.'[13]

The most plausible inference from the limited information we can gather on Patel's economic thought is that India would have chosen a markedly different strategy of development under him. Unlike Nehru, he would not have placed heavy industry at the centre of his economic-policy framework. The role of the public sector in industrial production would have been minimal, if any. The country would have also sought self-sufficiency in agriculture sooner than it did.

This overall strategy would have been free of both investment licensing and public-sector manufacturing. The resulting economy would have been far more reliant on markets from the beginning than was the case under Nehru and his successors. The only area where controls would have survived is imports. Though Patel expresses concern about the foreign-exchange shortage on more than one occasion, each time, he suggests a cut in imports as the only solution. There is no recognition in his speeches of the importance of expanding exports as an alternative. Nor does he recognize the need for occasional devaluation of the rupee to ensure that Indian goods remain competitive vis-à-vis their foreign counterparts.

This being acknowledged, the absence of investment licensing would have gone some distance towards minimizing the damage to efficiency and growth from import licensing. There are also hints of Patel being a fiscal conservative, which would have translated into lower inflation and hence greater competitiveness of domestic goods vis-à-vis foreign goods than was the case under Nehru.[14] More importantly, without the baggage of socialism, when the world moved to a flexible exchange-rate system in the early 1970s, it would have been easier for India to let the rupee depreciate and move away from import licensing. The transition to an open economy would thus have taken place nearly two decades earlier than it actually did.

One final question in considering this scenario is whether the socialist wing within the Congress would not have posed a challenge to Patel. The weight of evidence on this question is in favour of Patel prevailing over them. As we saw in Chapter 13, even after the death of Patel in December 1950, the conservative wing of Congress remained sufficiently powerful that the Draft Outline of the first plan, released in mid-1951, gave socialism nothing more than lip service. Frankel makes this point systematically, quoting extensively from the Draft Outline. To quote her,[15]

> The Directive Principles of State Policy were accepted as the guide to the 'economic and social pattern to be attained through planning.' However, the planners warned in an immediate caveat that 'a hasty implementation of measures intended to bring about economic equality, may, in the short run, affect savings and the level of production adversely.' Although the Draft Outline endorsed goals of social and institutional transformation, virtually all programmes included in the plan were justified by reference to a single yardstick: the economic goal of increasing production. The result was an approach to planning that limited the government's role to the creation of social capital and financial incentives for the expansion of private enterprise.

Frankel further points out, 'The planners did affirm the need to institute a system of controls on capital issues, industrial licensing, foreign exchange allocations, imports and exports, and prices; but they simultaneously conceded that "the expansion of industrial production during the period of the Plan would be largely the responsibility of the private sector".'[16] The Draft Outline also gave the highest priority to agriculture, rural development, irrigation and power. Furthermore, it ruled out a ceiling on existing holdings for the purpose of redistributing land to subsistence farmers, arguing that breaking up the larger farms into smaller ones might lead to a decline in production.

In the end, the conservatives lost to Nehru because he enjoyed the popular support necessary to win the general elections held from 25 October 1951 to 21 February 1952. But if Nehru had departed from the scene in December 1950 while Patel had stayed, the conservative wing would have remained in control of the party, and the future trajectory of the economy would have been closer to what I have described above.

But, of course, that was not to be. Being much younger than Patel, Nehru was the one who lived till May 1964 and got to lay down the foundation of the economic system in India. And the rest, as they say, is history.

Appendix 1

Statement of Industrial Policy, April, 1945[1]

The Government of India have issued the following statement on Industrial Policy:

1. The Government of India have reached a stage in their planning of industrial development when they consider it would be in the public interest to make an announcement of the conclusions reached by them on various aspects of policy. There has not been time to consult either provincial Governments which are, at present, constitutionally responsible for industrial development in Provinces or States between whom and British India a high degree of collaboration will be necessary if the maximum results are to be achieved from a vigorous industrial policy. Some of the proposals will eventually have to be placed before the Legislature for approval. Although, for these and other reasons, the conclusions reached are, to some extent, provisional, the Government of India consider that an announcement of their views may help to clear up the uncertainty which appears at present to be impeding plans of development by private industry.
2. Under the Government of India Act, 1935, the development of industries is a provincial subject, but is open to the Centre to declare by law that the development of certain industries under Central control

is expedient in the public interest and thereupon, the development of such industries becomes a Central subject. No such Act has, in fact, been passed by the Central Legislature with the consequence that the development of industries is at the moment wholly a provincial subject. In view of this, some explanation is necessary as to why the Government of India feel themselves called upon to issue a statement of their industrial policy. The reasons are two-fold. In the first place, the general economic policy pursued by the Government of India under their own constitutional powers exercises a profound influence over industrial development. It is a matter of history, for example, that the cotton textile, the iron and steel and the sugar industries have made rapid strides in India largely as a result of the fiscal policy pursued by the Central Government. In the second place, the progress of planning has made it abundantly clear that certain industries must be taken over under Central control in the interests of coordinated development. It was indeed contemplated by Parliament, when the Government of India Act was passed, that industries in which a common policy was desirable would be brought under Central control. Government consider that for achieving the foregoing object the following industries should be centralized, but before coming to a final decision they will consult the Provinces and the leading Indian States.

i. Iron and steel.
ii. Manufacture of prime movers.
iii. Automobiles and tractors and transport vehicles.
iv. Aircraft.
v. Ship-building and marine engineering.
vi. Electrical machinery.
vii. Heavy machinery, such as textiles, sugar, paper, mining, cement and chemical.

viii. Machine tools.
ix. Heavy chemicals and fine chemicals, chemical dyes, fertilizers and pharmaceutical drugs.
x. Electrochemical industry.
xi. Cotton and woolen textiles.
xii. Cement.
xiii. Power alcohol.
xiv. Sugar.
xv. Motor and aviation fuel.
xvi. Rubber manufacture.
xvii. Non-ferrous metals industry.
xviii. Electric power.
xix. Coal
xx. Radio engineering.

When the necessary legislation is passed by the Centre, the Government of India will have direct constitutional authority for shaping the progress of a number of industries of vital importance to the country's development. It may be pointed out, although the point is clear enough, that this arrangement has no long-range constitutional implications. It is intended to be in operation for so long as the present Constitution lasts; and to what extent it will survive beyond that period is a matter to be decided by the future.

3. The policy to be pursued by Government must be governed by what they consider to be the proper objectives of industrial development and the steps that will be necessary, in the conditions in which India will find herself after the war, to enable these objectives to be achieved. Government consider that the fundamental objects of industrialization are three-fold:
   i. To increase the national wealth by the maximum exploitation of the country's resources. It is well-known that there are considerable unused resources

of manpower and material, and clearly Government policy must be directed towards stimulating their fullest and most effective utilization.

ii. To make the country better prepared for defence. The experience of two wars has demonstrated the dangers, both to India and to the rest of the Commonwealth, inherent in India's dependence on overseas supplies for vital commodities required for defence.

iii. To provide a high and stable level of employment. At present the volume of industrial employment is comparatively speaking small, but if the country's industrial resources are developed to their maximum possible extent, industrial employment, including employment in ancillary trades and professions, will considerably affect the volume of total employment in the country. Government consider that their industrial policy should be directed towards maintaining employment at the highest possible degree of stability and volume.

It is axiomatic in Government's policy that the additional wealth created by industrial development should be distributed in a manner that may be regarded as socially equitable. Powers must be taken and consciously used to secure this purpose.

4. The attitude of Government towards industry in the past was, for many years, one of laissez-faire. Till the war of 1914-18 this policy was maintained in the belief, which was in accordance with the current economic doctrine, that industrial progress was best achieved by unregulated private enterprise. This attitude underwent some modification after the last war through the adoption of the policy of discriminating protection. The Secretary of State, Mr. Edwin Montague, in a dispatch to the Government of India in 1919 on the Fiscal Commission report, announced a new policy. He said,

'If the active participation by Government in industrial development is to be accepted as one of its legitimate functions a new policy is required.

With the quickening of political life that will follow the grant of constitutional reforms the demand for progress in administration and social reform may be expected to become insistent, and if progress is not to be hampered by want of funds the taxable capacity of the people will have to be increased. To this end the natural resources of India must be effectively utilized as new opportunities for the investment of capital present themselves, in order that the standard of comfort of the people may be raised, and the economic strength of the country may increase. Further, as the experience of the past few years has shown that in time of war, India cannot rely on outside sources for her needs, the matter is one in which political expediency, economic advantage and military security are coincident and accord with the interests of the Empire as a whole.

I accept the two fundamental principles, underlying the recommendations of the Commission; first, that in future Government should play an active part in the industrial development of the country; secondly, that Government cannot undertake this work unless provided with adequate administrative equipment and forearmed with reliable scientific and technical advice.'

This dispatch was soon followed by the Government of India Act, 1919, under which industries became a provincial subject. The Government of India, therefore, lost direct interest in industrial development and the Provinces had neither the financial nor the technical resources to stimulate development on any significant scale.

The Government of India consider that the continuance of their existing policy, in the conditions in which India will find herself after this war, will not meet the objectives of sound post-war development. Though industrially stronger than in 1939, India will find herself in a position of relative inferiority. In other countries technological advances have been immense and, as a result of the nature of modern warfare, there has been a striking increase in the total volume of skilled industrial labour. If India is to make rapid headway and if the standard of living of the masses is to be effectively raised, a vigorous and sustained effort is necessary in which the State no less than private industry must take a part.

5. Government have decided to take positive steps to encourage and promote the rapid industrialization of the country to the fullest extent possible. They attach particular importance to the development of those industries which constitute the foundation of modern industrial life, such as the iron and steel industry, the heavy engineering industry, the machine tool industry, the heavy chemical industry and so on. But while the Regulation and Development of these industries must take high priority, it must form part of a balanced plan in which due place is given to consumption goods industries. It is clear that if progress is to be achieved, the development of industry must be planned by Government in cooperation with the industry and every effort made to make the plan effective.
6. The formulation of a tariff policy appropriate to the post-war needs and conditions of the country is under active consideration. The subject, however, is one of great complexity, and will require a little further time for the Government of India to determine its policy and devise the machinery for implementing it. In the meantime, the position of industries which have been established or developed in wartime requires consideration. Some of these are covered by the announcement made in 1940 in regard to the grant of an assurance of post-war

protection to essential wartime industries. Outside the scope of this announcement, however, lie a large number of industries which have helped to sustain the national economy during an exceptionally difficult period. The provision of assistance to or protection of such of these industries as have been established on sound lines is likely to assume a measure of urgency during the period of transition. Government propose to set up machinery without delay for the investigation of the claims of such industries for assistance or protection. This is a short-term measure pending the formulation of a long-term tariff policy and the establishment of a permanent machinery for the purpose.

7. (i) A primary point in industrial policy is the extent to which the State will take part in industrial enterprise. In India, ordnance factories, public utilities and railways together forming a considerable proportion of the total industrial enterprise are already very largely State-owned and State operated. This arrangement will naturally continue. Further, Government have recently decided that the bulk generation of electric power should, as far as possible, be a State concern. This decision falls within the existing pattern of State and private enterprise. Apart from ordnance factories, public utilities and railways, basic industries of national importance may be nationalized provided adequate private capital is not forthcoming and it is regarded as essential, in the national interests, to promote such industries. For the purpose of Government policy, basic industries can be defined as including aircraft, automobiles and tractors, chemicals and dyes, iron and steel, prime movers, transport vehicles, electrical machinery, machine tools, electro-chemical and non-ferrous metal industries. It is contemplated also that Government may take over certain industries in which the tax element is much

more predominating than the profit element and it is necessary and convenient for the State to take over the industry. An example of such action in the past is 'Salt Manufacture'.

All other industries will be left to private enterprise under varying degrees of control. There may be no control except such as is required to ensure fair conditions for labor, in the case of such industries as those catering for ordinary consumers' demands and subject to free competition, while in the case of industries of a semi-monopolistic nature or which control scarce natural resources there may be a stricter control varying with the circumstances of each case.

The views expressed in this paragraph regarding the scope of nationalism will be discussed with the Provinces and also with the more important Indian States and a further statement issued as to whether the scope should be enlarged at all, and if so to what extent.

Within the field considered open for State enterprise the question whether the existing units which are privately owned should be taken over by the State will be examined on the merits of each type of such cases. The Reconstruction Committee of the Council has decided with regard to electricity undertakings that, as licenses fall due, they will as far as possible be taken over by the State or quasi-State organization. The case of coal will be examined and dealt with separately.

(ii) Certain industries of national importance such as ship-building and the manufacture of locomotives and boilers will be run by the State as well as by private capitalists.

(iii) Normally State enterprises will be managed by the State. In special cases the possibility of management through a private agency for a limited period may have to be explored.

(iv) In some cases, State enterprises may be operated through public corporations. In order to gain experience of management through public corporations, further experiments will be tried.

Government Assistance to Industry

8. Government have a primary responsibility, which they propose to discharge without delay as soon as war conditions allow, for developing certain prerequisites of industrial progress. One of them is the development of transport facilities. This is a matter in which both the Central and Provincial Governments as well as the Indian States are vitally interested and steps to ensure a co-ordinated policy have already been initiated and made considerable headway. Another prerequisite is the development of power. The Government of India have made good progress in ensuring co-ordinated development in this field. In many cases, power schemes-particularly where they are combined with irrigation-are the primary responsibility of Provinces, but where regional projects, which overrun Provincial and State boundaries, are considered necessary, the Government of India are taking action for the development of resources on a regional basis. The survey of mineral resources is another field where the responsibility falls squarely on the Central Government. Steps are being taken to extend the Geological survey and to put it on a footing where it can be of the maximum service to the country. Another pre-requisite of industrial progress is scientific and industrial research; the Government of India have already devoted considerable attention to it and they propose to take all steps which their resources will allow for seeing that it is maintained at a high level. Technical education, particularly through high-grade technological institutes, and technical training of personnel required

for skilled employment are also matters in which the Government of India have initiated action which will directly assist industrial progress.

9. In addition to discharging their responsibility for thus laying the foundation of industrial progress, the Government of India are prepared to assist industry in one or more of the following ways:

   i. Government will take part either by making loans or by subscribing a share of the capital in industrial undertakings which are considered to be of importance to the country's development, but for which adequate private capital may not be forthcoming. Within this category might fall such industries as those manufacturing aircraft, automobiles and tractors, chemicals and dyes, iron and steel, prime movers, transport vehicles, electrical machinery, machine tools, electro-chemical and non-ferrous metal industries. This list will be modified from time to time as circumstances warrant. Industries receiving this type of assistance will be subject to a greater degree of Government control than others. For example, Government might require representation on the Board of management and that their sanction should be obtained for incurring certain types of expenditure and for certain appointments.

      Government might provide in suitable cases capital equipment like buildings, services and/or machinery on terms to be settled on the merits of each case. This might in certain cases take the form of bulk Government orders for capital goods which might then be allocated to industrialists on suitable terms.

   ii. In special cases, industrial enterprise will be encouraged by guaranteeing a minimum dividend on capital or undertaking to meet revenue losses for a fixed number of years, subject to the condition that

Government would have a voice in the management and that a ceiling will be fixed for the return on capital. Where this procedure is followed, profits in subsequent years over and above the ceiling will be appropriated towards returning the funds paid by Government and after this has been done, such excess profits as continue to accrue will be divided by the Government and the Company in agreed proportions.

iii. Government will be prepared to give adequate financial support to research organizations set up by Industrial Associations representing organized industries and to provide for grants to Universities for approved schemes of research. Such assistance would be in addition to the direct Government organization of research as, for instance, through the Council of Scientific and Industrial Research.

iv. Subject to reasonable safeguards as to the quality and price, Government will continue to encourage Indian industry by buying its products in preference to others.

v. The Government of India are examining the question of the promotion of an Industrial Investment Corporation or a similar institution.

vi. Government will undertake to examine from time to time, the tax system with a view to ensuring that, while securing the ends of social justice and national budgetary interests, the taxation does not tend to act adversely on development.

vii. Government will assist in the procurement of capital goods required by industrialists. They propose to set up an organization in the UK and in the USA for this purpose.

viii. In certain branches of industry, the advice of experts is particularly essential. Government will help in making the services of such experts available to industry.

Licensing of Industry

10. Government have come to the conclusion that they must assume power to license industrial undertakings. They have at present no power except for emergency wartime controls, to regulate the growth of industry; normally a person may set up a factory wherever he likes and may manufacture in it whatever commodity he chooses. There are, of course, local laws which regulate the size of the buildings, the proportion of open space, public health needs and so forth and it is possible under these regulations to refuse permission to put up a factory building, but such refusal cannot be based on considerations of industrial development. One effect of this unregulated freedom to promote industrial enterprise has been the concentration of industry in certain areas, for instance, the manufacture of cotton textiles has been concentrated in Bombay and Ahmedabad, sugar in the United Provinces and Bihar, paper in Bengal. In some cases, there are good grounds for the concentration of particular industries in particular areas, but in many cases, it has been the result of fortuitous and haphazard growth. There are vast areas in this country which, though suitable for industrial development, have not been developed because industry has tended to flow in particular channels.
11. The effects of such concentration are economic, social as well as strategic. It seems unsound from the strategic point of view that so large a proportion of industry should be concentrated in a few cities which might well be vulnerable to attack. On the social side it is clear that concentration creates housing problems of a most acute type. Perhaps, an even more important consideration is that concentration deprives other areas

of the country of the beneficent effects of diversified economy. Lastly, it is not clear that concentration is necessarily economically sound. The markets for textiles, for instance, are situated all over India, and cotton, the main raw material, is also grown in various parts of India. From the point of view of the consumer, it would obviously be right to cut out unnecessary transportation costs and to locate manufacture where both the raw material and the market are situated. Even where concentration appears relatively cheap on the basis of financial costs of production and distribution, it would, in many cases, be found in the long run, both socially and economically cheaper to disperse industry, if regard is paid to the benefits of a widely spread industrial structure and its integration with agriculture.

12. Control over development would be necessary from another point of view. In an unregulated industrial economy there is likely to be a tendency for capitalists to go in for schemes which promise quick returns. This will lead to lopsided development-a scramble for some industries, with the danger of overproduction and excessive competition and inadequate attention to other industries which are equally necessary in the national interest. To overcome this difficulty, it would be necessary to fix targets, to allocate them on a regional basis, and to see that these targets are achieved.

13. As Government has no authority at present to do this, they will have to take powers by legislation. Government propose that they should take power to license the starting of new factories and the expansion of existing factories, for, without this power, planned industrial development will be quite impossible. At the same time in order to avoid unnecessary delays, it is proposed to set a monetary limit to the plants

or projects requiring license so that very small plants, moderate extension of existing plants or replacements which do not add to the output should not be subject to licensing. Details of this legislation are under consideration. Even on a preliminary examination, it is manifest that the power proposed to be taken by Government must be used in a manner that will command general public confidence. It is equally clear that the administration of the licensing system must be such as to assure Indian States that their legitimate desire for industrial development is not overlooked. It is accordingly proposed that a Board should be constituted at a high level to advise the Central Government in the matter of granting licences for industries specified in paragraph 2 above. Details of the personnel of the Board, its function, and other connected matters will be decided later.

Other Controls

14. In a planned economy it is impossible to do without controls. Government consider that such controls should be the very minimum required. They propose that apart from licensing control should be undertaken to achieve the following objects:
    i. To secure balanced investment in industry, agriculture and the social services. It will be necessary, after the war, to ensure that the available capital resources are utilized on a balanced plan of agricultural, industrial and other development and that inside the field of industrial development, a balance is kept between manufacture of capital and consumer goods. Agricultural development will be undertaken almost wholly under the auspices of the State. This is because the bulk of the holders of land

are poor and cannot themselves finance, at any rate, initially, improvements such as contour bunding and irrigation by lift pumps. In many cases it will be possible to recover the cost ultimately, but the capital expenditure will have to be advanced by the State. The State will also require to borrow heavy sums either directly for itself or on behalf of local authorities for financing road development, irrigation, electrical power, public health and other social services. On any reasonable estimate, the capital resources required for these purposes will be heavy, and it will be necessary to ensure that the State is in a position to mobilize them from the country's savings. This will make it necessary to maintain control over capital issues; for, otherwise, capital may flow excessively in one direction and lead to lopsided development.

ii. To secure for industrial workers a fair wage, decent conditions of work and living and a reasonable security of tenure. It is a fundamental objective of industrial development that it would enable the general standard of living to be raised. It would be a frustration of this objective if industrial workers do not get fair wages and decent working conditions. In the past, these matters were left largely to be settled between the employers and the workers, but it may be necessary for the State to intervene with statutory powers. This question is engaging the earnest attention of Government and the necessary legislation will be undertaken from time to time.

iii. To prevent excessive profits to private capital. In the case of private undertakings, subject to free competition, it would be a mistake to discourage enterprise by undue restriction of profits. The risks of such enterprise are considerable and if industrialists are to bear the losses, they must also be permitted to reap the profits. In the normal course, the tax system may be expected to prevent any excessive accumulation of profits. Where, however, conditions of free competition do not exist and as a consequence, excessive profits accrue, special steps would be necessary. These can only be considered on the facts of each case as it arises.

iv. To ensure the quality of industrial products in the interests of both internal and external markets. It is of the utmost importance to ensure good quality for the internal as well as the external markets. This involves standardization of products and administrative machinery to enforce standardization.

v. To ensure that unhealthy concentration of assets in the hands of a few persons or of a special community would be avoided. This may be secured by a judicious exercise of controls, such as capital issues control and the licensing machinery for the regionalization of industry.

vi. To require necessary technical training of personnel and to extend the benefit of such training to minorities and backward communities.

15. The Government of India propose without delay to enter into discussions with the Provinces and with the Indian States in the light of the policy stated above and are confident that it will be possible to evolve a machinery which will enable an agreed policy to be implemented in practice in a spirit of friendly cooperation on the part of all parties concerned.

Planning and Development Department,
New Delhi, 21 April, 1945.

Appendix 2

Government of India Resolution on Industrial Policy, 6 April 1948[1]

1. The Government of India have given careful thought to the economic problems facing the country. The nation has now set itself to establish a social order where justice and equality of opportunity shall be secured to all the people. The immediate objective is to provide educational facilities and health services on a much wider scale, and to promote a rapid rise in the standard of living of the people by exploiting the latent resources of the country, increasing production and offering opportunities to all for employment in the service of the community. For this purpose, careful planning and integrated effort over the whole field of national activity are necessary; and the Government of India propose to establish a National Planning Commission to formulate programmes of development and to secure their execution. The present statement, however, confines itself to Government's policy in the industrial field.
2. Any improvement in the economic conditions of the country postulates an increase in national wealth: a mere redistribution of existing wealth would make no essential difference to the people and would merely mean the distribution of poverty. A dynamic national policy must, therefore, be directed to a continuous

increase in production by all possible means, side by side with measures to secure its equitable distribution. In the present state of the nation's economy, when the mass of the people are below the subsistence level, the emphasis should be on the expansion of production, both agricultural and industrial; and in particular on the production of capital equipment, of goods satisfying the basic needs of the people, and of commodities the export of which will increase earnings of foreign exchange.

3. The problem of State participation in Industry and the conditions in which private enterprise should be allowed to operate must be judged in this context. There can be no doubt that the State must play a progressively active role in the development of industries, but ability to achieve the main objectives should determine the immediate extent of State responsibility and the limits to private enterprise. Under present conditions, the mechanism and the resources of the State may not permit it to function forthwith in Industry as widely as may be desirable. The Government of India are taking steps to remedy the situation; in particular, they are considering steps to create a body of men trained in business methods and management. They feel, however, that for some time to come, the State could contribute more quickly to the increase of national wealth by expanding its present activities wherever it is already operating and by concentrating on new units of production in other fields, rather than on acquiring and running existing units. Meanwhile, private enterprise, properly directed and regulated, has a valuable role to play.

4. On these considerations the Government have decided that the manufacture of arms and ammunition, the production and control of atomic energy, and the ownership and management of railway transport should be the exclusive monopoly of the Central Government.

Further, in any emergency, the Government would always have the power to take over any industry vital for national defence. In the case of the following industries, the State-which in this context, includes Central, Provincial and State Governments and other Public Authorities like Municipal Corporations-will be exclusively responsible for the establishment of new undertakings, except where, in the national interest, the State itself finds it necessary to secure the co-operation of private enterprise subject to such control and regulation as the Central Government may prescribe:

i. Coal (the Indian Coalfields Committee's proposals will be generally followed).
ii. Iron and Steel.
iii. Aircraft Manufacture.
iv. Shipbuilding.
v. Manufacture of telephone, telegraph and wireless apparatus, excluding radio receiving sets.
vi. Mineral Oils.

While the inherent right of the State to acquire any existing industrial undertaking will always remain, and will be exercised whenever the public interest requires it, Government have decided to let existing undertakings in these fields develop for a period of ten years, during which they will be allowed all facilities for efficient working and reasonable expansion. At the end of this period, the whole matter will be reviewed and a decision taken in the light of circumstances obtaining at the time. If it is decided that the State should acquire any unit, the fundamental rights guaranteed by the Constitution will be observed and compensation will be awarded on a fair and equitable basis.

Management of State enterprise will, as a rule, be through the medium of public corporations under the statutory control of the Central Government, who will assume such powers as may be necessary to ensure this.

5. The Government of India have recently promulgated a measure for the control by the State of the generation and distribution of electric power. This industry will continue to be regulated in terms of this measure.
6. The rest of the industrial field will normally be open to private enterprise, individual as well as co-operative. The State will also progressively participate in this field; nor will it hesitate to intervene whenever the progress of an industry under private enterprise is unsatisfactory. The Central Government have already embarked on enterprises like large river-valley developments, which are multi-purpose projects of great magnitude, involving extensive generation of hydro-electric power and irrigation on a vast scale, and are calculated in a comparatively short time to change the entire face of large areas in this country. Projects like the Damodar Valley Scheme, the Kosi Reservoir, the Hirakud Dam, etc., are in a class by themselves and can stand comparison with any of the major schemes in America or elsewhere. The Central Government have also undertaken the production of fertilizer on a very large scale and have in view other enterprises like the manufacture of essential drugs, and of synthetic oil from coal; many Provincial and State Governments are also proceeding on similar lines.
7. There are certain basic industries of importance, apart from those mentioned in paragraph 4, the planning and regulation of which by the Central Government is necessary in the national interest. The following industries whose location must be governed by economic factors of all-India import, or which require considerable investment or a high degree of technical skill, will be the subject of Central regulation and control:

i. Salt.
ii. Automobiles and tractors.
iii. Prime Movers.
iv. Electric Engineering.
v. Other heavy machinery.
vi. Machine tools.
vii. Heavy chemicals, fertilizers and pharmaceuticals and drugs.
viii. Electrochemical industries.
ix. Non-ferrous metals.
x. Rubber Manufactures.
xi. Power and industrial alcohol.
xii. Cotton and woolen textiles.
xiii. Cement.
xiv. Sugar.
xv. Paper and newsprint.
xvi. Air and Sea Transport.
xvii. Minerals.
xviii. Industries related to defense.

The above list cannot obviously be of an exhaustive nature. The Government of India, while retaining the ultimate direction over this field of industry, will consult the Governments of the Provinces and States at all stages and fully associate them in the formulation and execution of plans. Besides these Governments, representatives of Industry and Labour will also be associated with the Central Government in the Industrial Advisory Council and other bodies which they propose to establish, as recommended by the Industries Conference.

8. Cottage and small-scale industries have a very important role in the national economy, offering as they do scope for individual, village or cooperative enterprise, and means for the rehabilitation of displaced persons. These industries are particularly suited for the better utilization

of local resources and for the achievement of local self-sufficiency in respect of certain types of essential consumer goods like food, cloth and agricultural implements. The healthy expansion of cottage and small-scale industries depends upon a number of factors like the provision of raw materials, cheap power, technical advice, organized marketing of their produce, and, where necessary, safeguards against intensive competition by large-scale manufacture, as well as on the education of the worker in the use of the best available technique. Most of these fall in the Provincial sphere and are receiving the attention of the Governments of the Provinces and the States. The Resolution of the Industries Conference has requested the Central Government to investigate how far and in what manner these industries can be coordinated and integrated with large-scale industries. The Government of India accept this recommendation. It will be examined, for example, how the textile mill industry can be made complementary to, rather than competitive with the handloom industry, which is the country's largest and best-organized cottage industry. In certain other lines of production, like agricultural implements, textile accessories, and parts of machine tools, it should be possible to produce components on a cottage industry scale and assemble these into their final product at a factory. It will also be investigated how far industries at present highly centralized could be decentralized with advantage.

The Resolution of the Industries Conference has recommended that Government should establish a Cottage Industries Board for the fostering of small-scale industries. The Government of India accept this recommendation and propose to create suitable machinery to implement it. A Cottage and Small-scale

Industries Directorate will also be set up within the Directorate General of Industries and Supplies.

One of the main objectives will be to give a distinctly cooperative bias to this field of industry. During and before the last war, even a predominantly agricultural country like China showed what could be done in this respect, and her mobile industrial co-operative units were of outstanding assistance in her struggle against Japan. The present international situation is likely to lessen to a marked degree our chances of getting capital goods for large-scale industry, and the leeway must be made up by having recourse to small-size industrial co-operatives throughout the country.

9. The Government, however, recognize that their objective, viz., securing the maximum increase in production, will not be realized merely by prescribing the respective spheres of the State and of private enterprise in Industry: it is equally essential to ensure the fullest co-operation between labour and management and the maintenance of stable and friendly relations between them. A Resolution on this subject was unanimously passed by the Industries Conference which was held in December last. Amongst other things, the Resolution states:

> '. . . The system of remuneration to capital as well as labour must be so devised that, while in the interests of the consumers and the primary producers, excessive profits should be prevented by suitable methods of taxation and otherwise, both will share the product of their common effort, after making provision for payment of fair wages to labor, a fair return on capital employed in the industry and reasonable reserves for the maintenance and expansion of the undertaking.'

Government accept this Resolution. They also consider that labour's share of the profits should be on a sliding scale normally varying with production. They propose, in addition to the overall regulation of industry by the State, to establish machinery for advising on fair wages, fair remuneration for capital, and conditions of labour. They will also take steps to associate labour in all matters concerning industrial production.

The machinery which Government propose to set up will function at different levels, central, regional and unit. At the Centre, there will be a Central Advisory Council, which will cover the entire field of industry, and will have under it Committees for each major industry. These Committees may be split up into sub-committees dealing with specific questions relating to the industry, e.g. production, industrial relations, wage fixation, and distribution of profits. The regional machinery under the Provincial Governments will be Provincial Advisory Boards which, like the Central Advisory Council, will cover the entire field of industry within the province; they will have under them Provincial Committees for each major industry. The Provincial Committees may also be split up into various sub-committees dealing with specific questions relating to production, wage fixation and industrial relations. Below the Provincial Committees will come the Works Committees and the Production Committees attached to each major industrial establishment.

The Works Committees and the Production Committees will be bi-partite in character, consisting of representatives of employers and workers only, in equal numbers. All other Committees will be tri-partite, with representatives of Government, employers and workers. Government hope that the machinery proposed will substantially reduce the volume of industrial disputes. In the case of unresolved conflicts, Government trust that management and labour will, in their own interests and in the larger interests of the country, agree to settle them through recognized channels of conciliation and arbitration, which will be provided by Government. The Industrial Relations Machinery, both at the Centre and in the Provinces, is being strengthened, and permanent Industrial Tribunals are being established for dealing with major disputes.

The Government of India are also taking special steps to improve industrial housing as quickly as possible. A scheme for the construction of one million workers' houses in ten years is under contemplation, and a Housing Board is being constituted for this purpose. The cost will be shared in suitable proportions between Government, employers and labour, the share of labour being recovered in the form of a reasonable rent.

In order to ensure quick decisions on the various matters arising out of the Industrial Truce Resolution, Government are appointing a special officer.

10. The Government of India agree with the view of the Industries Conference that, while it should be recognized that participation of foreign capital and enterprise, particularly as regards industrial technique and knowledge, will be of value to the rapid industrialization of the country, it is necessary that the conditions under which they may participate in Indian industry should be carefully regulated in the national interest. Suitable legislation will be introduced for this purpose. Such legislation will provide for the scrutiny and approval by the Central Government of every individual case of participation of foreign capital and management in industry. It will provide that, as a rule, the major interest in ownership, and effective control, should always be in Indian hands; but power will be taken to deal with exceptional cases in a manner calculated to serve the national interest. In all cases, however, the training of

suitable Indian personnel for the purpose of eventually replacing foreign experts will be insisted upon.

11. The Government of India are fully alive to their direct responsibility for the development of those industries which they have found necessary to reserve exclusively for State enterprise. They are equally ready to extend their assistance to private or cooperative enterprise in the rest of the industrial field, and in particular, by removing transport difficulties and by facilitating the import of essential raw materials to the maximum possible extent. The tariff policy of Government will be designed to prevent unfair foreign competition and to promote the utilization of India's resources without imposing unjustifiable burdens on the consumer. The system of taxation will be reviewed and readjusted where necessary to encourage saving and productive investment and to prevent undue concentration of wealth in a small section of the population.

12. The Government of India hope that this elucidation of their intentions on fundamental aspects of industrial policy will remove all misapprehensions, and they are confident that a joint and intensive effort will now be made by labour, capital and the general public, which will pave the way for the rapid industrialization of the country.

Appendix 3

Industrial Policy Resolution, 30 April 1956[1]

1. The Government of India set out in their Resolution dated 6 April 1948 the policy which they proposed to pursue in the industrial field. The Resolution emphasized the importance to the economy of securing a continuous increase in production and its equitable distribution, and pointed out that the State must play a progressively active role in the development of Industries. It laid down that besides arms and ammunition, atomic energy and railway transport, which would be the monopoly of the Central Government, the State would be exclusively responsible for the establishment of new undertakings in six basic industries-except where, in the national interest, the State itself found it necessary to secure the cooperation of private enterprise. The rest of the industrial field was left open to private enterprise though it was made clear that the State would also progressively participate in this field.
2. Eight years have passed since this declaration on industrial policy. These eight years have witnessed many important changes and developments in India. The constitution of India has been enacted, guaranteeing certain Fundamental Rights and enunciating Directive Principles of State Policy. Planning has proceeded on an organized basis, and the First Five Year Plan has recently been completed. Parliament has accepted the socialist

pattern of society as the objective of social and economic policy. These important developments necessitate a fresh statement of industrial policy, more particularly as the Second Five Year Plan will soon be placed before the country. This policy must be governed by the principles laid down in the Constitution, the objective of socialism, and the experience gained during these years.

3. The Constitution of India, in its preamble, has declared that it aims at securing for all its citizens:

'JUSTICE, Social, economic and political;
LIBERTY of thought, expression, belief, faith and worship;
EQUALITY of status and opportunity; and to promote among them all;
FRATERNITY assuring the dignity of the individual and the unity of the Nation.'

In its Directive Principles of State Policy, it is stated that-

'The State shall strive to promote the welfare of the people by securing and protecting as effectively as it may a social order in which justice, social, economic and political, shall inform all the institutions of the national life.'

Further that-

'The State shall, in particular, direct its policy towards securing-

i. that the citizens, men and women equally, have the right to an adequate means of livelihood;
ii. that the ownership and control of the material resources of the community are so distributed as best to subserve the common good;
iii. that the operation of economic system does not result in the concentration of wealth and means of production to the common detriment;
iv. that there is equal pay for equal work for both men and women;

v. that the health and strength of workers, men and women, the tender age of children are not abused and that citizens are not forced by economic necessity to enter vocations unsuited to their age or strength;

vi. that childhood and youth are protected against exploitation and against moral and material abandonment.'

4. These basic and general principles were given a more precise direction when Parliament accepted in December 1954, the socialistic pattern of society as the objective of social and economic policy. Industrial policy, as other policies, must therefore, be governed by these principles and directions.

5. In order to realize this objective, it is essential to accelerate the rate of economic growth and to speed up industrialization and, in particular, to develop heavy industries and machine-making industries, to expand the public sector, and to build up a large and growing cooperative sector. These provide the economic foundations for increasing opportunities for gainful employment and improving living standards and working conditions for the mass of the people. Equally, it is urgent, to reduce disparities in income and wealth exist, today, to prevent private monopolies and concentration of economic power in different fields in the hands of small numbers of individuals. Accordingly, the State will progressively assume a predominant and direct responsibility for setting up new industrial undertakings and for developing transport facilities. It will also undertake State trading on an increasing scale. At the same time, as an agency for planned national development, in the context of [the] country's expanding economy, the private sector will have the opportunity to develop and expand. The principle of cooperation should be applied whenever possible and a steadily

increasing proportion of the activities of the private sector developed along cooperative lines.

6. The adoption of the socialist pattern of society as the national objective, as well as the need for planned and rapid development, require that all industries of basic and strategic importance, or in the nature of public utility services, should be in the public sector. Other industries which are essential and require investment on a scale which only the State, in present circumstances, could provide, have also to be in the public sector. The State has, therefore, to assume direct responsibility for the future development of industries over a wide area. Nevertheless, there are limiting factors which make it necessary at this stage for the State to define the field in which it will undertake sole responsibility for further development, and to make a selection of industries in the development of which it will play a dominant role. After considering all aspects of the problem in consultation with the Planning Commission, the Government of India have decided to classify industries into three categories, having regard to the part which the State would play in each of them. These categories will inevitably overlap to some extent and too great a rigidity might defeat the purpose in view. But the basic principles and objectives have always to be kept in view and the general directions hereafter referred to be followed. It should also be remembered that it is always open to the State to undertake any type of industrial production.
7. In the first category will be industries the future development of which will be the exclusive responsibility of the State. The second category will consist of industries which will be progressively state-owned and in which the State will, therefore, generally take the initiative in establishing new undertakings, but in which private enterprise will also be expected to supplement the

efforts of the State. The third category will include all the remaining industries, and their future development will, in general, be left to the initiative and enterprise of the private sector.

8. Industries in the first category have been listed in Schedule-A of this Resolution. All new units in these industries, save where their establishment in the private sector has already been approved, will be sent only by the State. This does not preclude the expansion of the existing privately owned units, or the possibility of the State securing the cooperation of private enterprise in the establishment of new units when the national interests so require. Railways and air transport, arms and ammunition and atomic energy will however, be developed as Central Government monopolies. Whenever cooperation with private enterprise is necessary, the State will ensure, either through majority participation in the capital or otherwise, that it has the requisite powers to guide the policy and control the operations of the undertakings.
9. Industries in the second category will be those listed in Schedule-B. With a view to accelerating their future development, the State will increasingly establish new undertakings in these industries. At the same time, private enterprise will also have the opportunity to develop in this field, either on its own or with State participation.
10. All the remaining industries will fall in the third category, and it is expected that their development will be undertaken ordinarily through the initiative and enterprise of the private sector, though it will be open to the State to start any industry even in this category. It will be the policy of the State to facilitate and encourage the development of these industries in the private sector, in accordance with the programs formulated in successive Five Year Plans, by ensuring the

development of transport, power and other services, and by appropriate fiscal and other measures. The State will continue to foster institutions to provide financial aid to these industries, and special assistance will be given to enterprises organized on cooperative lines for industrial and agricultural purposes. In suitable cases, the State may also grant financial assistance to the private sector. Such assistance, especially when the amount involved is substantial, will preferably be in the form of participation in equity capital, though it may also be in part, the form of debenture capital.

11. Industrial undertakings in the private sector have necessarily to fit into the framework of the social and economic policy of the State and will be subject to control and regulation in terms of the Industries (Development and Regulation) Act and other relevant legislation. The Government of India, however, recognize that it would, in general, be desirable to allow such undertakings to develop with as much freedom as possible, consistent with the targets and objectives of the national plan. When there exist in the same industry both privately and publicly owned units, it would continue to be the policy of the State to give fair and nondiscriminatory treatment to both of them.

12. The division of industries into separate categories does not imply that they are being placed in water-tight compartments. Inevitably, there will not only be an area of overlapping but also a great deal of dovetailing between industries in the private and the public sectors. It will be open to the State to start any industry not included in Schedule-A and Schedule-B when the needs of planning so require or there are other important reasons for it. In appropriate cases, privately owned units may be permitted to produce an item falling within Schedule-A for meeting their own requirements or as

byproducts. There will be ordinarily no bar to small privately owned units undertaking production, such as the making of launches and other lightcraft, generation for power for local needs and small-scale mining. Further, heavy industries in the public sector may obtain some of their requirements of lighter components from the private sector, while the private sector in turn would rely for many of its needs on the public sector. The same principle would apply with even greater force to the relationship between large-scale and small-scale industries.

13. The Government of India would, in this context, stress the role of cottage and village and small-scale industries in the development of the national economy. In relation to some of the problems that need urgent solutions, they offer some distinct advantages. They provide immediate large-scale employment; they offer a method of ensuring a more equitable distribution of the national income and they facilitate an effective mobilization of resources of capital and skill which might otherwise remain unutilized. Some of the problems that unplanned urbanization tends to create will be avoided by the establishment of small centers of industrial production all over the country.

14. The State has been following a policy of supporting cottage and village and small-scale industries by restricting the volume of production in the large-scale sector, by differential taxation, or by direct subsidies. While such measures will continue to be taken, whenever necessary, the aim of the State Policy will be to ensure that the decentralized sector acquires sufficient vitality to be self-supporting and its development is integrated with that of large-scale industry. The State will, therefore, concentrate on measures designed to improve the competitive strength of the small-scale producer.

For this it is essential that the technique of production should be constantly improved and modernized, the pace of transformation being regulated so as to avoid, as far as possible, technological unemployment. Lack of technical and financial assistance, of suitable working accommodation and inadequacy of facilities for repair and maintenance are among the serious handicaps of small-scale producers. A start has been made with the establishment of industrial estates and rural community workshops to make good these deficiencies. The extension of rural electrification, and the availability of power at prices which the workers can afford will also be of considerable help. Many of the activities relating to small-scale production will be greatly helped by the organization of industrial cooperatives. Such cooperatives should be encouraged in every way and the State should give constant attention to the development of cottage and village and small-scale industry.

15. In order that industrialization may benefit the economy of the country as a whole, it is important that disparities in levels of development between different regions should be progressively reduced. The lack of industries in different parts of the country is very often determined by factors such as the availability of the necessary raw material and other natural resources. A concentration of industries in certain areas has also been due to the ready availability of power, water supply and transport facilities which has been developed there. It is one of the aims of national planning to ensure that these facilities are steadily made available to areas which are at present lagging behind industrially or where there is greater need for providing opportunities for employment provided the location is otherwise suitable. Only by securing a balanced and coordinated development, of the industrial and the agricultural economy in each region, can the entire country attain higher standards of living.

16. This program of industrial development will make large demand on the country's resources of technical and managerial personnel. To meet these rapidly growing needs for the expansion of the public sector and for the development of the village and small-scale industries, proper managerial and technical cadres in the public services are being established. Steps are also being taken to meet shortages at supervisory levels, to organize apprenticeship schemes of training on a large scale both in public and in private enterprises, and to extend training facilities in business management in universities and other institutions.
17. It is necessary that proper amenities and incentives should be provided for all those engaged in industry. The living and working conditions of workers should be improved and their standards of efficiency raised. The maintenance of industrial peace is one of the prime requisites of industrial progress. In a socialist democracy, labour is a partner in the common task of development and should participate with enthusiasm. Some laws governing industrial relations have been enacted and a broad common approach has developed with growing recognition of the obligations of both management and labour. There should be joint consultation and workers and technicians should wherever possible, be associated progressively in management. Enterprises in the public sector have to set an example in this respect.
18. With the growing participation of the State in industry and trade, the manner in which these activities should be conducted and managed assumes considerable importance. Speedy decisions and a willingness to assume responsibility are essential if these enterprises are to succeed. For this wherever possible, there should be decentralization of authority and their management should be along business lines. It is to be expected that

public enterprises will augment the revenues of the State and provide resources for further development in fresh fields. But such enterprises may sometimes incur losses. Public enterprises have to be judged by their total results and in their working they should have the largest possible measure of freedom.

19. The Industrial Policy Resolution of 1948 deals with a number of other subjects which have since been covered by suitable legislation or by authoritative statement of policy. The division of responsibility between Central Government and the State Governments in regard to industries has been set out in the Industries (Development and Regulation) Act. The Prime Minister, in his statement in Parliament on 6 April, 1949, has enunciated the policy of the State in regard to foreign capital. It is, therefore, not necessary to deal with these subjects in this resolution.
20. The Government of India trust that this statement of their Industrial Policy will receive the support of all sections of the people and promote the rapid industrialization of the country.

Schedule A

1. Arms and ammunition and allied items of defense equipment.
2. Atomic energy.
3. Iron and Steel.
4. Heavy castings and forgings of iron and steel.
5. Heavy plant and machinery required for iron and steel production, for mining, for machine tool manufacture and for such other basic industries as may be specified by the Central Government.
6. Heavy electrical plant including large hydraulic and steam turbines.

7. Coal and lignite.
8. Mineral oils.
9. Mining of iron ore, manganese ore, chrome-ore, gypsum, sulphur, gold and diamond.
10. Mining and processing of copper, lead, zinc, tin, molybdenum and wolfram.
11. Minerals specified in the Schedule to the Atomic Energy (Control of Production and Use) Order, 1953.
12. Aircraft.
13. Air Transport.
14. Railway Transport.
15. Ship Building.
16. Telephones and telephone cables, telegraph and wireless apparatus (excluding radio receiving sets).
17. Generation and distribution of electricity.

Schedule B

1. All other minerals except minor minerals as defined in Section 3 of the Minerals Concession Rules, 1949.
2. Aluminum and other non-ferrous metals not included in Schedule A.
3. Machine tools.
4. Ferro alloys and tool steels.
5. Basic and intermediate products required by chemical industries such as the manufacture of drugs, dye-stuffs and plastics.
6. Antibiotics and other essential drugs.
7. Fertilizers.
8. Synthetic rubber.
9. Carbonization of coal.
10. Chemical pulp.
11. Road transport.
12. Sea transport.

Appendix 4

Statement Made by The Prime Minister in The Constituent Assembly of India (Legislative) 6 April 1949[1]

The policy as regards participation of foreign capital has already been announced in broad terms in Government's resolution of the 6th April 1948. The stress on the need to regulate, in the national interest, the scope and manner of foreign capital arose from past association of foreign capital and control with foreign domination of the economy of the country. But circumstances today are quite different. The object of our regulation should therefore be the utilization of foreign capital in a manner most advantageous to the country. Indian capital needs to be supplemented by foreign capital not only because our national savings will not be enough for the rapid development of the country on the scale we wish, but also because in many cases scientific, technical and industrial knowledge and capital equipment can best be secured along with foreign capital.

In this context, foreign investors would no doubt wish to have some clear indication of our policy on certain matters, like the repatriation of capital, the remittance of profits, and the treatment of foreign enterprise vis-a-vis Indian enterprise. I propose to make the policy of Government quite clear in this matter.

In the first place, I would like to state that Government would expect all undertakings, Indian or foreign, to conform to the general requirements of their industrial policy. As regards existing foreign interests, Government do not intend to place any restrictions or impose any conditions which are not applicable to similar Indian enterprise. Government would also so frame their policy as to enable further foreign capital to be invested in India on terms and conditions that are mutually advantageous.

Secondly, foreign interests would be permitted to earn profits, subject only to regulations common to all. We do not foresee any difficulty in continuing the existing facilities for remittance of profits, and Government have no intention to place any restriction on withdrawal of foreign capital investments, but remittance facilities would naturally depend on foreign exchange considerations. If, however, any foreign concerns come to be compulsorily acquired, Government would provide reasonable facilities for the remittance of proceeds.

Thirdly, if and when foreign enterprises are compulsorily acquired, compensation will be paid on a fair and equitable basis as already announced in Government's statement of policy. Government have stated before that, as a rule, the major interest in ownership and effective control of an undertaking should be in Indian hands. They have also stated that power will be taken to deal with exceptional cases in a manner calculated to serve the national interest. Obviously there can be no hard and fast rule in this matter. Government will not object to foreign capital having control of a concern for a limited period, if it is found to be in the national interest and each individual case will be dealt with on its merits. In the matter of employment of personnel, Government would not object to the employment of non-Indians in posts requiring technical skill and experience, when Indians of requisite qualifications are not available, but they attach vital importance to the training and employment of Indians even for such posts in the quickest possible manner.

I should like to add a few words about British interests in India which naturally form the largest part of foreign investments in India. Although it is the policy of the Government of India to encourage the growth of Indian industry and commerce (including such services like Banking, Shipping and Insurance) to the best of their ability, there is and will still be considerable scope for the investment of British capital in India. These considerations will apply equally to other existing non-Indian interests. The Government of India have no desire to injure in any way British or other non-Indian interests in India and would gladly welcome their contribution in a constructive and cooperative role in the development of India's economy.

Notes

1. Introduction

1 Harrison 1960.
2 Nehru 1946, 397.
3 Bhagwati and Desai 1970.
4 Bauer 1961.
5 See the section titled 'Law and Judiciary' in Chapter 13.
6 See the section titled 'Law and Judiciary' in Chapter 13.

2. Nehru: From Radical to Fabian Socialist

1 For example, Mohan 1975 (p. 184) observes, 'Notwithstanding this upbringing, during his days at Eton and Cambridge, he exposed himself to new ideas—especially those of socialism, and of Fabian Socialism in particular.' Similarly, Abadi 1993 (p. 13) notes, 'Nehru's interest in socialism began in his college days in England where he imbibed Fabian socialist ideas.' In a more recent contribution, Menon 2022 (p. 33) also traces the Fabian origins of Nehru's socialism to his days in London as a law student.
2 Nehru 1936a, 25.
3 Gopal 1976, 24.
4 Gopal 1976, 24.
5 Morris died in 1896. Details on his life and numerous contributions can be found in McCarthy 1994.
6 Gopal 1976, 27.
7 See the concluding paragraph in Gopal 1976 on p.? 34.

8 Gopal 1976, 109.
9 Gopal 1972, 222.
10 Nayar 1972, 113, footnote 88.
11 As quoted in Gopal 1976, 156,
12 Nehru 1934, 25.
13 Nehru 1934, 24. Nehru later combined the three articles into a single pamphlet titled *Whither India*, reproduced under the same title in Nehru 1934, pp. 1–24.
14 In a long story on an interview Nehru gave to some visiting foreign delegates in mid-December 1933, the *Free Press Journal* had accused Nehru of having expressed a clear preference for fascism over communism. Sharply reacting to this story, Nehru issued a press release in which he denounced the *Journal*, pointing out that the report was so full of errors that it could not be corrected. 'But one thing I wish to clear up and that is my attitude to Fascism and Communism. I do believe that fundamentally the choice before the world today is one between some form of Communism and some form of Fascism, and I am all for the former, that is Communism. . . . There is no middle road between Fascism and Communism. One has to choose between the two and I choose the Communist ideal.' (Nehru 1934, pp. 125–6).
15 By this time, the British government was sufficiently alarmed by Nehru's views that a 1934 pamphlet circulated by the United Provinces government described him as 'the high priest of communism'. See Gopal 1976, 188.
16 Nehru 1936b.
17 Nehru 1936b.
18 Nehru 1936b.
19 For a detailed discussion of the battle between Nehru and the industrialists, see Chandra 1975. Narrating the impact of the Lucknow address on the Bombay business community, Gopal writes, 'such unhesitant exposition of his intellectual and emotional commitment to the socialist ideal

naturally roused resentment. Bombay was the heart of "big business" and there were reactive tremors to "the storm of communism" that was passing over the city. Twenty-one leading businessmen issued a manifesto condemning Jawaharlal's "destructive and subversive program" which, according to them, would create disorders and impede the achievement of self-government'. (Gopal 1976, 211).

20 The election manifesto of the Congress, primarily drafted by Nehru, had rejected the Government of India Act of 1935. For Nehru, the only reason to send Congressmen to the legislatures was to seek an end to this act. He was opposed to Congress members forming governments after election victories. However, once they had won the elections, attracted by prospects of holding ministerial positions, almost all of them changed their tune and proceeded to form governments. Unfortunately for Nehru, Gandhi put his seal of approval on these governments. As a loyal member of the Congress, Nehru went along and did not express his disapproval publicly at any point in time. For further details, see Gopal 1976, chapters 14–15, especially pp. 214–31.

21 Mishra 2014, 1.

22 Mishra 2014, 1–2.

23 As reproduced in the text, the quotation is from Nehru 1946, 396. Nehru does not provide the source of the quotation, but its first sentence is also quoted in Lockwood 2011, who attributes it to the resolution of the Industries Ministers' Conference. Planning Commission 1997 provides a compilation of the contributions of Subhas Chandra Bose to Indian planning. This document also includes the address Bose delivered at the Industries Ministers' Conference in Delhi on 2 October 1938 and the transcript of a question-and-answer session between Bose and Professor Meghnad Saha on 31 August 1938. In reply to one of the questions by Saha in this session, Bose explicitly mentions the need for a

national planning commission after achieving freedom. To quote him, 'I have no doubt that when we have a national government for the whole country, one of the first things we shall have to do is to appoint a National Planning Commission for the whole country' (Planning Commission 1997, 72).

24 In a letter dated 19 October 1938, Bose wrote to Nehru, 'I hope you will accept the Chairmanship of the Planning Committee. You must if it is to be a success.' See Planning Commission 1997, 86.
25 Nehru 1946, 395.
26 Chakrabarty 1992, 282.
27 Nehru 1946, 395.
28 Nehru 1946, 396.
29 See details in Nehru 1946, pp. 401-2.
30 Gopal 1976, pp. 247-8.
31 Two jail terms separated by eight months from 5 December 1941 to 8 August 1942 took up most of his days between 30 October 1940 and 15 June 1945.
32 Choudhary 1987, 35.
33 Nehru 1958a, 107, unnumbered footnote.
34 Nehru 1958a, 109.
35 Nehru 1958a, 126.
36 Nehru 1958a, pp. 140–1.
37 *Times of India* 1948a (8 April), 5.
38 Choudhary 1987, 34-35.
39 Nehru 1958a, 116.
40 Nehru 1958a, pp. 116-7.
41 The four members were: Purshotamdas Thakurdas, A.D. Shroff, Walchand Hirachand and Ambalal Sarabhai.
42 Nehru 1946, pp. 399-400.
43 Nehru 1946, 400.
44 Times of India 1948a, 5.
45 Kidron 1965, 83.
46 Kidron 1965, pp. 83–84.

47 Gill 1959, 223.
48 Frankel 2004, 165.
49 This account is from Gopal 1976, pp. 110–12.
50 Like the previous one, this account, including the quotation from Gandhi's letter, is based on Gopal 1976, pp. 208–09.

3. The Nehru Development Model

1 The Mahalanobis Model, named after its author Prasanta Chandra Mahalanobis and familiar to all serious students of Indian economic planning, is essentially a formalization of Nehru's core ideas. At Nehru's urging, Mahalanobis had authored the Draft Plan frame for the Second Five-Year Plan, the precursor to the actual Second Five-Year Plan. It is this plan that implemented in earnest Nehru's vision for the Indian economy. Mahalanobis has brought together some of the early history of formulating this plan, his formal model and broader features of the proposed framework in a long paper (Mahalanobis 1955, 3–130) published in the journal *Sankhya*, which he had founded in 1933.
2 Illustrative of his constant evolution is this statement in the preface to *The Discovery of India* (Nehru 1946, 10): 'I do not know how other authors feel about their writings, but always I have a strange sensation when I read something that I had written some time previously. . . . I recognize it of course, but not wholly; it seems almost that I was reading some familiar piece written by another, who was near to me and yet who was different. Perhaps that is the measure of the change that has taken place in me.' As we will see below, Nehru's ideas on socialism also underwent a dramatic change before Independence but not subsequently.
3 Panagariya 2008, Ch 1-3.
4 Nehru was not unaware of the human cost the Soviet Union had paid. Nor did he approve of its coercion of its citizenry. Thus, for example, while referring to the Soviet experience

in his Presidential Address to the Congress at its Lucknow session in 1936b, he had stated, 'Much has happened there which has pained me greatly and with which I disagree, but I look upon that great and fascinating unfolding of a new order and a new civilization as the most promising feature of our dismal age.' He probably thought that with some modification, it would be possible to accomplish what the Soviet Union had accomplished without human sacrifice and resorting to coercive methods.

5 Nehru 1946, 400.

6 Nehru 1934, 6.

7 Nehru 1934, 20.

8 Nehru 1946, 397.

9 Nehru 1946, 397.

10 Nehru 1946, 397–8.

11 Planning Commission 1952, 8, paragraph 4. India's fiscal year begins on 1 April and ends on 31 March.

12 Nehru 1964, pp. 137–8.

13 To quote him directly, 'Capitalism has led to imperialism and to the conflicts of imperialist powers in search for colonial areas for exploitation, for areas of raw produce and for markets for manufactured goods. It has led to ever-increasing conflicts with the rising nationalism of colonial countries, and to social conflicts with powerful movements of the exploited working class.' (Nehru 1934, 15).

14 Nehru 1934, pp. 8–9.

15 Nehru 1946, 398.

16 Nehru 1958b, 18.

17 Nehru 1958b, 19.

18 Nehru 1946, 397.

19 Nehru 1958b, pp. 17–18.

20 By way of clarification, I may note that serious discussions on development strategy officially began only when formulating the Second Five-Year Plan. Planners had not devoted enough time to such discussions at the time of the

launch of the First Five-Year Plan, which spanned 1951–52 to 1955–56—the first two years of this plan had already elapsed when the formal plan document was approved. The plan was a collection of projects under implementation, launched in prior years.

21 Nehru 1946, 406.
22 Nehru 1946, 407.
23 Nehru 1946, pp. 407–8.
24 Nehru 1946, 408.
25 I have taken the quote from Nayar 1972, pp. 127-8, who translated it from Hindi to English.
26 Nehru 1958b, 24.
27 Nehru 1958b, pp. 87–8.
28 Nehru 1964, 136.
29 Nehru 1958b, 41.
30 Nehru 1958b, pp. 41–2.
31 Nehru 1958b, 40.
32 Nehru 1946, pp. 402–9.
33 Nehru 1946, 406.
34 For instance, he opened his speech at the All-India Congress Committee on 4 January 1957, thus, 'Planning essentially consists in balancing: the balancing between industry and agriculture, the balancing between heavy industry and light industry, the balancing between cottage industry and other industry. If one of them goes wrong then the whole economy is upset.' (Nehru 1958b, 51.)
35 Nehru 1954, 84.
36 Nehru 1954, 84. Nehru again highlighted the small industry as a source of employment in his speech at the Associated Chamber of Commerce in Calcutta on 14 December 1953. He noted, 'Looked at from the point of view of nineteenth century economics, we could well . . . go on developing industrially, accumulating reserves for investment and the like, but at a cost in human terms which no government can possibly face today. Take a simple fact. I speak subject

to correction as to figures, but I believe that even now there are far more people employed in the handloom and hand-weaving industry in India than in all the organized industries. Are we to ignore these millions simply because of some economic theory? An autocratic or authoritarian government might do it; it might enforce its will at a terrific cost. But no democratic government will do it.' [Nehru 1958b, 62.]

37 Nehru 1958b, pp. 51–2.

38 Referring to a media interview by Gandhi, Nehru wrote, 'He seemed to think that this [zamindari] was a very desirable part of rural and national economy. This was a great surprise to me for the big zamindaris and taluqas have very few defenders today. All over the world they have been broken up, and even in India most people recognize that they cannot last long.' (Nehru 1936a, pp. 477–8) Later in the autobiography, he revisited the issue stating, 'It hardly seems a matter for argument that this semi-feudal system is out of date and is a great hindrance to production and general progress. It conflicts even with a developing capitalism, and almost all over the world large landed estates have gradually vanished and given place to peasant proprietors.' (Nehru 1936a, pp. 534–5)

39 The quote is from Nehru 1946, 396.

40 Nehru 1954, 89.

41 Nehru 1958b, 11.

42 Nehru 1958b, 100.

43 Nehru 1964, pp. 136–7.

44 Nehru 1954, 87.

45 Panagariya 2008, chapter 2.

46 Britain had owed India a substantial sum in pound sterling accumulated on account of its balance-of-payments surpluses during the Second World War. These sterling balances were available to India for imports from countries willing to accept pound sterling in payment.

47 For a detailed discussion of the points in this paragraph, see Frankel 2005, 190-96.
48 The discussion of the community development programme up to this point relies on Desai 1958.
49 Neale 1985, pp. 677–8.
50 Nehru 1958b, 23.
51 Nehru 1958b, 25.
52 Neale 1985, 690.
53 Gill 1959, 223.

4. Other Contemporary Influential Voices

1 An exception was economist Milton Friedman, who pointed to the folly of prioritizing the development of heavy industries over light industries. But unlike most of the other foreign experts who the Indian establishment had invited, he had been sent by the United States government. As such, the chances that the Indian government would accept his advice were nil.
2 Although the First Five-Year Plan began on 1 April 1951, the plan document was completed towards the end of 1952, with the Parliament considering it on 8 December 1952. As Bhagwati and Desai put it, the plan was 'very much a collection of many *overhead* projects' (Bhagwati and Desai 1970, 233). At the beginning of 1951–52, the Planning Commission was still taking shape. Even the first general election for the Parliament was concluded in February 1952.
3 I have taken the biographical details of Mahalanobis from Mahalanobis 1955 and Mahalanobis 1961. For a more detailed sketch of Mahalanobis and his contributions to Indian planning, see Menon 2022.
4 Mahalanobis 1961, 3, paragraph 13.
5 Mahalanobis 1955. This paper also provides the contemporary history of the developments surrounding the Draft Plan-frame in addition to reproducing the Draft

Plan-Frame, the memorandum by the Panel of Economists in full, and excerpts from the working paper. The working paper, entitled 'The Second Five Year Plan—A Tentative Framework,' covered much the same ground as the Draft Plan-frame and was prepared alongside it under the guidance of Mahalanobis by economists at the Ministry of Finance, the Planning Commission and the Indian Statistical Institute.

6 Mahalanobis 1955, 51.
7 Feldman 1928, 1929.
8 Mahalanobis 1953, 309.
9 The Mahalanobis Model generated considerable academic interest among economists. A recent book by Ghate, Gopalakrishnan and Grover 2022 brings some of these contributions together with a numerically solvable computation element added to each of them.
10 Mahalanobis 1955, 28.
11 Mahalanobis 1955, 29. The 11 per cent rate, to be achieved by the end of the Second Five-Year Plan, corresponded to the average investment rate in the United Kingdom during 1870–1913.
12 Mahalanobis 1955, 19.
13 Mahalanobis 1955, 51.
14 Mahalanobis 1955, pp. 51–2.
15 Mahalanobis 1955, 52–3.
16 Mahalanobis 1955, 53.
17 Mahalanobis 1955, 53.
18 Mahalanobis 1955, 53.
19 Mahalanobis 1955, 55.
20 The states and union territories were: Gujarat, Maharashtra, Delhi, Uttar Pradesh, Madhya Pradesh, Tamil Nadu (Madras at the time), West Bengal and Kerala.
21 Later, the Planning Commission brought together these papers; some others by Government of India bodies such as the Reserve Bank of India, CSO and Economic Division of the Planning Commission; the Draft Plan-frame and an

associated background paper; memorandum by the Panel of Economists and the dissent note by Shenoy in a 650-page-long document (Planning Commission 1955).

22 The memorandum can be found in its entirety in Planning Commission 1955, pp. 1–18 and Mahalanobis 1955, pp. 112–130.

23 Mahalanobis 1955, 111.

24 Mahalanobis 1955, 8.

25 Planning Commission 1955, 1. Going by this collection by the Planning Commission, panel members and their associates submitted thirty-three papers, while economists from various arms of the Government of India submitted another ten.

26 Planning Commission 1955, 3.

27 Planning Commission 1955, 4.

28 Planning Commission 1955, 4.

29 Planning Commission 1955, 4.

30 Planning Commission 1955, 4. Rs 200 crore (Rs 2 billion) is the approximate annual financing through money creation recommended by the Draft Plan-frame.

31 Planning Commission 1955, 6.

32 Planning Commission 1955, 12.

33 Planning Commission 1955, 12.

34 Planning Commission 1955, 13.

35 Planning Commission 1955, 14. The reference here is to the Industries (Development and Regulation) Act of 1951, which provided for licensing industrial units with investment above a relatively low threshold in many industries.

36 Planning Commission 1955, 15.

37 Planning Commission 1955, 15.

38 Planning Commission 1955, 16.

39 Planning Commission 1955, 17.

40 Planning Commission 1955, 18.

41 Planning Commission 1955, 18.

42 These lectures were later published in book form as *Prices and Production*.

43 In a 2003 interview, Shenoy's daughter, Sudha Shenoy (Shenoy 2003, pp. 1–2), describes her father's conversion to the Austrian School of Economics thus: 'My father, B.R. Shenoy, was a graduate student at the London School of Economics in January 1931 when F.A. Hayek delivered his lectures on prices and production. My father said that Hayek still had a thick Viennese accent at the time. . . . My father couldn't really follow because of the accent, but he could tell that there was something there. After studying the Austrian theory, he said that he was immunized against every other framework.'
44 According to Sudha Shenoy (Shenoy 2003, 2), 'Nehru got very upset' by the dissent note filed by her father.
45 Shenoy 1955a, pp. 21–32.
46 Planning Commission 1955, 22.
47 Planning Commission 1955, 25.
48 Chapter 8 of Part VI (pp. 483–98) in Planning Commission 1955.
49 Shenoy 1955b, pp. 488–9.
50 Shenoy 1955b, 489.
51 Shenoy 1955a, 29.
52 Shenoy 1955a, 30.
53 Shenoy 1955a, 30.
54 Shenoy 1955a, 31.
55 Panagariya 2021.
56 I use the Bombay School of Economics to refer to economists C.N. Vakil, R. Brahmananda, and their followers. In particular, I exclude from this school panel members M.L. Dantwala and D.T. Lakdawala, who also served on the Bombay School of Economics faculty but did not oppose the basic strategy of the Draft Plan-frame.
57 Vakil and Brahmananda 1955a.
58 Vakil and Brahmananda 1956. Ghate et al. 2022, Ch. 7 provide a numerically computable dynamic version of this model.

59 Vakil and Brahmananda 1955a, 142.
60 Vakil and Brahmananda 1955a, 145
61 Vakil and Brahmananda 1955a, 145.
62 Vakil and Brahmananda 1955a, 146.
63 Vakil and Brahmananda 1955b.
64 Vakil and Brahmananda 1955b, 529.
65 Vakil and Brahmadanda 1955b, 529.
66 Krishnamurthi 1955, 574.
67 Krishnamurthi 1955, 575.
68 Krishnamurthi 1955, 575.
69 Mahalanobis 1955, 7.
70 Friedman 2000, 1.
71 I have discussed some of the points in the text in Panagariya 2001 earlier.
72 Friedman 1955.
73 Friedman 1955, pp. 29–30.
74 Bhagwati and Desai 1970, chapters 15 and 16. In the book, there is no indication that the authors had seen the memorandum by Milton Friedman.
75 To quote Lockwood 2011, pp. 624–25, 'In the interwar period, the economic interests of the Indian bourgeoisie were repeatedly confronted with a political obstacle in the shape of the British state. If economic interests were to be pursued from this point, the political obstacle has to be removed. A political strategy was therefore economically necessary. This began with attempts to pressure the existing state for reforms but developed into the demand for a new (Indian national) state. In this way, the hard-headed pursuit of profit led to nationalist politics.'
76 Purshotamdas Thakurdas et al. 1945. There were eight authors of the document; the other seven were J.R.D. Tata, G.D. Birla, Ardeshir Dalal, Shri Ram, Kasturbhai Lalbhai, A.D. Shroff and John Mathai. Two of the eight authors, Purshotamdas Thakurdas and A.D. Shroff, were also members of the National Planning Committee of the

Congress. John Mathai was an economist who served as India's Minister of Railways from 15 August 1947 to 22 September 1948 and the Minister of Finance from 22 September 1948 to 1 June 1950.

77 Purshotamdas Thakurdas et al 1945, 66.

78 Purshotamdas Thakurdas et al. 1945, 65. The reader may note the close resemblance between this discussion of poverty reduction as the objective and growth as a key instrument and the discussions in the National Planning Committee along similar lines described in the previous chapter.

79 Purshotamdas Thakurdas et al. 1945, pp. 9–10.

80 Purshotamdas Thakurdas et al. 1945, 90.

81 Purshotamdas Thakurdas et al. 1945, 10.

82 Purshotamdas Thakurdas et al. 1945, 10. Later, the plan reiterated these points stating, 'It is an essential part of our plan for the organization of industries that adequate scope should be provided for small-scale and cottage industries along with large-scale industries. This is important not merely as a means of affording employment but also of reducing the need for capital, particularly of external capital, in the early stages of the plan.' (Purshotamdas Thakurdas et al. 1945, pp. 48–49)

83 Purshotamdas Thakurdas et al. 1945, 32.

84 Purshotamdas Thakurdas et al. 1945, 66.

85 Purshotamdas Thakurdas et al. 1945, 68.

86 Purshotamdas Thakurdas et al. 1945, 90.

87 Purshotamdas Thakurdas et al. 1945, 94.

88 Purshotamdas Thakurdas et al. 1945, 94.

89 Frankel 2005, 129.

90 *Times of India* 1955a (23 July).

91 *Times of India* 1956a (11 February).

92 Shroff 1956, 8.

93 Nayar 1972, pp. 149–50 (see, especially, footnote 161 on p. 150).

94 See the main page of the forum's website at https://indianliberals.in/periodicals/forum-of-free-enterprise/,

(accessed 12 October 2023) which also provides articles by many of its [forum's] contributors in pdf.

95 Masani 1961, 1.

96 Masani 1961, 2.

97 Shroff 1956, pp. 4–5.

98 Shroff 1956, pp. 10–11.

99 Later, close to the mid-1960s, he did question and criticize the more basic features of the model, such as the centrality of heavy industries to the neglect of light industries and autarkic trade policies. However, by then, it was too little too late. Moreover, his most trenchant critique (Shenoy 1964, 467–74) was published in an obscure American journal. While interesting from a history of thought viewpoint, it is unlikely that it reached many Indian readers then.

100 Nayar 1972, 150.

5. Industrial and Labour Policies

1 One important exception is a former bureaucrat, Sharad Marathe, who, in his book (Marathe 1989), provides not only its detailed discussion but also reproduces the original document in an appendix. Because this book is out of print, I have reproduced SIP 1945 from it in Appendix 1 of the present volume.

2 Statement of Industrial Policy 1945, paragraph 4, Appendix 1 of this volume.

3 Statement of Industrial Policy 1945, paragraph 5, Appendix 1 of this volume.

4 Statement of Industrial Policy 1945, paragraph 11, Appendix 1 of this volume.

5 Statement of Industrial Policy 1945, paragraph 12, Appendix 1 of this volume.

6 Statement of Industrial Policy 1945, paragraph 13, Appendix 1 of this volume.

7 Soon after the Statement of Industrial Policy of 1945 was released, critics charged that it had been influenced by the London industrialists and the secretary of state for India, L.S. Amery. These charges led Dalal to publicly state that the proposals made by the government in the statement 'were thought out by me alone' (*Times of India* 1945a, 7).

8 The members included Maulana Abul Kalam Azad, Jayaprakash Narayan, N.G. Ranga, Gulzari Lal Nanda, J.C. Kumarappa, Achyut Patwardhan and Shankarrao Deo. Later, the committee also co-opted John Mathai as a member.

9 Given the difficulty of accessing the full text of IPR 1948, which I experienced, I have reproduced it in Appendix 2. While I have taken it from *Fiscal Commission 1949–50* (Government of India 1950a, pp. 410–16), it can also be found in the now out-of-print book Hazari 1986, pp. 119–26.

10 IPR 1948, which appears as Appendix 2.

11 IPR 1948, which appears as Appendix 2.

12 IPR 1948, which appears as Appendix 2.

13 IPR 1948, which appears as Appendix 2

14 I reproduce IPR 1956 and associated schedules A and B in Appendix 3 for ready reference. I take the main text of the resolution from https://dpiit.gov.in/sites/default/files/chap001%20%2013.pdf and the schedules from Marathe 1989, pp. 323-4.

15 IPR 1956, which is reproduced as Appendix 3.

16 IPR 1956, which is reproduced as Appendix 3.

17 IPR 1956, which is reproduced as Appendix 3.

18 As quoted in Marathe 1989, 67. Marathe also provides a more detailed history of the bill, originally titled the Industries (Development and Control) Bill of 1949. It was at the behest of a select committee that the word 'regulation' replaced 'control' (Marathe 1989, 68).

19 According to Marathe 1989, 82, 'The original First Schedule to the act was fairly broad with categorization

such as "Iron and Steel and products thereof". The schedule was drastically revised in 1956 and, to a lesser extent, by subsequent amendments in 1962, 1973, and 1979. The result of these amendments was twofold. First, certain categories of industrial activity were added to the schedule. Second, and more important, the description of industrial activity was given much more detail.'

20 Marathe, 1989.
21 Marathe 1989, pp. 86–87.
22 Hazari 1967, 11, paragraph 14.7.
23 Indian National Congress 1954, 8.
24 For example, see Panagariya 2020, pp. 97–102.
25 Lewis 1962, 226.
26 Lewis 1962, 226.

6. Implementation: Target-Setting and Industrial Licensing

1 Government reports covering various aspects of the system as it operated include Government of India 1964, 1965a to 1965c, 1966b, 1967 and 1969. Relevant parliamentary committee reports include Lok Sabha 1967, 1968 and 1972.
2 Beginning on 1 January 2015, the NITI Aayog replaced the Planning Commission. This was done in recognition that with the abolition of investment and import licensing, prices now guided the allocation of investment and the flow of imports. Therefore, the relevant institution had to focus on guidance on policy rather than the allocation of investment through five-year plans.
3 The July 1951 date is noted in the Introduction to the First Five-Year Plan, while 15 December 1952 is the date of Nehru's speech (Nehru 1954, pp. 80–91) when presenting the plan to the Parliament.
4 Nehru 1954, 89.
5 Government of India 1952, paragraph 2 in the Introduction.

6 Nehru 1954, 80.
7 Nehru 1954, 88.
8 Government of India 1952, paragraph 7 in chapter 29.
9 Government of India 1952, paragraph 25 of chapter 29.
10 Mahalanobis had to make certain assumptions to convert the four-sector allocations derived from the model into six-sector allocations reported in the Draft Plan-frame. For details, see Mahalanobis 1955, chapter 4, especially paragraph 32 to 35. In the table associated with this paragraph, Mahalanobis compares the allocations derived from his four-sector model and those included in the Draft Plan-frame.
11 Komiya 1959. In the words of Bhagwati and Desai (p. 237), 'as Komiya pointedly noted, the Mahalanobis solution was inefficient, in that it was situated in the interior of the feasibility locus between incremental output and incremental employment.'
12 In his formal model, Mahalanobis had confined himself to allocating the total economy-wide investment. In the Draft Plan-frame, he divided this total investment into its public and private components and allocated each to six different sectors. These six sectors can be collapsed into four to make his public-sector allocations comparable to those in the final plan. When this is done, only the allocations to agriculture, irrigation and power match between the Draft Plan-frame and the final plan. The allocation to industry is significantly smaller, and to transport and communication significantly larger in the latter than in the former. A similar comparison between private sector allocations is not possible due to differences in classifications of sectors in the Draft Plan-frame and the final plan.
13 Bhagwati and Desai 1970, 240.
14 Government of India 1969, paragraph 6.13, 104.
15 See Government of India 1969, Table II, 105.
16 Government of India 1969, paragraph 6.14, 104.

17 Government of India 1969, the second half of Table II titled 'Schedule B,' 106.

18 Government of India 1969, paragraph 6.17, 107.

19 Immediately following the Second World War, the DGTD was created as the Development Wing of the Directorate General of Industries and Supply within the Ministry of Industry and Supply. Its principal objective was to coordinate industrial development in the country. In 1951, the Development Wing became a separate office under the Ministry of Commerce and Industry and retained that status till early November 1962. Then, in mid-November 1962, it was redesigned and redesignated as DGTD and placed under the Ministry of Economic and Defence Coordination. Subsequently, it was moved to the Ministry of Supply and Technical Development and Materials Planning. For further details, see Lok Sabha 1972, 1.

20 Lok Sabha 1972, paragraph 2.2, 7.

21 *Times of India* 1952b (4 June).

22 For details on this point, see Panagariya 2008, chapter 2, especially pp. 34–40.

23 For instance, as early as May 1953, with rare exceptions, the government rejected applications for installing additional looms [*Times of India* 1953f, 5 (27 May)].

24 Shroff 1956, pp. 4–5.

25 Marathe 1989, 51. These numbers should be viewed as indicative of the trend. As R.K. Hazari pointed out in his interim report (Hazari 1966, pp. 13–14, especially paragraphs 11.2 to 11.6), available records on the number of applications and approvals suffer numerous deficiencies and limitations.

26 Marathe 1989, 84.

27 According to the Hazari report (Government of India 1967, 11, paragraph 14.9), procedures for considering licence proposals from state and local governments and public-sector corporations were different from those

applying to private-sector undertakings. Many of the large investment proposals by these entities did not go to the Licensing Committee, the key authority in charge of licence applications submitted by private-sector entities.

28 Government of India 1969, 35, paragraphs 3.54 and 3.55.

29 Government of India 1966b, paragraph 1, 41.

30 Government of India 1966b, 42.

31 Government of India 1966b, 43.

32 Government of India 1966b, 43. The Dutt committee later echoed this indictment of the registration process by the Mathur study team (see Government of India 1969, 36).

33 Government of India 1967, 11, paragraph 14.8.

34 Government of India 1967, 11, paragraph 14.11.

35 Government of India 1964, Annexure II, paragraph 5, 8.

36 Unless otherwise noted, the discussion of licensing procedures in this section is based on Government of India 1969 (Dutt Committee), pp. 29–31. Occasionally, I also draw on Lok Sabha 1967 (chapter III), which provides some details not available in the Dutt Committee report.

37 See Government of India 1969, paragraph 3.75, 40 and Lok Sabha 1967, paragraph 3.2, 133.

38 The committee was set up on 5 September 1952 by the Ministry of Commerce and Industry (Lok Sabha 1967, paragraph 3.13, 137) following the notification of the rules and regulations relating to IDRA 1951.

39 For further details, see Lok Sabha 1967, paragraph 3.4, 134.

40 *Times of India* 1952c (19 November).

41 For further historical details, see Lok Sabha 1972, 1 and the Government of India 1969, pp. 40–41.

42 Government of India 1965c, 4.

43 Government of India 1965c, pp. 4–5.

44 Bhagwati and Desai 1970, pp. 252–72.

45 Lok Sabha 1967, 136.

46 Government of India 1967, paragraph 13.2, 8.

47 Lok Sabha 1967, 154.
48 Lok Sabha 1967, paragraph 7.18, 248.
49 Some of these harmful effects of the controls were documented in a report authored by economist K.N. Raj in his report on steel industries. See Government of India 1963.

7. A Liberal Import Regime: 1882–1956

1 Chaudhuri 1983, 868.
2 Government of India 2020, paragraphs 1.2.9 and 1.2.10, 8.
3 Chaudhuri 1983, 868.
4 Government of India 2020, paragraphs 1.5.3 and 1.6.1, 13.
5 Wagle 1981, pp. 123–4 and footnote 21 on 124.
6 Government of India 2020, Paragraphs 1.7.10, 1.7.11 and 1.8.4, pp. 15–19.
7 Chaudhuri 1983, 866.
8 Chaudhuri 1983, 869.
9 *Times of India* 1940a (13 January).
10 This section draws heavily on Reserve Bank of India 1970, chapter 12.
11 Canada, Newfoundland and Hong Kong were excluded because they had closer financial and trading relations with countries other than the United Kingdom.
12 Reserve Bank of India 1997, 595.
13 *Times of India* 1939a (11 September).
14 *Times of India* 1939b (27 November).
15 Reserve Bank of India 1970, pp. 365–66.
16 *Times of India* 1940b (22 May).
17 *Times of India* 1940c (25 October).
18 *Times of India* 1940d (28 December).
19 *Times of India* 1941a (10 May)
20 *Times of India* 1941b (22 July).
21 Bhagwati and Desai 1970, 2811.

22 *Times of India* 1942a (11 May) and *Times of India* 1942b (10 August).

23 *Times of India* 1943a (24 July).

24 *Times of India* 1946a (16 May), 1946b (30 May), 1946c (20 June) and 1946d (17 July).

25 *Times of India* 1946b (30 July).

26 *Times of India* 1949a (27 February), 7.

27 For completeness, I may note that around the same time, *Fiscal Commission 1949–50* took a more positive view of protection. Concluding its assessment of protection provided during interwar years, it noted, 'It is our view that if world factors had been more favorable, and the policy of protection had been more broadly conceived and liberally implemented in a constitutional atmosphere more in harmony with national aspirations, the gaps in Industrial set-up would have been perhaps fewer. As it is, the policy of protection has enabled a few big industries like steel, sugar, paper, cotton textiles and matches to establish themselves firmly' (Government of India 1950a, 85). Luckily, the commission report had minimal effect on the import policy.

28 Reserve Bank of India 1997, 597.

29 For a detailed history of these negotiations, see Reserve Bank of India 1997, pp. 595–607.

30 My account of trade policy during 1945–47 draws heavily on the Reserve Bank of India 1970, pp. 643–9.

31 B.K. Nehru, who served as a Joint Secretary in the Ministry of Finance during 1947–49, details the circumstances leading to the introduction of foreign exchange budgeting in his autobiography (Nehru 1997, 214). According to Lok Sabha 1968 (paragraph 9.2, 250), the first foreign-exchange budget covered the shipping period July–December 1947. However, the practice was discontinued in 1953 due to the improved foreign-exchange situation. A report in the *Times*

of India (1950a) (1 July) testifies to the existence of the budget for the July–December 1950 period.

32 *Times of India* 1948b (24 January).

33 *Times of India* 1948c (4 July), 1948d (4 September) and 1948e (15 September).

34 *Times of India* 1949b (27 February) and 1949c (27 August).

35 *Times of India* 1950b (2 March).

36 *Times of India* 1950c (15 June).

37 *Times of India* 1950d (4 July).

38 A long write-up in the *Times of India* 1950e (24 October) provides a detailed account of the committee's recommendations.

39 *Times of India* 1951a 5 (January).

40 *Times of India* 1951b (13 March).

41 See *Times of India* 1951c (29 December) for import policy in the first half of 1952 and *Times of India* 1952a (18 June) for that in the second half.

42 *Times of India* 1953a. The government had constituted the Import Advisory Council on 27 September 1948. It consisted of representatives of government departments, including industry and commerce, and members of the Legislative Assembly (Reserve Bank of India 1970, 649).

43 *Times of India* 1953b (25 June).

44 *Times of India* 1953d (1 December).

45 *Times of India* 1953d (29 November).

46 *Times of India* 1953e (31 December).

47 *Times of India* 1954a (30 June).

48 *Times of India* 1954b (12 September).

49 *Times of India* 1954c (31 December).

50 *Times of India* 195a (30 June).

51 See *Times of India* 1956b (1 January) for January–June policy and *Times of India* 1956c (1 July) for July–December policy.

52 *Times of India* 1956d (1 June).

8. A Highly Restrictive Import Regime: 1957–1964

1 B. K. Nehru 1997, 279.

2 *Times of India* 1956e (30 December, 11).

3 The timing of the reintroduction of foreign-exchange budgeting, which would be central to the trade regime turning autarkic in the subsequent three decades, is recorded in Lok Sabha 1968, paragraph 9.15, 258. B.K. Nehru, who had returned to the finance ministry in 1954, describes the decision to bring back foreign-exchange budgeting in these words (Nehru 1997, 279), 'Once again, I had to take the initiative and re-establish the whole control mechanism through the foreign exchange budget that I had invented nine years earlier.'

4 *Times of India* 1956f (30 December, 1).

5 *Times of India* 1956e (30 December, 1).

6 Media reports suggest that the year of the foreign-exchange budget was simultaneously aligned with the financial year. For example, *Times of India* 1958a and 1958b refer to the foreign-exchange budget for the period April–September 1958, which corresponds to the first half of the fiscal year 1957–58.

7 *Times of India* 1957a (30 June).

8 *Times of India* 1957b (1 October).

9 Times of India 1957c (2 October).

10 *Times of India* 1958a (1 April).

11 See Tables 142 of RBI Handbook of Statistics on Indian Economy, 2010 at https://rbi.org.in/Scripts/AnnualPublications.aspx? head=Handbook+of+Statistics+on+Indian+Economy.

12 *Times of India* 1958h (1 November).

13 *Times of India* 1959b (1 April).

14 *Times of India* 1959c (1 October).

15 Details of import policies in 1960–61 can be found in *Times of India* 1960a (1 April) and 1960b (2 October) and those

of the policies in 1961–62 in *Times of India* 1961c (2 April) and 1961d (1 October).

16 *Times of India* 1962a (20 March).

17 *Times of India* 1962b (1 April) and 1962c (1 April).

18 *Times of India* 1962d (4 April).

19 *Times of India* 1962e (26 December).

20 *Times of India* 1963a (23 April).

21 *Times of India* 1957d (22 August) and 1958c (21 March).

22 Shenoy 1958.

23 *Times of India* 1958d (25 June).

24 *Times of India* 1958e.

25 Shroff 1958, 4.

26 Shroff 1958, 4.

27 In this context, see the detailed analysis of the 1966 devaluation in Bhagwati and Srinivasan 1975, chapters 5–11.

28 The discussion of the import licensing and foreign-exchange-allocation regimes below is based on two excellent reports by the study team headed by H.C. Mathur (the Mathur study team), each issued in two parts. The first of these reports focuses on the licensing regime (Government of India 1965a and 1965b) and the second on the foreign-exchange-allocation regime (Government of India 1965c and 1966b). Additional relevant details are available in Lok Sabha 1968.

29 Bhagwati 1962 provides a comprehensive list of the types of import licences during this time. In Table I, he also reports the dollar value of each licence category from the first half of the calendar year 1951 to the first half of the financial year 1960–61. The data show a sharply declining share of established importer licences reflecting the tightening of imports of consumer goods items.

30 Government of India 1965a, paragraph 42, pp. 32–33.

31 A comprehensive list of industries in category (b) and corresponding sponsoring authorities can be found in Government of India 1965a, Appendix VII, pp. 103–04.

There are twenty-one industries and nineteen sponsoring authorities on this list.

32 Government of India 1965a, paragraphs 67 and 68, pp. 41–42.

33 Government of India 1965a, paragraphs 3–6, pp. 13–15.

34 This last fact is based on the list of authorities responsible for foreign-exchange allocation for private-sector imports of different products and users in the last column of Appendix III in Government of India 1965c, pp. 90–91.

35 Government of India 1965a, 51.

36 Government of India 1965a, paragraph 1, 49.

37 Government of India 1965a, paragraph 4, 50.

38 Government of India 1965b, paragraph 1, 4.

39 Government of India 1965b, paragraph 6, 6.

40 Government of India 1965b, paragraph 2, 4.

41 Government of India 1965b, paragraph 3, 5.

42 Government of India 1965b, paragraph 5, pp. 5–6.

43 Government of India 1965b, paragraph 30, 16.

44 Government of India 1965b, paragraph 5, pp. 18–19.

45 Government of India 1965b, paragraph 7, 20.

46 Government of India 1965b, paragraph 12, 24.

47 Government of India 1965b, paragraph 19, 26.

48 Lok Sabha 1968, paragraph 9.7, pp. 252–53.

49 Therefore, four months of the relevant six-month period would have already passed before the DEA made these allocations. It took several more months before the import licences were granted, and the undertakings could affect imports. This fact meant that they had to maintain sufficient inventories from allocations in the previous periods to carry on their production activities in the interim.

50 These allocations are described in Bhagwati and Desai 1970, 284. The allocation to the Economic Adviser, Ministry of Industry is discussed in detail in Government of India 1965c, paragraph 4, 12. Implicitly, this report also discusses the direct allocation to the Iron and Steel controller in paragraph 6 on 13. Finally, the report notes the allocation to administrative ministries by the DEA in paragraph 1, 56.

51 Lok Sabha 1968, 253 states, 'Imports of capital equipment are normally allowed only against some foreign loans/ credits, though a few exceptions have been made here and there.' Government of India 1965c, paragraph 3, 45, notes four sources of foreign exchange for capital goods imports by private-sector undertakings: financial collaboration with a foreign party, foreign loan, government credit and free exchange.
52 Government of India 1965c, paragraph 3–4, pp. 11–12.
53 Government of India 1965c, paragraph 4, 12. For a full list of recipients of these distributions from the Economic Adviser, Industry Ministry, see Appendix III, pp. 90–91 of this report.
54 The second and third steps are described in greater detail in Government of India 1965c, 19 (paragraph 19) and 21–22 (paragraph 24), respectively.
55 See Government of India 1965c, 6 (paragraph 7). On page 4 (paragraph 1), the report further notes that the development and assistant development officers in the directorates were all engineers or technical personnel.
56 Government of India 1965a, paragraph 2, 26.
57 Lok Sabha 1968, paragraph 9.18, 260.
58 Readers interested in more details are encouraged to consult chapters 15 and 16 in Bhagwati and Desai.
59 Lok Sabha 1968, paragraph 9.10, pp. 256–7.
60 Lok Sabha 1968, paragraph 10, 257.
61 Government of India 1965c paragraph 4, 12.
62 For full details, see Bhagwati and Desai 1970, pp. 287–93.
63 Government of India 1965c, paragraph 22, 109.
64 Government of India 1965a, paragraph 2, 13.
65 Government of Indi 1965a, paragraph 23(ii), 22.
66 Government of India 1965a, paragraph 4, 14.
67 Government of India 1965a, paragraph 4, 50.
68 Government of India 1965a, paragraph 5, pp. i–ii.
69 Government of India 1965c, paragraph 2, 26 and Government of India 1965a, paragraph 54, 36.

70 Case studies on licences for raw materials and components by other applicants, such as the SSI undertakings and non-SSI undertakings in industries listed in Schedule I of IDRA 1951 and belonging to sponsoring authorities other than the DGTD can be found in Appendix IV of Government of India 1965a, pp. 86-90.
71 See Government of India 1965a, Appendix V, 91–98 for these estimates and additional details.
72 Government of India 1965b, paragraph 7, 6.
73 Government of India 1965b, paragraph-8, 6.
74 Government of India 1965b, paragraph 13, 7.

9. Export and Foreign Investment Policies

1 Singh 1964 and Bhagwati and Desai 1970.
2 When devaluation did come in June 1966, as Bhagwati and Desai correctly point out, its timing turned out to be ill-fated, for its positive impact was drowned in massive negative impact wrought by two back-to-back droughts around the same time.
3 Government of India 1949, 16.
4 *Times of India* 1940f (12 August) and 1940g (3 December).
5 *Times of India* 1944a (3 July).
6 *Times of India* 1943a (24 July).
7 Government of India 1949, 16.
8 *Times of India* 1946e (23 April) and 1946f (30 July).
9 Government of India 1949, i.
10 Government of India 1949, 8.
11 Government of India 1949, 8.
12 Government of India 1949, 8–9.
13 Government of India 1949, 9.
14 Government of India 1949, 11.
15 Government of India 1949, 12.
16 Government of India 1949, 16.

17 Government of India 1949, pp. 16–17.
18 Bhagwati and Desai 1970, 368.
19 Bhagwati and Desai 1970, 378.
20 For example, at a conference on the promotion of exports organized by the Federation of Indian Chambers of Commerce and Industry on 29 January 1959, the Minister for Commerce and Industry, Lal Bahadur Shastri, went so far as to say that if the situation warranted, the Government of India might take the 'extreme step' of compelling manufacturers to export certain proportion of their output (*Times of India* 1959a (30 January)). Two years later, on 29 March 1961, the Minister of Finance Morarji Desai said at a conference that increased exports were vital to the country's economy and that industrialists and producers should share the responsibility with the government (*Times of India* 1961a (29 March)). Earlier, the *Economic Survey 1957–58* of the Government of India (pp. 15–16, paragraphs 35–36) had underlined the need for export expansion, stating, 'Every effort will have to be made to promote exports; the sacrifice this involves in terms of domestic consumption is the price which has inevitably to be paid.' Media articles underlining the importance of exports around this time include the *Times of India* 1957f (26 April), Times of India 1958f (8 February), Verghese (1958 and 1960), and Shenoy (1959).
21 *Times of India* 1958f (8 February).
22 Shenoy 1959. Less than a year earlier, Verghese (1958) had arrived at almost an identical conclusion stating, 'Despite such promotional measures as have been adopted during the past few years, export earnings have by and large been stagnant around Rs. 600 crores.'
23 Bhagwati and Desai 1970, Table 18.2, 371.
24 The list of export-promotion measures in 1962–63 in the text is taken entirely from the *Economic Survey 1962–63* of the Government of India, 41, paragraphs 116–18.

25 *Economic Survey 1963–64* of the Government of India, 34, paragraph 73.
26 Bhagwati and Desai 1970, 406.
27 Bhagwati and Desai, Table 18.1, 370.
28 I reproduce the text of the statement in Appendix 4 in this volume. It is taken from *the Fiscal Commission 1949–50* (Government of India 1950a, pp. 417–18). Parts of the statement are also quoted in the *Times of India* 1949d (7 April) and Kidron 1965, 101.
29 See the 'Neo-Swadeshism' section in Kidron 1965, pp. 103–10.
30 Kidron 1965, 102.
31 Government of India 1950b, 9.
32 Government of India 1950b, pp. 9–10.
33 Kidron 1965, 102.
34 *Times of India* 1957g (21 September).
35 *Times of India* 1958g (10 February).
36 Kidron 1965, pp. 158–59.
37 *Times of India* 1961b.

10. Growth, Industrialization and Poverty

1 As reported in Nayyar 2006, Sivasubramonian 2000 places the growth rate of national income in India from 1900–01 to 1946–47 at 1.03 per cent and that in per-capita income over the same period at 0.24 per cent.
2 Singh 1964. In particular, see Section E, Chapter III on jute, Section D of Chapter IV, and Section A of Chapter V.
3 Based on the figures in the table on p. 11 of *Economic Survey 1958–59*, Government of India.
4 Based on the table on 12 in *Economic Survey 1960–61*, Government of India.
5 Lok Sabha 1968, paragraph 8.19, 241.
6 Niranjan Ramakrishnan 2005.
7 Lok Sabha 1990, 43.

8 Datt 1998.
9 Kwan S. Kim 1991, 55 (footnote 57).
10 Specifically, see Panagariya 2008, chapters 1–3.
11 Friedman 1955, 23.
12 All data in this paragraph are from Singh 1964, Table V.1, 74.
13 Bhagwati and Desai 1970, 388.
14 Bauer 1961, pp. 51–52.
15 Shenoy provided concrete examples of the high domestic production costs relative to those abroad in import-competing products. To quote him, 'The landed cost of imported penicillin is 2 cents per million units, while the estimated cost of production in India is 26 cents per million units. The import of refrigerator is banned. The cost of refrigerator in India is $473. The cost of a comparable refrigerator in England is about $190' (Shenoy 1964, 471). Recall that the presence of large import premiums noted earlier on the authority of Bhagwati and Desai in Table 8 points in the same direction.

11. The Political Leadership I: 1950–84

1 The account of Masani speech from Lok Sabha Secretariat 1963a, pp 1281–305.
2 Nehru's quotes in the text that follows are from his speech in Lok Sabha Secretariat 1963b, pp. 2191–221.
3 Lok Sabha Secretariat 1963a, 1288.
4 Lok Sabha Secretariat 1963b, 1917.
5 Frankel 2005, pp. 246–92.
6 Patel 2002, 98.
7 Patel 2002, 108.
8 Frankel 2005, 247.
9 Shastri 1974, 3.
10 Shastri 1974, 15.
11 Shastri 1974, 67.

12 Shastri 1974, 67.
13 Shastri 1974, 68.
14 Shastri 1974, 68.
15 For a detailed discussion of political and economic developments during the Shastri era, see Frankel 2005, pp. 246–92.
16 Shastri 1974, 88.
17 For food import figures in this paragraph, see Panagariya 2008, Table 3.3, 72.
18 Patel 2002, 107–08.
19 This account is based on Frankel 2005, 298.
20 Frankel 2005, 299.
21 See Frankel 2005, 288–90, for a detailed discussion of the thinking among Syndicate members.
22 Frankel 2005, 397–433, provides a detailed account of the struggle for power between IG and the Syndicate, the critical role played by the Young Turks in it and the evolution of CFSA.
23 The first quotation is on p. 435, and the second is on p. 434 in Guha 2007.
24 Kaviraj 1986, 1697.
25 Patel 2002, 110.
26 Frankel 2005, 289–90.
27 This description is due to T.N. Kaul, who had served as India's ambassador to the Soviet Union in the 1960s. According to Kaul, IG rejected his suggestion of B.K. Nehru as a possible replacement for Jha for the same reason. For details, Jairam Ramesh 2018, 126.
28 Patel 2002, 107.
29 Ramesh 2018, 52.
30 Haksar joined IG's office on 6 May 1967 (Ramesh 2018, 133). The Congress Working Committee approved the Ten Point Programme at the initiative of the party high command, with the All India Congress Committee adopting it at its session on 23 June 1967 (Frankel 2005, 397–98).

According to Frankel (p. 398), 'The Ten-Point Program, apart from the proposal to remove privileges enjoyed by ex-rulers, did no more than reiterate longstanding policies of the Congress party.' The proposal for the removal of princely privileges had come from Atulya Ghosh, a member of the Syndicate, in a note dated 12 May 1967 (Frankel 2005, 397). Given this timeline and process, Haksar had no chance to influence the Ten Point Programme.

31 The account of the Industrial Policy Statement of 1977 in the following paragraph is based entirely on *Times of India* 1977a, 1 and 15 [24 December].

32 *Time* 1977.

33 Lal 1978, p. 8.

34 Frankel 2005, 580.

35 The discussion of the 1980 industrial policy statement below is based on *Times of India* 1980a, 1 and 8 [24 July].

36 For details, see Panagariya 2008, pp. 82–3 and 85–89.

37 Kohli 1989, 308.

38 Manor 1988, pp. 71–91.

39 Panagariya 2008, 81.

40 Jha 1982.

12. The Political Leadership II: 1985–2023

1 Jain 1985.

2 Bhagwati 1993, 79.

3 Gandhi 1987.

4 Gandhi 1987, 6.

5 Gandhi 1987, 260.

6 Gandhi 1987, 206–07.

7 Gandhi 1987, 131.

8 Gandhi 1987, 94.

9 Gandhi 1987, 95.

10 Gandhi 1987, 96.

11 Gandhi 1987, 96.

12 Gandhi 1987, 97.
13 Gandhi 1987, 97.
14 Gandhi 1987, 98.
15 Gandhi 1987, 99.
16 Gandhi 1987, 101.
17 Gandhi 1987, 101.
18 Kohli 1989, 313.
19 *Times of India* 1985a (5 May).
20 *Times of India* 1986a [6 March].
21 Jha 1986 [*TOI* 5 March].
22 Gandhi 1989, 205.
23 Gandhi 1989, 155.
24 Gandhi 1989, 202.
25 Gandhi 1989,173.
26 Gandhi 1989, 181.
27 *Times of India* 1990a [2 June].
28 Economist Rakesh Mohan, who had been actively involved in drafting this policy, offers a more detailed and, at one point, comical account of how the implementation of the policy met its demise (Mohan 2017, 21–22).
29 I discuss the policy in Panagariya 2008, pp. 99–100, and reproduce the full document in Appendix 1, pp. 455–59 of the same book. For a newspaper account of the policy, see *Times of India* 1990b [2 June].
30 Jairam Ramesh, who worked on an earlier draft of the new industrial policy, had recommended including an exit policy. But Rao removed this provision from the final version of the policy, possibly to avoid political backlash. Similarly, Ramesh and Rakesh Mohan had wanted to see the list of items reserved for small-scale enterprises trimmed but were unsuccessful in persuading Rao. See Ramesh 2015, chapter 15.
31 Ramesh 2015, chapters 6–16.
32 Ramesh 2015, 90. Ramesh bases this description on the authority of A.N. Verma, who had attended the meeting as the prime minister's principal secretary.

33 The episode is described in detail in C.G. Somiah 2010. Somiah had served as the member secretary of the Planning Commission when this incident occurred.

34 In a nutshell, this is Rao's portrait that emerges from Vinay Sitapati's biography.

35 For details, see Ramesh 2015, chapter 15.

36 Reservations among industrialists along these lines continued to be expressed till later. In mid-1993, a group of industrialists led by Rahul Bajaj submitted a five-page memorandum to the finance minister in which it welcomed industrial liberalization but voiced concern regarding opening the door to foreign investors and import-duty cuts. 'The phrase made popular by this group . . . was "level playing field", which came to be seen as a euphemism for protection from foreign competition. The club actually met only once formally and submitted a five-page memorandum to the finance minister' (Ramesh 2015, 103, footnote 64).

37 As a staff member of the World Bank during 1989–93, I have first-hand knowledge that after the first year, the institution had no leverage over Indian policy. In March 1993, I was part of a World Bank loan mission that sought the liberalization of consumer goods imports by India as a condition of the proposed loan. The government categorically refused to oblige the mission. Yet, the loan was advanced. Already, the World Bank needed India more than India needed it.

38 Sitapati 2015, 49.

39 Sitapati 2015, 59.

40 Ramesh 2015, 137.

41 Sitapati 2015, 45.

42 Ramesh 2015, 138.

43 I have not had access to this paper. As such, in describing its relevant contents, I have relied on a long quote from the paper in Ramesh 2015, chapter 21.

44 Ramesh 2015, pp. 138–39.

45 Sitapati 2015, 60.
46 Sitapati 2015, 67.
47 Rao did have prior inputs from at least two sources: an eight-page note prepared by bureaucrats of the outgoing government and shared by Cabinet Secretary Naresh Chandra on 20 June and discussions at a meeting attended by a select group of individuals, including MMS on 21 June.
48 Rao 1993, 3.
49 Rao 1993, 4.
50 Rao 1993, 169.
51 Rao 1993, 169.
52 Rao 1993, 158.
53 Rao 1993, 158.
54 Rao 1993, 160.
55 Lok Sabha Secretariat 1991, 411.
56 Rao 1993, 160.
57 Rao 1993, 161.
58 Rao 1993, 162.
59 Rao 1993, 163.
60 Rao 1993, 164.
61 Rao 1993, 165.
62 This speech can be found in the appendix of Baru 2016, 163–97.
63 The quotes in this paragraph are from paragraph 31 of the appendix in Baru 2016, 176–77.
64 Ramesh 2015, 137.

13. Institutions and the Business Community

1 I base the account below on Government of India 1969, 3–4, paragraphs 1.01–1.03.
2 Planning Commission 1964, paragraph 73, 54–5.
3 Government of India 1965d, i.
4 Government of India 1965d, 7.
5 Government of India 1965d, 8.
6 Hazari 1966, paragraph 9.2,7.

7 Tooley 2009.
8 This section is based primarily on the very detailed discussion of the role of the Planning Commission spread throughout the text in Frankel 2005.
9 Frankel 2005, 86.
10 Frankel 2005, 113.
11 Frankel 2005, 114.
12 Frankel 2004, 145.
13 Frankel 2005, 250.
14 Frankel 2005, 252.
15 As quoted in Frankel 2005, 310.
16 Somiah 2010, 117–18.
17 Somiah 2010, 118.
18 Somiah 2010, 118.
19 This discussion is based on a conversation between the author and a family member of the judge.
20 Sanyal 2006, 9. The final Supreme Court judgment on the case 'Bharat Forge Co. Ltd vs Uttam Manohar Nakate on 18 January, 2005' can be found at https://indiankanoon.org/doc/763806/ (accessed on 5 June 2023).
21 Mehta 1994, as quoted in Datta Chaudhuri 1996.
22 Sarkar 2017, 205.
23 Frankel 2005, 129.
24 *Times of India* 1955a (23 July).
25 *Times of India* 1962f (26 March).
26 *Times of India* 1962g (6 May).
27 *Times of India* 1963b (18 March).
28 *Times of India* 1963c (25 September).
29 *Times of India* 1964 (17 August).
30 Frankel 2005, 269–71.
31 *Times of India* 1966a (15 March).
32 *Times of India* 1966b (17 April).
33 *Times of India* 1966c (27 April).
34 This account of the encounter between Tata and the industry minister is based entirely on the *Times of India* 1966d (15 October).

35 *Times of India* 1970a (15 March).
36 *Times of India* 1972 (6 March).
37 *Times of India* 1974 (23 December).
38 *Times of India* 1977b (5 October).
39 *Times of India* 1978 (2 December) and 1979 (27 December).
40 *Times of India* 1980b (20 January).
41 *Times of India* 1982 (15 December).
42 *Times of India* 1983 (3 April).
43 *Times of India* 1984 (9 April).
44 *Times of India* 1985b (17 March).
45 *Times of India* 1990c (28 August).

14. Economists and Other Policy Analysts

1 Friedman 2000, 1. Interestingly, Mahalanobis does acknowledge the debt to a large number of distinguished foreign economists who visited India during the preparation of his Draft Plan-frame (Mahalanobis 1955, 7, paragraph 17), but the article makes no mention of Friedman anywhere.
2 Bauer 1961, Shenoy 1968 and Bhagwati and Desai 1970.
3 Lokanathan 1962, 195–58.
4 Another contemporary review of Bauer's book by the United States-based Indian economist Subbiah Kannappan (Kannappan 1962, 249–50) was more sympathetic but reached the same conclusion. To wit, 'It is thus not enough to build a case against Indian planning; it is indispensable to develop an alternative' and 'Thus, despite substantial agreement with Bauer's analysis of the drawbacks in Indian planning, the reviewer must reject his conclusions, . . .'
5 Bhagwati 1969, 636.
6 The reviews include Alagh 1971, Bagchi 1971, Desai 1971, Medhora 1971, Singh 1972 and Swamy 1972. In the following text, I briefly reference only three of these six reviews.
7 Alagh 1971, 1681.

8 Medhora 1971, 1690.
9 Singh 1972, 414.
10 Singh 1972, 415.
11 Singh 1972, 417.
12 Khusro 1984, 12.
13 Khusro 1984, 10.
14 In passing, I also mention here the work of the committee on steel control chaired by eminent economist K.N. Raj. The committee provided useful suggestions for rationalizing a convoluted system of pricing and distribution in steel. Nevertheless, the recommendations still amounted to replacing one administrative system with another and relying on the good intentions of the bureaucracy and other actors involved in the distribution chain.
15 Planning Commission 1964, 54–55.
16 Government of India 1965d, 6–7.
17 Government of India 1965d, 8.
18 Government of India 1965d, chapters 7 and 9.
19 Hazari 1966, 6 (paragraph 9.2, especially the table in this paragraph).
20 Hazari 1967, 25, paragraph 29.1.
21 Government of India 1969, 184 (paragraph 8.08).
22 Government of India 1969, 188–89 (paragraphs 8.22–8.26).
23 Patel 1987, 2017–18.
24 The quote in the text is from a summary of the report on the Associated Cement Companies for the year ending 31 July 1969 by its chairman Palkhivala, as reproduced in the *Times of India* 1970b [22 January].
25 The quote is from Sau 1972, 1572. As it later turned out, this was a false claim. In fact, Mao struggled to achieve rapid growth by extracting surplus from agriculture in the countryside for investment in urban-based industries. But the effort backfired, with millions of Chinese losing their lives without significant growth or reduction in poverty.

Had Mao succeeded, Deng Xiaoping would not have had to make a U-turn on his policies to accelerate growth beginning in the late 1970s.

26 The quote is from Ranidev 1973, 834.
27 The evolution of the fifth plan, as described in this paragraph, can be found in the *Economic and Political Weekly* 1976, pp. 1641–42.
28 Bimal Jalan 1972.
29 Bhagwati and Panagariya 2013.
30 Government of India 1984.
31 This paragraph is based on Center for Civil Society, undated,3; *Economic Survey 1987-88*, Ministry of Finance, Government of India, paragraphs 5.28 and 5.29, pp. 48-9; *Economic Survey 1988-89*, Ministry of Finance, Government of India, paragraph 5.46,67; and correspondence with Vijay Kelkar.
32 In 1975, they had jointly authored the first major book on India's trade policy as a part of the major NBER project on foreign trade regimes and economic development (Bhagwati and Srinivasan 1975).
33 Sen 1982, 4.
34 Sen 1982, 6.
35 Sen 1982, 6.
36 Sen 1982, 6.
37 Devaki Jain, Ashok Mitra et al. 1983, 3.
38 Sau 1983, 235.
39 See, in particular, Sau 1972, 1577, where he says, 'The very process of India's independence from the British rule and the subsequent parliamentary democracy have thrown the petty bourgeoisie (lower-middle-class) and rich peasantry into the citadel of political power.... The numerical strength coupled with a balancing act between the workers and peasants on the one hand and the big bourgeoisie and remnants of feudalism on the other facilitates the continuation of their power.'
40 Tata 1991.

41 Jalan 1991, 11.
42 Lal 1992.
43 Bhagwati 1993.
44 Bhagwati 1993, Desai 1993 and Joshi and Little 1994 and 1996.
45 Panagariya 1994, 221.
46 Drèze and Sen 1996, vii.
47 Bhagwati 1998, 198.
48 Bhagwati 1998,199.
49 See Khatkhate 2006, Panagariya 2004a; and Bhagwati and Panagariya 2013 for refutations of the first, second and third claims.
50 Drèze and Sen 2013 and Bhagwati and Panagariya 2013.
51 Rajadhyaksha 2013.

15. An Afterthought

1 Patel 1948, 50.
2 Patel, 1948, 51.
3 Patel 2017, 94–95.
4 Patel 2017, 95.
5 Patel 2017, 95–96.
6 Patel 2017, 97–98 for the longer quote in this paragraph and p. 98 for the shorter one.
7 Patel 2017, 99.
8 Patel 2017, 99.
9 Patel 2017, 108.
10 Patel 2017, 113.
11 Patel 2017, 121.
12 Patel 2017, 121.
13 Patel 2017, 122.
14 For example, in the speech entitled 'The Economic Situation', delivered on 11 November 1949, Patel stated, 'With our incomes shrinking and the prospect of further shrinkage, unless we stage a quick recovery, we must cut down our expenditure in order to balance our budget.' (Patel 2017, 106–07).

15 Frankel 2005, 85. I have deleted a footnote referencing p. 11 of the Draft Outline of the first plan as the source of the quotes within this quote.
16 Frankel 2005, 86. I have deleted a footnote referencing p. 152 of the Draft Outline of the first plan as the source of the quote within this quote.

Appendix 1: Statement of Industrial Policy, April, 1945

1 This statement is reproduced (with permission) from Marathe 1989, 308–22, Appendix I.

Appendix 2: Government of India Resolution on Industrial Policy, 6 April 1948

1 This statement is reproduced from Government of India 1950a, 410–16, Appendix III.

Appendix 3: Industrial Policy Resolution, 30 April 1956

1 The text of this statement is reproduced from https://dpiit.gov.in/sites/default/files/chap001%20%2013.pdf and Schedules A and B (with permission) from Marathe 1989, pp. 323–24.

Appendix 4: Statement Made by the Prime Minister in the Constituent Assembly of India (Legislative), 6 April 1949

1 This statement is reproduced from Government of India 1950a, 417–18, Appendix IV.

References

Abadi, Jacob, 1993. 'India's Economic Policy Since Nehru: The Failure of Democratic Socialism and the March Toward Free Trade,' *Journal of Third World Studies* 10(2), pp. 12–35.

Alagh, Yogendra K., 1971. 'Indian Industrialization: Fact and Fiction', *Economic and Political Weekly* 6(30/32), Special Number, July, pp. 1677–79 and 1681–82.

Bagchi, Amiya, 1971. 'The Theory of Efficient Neocolonialism', *Economic and Political Weekly* 6(30/32), Special Number, July, pp 1669–71 and 1673–76.

Baru, Sanjaya, 2016. *1991: How P.V. Narasimha Rao Made History*, New Delhi: Aleph Book Company.

Bauer, P.T., 1961. *Indian Economic Policy and Development*, London: George Allen and Unwin Ltd.

Bhagwati, Jagdish. 1962. 'Indian Balance of Payments Policy and Exchange Auctions,' *Oxford Economic Papers*, New Series, Vol. 14, No. 1, pp. 51–68.

Bhagwati, Jagdish, 1969. '*Indian Economic Policy*. by B.R. Shenoy; *The Crisis of Indian Planning. Economic Policy in the 1960's*. by P. Streeten and M. Lipton,' *The Economic Journal* 79(315), pp. 634–39.

Bhagwati, Jagdish, 1993. *India in Transition: Freeing the Economy*, Oxford: Clarendon Press.

Bhagwati, Jagdish, 1998. 'Reviews: *India's Economic Reforms: 1991–2001*. By Joshi (Vijay) and Little (I.M.D.) and *India: Economic Development and Social Opportunity*. By Drèze (Jean) and Sen (Amartya),' *Economic Journal* 108, January, pp. 196–200.

Bhagwati, Jagdish and Padma Desai. 1970. *India: Planning for Industrialization*, London: Oxford University Press.

Bhagwati, Jagdish and Arvind Panagariya, 2013. *Why Growth Matters: How Economic Growth in India Reduced Poverty and the Lessons for Other Developing Countries*, New York: Public Affairs.

Bhagwati, Jagdish and T.N. Srinivasan, 1975. *Foreign Trade Regimes and Economic Development: India*, New York: National Bureau of Economic Research.

Center for Civil Society, undated, 'The Decontrol of Drug Prices in India: Implications for the Indian Pharma Industry,' available at https://ccs.in/sites/default/files/2022-10/Drudgery%20of%20Drug%20Price%20Controls%20Who%20Benefits%20.pdf (accessed 23 June 2023).

Chakrabarty, Bidyut, 1992. Jawaharlal Nehru and Planning, 1938-41: India at the Crossroads. *Modern Asian Studies* 26(2), 275–87.

Chandra, Bipan, 1975. 'Jawaharlal Nehru and the Capitalist Class, 1936,' *Economic and Political Weekly* 10(33–35), Special Number, pp. 1307–24.

Chaudhuri, K.N., 1983. 'Foreign Trade and Balance of Payments (1757–1947).' In Dharma Kumar, ed., *The Cambridge Economic History of India, Volume 2*: c. 1757 – c. 1970, Cambridge: Cambridge University Press.

Choudhary, Valmiki (ed.), 1987. *Dr. Rajendra Prasad: Correspondence and Selected Documents*, Volume 8, New Delhi: Allied Publishers Private Limited.

Datt, Gaurav, 1998. 'Poverty in India and Indian States: An Update,' FCND Discussion Paper No. 47, International Food Policy Research Institute, July. Available at: file:///Users/arvindpanagariya/Downloads/Poverty_in_India_and_Indian_states%20(1).pdf (accessed 29 July 2023).

Datta Chaudhuri, Mrinal (1996). 'Labor Markets as Social Institutions in India,' IRIS-India Working Paper No. 10, Center on the Institutional Reform and Informal Sector, University of Maryland at College Park.

Desai, A.R. 1958, 'Community Development Projects—A Sociological Analysis,' *Sociological Bulletin* 7(2), pp. 152–66.

Desai, Ashok, 1993. *My Economic Affair*, New Delhi: Wiley Eastern Limited.

Desai, V.V., 1971. 'Neglect of Implications of Self-Sufficiency Goal,' *Economic and Political Weekly* 6(30/32), Special Number, July, pp. 1683 and 1685–86.

Drèze, Jean and Amartya Sen, 1996. *India: Economic Development and Social Opportunity*, Oxford and New York: Clarendon Press.

Drèze, Jean, and Amartya Sen. 2013. *An Uncertain Glory: India and Its Contradictions*, Princeton, NJ: Princeton University Press.

Economic and Political Weekly, 1976. 'Story the Cuts Tell,' Volume 11, No. 42, 16 October, pp. 1641–42.

Feldman, Grigory Alexandrovich, 1928. 'On the Theory of Growth Rates of National Income'. *Planovoe Khozyaistvo*, No. 11.

Feldman, Grigory Alexandrovich, 1929. 'An Analytical Method for Constructive Perspective Plans'. *Planovoe Khozyaistvo*, No 12.

Frank, Katherine, 2011. *Indira: The Life of Indira Gandhi*, New Delhi: HarperCollins, p. 162.

Frankel, Francine, 2005. *India's Political Economy 1947–2004: The Gradual Revolution*, New Delhi: Oxford University Press.

Friedman, Milton, 1955. 'A Memorandum to the Government of India.' In Parth Shah, ed., *Milton Friedman on India*, 2000, New Delhi: Center for Civil Society, pp. 21–33. https://ccs.in/download.php?file=sites/all/books/com_books/friedman-on-india.pdf (accessed 23 February 2022).

Friedman, Milton, 2000. 'Preface.' In Parth Shah, ed., *Milton Friedman on India*, 2000, New Delhi: Center for Civil Society, pp. 1–2. https://ccs.in/download.php?file=sites/

all/books/com_books/friedman-on-india.pdf (accessed 23 February 2022).

Gandhi, Rajiv, 1987. *Rajiv Gandhi: Selected Speeches and Writings*, Volume I, 31 October 1984 to 31 December 1985, Government of India: Publications Division, Ministry of Information and Broadcasting. [All page numbers in the text are from the 1991 deluxe edition.]

Gandhi, Rajiv, 1989. *Rajiv Gandhi: Selected Speeches and Writings*, Volume III, 1st January 1987—31 December 1987, Government of India: Publications Division, Ministry of Information and Broadcasting. [All page numbers in the text are from the April 1992 deluxe edition.]

Ghate, Chetan, Pawan Gopalakrishnan and Srishti Grover, 2022. *The Mahalanobis Model: A Macrodynamics Approach*, Singapore: Springer.

Gill, K.S., 1959. 'The Nagpur Resolution,' *The Economic Weekly*, Annual Number, January, pp. 223–28.

Gopal, Sarvepalli (Editor), 1972. *Selected Works of Jawaharlal Nehru*, Volume Three, New Delhi: Orient Longman.

Gopal, Sarvepalli, 1976. *Jawaharlal Nehru: A Biography*, Volume One, 1889–1947, Bombay: Oxford University Press.

Government of India, 1948. 'Government of India Resolution on Industrial Policy, 6 April, 1948.' In Hazari, R.K., 1986, *Essays on Industrial Policy*, New Delhi: Concept Publishing Company, Appendix 1, pp. 119–26.

Government of India, 1949. *Report of Export Promotion Committee*, New Delhi: Ministry of Commerce. https://indianculture.gov.in/flipbook/1008 (accessed 29 July 2022).

Government of India, 1950a. *Fiscal Commission 1949–50*, New Delhi: Government of India Press. Available at: https://dspace.gipe.ac.in/xmlui/handle/10973/52266 (accessed 22 August 2022).

Government of India, 1950b. 'Budget 1950–51: Finance Minister's Speech,' 28 February.

Government of India, 1952. *First Five Year Plan*, New Delhi: Planning Commission. Available at https://niti.gov.in/

planningcommission.gov.in/docs/plans/planrel/fiveyr/index5.html.

Government of India, 1956. 'Industrial Policy Resolution (30th April 1956).' In *Report of the Industrial Licensing Policy Inquiry Committee* (Dutt Committee), New Delhi: Ministry of Industrial Development, Internal Trade and Company Affairs, 1969, Appendix I-A. Available at https://dspace.gipe.ac.in/xmlui/handle/10973/52318 (accessed 29 April 2022).

Government of India, 1963. *Report of Steel Control*, Ministry of Steel and Heavy Industries.

Government of India, 1964. *Final Report of the Industrial Development Procedures Committee*, Ministry of Industry, New Delhi: Government of India Press (Swaminathan Committee Report). Available at https://archive.org/details/dli.csl.565 (accessed 3 September 2022).

Government of India, 1965a. *Report of the Study Team on Import and Export Trade Control Organization: Part I*, Ministry of Commerce, New Delhi, New Delhi (Mathur Committee).

Government of India, 1965b. *Report of the Study Team on Import and Export Trade Control Organization: Part II*, Ministry of Commerce, New Delhi, New Delhi (Mathur Committee).

Government of India, 1965c. *Report of the Study Team on Directorate General of Technical Development: Part I*, Ministry of Industry and Supply, New Delhi (Mathur Committee Report Part I). Available at https://indianculture.gov.in/report-study-team-directorate-general-technical-development (accessed 8 September 2022).

Government of India, 1965d. *Report of the Monopolies Inquiry Commission*, Volumes I and II, Ministry of Finance, New Delhi. Available at https://archive.org/details/dli.ministry.21164 (accessed 4 June 2023).

Government of India, 1966a. Report of the Education Commission: 1964–66, New Delhi: Ministry of Education. Available at https://archive.org/download/ReportOfTheE

ducationCommission1964-66D.S.KothariReport/48.Jp-ReportOfTheEducationCommission1964-66d.s.kothari.pdf (accessed 18 March 2023).

Government of India, 1966b. *Report of the Study Team on Directorate General of Technical Development: Part II*, Ministry of Supply and Technical Development, New Delhi (Mathur Committee Report Part II). Available at https://indianculture.gov.in/report-study-team-directorate-general-technical-development-part-ii (accessed 8 September 2022).

Government of India, 1967. *Industrial Planning and Licensing Policy: Volume I*, Planning Commission, New Delhi (Hazari Committee). Available at https://archive.org/details/dli.ministry.14791 (accessed 17 September 2022).

Government of India, 1969. *Report of the Industrial Licensing Policy Inquiry Committee*, Ministry of Industrial Development, Internal Trade and Company Affairs, New Delhi, July (Dutt Committee). Main report at https://archive.org/details/dli.ministry.20967 (accessed 8 September 2022).

Government of India, 1984. *Report of the Committee on Trade Policies*, Ministry of Commerce, New Delhi, December.

Government of India, 2017. *Agricultural Statistics at a Glance 2016*, Department of Agriculture, Cooperation & Farmer Welfare, Ministry of Agriculture & Farmer Welfare, New Delhi.

Government of India, 2020. *Role and Structure of the Tariff Commission*, New Delhi: Tariff Commission. Available at https://tc.nic.in/site/writereaddata/siteContent/202010261422447479Document%20on%20the%20Tariff%20Commission%20Volume%201.pdf (accessed 29 April 2022).

Guha, Ramchandra, 2007. *India after Gandhi*, New Delhi: Picador.

Harrison, Selig S., 1960. *India: The Most Dangerous Decades*, Princeton, N.J.: Princeton University Press.

Hazari, R.K., 1966. *Industrial Planning and Licensing Policy: Interim Report to the Planning Commission*, Bombay: University of Bombay. Available at: https://hemindrahazari.com/wp-content/uploads/2022/07/INDUSTRIAL-PLANNING-AND-LICENSING-POLICY.pdf (accessed 17 September 2022).

Hazari, R.K., 1967. *Industrial Planning and Licensing Policy: Final Report to the Planning Commission*, Bombay: University of Bombay. Available at https://archive.org/details/dli.ministry.14793 (accessed 15 June 2023).

Hazari, R.K., 1986. *Essays on Industrial Policy*, New Delhi: Concept Publishing Company, Appendix 1, pp. 119–26.

IDRA 1951 [The Industries (Development and Regulation) Act, 1951], Ministry of Industry, Government of India, New Delhi.

Indian National Congress, 1954. *Resolutions on Economic Policy and Program 1924–54*, New Delhi: All India Congress Committee.

Inoue, Kyoko, 1992. 'The Initial Formulation of Industrial Policy.' No. 27, Occasional Working Papers Series, Institute of Developing Economies, Japan External Trade Organization (IDE-JETRO), pp. 4–24. Available at https://ir.ide.go.jp/?action=repository_uri&item_id=40338&file_id=26&file_no=1 (accessed 23 April 2022).

Jain, Devaki, Ashok Mitra, Benedict Stavis, and K.N. Raj, reply by Amartya Sen, 1983. 'How is India Doing?' An Exchange,' *New York Review of Books*, 3 March.

Jain, Girilal, 1985. 'The Rajiv Phenomenon I—India's Search for a Monarch,' *Times of India*, 19 March, p. 8.

Jalan, Bimal, 1991. *India's Economic Crisis: The Way Ahead*, New York: Oxford University Press.

Jha, Prem Shankar, 1982. 'The End of the Tunnel: Return to Sanity in Economic Policy,' *Times of India*, 19 April, p. 8.

Jha, Prem Shankar, 1986. 'A Missed Opportunity I: What the Budget Should Have Done,' *Times of India*, 5 March, p. 8.

Jalan, Bimal, 1972. 'GNP!', *Economic and Political Weekly* 7(23), Jun. 3, pp. 1112–13.

Joshi, Vijay and Ian M.D. Little, 1994. *India: Macroeconomics and Political Economy: 1961–91*. Washington, DC: World Bank.

Joshi, Vijay and Ian M.D. Little, 1996. *India's Economic Reforms: 1991–2001*, Oxford and New York: Clarendon Press.

Kannappan, Subbiah, 1962. 'Reviewed Work: Indian Economic Policy and Development. by Peter T. Bauer,' *The Journal of Asian Studies* 21(2), February, pp. 249–50.

Kaushik, R.K., 2012. 'The Men who Ran the Raj,' *Hindustan Times*, 17 April, Chandigarh edition, Available at https://www.hindustantimes.com/chandigarh/the-men-who-ran-the-raj/story-S6yQeWGkqIw7xzgRhH5wIO.html (accessed 3 June 2023).

Kaviraj, Sudipto, 1986. 'Indira Gandhi and Indian Politics,' *Economic and Political Weekly*, 20–27 September 1986, Vol. 21, No. 38/39, pp. 1697–1708.

Khatkhate, Deena, 2006. 'Indian Economic Reform: A Philosopher's Stone,' *Economic and Political Weekly* 41(22), pp. 2203–5.

Khusro, A.M., 1984. 'Economists and Indian Development,' *The Indian Economic Journal* 32(1), pp. 1–36.

Kidron, Michael, 1965. *Foreign Investments in India*, London: Oxford University Press.

Kim, Kwan S., 1991. 'The Korean Miracle Revisited: Myths and Realities in Strategy and Development,' Working Paper 166, The Helen Kellogg Institute for International Studies, University of Notre Dame.

Kohli, Atul, 1989. 'Politics of Economic Liberalization in India,' *World Development* 17(3), pp. 305–28.

Komiya, Ryutaro, 1959. 'A Note on Professor Mahalanobis' Model of Indian Economic Planning,' *Review of Economics and Statistics* 41(1), pp. 29–35.

Krishnamurthi, B.V., 1955. 'The Public and Private Sectors.' In Planning Commission, ed., 1955, *Papers Relating to the*

Formulation of the Second Five Year Plan, Government of India, 574–76. https://dspace.gipe.ac.in/xmlui/handle/10973/39656 (accessed 1 January 2022).

Kwait, Natasha, undated. 'Occupational Structure of India: An Overview,' at https://www.economicsdiscussion.net/india/occupational-structure-in-india-an-overview/19135 (accessed 1 October 2023).

Lal, Deepak, 1978. 'Janata's Industrial Policy I – A New Caste System,' *Times of India*, 9 January, p. 8.

Lal, Deepak, 1992. 'Review of *India's Economic Crisis—The Way Ahead* by Bimal Jalan,' Finance and Development 29(3), 1 September, p. 48.

Lewis, John P., 1962. *Quiet Crisis in India*, Washington, DC: Brookings Institution.

Lockwood, David, 2011. 'Was the Bombay Plan a Capitalist Plot?', *Proceedings of the Indian History Congress* 72, PART-I, pp. 618–31.

Lokanathan, P.S., 1962. 'Reviewed Works: Indian Economic Policy and Development by P.T. Bauer; India and the West by Barbara Ward,' *India Quarterly* 18(2), April–June, pp. 195–98.

Lok Sabha Secretariat, 1963a. *Lok Sabha Debates*, third series, Vol XIX, 19 August. Available at https://eparlib.nic.in/handle/123456789/3058?view_type=search (accessed 16 April 2023).

Lok Sabha Secretariat, 1963a. *Lok Sabha Debates*, third series, Vol XIX, 21 August. Available at https://eparlib.nic.in/handle/123456789/3058?view_type=search (accessed 16 April 2023).

Lok Sabha Secretariat, 1963c. *Lok Sabha Debates*, third series, Vol XIX, 22 August. Available at https://eparlib.nic.in/handle/123456789/2906?view_type=search (accessed on 16 April 2023).

Lok Sabha Secretariat, 1967. *Estimates Committee (1967–68): Ninth Report on Industrial Licensing*, Lok Sabha Secretariat, New Delhi, July. Available at https://eparlib.nic.

in/handle/123456789/57705?view_type=search (accessed 3 September 2022).

Lok Sabha Secretariat, 1968. *Estimates Committee (1967–68): Thirtieth Report on Foreign Exchange*, Lok Sabha Secretariat, New Delhi, January. Available at https://eparlib.nic.in/handle/123456789/57701?view_type=search (accessed 3 September 2022).

Lok Sabha Secretariat, 1972. *Estimates Committee (1971–72): Seventeenth Report on Directorate General of Technical Development*, Lok Sabha Secretariat, New Delhi, April. Available at https://eparlib.nic.in/handle/123456789/57757?view_type=search (accessed 3 September 2022).

Lok Sabha Secretariat, 1990. *Eminent Parliamentarians Monograph Series: Dr. Rammanohar Lohia*, New Delhi: Lok Sabha Secretariat. Available at: https://eparlib.nic.in/bitstream/123456789/58682/1/Eminent_Parliamentarians_Series_Ram_Manohar_Lohia.pdf (accessed 16 March 2023).

Lok Sabha Secretariat, 1991. *Lok Sabha Debates*, 10th series, Vol. IV, No. 32, 26 August. Available at https://eparlib.nic.in/bitstream/123456789/3448/1/lsd_10_1_26-08-1991.pdf.

Mahalanobis, P.C., 1953. 'Some Observations on the Process of Growth of National Income,' *Sankhya* 12(4), pp. 307–12.

Mahalanobis, P.C., 1955. 'The Approach of Operational Research to Planning in India,' *Sankhya* 16(1/2), pp. 3–130.

Mahalanobis, P.C., 1961. *Talks on Planning*, London: Asia Publishing House. Also available at http://library.isical.ac.in:8080/jspui/handle/10263/6903 (accessed 6 January 2022).

McCarthy, Fiona, 1994. *William Morris: A Life for Our Time*, London: Faber & Faber.

Manor, James, 1988. 'Parties and the Party System,' in Atul Kohli, ed., *India's Democracy: An Analysis of Changing Stare-Society Relations*. Princeton, NJ: Princeton University Press.

Marathe, Sharad, 1989, *Regulation and Development: India's Policy Experience with Controls over Industry*, second edition, New Delhi: Sage Publications.

Masani, M.R., 1961. 'The Future of Free Enterprise in India,' Mumbai: Forum of Free Enterprise. Available at https://indianliberals.in/content/the-future-of-free-enterprise-in-india-by-m-r-masani-m-p-jun-8-1961/ (accessed 21 August 2022).

Medhora, Phiroze, 1971. 'Misplaced Accent on External Balance,' *Economic and Political Weekly* 6(30/32), Special Number, July, pp. 1687–90.

Mehta, T.U. 1994. 'Contribution of Judiciary to Industrial Equity', in D.S. Saini, ed; *Labor Judiciary, Adjudication and Industrial Justice*, New Delhi: Oxford and International Book House Publishing Co.

Menon, Nikhil, 2022. *Planning for Democracy: Modern India's Quest for Development*, Cambridge, UK: Cambridge University Press.

Mishra, Girish, 2014. 'Nehru and the Planning Commission,' *Mainstream* LII(47), 15 November 1-4. At http://www.mainstreamweekly.net/article5320.html (accessed 12 October 2023).

Mohan, Jag, 1975. 'Jawaharlal Nehru and his Socialism,' *India International Centre Quarterly* 2(3), pp. 183–92.

Mohan, Rakesh, 2017. 'The Road to the 1991 Industrial Policy Reforms and Beyond: A Personalized Narrative from the Trenches,' in Mohan, Rakesh, ed., *India Transformed: 25 Years of Economic Reforms*, Gurgaon: Penguin Random House India Pvt. Ltd.

National Planning Committee, 1939. 'Resolutions of the Conference of Ministers of Industries: 2–3 October 1930,' *Abstract of Proceedings*, Number 1, Bombay.

Nayar, Baldev Raj, 1972. *The Modernization Imperative and Indian Planning*, Delhi: Vikas Publications.

Nayyar, D., 2006. 'Economic Growth in Independent India: Lumbering Elephant or Running Tiger?', *Economic and Political Weekly* 41(15), pp. 1451–58.

Neale, Walter C., 1985. 'Indian Community Development, Local Government, Local Planning, and Rural Policy Since 1950,' *Economic Development and Cultural Change* 33(4), pp. 677–98.

Nehru, B.K. 1997. *Nice Guys Finish Second*. New Delhi: Viking.

Nehru, Jawaharlal, 1934. *Recent Essays and Writings: On the Future of India, Communalism and Other Subjects*, Allahabad: Kitabistan, second impression, May.

Nehru, Jawaharlal, 1936a. *An Autobiography*, 1942 edition, New Delhi: Jawaharlal Nehru Memorial Fund.

Nehru, Jawaharlal, 1936b. 'Presidential Address to the Indian National Congress,' *The Labor Monthly* 18(5), May, pp. 282–305. https://www.marxists.org/history/international/comintern/sections/britain/periodicals/labour_monthly/1936/05/x01.htm

Nehru, Jawaharlal, 1946. *The Discovery of India*, New Delhi: Oxford University Press (Centenary Edition 1989, sixth impression 1994).

Nehru, Jawaharlal, 1958a. *Jawaharlal Nehru's Speeches*, Volume One: September 1946—May 1949, New Delhi: The Publication Division, Government of India [Second Edition].

Nehru, Jawaharlal, 1954. *Jawaharlal Nehru's Speeches*, Volume Two: August 1949—February 1953, New Delhi: The Publication Division, Government of India [Fourth Impression, June 1964].

Nehru, Jawaharlal, 1958b. *Jawaharlal Nehru's Speeches*, Volume Three: March 1953—August 1957, New Delhi: The Publication Division, Government of India [Reprinted October 1970].

Nehru, Jawaharlal, 1964. *Jawaharlal Nehru's Speeches*, Volume Four: September 1957—April 1963, New Delhi: The Publication Division, Government of India.

Panagariya, Arvind, 1994. 'India: A New Tiger on the Block?', *Journal of International Affairs*, 48/1: 193–221.

Panagariya, Arvind, 2001. 'Heed these words of wisdom,' *Economic Times*, 24 October.

Panagariya, Arvind, 2004a. 'Growth and Reforms during 1980s and 1990s,' *Economic and Political Weekly* 39(25), 19–25 June, pp. 2581–94.

Panagariya, Arvind, 2004b. 'Vote Against Reform?' *Economic and Political Weekly*, 39(21), 22–28 May, pp. 2079–81.

Panagariya, Arvind, 2008. *India: The Emerging Giant*, New York: Oxford University Press.

Panagariya, Arvind, 2020. *New India: Reclaiming the Lost Glory*, New York: Oxford University Press.

Panagariya, Arvind, 2021. 'Real Cost of MSP for All Crops,' *Times of India*, 9 December.

Panel of Economists, 1955. 'The Second Five Year Plan: Basic Considerations relating to the Plan Frame.' In Planning Commission, ed., 1955, *Papers Relating to the Formulation of the Second Five Year Plan*, Government of India, 1–18.

Panjabi, B.L., 1940. 'Effects of the War on the Indian Financial System,' *Times of India*, 25 October, p. 35.

Patel, I.G., 1987. 'On Taking India into the Twenty-First Century,' Modern Asian Studies, Vol. 21, No. 2, pp. 209–31.

Patel, I.G., 2002. *Glimpses of Indian Economic Policy: An Insider's View*, New Delhi: Oxford University Press.

Patel, Vallabhbhai, 1948. 'Good out of Evil,' in Saggi, P.D., ed., *Life and Work of Sardar Vallabhbhai Patel*, 2010, World Public Library Association. Available at https://ksschool.org.in/lifeworkofsardar00sagguoft.pdf (accessed 13 August 2023).

Patel, Vallabhbhai, 2017. *For a United India—Speeches of Sardar Patel 1947–1950*, Publication Division, Government of India, New Delhi.

Planning Commission, ed., 1955, *Papers Relating to the Formulation of the Second Five Year Plan*, Government of

India: https://dspace.gipe.ac.in/xmlui/handle/10973/39656 (accessed 1 January 2022).

Planning Commission, 1952. *First Five Year Plan*, New Delhi.

Planning Commission, 1961. *Third Five Year Plan*, New Delhi.

Planning Commission, 1964. *Distribution of Income and Wealth and Concentration of Economic Power, Part I*, February, New Delhi. Available at http://library.isical.ac.in:8080/jspui/bitstream/10263/2062/1/314.pdf (accessed 4 June 2023).

Planning Commission, 1997. *Subhas Chandra Bose: Pioneer of Indian Planning*, New Delhi: http://14.139.60.153/bitstream/123456789/9021/1/0085_Subhash%20Chandra%20Bose%20Pioneer%20Of%20Indian%20Planning.pdf

Purshotamdas Thakurdas et al., 1945. titled *Memorandum Outlining a Plan of Economic Development for India*, London: Penguin Books. http://www.isec.ac.in/Plan_%20of_%20economic_%20development_%20for_%20India.pdf (accessed 7 March 2022).

Rajadhyaksha, Niranjan, 2013. 'Gandhi vs Modi is Actually Sen vs Bhagwati,' *Mint*, 10 July, available at https://www.livemint.com/Politics/LKb8rZi6t6t7TRYOVKKKyH/Gandhi-vs-Modi-is-actually-Sen-vs-Bhagwati.html (accessed 12 October 2013).

Ramakrishnan, Niranjan, 2005. 'The Che of Non-violence,' Counterpunch, 23 March. Available at https://www.counterpunch.org/2005/03/23/the-che-of-non-violence/ (accessed 16 March 2023).

Ramesh, Jairam, 2015. *To the Brink and Back: India's 1991 Story*, New Delhi: Rupa Publications India Pvt. Ltd.

Ramesh, Jairam, 2018. *Intertwined Lives: P.N. Haksar and Indira Gandhi*, India: Simon and Schuster (page numbers in the text from Apple Books edition).

Ranadive, K.R., 1973. 'Growth and Social Justice: Political Economy of "Garibi Hatao"' *Economic and Political Weekly* 8(18), 5 May, pp. 834–41.

Rao, P.V. Narasimha, 1993. *P.V. Narasimha Rao: Selected Speeches 1991–92*, New Delhi: Information and Broadcasting Ministry, Government of India.

Reserve Bank of India, 1970. *History of the Reserve Bank of India, Volume 1 (1935–51)*, Bombay: Reserve Bank of India. https://www.rbi.org.in/scripts/RHvol-1.aspx (accessed 17 May 2022).

Reserve Bank of India, 1997. *History of the Reserve Bank of India, Volume 2 (1951–67)*, Bombay: Reserve Bank of India. https://www.rbi.org.in/scripts/RHvol-2.aspx (accessed 17 May 2022).

Sanyal, Sanjeev. 2006. 'Post-liberalization India and the Importance of Legal Reform'. http://www.idfresearch.org/gov_parent/Sanjeev%20Sanyal%20Indian%20Legal%20Reforms%20Jul06.pdf (accessed 20 December 2011).

Sarkar, Santanu, 2017. 'Changing Judicial Pronouncements on Impugned Discharge & Dismissal under Industrial Disputes Act, 1947,' *The Indian Journal of Industrial Relations* 53(2), October, pp. 200–08.

Sau, Ranjit, 1972. 'The 'New Economics,' *Economic and Political Weekly* 7(31/33), Special Number, August, pp. 1571–73, 1575 and 1579–80.

Sau, Ranjit, 1983. 'Growth, Stagnation and Fluctuation in Indian Economy,' *Economic and Political Weekly* 1897, 12 February, pp. 234–37.

Sen, Amartya, 1982. 'How is India Doing?' *New York Review of Books*, 16 December.

Sharma, G.D. 1974. *Streamlined Procedures of Industrial Licensing, Law & Regulations*. Delhi: Press Publications Agency.

Shastri, Lal Bahadur, 1974 [2007 reprint]. *Selected Speeches of Lal Bahadur Shastri*, Publications Division, Ministry of Information and Broadcasting, Government of India.

Shenoy, B.R., 1955a. 'The Second Five Year Plan: A Note of Dissent on the Basic Considerations Relating to the Plan Frame.' In Planning Commission, ed., 1955, *Papers Relating to the Formulation of the Second Five Year Plan*, Government of India, 21–32.

Shenoy, B.R., 1955b. 'Deficit Financing and Indian Economic Development.' In Planning Commission, ed., 1955, *Papers Relating to the Formulation of the Second Five Year Plan*, Government of India, 483–98.

Shenoy, B.R., 1958. 'Foreign Exchange Crisis: Devaluation Only Remedy,' *Times of India*, 5 May, p. 6.

Shenoy, B.R., 1959. 'Problems of Export Promotion,' *Times of India*, 30 June, p. I and p. XX.

Shenoy, B.R., 1964. 'A report on Ten Years of Planning in India,' *New Individualist Review* 3(2), 467–74.

Shenoy, B.R., 1968. *Indian Economic Policy*, Bombay: Popular Prakashan.

Shenoy, B.R., 1975. '25 Years of Planning,' in R.K. Amin and Parth J. Shah, ed., *Theoretical Vision: B.R. Shenoy*, 2004, New Delhi: Center for Civil Society, chapter 3.

Shenoy, Sudha, 2003. 'An Interview with Sudha Shenoy,' Austrian Economics Newsletter, Auburn, Ala.: Ludwig von Mises Institute.

Shroff, A. D., 1956. 'Has Private Enterprise Failed?' Speech delivered at the Commerce Graduates' Association, Bombay, 23 October. Available at https://indianliberals.in/content/has-private-enterprise-failed-by-a-d-shroff-october-23-1956/ (accessed 21 August 2022).

Shroff, A.D., 1958. 'The Foreign Exchange Crisis & Some Remedies,'. Based on a speech at the Rotary Club, Bombay, on 29 July 1958, Forum for Free Enterprise. Available at https://indianliberals.in/bn/content/the-foreign-excahnge-crisis-some-remedies-by-a-d-shroff-aug-6-1958/.

Singh, Manmohan, 1964. *India's Export Trends and the Prospects for Self-sustained Growth*, London: Oxford University Press.

Singh, Manmohan, 1972. 'Jagdish N. Bhagwati and Padma Desai, India: Planning for Industrialization:

Industrialization and Trade Policies Since 1951,' *The Indian Economic and Social History Review* 9(4), December, pp. 413–17.

Sitapati, Vinay, 2015. *Half-Lion: How P.V. Narasimha Rao Transformed India*, New Delhi: Penguin Books (page numbers in the text from the Apple Books edition).

Sivasubramonian, S., 2000. *The National Income of India during the Twentieth Century*, Oxford University Press, Delhi.

Somiah, C.G., 2010. *The Honest Always Stand Alone*, New Delhi: Niyogi Books.

Spencer, Daniel, 1959. 'India, Mixed Enterprise and Western Business: Experiments in Controlled Change for Growth and Profit,' The Hague: Martinus Nijhoff.

Swamy, Subramaniam, 1972. 'Jagdish N. Bhagwati and Padma Desai, India: Planning for Industrialization: Industrialization and Trade Policies Since 1951,' *India Quarterly* 28(2), April, pp. 168–69.

Tata, J.R.D., 1991. 'Berlin Walls Should Fall,' *Times of India*, 1 August, pp. 1 and 18.

Time, 1977. 'Business: IBM Withdraws from India,' 28 November. Available at https://content.time.com/time/subscriber/article/0,33009,919167,00.html (accessed 25 January 2024).

Times of India, 1939a. 'Prohibition of exports: Arms and Fuel,' 11 September, p. 9.

Times of India, 1939b. 'Indian Exports Control: Revised Notification,' 27 November, p. 9.

Times of India, 1940a. 'Tax-Burden Associated with Tariff Duties: Highest on General Consumption Articles,' 13 January, p. 4.

Times of India, 1940b. 'Import Restrictions,' 22 May, p. 6.

Times of India, 1940c. 'Import Control: Measures to Conserve Exchange and Freight,' 25 October, p. 40.

Times of India, 1940e. 'Import Control List Extended: Paper and Chrome Compounds,' 28 December, p. 7.

Times of India, 1940f. 'Exports of Mica from India: Changes in System of Control,' 12 August, p. 4.

Times of India, 1940g. 'Coffee Control in India: Plan for Surplus Pool,' 3 December, p. 5.

Times of India, 1941a. 'Conserving Foreign Exchange: Import Control Extended,' 10 May 1941, p. 6.

Times of India, 1941b. 'Import Control Extended', Government of India Notification, 22 July, p. 5.

Times of India, 1942a. 'Curtailment of Imports: Government Scheme,' 11 May, p. 4.

Times of India, 1942b. 'Imports and Use of Sizing Goods: New Control Order,' 10 August, p. 4.

Times of India, 1943a. 'Export and import Control: Plea for Revision,' 24 July, p. 7.

Times of India, 1944a. 'Control of Textile Export Prices: Promoting Healthy Overseas Trade,' 3 July, p. 4.

Times of India, 1945a. 'Sir A. Dalal on his Plan: Outside Influence Denied,' 16 May, p. 7.

Times of India, 1946a. 'Import Control Excuses,' 15 May, p. 6.

Times of India, 1946b. 'End Import Control,' 30 May, p. 6.

Times of India, 1946c. 'Blocked Imports,' 20 June p.6.

Times of India, 1946d. 'More Import Muddles,' 17 July, p. 6.

Times of India, 1946e. 'More Articles Freed for Exports: Govt.'s Control Policy,' 23 April, p. 3.

Times of India, 1946f. 'More Articles Decontrolled: Export Policy under Constant Review,' 30 July, p. 1.

Times of India, 1948a. 'Policy Will Not be Approved': Mr. Shah's Criticism,' 8 April, p. 5.

Times of India, 1948b. 'India's New Import Policy: Monetary Ceilings to be Raised,' 24 January, p. 7.

Times of India, 1948c. 'Import of Certain Goods: Removal of Control,' 4 July, p. 9.

Times of India, 1948d. 'Import Controls Relaxed Further: More Goods Allowed on Open General License,' 4 September, p. 1.

Times of India, 1948e. 'Imports to India: Control Removed Over More Categories,' 15 September, p. 4.

Times of India, 1949a. 'Import Advisory Council Confers in Delhi: Mr. Neogy on Liberalization Policy,' 27 February, p. 7.

Times of India, 1949b. 'More Controls on Imports from Dollar and Hard Currency Areas: Revised Policy Announces,' 27 February, p. 9.

Times of India, 1949c. 'Open General License No. XVI: Release of Full Text,' 27 August, p. 6.

Times of India, 1949d. 'No Restrictions in India on Foreign Capital: Pandit Nehru Defines Policy,' 7 April, p. 3.

Times of India, 1950a. 'Foreign Exchange Budget: Ceiling for Imports,' 1 July, p. 5.

Times of India, 1950b. 'Liberalization of Import Policy: Larger Intake of Raw Materials,' 2 March, p. 1.

Times of India, 1950c. 'Decentralization of Licensing Authority: New Import Program for July-December,' 15 June, p. 1.

Times of India, 1950d. 'Import Control System: Terms of reference of Inquiry Committee,' 4 July, p. 1.

Times of India, 1950e. 'Control on Import Licenses: Committee Suggests Decentralization,' 24 October, p. 1 (continued on p. 9)

Times of India, 1951a. 'Maintaining Stable Level of Imports: Delhi Decision on Inquiry Committee's Report,' 5 January, p. 1.

Times of India, 1951b. 'Liberalization of Import Policy for 1951: Delhi Announces Steps for Flow of Essential Goods to India,' 13 March, p. 1.

Times of India, 1951c. 'Current Topics: Import Policy, Middle Class Living,' 29 December, p. 4.

Times of India, 1952a. 'Supplies of Essential Goods Assured: Impact of New Import Control Policy,' 18 June, p. 3.

Times of India, 1952b. 'Industrial Control,' 4 June, p. 4.

Times of India, 1952c. 'Manufacturing of Consumer Goods by Foreign Firms: Government Policy Regarding Grant of Licenses,' 19 November, p. 9.

Times of India, 1953a. 'Drastic Cuts in Imports Ruled Out: Steps to Avoid Delays in Policy Announcements,' 23 May, p. 5.

Times of India, 1953b. 'Further Liberalization of Imports: Stability Marks Policy for Next Half Year,' 25 June, p. 5.

Times of India, 1953c. 'Trade Policy,' 1 December, p. 6.

Times of India, 1953d. 'No Checks on Imports for Protection,' 29 November, p. 1.

Times of India, 1953e. 'Industrial Equipment & Raw Materials: Liberal Import Policy,' 31 December, p. 4.

Times of India, 1953f. 'Survey of Idle Industrial Capacity: Forthcoming Talks by Advisory Council,' 27 May, p. 5.

Times of India, 1954a. 'Import Policy for July-December Liberalized: Quota Raised for 60 Items,' 30 June, p. 5.

Times of India, 1954b. 'Import Control Relaxed but Duty Raised,' 12 September, p. 1.

Times of India, 1954c. 'Two innovations for Import Policy: Profit Margins on sales: Move for Monopoly Trade,' 31 December, p. 1.

Times of India, 1955a. 'Plea to Raise 2nd Plan Target: Textile Mill Production,' 23 July, p. 11.

Times of India, 1955b. 'Import Policy for Next Half of 1955: Less Quota for Items Manufactured Here,' 30 June, p. 1.

Times of India, 1956a. 'Emphasis on Industries: Draft 2nd Plan Welcomed,' 11 February.

Times of India, 1956b. 'New Import Policy Causes Sharp Rise in Caustic Soda and Sodium Bicarbonate [Prices],' 1 January, p. 12.

Times of India, 1956c. 'New import Policy Aims at Developing India's Industrial Potential,' 1 July, p. 11.

Times of India, 1956d. 'State Trading Corporation: Board to Meet,' 1 June, p. 5.

Times of India, 1956e. 'New Import Policy Geared to Needs of National Plan,' 30 December, p. 11.

Times of India, 1956f. 'Drastic Cuts in Imports: Many Items Affected: New Policy,' 30 December, p. 1.

Times of India. 1957a. 'Established Importers Will Get No New Licenses: Policy for Next Three Months,' 30 June, p. 1 and 9.

Times of India. 1957b. 'Govt. Imposes Drastic Cuts on. Imports: Rs. 100-Crore Saving in Foreign Exchange,' 1 October, p. 1 and 7.

Times of India, 1957c. 'Import Policy,' 2 October, p. 6.

Times of India, 1957d. 'No Cause for Alarm, Says Mr. Desai: Steps to Preserve Foreign Exchange Explained,' 22 August, p. 1.

Times of India, 1957e. 'No Devaluing Rupee to Surmount our Hurdles: Foreign Exchange a Secondary Issue,' 25 August, p. 1.

Times of India, 1957f. 'Imbalance in Foreign Trade: Case for Export Promotion,' 26 April, p. 6.

Times of India, 1957g. 'Move to Attract U.S. Investment: Terms of Convertibility Pact Signed by India,' 21 September, p. 7.

Times of India, 1958a. 'Import Quotas for Several Items Liberalized: Bid to Meet Crises in Essential Industries,' 1 April, p. 1.

Times of India, 1958b. 'Tailoring Imports to Fit Foreign Exchange Budget: Govt.'s Measures to Mitigate Hardship,' 1 July, p. 7.

Times of India, 1958c. 'Demand for Inquiry is Rejected: Crisis in Foreign Exchange,' 21 March, p. 1.

Times of India, 1958d. 'No Short Cut,' 25 June, p. 6.

Times of India, 1958e. 'Indian Govt. is Trying for Large Credits to Plan Ahead: Economy Very Sound, Asserts Mr. Nehru,' 4 July, p. 5.

Times of India, 1958f. 'Export Promotion Target Raised: Government Steps begin to Show Results,' 8 February, p. 1.

Times of India, 1958g. 'CEAT Tires of India,' 10 February, p. 4.

Times of India, 1958h. 'Import Policy Liberalized: Sequel to Promise of External Aid,' 1 November.

Times of India, 1959a. 'Union Minister Warns of "Extreme Step,"' 30 January, p. 1.

Times of India, 1959b. 'Little Change Made in Import Policy: Quotas Increased for Some Items,' p. 1.

Times of India, 1959c. 'Import Quotas for Machinery Parts Enhanced: Minor Adjustments in Other Items,' p. 1.

Times of India, 1960a. 'Foreign Exchange Allocation Raised: Main Features of New Import Policy,' 1 April, p. 1.

Times of India, 1960b. 'Further Cuts in Imports Announced: Cotton Fabrics, Raw Film and Auto "Spares" Affected,' 2 October, p. 1.

Times of India, 1961a. 'Exports are Vital for Economic Growth: "Sell or Sink" Slogan,' 29 March, p. 7.

Times of India, 1961b. 'Indian Investment Center to be Opened,' 16 February, p. 3.

Times of India, 1961c. 'Import Restrictions to Stay: Additional Quotas for Users who Increase Exports,' 2 April, p. 1.

Times of India, 1961d. 'Import Policy Linked with Exports,' 1 October, p. 1.

Times of India, 1962a. 'Urgency of Exports not Sufficiently Realized: Mudaliar Committee Calls for Sales Tax Remission,' 20 March, p. 1 and p. 9.

Times of India, 1962b. 'Import Quotas for 65 Items Cut or Banned,' 1 April, p. 9.

Times of India, 1962c. 'More Newsprint for Papers: New Import Policy: Annual Licensing System Revived,' 1 April, p. 1.

Times of India, 1962d. 'Import Policy,' 4 April, p. 6.

Times of India, 1962e. 'Import Policy,' 26 December, p. 8.

Times of India, 1962f. 'Realistic Price Policy to Cover Essential Goods: FICCI Urges Govt. to Take Steps—Obstacles to Higher Output Must Go,' 26 March, p. 1.

Times of India, 1962g. 'Licensing Policy Needs Probe,' 6 May, p. 1.

Times of India, 1963a. 'Imports Liberalized During 1963–64: Near-Doubling in Number of Items: Liquor Ban Off,' 23 April, p. 1.

Times of India, 1963b. 'Private Sector Needs Greater Encouragement: FICCI Wants Govt. to Shed Dogmas,' 18 March, p. 1.

Times of India, 1963c. 'Committee to Review Operation of Controls: Gearing up Growth of Industries is Aim,' 25 September, p. 1.

Times of India, 1964. 'Further Curbs will Hit Development, Little Scope Now for Monopoly, Says FICCI,' 17 August, p. 8.

Times of India, 1966a. 'Review Controls on Industry & Trade: FICCI Urges Govt. to Reorient its Policy,' 15 March, p. 1.

Times of India, 1966b. 'FICCI Calls for Relaxation of Controls,' 17 April, p. 7.

Times of India, 1966c. 'Best use of Plan Funds Vital, Affirms FICCI,' 27 April, p. 9.

Times of India, 1966d. 'Industry to be Freed of More Licensing Curbs: Diversified Output Will be Possible,' 15 October, p. 1.

Times of India, 1970a. 'PM Urges Trade to Support Socialist Plans,' 15 March, p. 1.

Times of India, 1970b. 'The Associated Cement Companies Limited: Extracts from the Statement of the Chairman, Mr. N.A. Palkhivala,' 22 January, p. 4.

Times of India, 1972. 'Abolish Licensing for Core Units, Says FICCI,' 6 March, p. 4.

Times of India, 1974. 'Big Recession Ahead, FICCI Warns Govt.,' 23 December, p. 1.

Times of India, 1977a. 'Rural Bias in Industrial Policy: 324 New Items Reserved for Small Industry,' 24 December, p. 1 and p. 15.

Times of India, 1977b. 'FICCI Panel Suggests Steps for Growth,' 5 October, p. 14.

Times of India, 1978. 'Limit Scope of Licensing: FICCI,' 2 December, p. 13.

Times of India, 1979. 'Reorient Licensing Policies: FICCI,' 27 December, p. 4.

Times of India, 1980a. 'Industrial Policy Statement: New Deal for Private Sector; Boost to Output,' 24 July, p. 1 and p. 8.

Times of India, 1980b. 'Scrap Licensing: FICCI,' 20 January, p. 9.

Times of India, 1982. 'Relax Licensing Policy,' 15 December, p. 9.

Times of India, 1983. 'Call for Change in Monopolies Act,' 3 April, p. 1.

Times of India, 1984. 'More Funds for Power,' 9 April, p. 1.

Times of India, 1985a. 'Talks Offer on Gujarat,' 5 May, p. 1.

Times of India, 1985b. 'Bold, Realistic, Feels Trade,' 17 March, p. 9.

Times of India, 1986. 'Budget Won't Spur Growth: Palkhivala,' 6 March, p. 9.

Times of India, 1990a. 'Industrial Policy More Liberalized: Ajit Singh,' 2 June, p. 13.

Times of India, 1990b. 'New Policy on Small-scale Industries,' 2 June, p. 7.

Times of India, 1990c. 'FICCI Puts up a Brave Front,' 28 August, p. 17.

Tooley, J. 2009. *The Beautiful Tree, A Personal Journey Into How The World's Poorest People Are Educating Themselves*. London: Penguin Books.

Vakil, C.N., and P.R. Brahmananda, 1955a. 'Investment Pattern in the Second Five Year Plan.' In Planning Commission, ed., 1955, *Papers Relating to the Formulation of the Second Five Year Plan*, Government of India, pp. 139–48.

Vakil, C.N., and P.R. Brahmananda, 1955b. 'Institutional Implications of a Bolder Plan.' In Planning Commission, ed., 1955, *Papers Relating to the Formulation of the Second Five Year Plan*, Government of India, pp. 513–29.

Vakil, C.N., and P.R. Brahmananda, 1956. 'Planning for an Expanding Economy.' Bombay, India: Vora and Co.

Verghese, B.G., 1958. 'The National Scene: Export or Perish,' *Times of India*, 8 February. 28 May, p. 6.

Verghese, B.G. 'Plans and Perspectives: Prosperity through Exports,' *Times of India*, 20 April, p. 8.

Wagle, Dileep M., 1981. 'Imperial Preference and the Indian Steel Industry,' *The Economic History Review* 34(1), New Series, pp. 120–31.

Index

B

C

L

M

R

S